America's
TEST KITCHEN

ALSO BY THE EDITORS AT AMERICA'S TEST KITCHEN

The Cook's Illustrated Cookbook

The America's Test Kitchen Menu Cookbook

Pasta Revolution

Slow Cooker Revolution

The Best Simple Recipes

The America's Test Kitchen Healthy
Family Cookbook

The America's Test Kitchen Family Baking Book

The America's Test Kitchen Family Cookbook

THE COOK'S COUNTRY SERIES:

From Our Grandmothers' Kitchens

Cook's Country Blue Ribbon Desserts

Cook's Country Best Potluck Recipes

Cook's Country Best Lost Suppers

Cook's Country Best Grilling Recipes

The Cook's Country Cookbook

America's Best Lost Recipes

THE TV COMPANION SERIES:

The Complete America's Test Kitchen TV
Companion Cookbook 2001–2012

America's Test Kitchen: The TV Companion
Cookbook (2009, 2011, and 2012 Editions)

Behind the Scenes with America's Test Kitchen

Test Kitchen Favorites

Cooking at Home with America's Test Kitchen

America's Test Kitchen Live!

Inside America's Test Kitchen

Here in America's Test Kitchen

The America's Test Kitchen Cookbook

AMERICA'S TEST KITCHEN ANNUALS:

The Best of America's Test Kitchen
(2007–2012 Editions)

Cooking for Two (2010–2012 Editions)

Light & Healthy (2010–2012 Editions)

THE BEST RECIPE SERIES:

The New Best Recipe

More Best Recipes

The Best One-Dish Suppers

Soups, Stews & Chilis

The Best Skillet Recipes

The Best Slow & Easy Recipes

The Best Chicken Recipes

The Best International Recipe

The Best Make-Ahead Recipe

The Best 30-Minute Recipe

The Best Light Recipe

The Cook's Illustrated Guide
to Grilling and Barbecue

Best American Side Dishes

Cover & Bake

Steaks, Chops, Roasts & Ribs

Baking Illustrated

Italian Classics

American Classics

FOR A FULL LISTING OF ALL OUR BOOKS
OR TO ORDER TITLES:

http://www.cooksillustrated.com

http://www.americastestkitchen.com

or call 800–611–0759

PRAISE FOR OTHER AMERICA'S TEST KITCHEN TITLES

"The perfect kitchen home companion. The practical side of things is very much on display . . . cook-friendly and kitchen-oriented, illuminating the process of preparing food instead of mystifying it."
THE WALL STREET JOURNAL ON *THE COOK'S ILLUSTRATED COOKBOOK*

"If this were the only cookbook you owned, you would cook well, be everyone's favorite host, have a well-run kitchen, and eat happily every day."
THECITYCOOK.COM ON *THE AMERICA'S TEST KITCHEN MENU COOKBOOK*

"This book upgrades slow cooking for discriminating, 21st-century palates— that is indeed revolutionary."
THE DALLAS MORNING NEWS ON *SLOW COOKER REVOLUTION*

"Forget about marketing hype, designer labels, and pretentious entrées: This is an unblinking, unbedazzled guide to the Beardian good-cooking ideal."
THE WALL STREET JOURNAL ON *THE BEST OF AMERICA'S TEST KITCHEN 2009*

"Expert bakers and novices scared of baking's requisite exactitude can all learn something from this hefty, all-purpose home baking volume."
PUBLISHERS WEEKLY ON *THE AMERICA'S TEST KITCHEN FAMILY BAKING BOOK*

"Scrupulously tested regional and heirloom recipes."
THE NEW YORK TIMES ON *THE COOK'S COUNTRY COOKBOOK*

"If you're hankering for old-fashioned pleasures, look no further."
PEOPLE MAGAZINE ON *AMERICA'S BEST LOST RECIPES*

"This tome definitely raises the bar for all-in-one, basic, must-have cookbooks. . . . Kimball and his company have scored another hit."
THE OREGONIAN ON *THE AMERICA'S TEST KITCHEN FAMILY COOKBOOK*

"A foolproof, go-to resource for everyday cooking."
PUBLISHERS WEEKLY ON *THE AMERICA'S TEST KITCHEN FAMILY COOKBOOK*

"The strength of the Best Recipe series lies in the sheer thoughtfulness and details of the recipes."
PUBLISHERS WEEKLY ON *THE BEST RECIPE SERIES*

"These dishes taste as luxurious as their full-fat siblings. Even desserts are terrific."
PUBLISHERS WEEKLY ON *THE BEST LIGHT RECIPE*

"Further proof that practice makes perfect, if not transcendent. . . . If an intermediate cook follows the directions exactly, the results will be better than takeout or Mom's."
THE NEW YORK TIMES ON *THE NEW BEST RECIPE*

"Like a mini–cooking school, the detailed instructions and illustrations ensure that even the most inexperienced cook can follow these recipes with success."
PUBLISHERS WEEKLY ON *BEST AMERICAN SIDE DISHES*

"Makes one-dish dinners a reality for average cooks, with honest ingredients and detailed make-ahead instructions."
THE NEW YORK TIMES ON *COVER & BAKE*

"Sturdy, stick-to-your-ribs fare that deserves a place at the table."
THE OREGONIAN ON *COOK'S COUNTRY BEST LOST SUPPERS*

"The best instructional book on baking this reviewer has seen."
THE LIBRARY JOURNAL (STARRED REVIEW) ON *BAKING ILLUSTRATED*

Simple

WEEKNIGHT FAVORITES

MORE THAN 200
NO-FUSS,
FOOLPROOF
MEALS

BY THE EDITORS AT
America's Test Kitchen

PHOTOGRAPHY BY
Daniel J. van Ackere

AMERICA'S TEST KITCHEN
17 Station Street, Brookline, MA 02445

Library of Congress
Cataloging-in-Publication Data
Simple weeknight favorites : more than
200 no-fuss, foolproof meals / by the editors
at America's Test Kitchen ; photography by
Daniel J. van Ackere — 1st Edition.
    pages cm.
 Includes index.
 ISBN 978-1-936493-06-7
 1. Cooking, American. 2. Cookbooks.
 I. America's test kitchen (Television program)
 TX715.S61175 2012
 641.5973--dc23
            2011042143

Manufactured in the United States
10 9 8 7 6 5 4 3 2 1

Distributed by America's Test Kitchen
17 Station Street, Brookline, MA 02445

EDITORIAL DIRECTOR: Jack Bishop

EXECUTIVE EDITOR: Elizabeth Carduff

EXECUTIVE FOOD EDITOR: Julia Collin Davison

SENIOR EDITOR: Louise Emerick

RECIPE DEVELOPMENT: Erika Bruce, Matthew Card, Danielle
DeSiato-Hallman, Eva Katz, Sean Kenniff, Rebeccah Marsters,
Maria del Mar Sacasa, Sarah Wilson

EDITORIAL ASSISTANT: Alyssa King

DESIGN DIRECTOR: Amy Klee

ART DIRECTOR: Greg Galvan

ASSOCIATE ART DIRECTOR: Matthew Warnick

PHOTOSHOOT KITCHEN TEAM:

    ASSOCIATE EDITOR: Yvonne Ruperti

    ASSISTANT TEST COOKS: Daniel Cellucci, Danielle DeSiato-Hallman

FRONT COVER PHOTOGRAPH: Daniel J. van Ackere

STAFF PHOTOGRAPHER: Daniel J. van Ackere

ADDITIONAL PHOTOGRAPHY: Kate Kelley, Anthony Tieuli

FOOD STYLING: Marie Piraino

PRODUCTION DIRECTOR: Guy Rochford

SENIOR PRODUCTION MANAGER: Jessica Quirk

SENIOR PROJECT MANAGER: Alice Carpenter

PRODUCTION AND TRAFFIC COORDINATOR: Kate Hux

ASSET AND WORKFLOW MANAGER: Andrew Mannone

PRODUCTION AND IMAGING SPECIALISTS: Judy Blomquist, Heather Dube,
Lauren Pettapiece

COPYEDITOR: Cheryl Redmond

PROOFREADER: Christine Corcoran Cox

INDEXER: Elizabeth Parson

PICTURED ON FRONT COVER: Antipasto Pizza with Arugula Salad (page 280)

PICTURED OPPOSITE TITLE PAGE: Cola-Glazed Pork Chops with Mustard
Greens (page 140)

PICTURED ON BACK OF JACKET: Quick Sausage Ragu with Gemelli
(page 212), Chili-Glazed Salmon with Bok Choy (page 175), Steak and
Zucchini Tostadas (page 108), Prosciutto-Wrapped Chicken with Sage
Butter (page 66)

Contents

Welcome to
America's Test Kitchen
viii

Introduction
ix

Soups & Stews
2

Salads
26

Poultry
52

Beef
92

Pork
122

Seafood
154

Vegetarian Entrées
186

Fire Up the Grill
246

Pasta & Risotto
208

Pizzas & Sandwiches
274

Stir-Fries, Curries
& Asian Noodles
298

Index
327

Welcome to America's Test Kitchen

This book has been tested, written, and edited by the folks at America's Test Kitchen, a very real 2,500-square-foot kitchen located just outside of Boston. It is the home of *Cook's Illustrated* magazine and *Cook's Country* magazine and is the Monday-through-Friday destination for more than three dozen test cooks, editors, food scientists, tasters, and cookware specialists. Our mission is to test recipes over and over again until we understand how and why they work and until we arrive at the "best" version.

We start the process of testing a recipe with a complete lack of conviction, which means that we accept no claim, no theory, no technique, and no recipe at face value. We simply assemble as many variations as possible, test a half-dozen of the most promising, and taste the results blind. We then construct our own hybrid recipe and continue to test it, varying ingredients, techniques, and cooking times until we reach a consensus. The result, we hope, is the best version of a particular recipe, but we realize that only you can be the final judge of our success (or failure).

As we like to say in the test kitchen, "We make the mistakes, so you don't have to."

All of this would not be possible without a belief that good cooking, much like good music, is indeed based on a foundation of objective technique. Some people like spicy foods and others don't, but there is a right way to sauté, there is a best way to cook a pot roast, and there are measurable scientific principles involved in producing perfectly beaten, stable egg whites. This is our ultimate goal: to investigate the fundamental principles of cooking so that you become a better cook. It is as simple as that.

You can watch us work (in our actual test kitchen) by tuning in to *America's Test Kitchen* (www.americastestkitchentv.com) or *Cook's Country from America's Test Kitchen* (www.cookscountrytv.com) on public television, or by subscribing to *Cook's Illustrated* magazine (www.cooksillustrated.com) or *Cook's Country* magazine (www.cookscountry.com). We welcome you into our kitchen, where you can stand by our side as we test our way to the "best" recipes in America.

Introduction

Every time someone offers a "simple" solution, I tend to walk quickly in the other direction, having found, as you probably have, that simple answers are not always the best. In fact, "simple" recipes are usually the hardest, since long ingredient lists and lengthy cooking times obscure deficiencies in ingredients and technique. Beef stew is inevitably decent whereas a four-ingredient pasta dish or a quick chicken bake can be woefully unsatisfying.

So creating simple recipes and menus is anything but simple. For starters, we learned to use the same ingredient in two or three different ways in the same menu. For Orange-Ginger Pork Tenderloin and Carrot Salad we used orange juice in both the glaze and the salad dressing. We tested convenience supermarket ingredients and discovered which ones are worth buying to save time (pizza dough and ready rice work well; don't even think about store-bought tostadas or teriyaki sauce). We learned to streamline our preparation methods as well: We used the same pot to boil potatoes and then cauliflower; we started risotto in the microwave so there would be only five minutes of stovetop stirring; and we used creamed corn, instead of a classic French roux of butter and flour, to thicken our Spicy Chicken and Corn Chowder.

Of course, creativity also comes into play here, since an interesting pairing of ingredients can turn a quick recipe into a great one. Turning Italian meatballs into a Greek-style dinner, using pine nuts and Parmesan for a crust on weeknight chicken, and turning a classic American sandwich into Indian-inspired Curried Chicken Sandwiches with Apple Raita are just three examples.

With some cookbooks, I feel intimidated, much like the flatlander who stops at the Vermont country store and asked an old-timer whether he could tell him how to get to the famous covered bridge. "Yup," replied the old-timer, giving him a hard look. "I could, but I don't know if you'd ever make it."

We have taken a more welcoming approach with *Simple Weeknight Favorites* by simplifying the problem of "What's for dinner?" and giving lots of no-nonsense, easy-to-follow options that are a lot better than the usual suspects. We have every confidence that you will make it to where you are headed. Enjoy.

CHRISTOPHER KIMBALL
Founder and Editor,
Cook's Illustrated and *Cook's Country*
Host, *America's Test Kitchen* and
Cook's Country from America's Test Kitchen

ESCAROLE, LINGUIÇA, AND WHITE BEAN SOUP

Soups & Stews

4   Quick All-American Chili with Cheesy Cornbread

6   Quick Guinness Beef Stew

7   Quick Chicken Pozole

9   Thai Coconut Curry Soup with Chicken

10   Spicy Chicken and Corn Chowder

11   Matzo Ball Soup with Chicken and Asparagus

12   Cambodian Chicken Soup

14   White Chicken Chili

15   Escarole, Linguiça, and White Bean Soup

16   Smoky Chorizo, Chickpea, and Spinach Soup

19   Gazpacho with Avocado and Crab

20   Quick Bouillabaisse

21   Shrimp Tortilla Soup

22   Quick Black Bean Soup

24   Creamy White Bean Soup with Kale Pesto

25   Moroccan Sweet Potato Soup

Quick All-American Chili with Cheesy Cornbread

Serves 4

✔ **WHY THIS RECIPE WORKS:** Who says you have to simmer chili for hours to get a spicy, full-flavored batch? To coax out the most flavor possible, we make sure the onions are softened and the spices are bloomed before adding the meat, beans, and tomatoes to the pot, and breaking apart the beef while it cooks prevents oversize chunks of meat in the final chili. For the perfect accompaniment, cornbread is an easy choice. To save time, we use fresh-baked cornbread from the supermarket bakery, then we top it with some shredded cheddar. Three minutes under the broiler not only melts the cheese topping to bubbly perfection, but also heats the cornbread through. This should be done just before serving the chili so that the cornbread is warm when it's time to eat.

2	tablespoons vegetable oil
1	onion, chopped
3	tablespoons chili powder
4	garlic cloves, minced
2	teaspoons ground cumin
1½	pounds 85 percent lean ground beef
2	(14.5-ounce) cans diced tomatoes
2	(15-ounce) cans red kidney beans, rinsed
	Salt and pepper
8	ounces cheddar cheese, shredded (2 cups)
1	(1-pound) package prepared cornbread, cut into 4 pieces

1. Adjust oven rack to middle position and heat oven to broil. Heat oil in Dutch oven over medium-high heat until shimmering. Add onion and cook until softened, about 4 minutes. Add chili powder, garlic, and cumin, and cook until fragrant, about 30 seconds. Add beef and cook until no longer pink, about 5 minutes, breaking up chunks with wooden spoon. Add tomatoes and beans and cook until thickened, about 15 minutes. Season with salt and pepper to taste.

2. Sprinkle 1 cup cheddar over cornbread and transfer to baking sheet. Broil until cheese is melted and bubbly and cornbread is heated through, about 3 minutes. Serve with chili, passing remaining cheddar at table.

EASY ALL-AMERICAN CHILI

After onion has softened and garlic, chili powder, and cumin are fragrant, add ground beef and cook until no longer pink, breaking up any chunks with wooden spoon. Add diced tomatoes and beans and simmer for 15 minutes. Season with salt and pepper to taste.

Quick Guinness Beef Stew

Serves 4 to 6

✔ **WHY THIS RECIPE WORKS:** One of the defining characteristics of beef stew is that it cooks for a long time to break down a tough cut of meat and allow all the flavors in the pot to meld. But what if you don't have time to sit around and wait? We replace slow-to-tenderize beef chuck with quick-cooking yet equally beefy sirloin steak tips, and browning the meat first ensures that it is thoroughly cooked through despite the shortened cooking time. The beer in this Irish-inspired recipe adds a great malty flavor; our tasters preferred Guinness Draught since it's sweeter and mellower than Guinness Extra Stout.

1½ **pounds sirloin steak tips,**
   trimmed and cut into 1-inch
   pieces
   Salt and pepper
2 **tablespoons vegetable oil**
2 **tablespoons unsalted butter**
2 **carrots, peeled and sliced**
   ½ inch thick
2 **parsnips, peeled and sliced**
   ½ inch thick
1 **cup frozen pearl onions, thawed**
¼ **cup all-purpose flour**
2 **cups beef broth**
¾ **cup Guinness Draught**

1. Pat steak dry with paper towels and season with salt and pepper. Heat oil in Dutch oven over medium-high heat until just smoking. Cook beef until well browned all over, 6 to 8 minutes. Transfer to plate.

2. Melt butter in now-empty pot. Add carrots, parsnips, onions, and ½ teaspoon salt and cook until browned, 6 to 8 minutes. Stir in flour and cook until golden, about 1 minute. Add broth, beer, and beef, along with any accumulated juices, and bring to boil. Reduce heat to medium-low and simmer, covered, until beef and vegetables are tender, about 10 minutes. Serve.

SMART SHOPPING BUYING STEAK TIPS
Steak tips can be cut from various muscles in the sirloin and round and cost about $5 per pound. After tasting 50 pounds of cheap steak tips, tasters had a clear favorite: a single muscle that butchers call flap meat and that is typically labeled "sirloin tips." Cut from the area just before the hip, flap meat has a distinct longitudinal grain and a deep, robust beefiness. This large steak is most often sold in strips or cubes, but we suggest buying the whole steak and cutting it yourself to ensure uniform pieces.

Quick Chicken Pozole

Serves 4

✔ **WHY THIS RECIPE WORKS:** *Pozole,* also spelled posole, is a thick, hearty Mexican stew made with various cuts of pork or chicken, hominy, onion, and garlic. Pozole comes in three varieties, two made with chiles (dried red or fresh green) and a third, called white pozole, made without chiles. Most traditional recipes take upward of 12 hours to execute. One key to our 30-minute pozole is swapping out obscure cuts of meat in favor of an already-cooked rotisserie chicken, and we wait to add the chicken until just before serving to ensure it does not overcook. We also opt for canned hominy rather than the traditional dried variety. Pozole is usually seasoned with fresh Mexican oregano, which can be difficult to find, but Mediterranean oregano works just as well. A few tablespoons of lime juice lend a final touch of freshness and contrasting acidity. Pozole can be served with a variety of garnishes, including diced avocado, thinly sliced cabbage or romaine lettuce, minced onion, red pepper flakes, diced radishes, lime wedges, and tortilla chips.

1 tablespoon vegetable oil

1 onion, chopped fine

2 garlic cloves, minced

1 tablespoon chili powder

4 cups low-sodium chicken broth

1 (14.5-ounce) can diced tomatoes

1 (15-ounce) can white or yellow hominy, rinsed

2 teaspoons minced fresh oregano

1 (2½-pound) rotisserie chicken, skin and bones discarded, meat shredded into bite-size pieces (3 cups)

2 tablespoons lime juice
   Salt and pepper

1. Heat oil in Dutch oven over medium-high heat until shimmering. Add onion and cook until softened, about 3 minutes. Add garlic and chili powder and cook until fragrant, about 30 seconds.

2. Add broth, tomatoes, hominy, and oregano and cook until tomatoes are soft and flavors meld, about 15 minutes. Add chicken and lime juice and cook until heated through, about 1 minute. Season with salt and pepper to taste and serve.

SMART SHOPPING ROTISSERIE CHICKEN
While we prefer to roast our own bird when it is destined to be the dinnertime centerpiece, it's hard to beat the convenience of an already-cooked rotisserie chicken from the supermarket when in need of cooked meat for a quick recipe like a weeknight soup or stew. A typical rotisserie chicken weighs about 2½ pounds and yields anywhere from 3 to 4 cups of picked meat. When buying a bird for use in a recipe such as this one, make sure to choose one that is plain and simply oven-roasted, as many supermarkets offer rotisserie chickens that have seasonings added (such as garlic and herbs) or are glazed.

Thai Coconut Curry Soup with Chicken

Serves 4

✔ **WHY THIS RECIPE WORKS:** Thai curries are time-consuming dishes to prepare purely because of the work needed to make the curry paste. We have found that using store-bought curry paste saves us from a lot of shopping and prep work and delivers good results. We speed up our recipe even more by poaching the chicken in a separate saucepan while we start building the soup in a Dutch oven, then we add the cooked chicken to the pot at the end. A combination of snow peas and sweet potatoes adds color and texture, and cooking the sweet potatoes in the soup base—a combination of curry paste, ginger, coconut milk, and broth—infuses both components with flavor. Because snow peas cook quickly, we wait until the sweet potatoes are almost tender before stirring them in.

3	tablespoons fish sauce
2	(6-ounce) boneless, skinless chicken breasts, trimmed
1	tablespoon vegetable oil
2	tablespoons Thai green curry paste
2	tablespoons grated fresh ginger
1½	pounds sweet potatoes, peeled and cut into ½-inch cubes
4	cups low-sodium chicken broth
1	(14-ounce) can coconut milk
2	teaspoons sugar
2	cups snow peas, strings removed and cut in half on bias
3	tablespoons lime juice (2 limes)
¼	cup chopped fresh cilantro

1. Bring 1 quart water to simmer in large saucepan. Add 1 tablespoon fish sauce and chicken and simmer, covered, over medium-low heat until chicken registers 160 degrees, 10 to 15 minutes. Transfer chicken to plate and shred into bite-size pieces.

2. Meanwhile, heat oil in Dutch oven over medium-high heat until shimmering. Add curry paste and ginger and cook until fragrant, about 30 seconds. Stir in sweet potatoes, chicken broth, and coconut milk and simmer until sweet potatoes are almost tender, 8 to 10 minutes.

3. Add remaining 2 tablespoons fish sauce, sugar, and snow peas and cook until snow peas are bright green and tender, about 4 minutes. Stir in chicken, lime juice, and cilantro and cook until chicken is heated through, about 1 minute. Serve.

QUICK PREP TIP
SHREDDING MEAT
Holding 1 fork in each hand with tines facing down, insert tines into meat. Gently pull forks away from each other, breaking meat apart and into bite-size strands.

Spicy Chicken and Corn Chowder

Serves 4

✔ **WHY THIS RECIPE WORKS:** Chowders usually rely on a roux of flour and butter for thickening; for ease we turn to creamed corn, a move that also reinforces the fresh corn's flavor. Simmering the broth and creamed corn for just five minutes until the mixture is slightly reduced gives this soup the right consistency without the need for the fussy roux. By poaching the chicken in a separate pan while we sauté the other components in a Dutch oven, we keep the recipe moving. A combination of chopped jalapeño and cayenne pepper creates two levels of heat in this spicy dish. For a milder flavor, you can reduce the cayenne to ¼ teaspoon.

2 **cups low-sodium chicken broth**
2 **(6-ounce) boneless, skinless chicken breasts, trimmed**
Salt and pepper
4 **slices bacon, chopped**
1 **onion, chopped fine**
4 **ears corn, kernels cut from cobs**
1 **jalapeño chile, stemmed, seeded, and chopped fine**
½ **teaspoon cayenne pepper**
2 **(15-ounce) cans creamed corn**
½ **cup half-and-half**
Chopped fresh chives
Lime wedges

1. Bring chicken broth to boil in medium saucepan. Season chicken with salt and pepper and add to saucepan with broth. Simmer, covered, over medium–low heat until meat registers 160 degrees, 10 to 15 minutes, flipping chicken halfway through cooking. Transfer chicken to plate and reserve broth. Using 2 forks, shred chicken into bite–size pieces.

2. Meanwhile, cook bacon in Dutch oven over medium heat until crisp, 5 to 7 minutes. Using slotted spoon, transfer bacon to paper towel–lined plate. Cook onion, corn kernels, jalapeño, cayenne, ½ teaspoon salt, and ¼ teaspoon pepper in bacon fat until vegetables are softened and golden brown, 4 to 5 minutes.

3. Add reserved broth and creamed corn to pot and bring to boil. Simmer over medium heat until slightly thickened, about 5 minutes. Stir in half-and-half, bacon, and shredded chicken and cook until warmed through, about 2 minutes. Season with salt and pepper to taste. Serve with chives and lime wedges.

QUICK PREP TIP HALF-AND-HALF SUBSTITUTES
Curious whether we could find a substitute for half-and-half since it's not something we always have on hand, we decided to run a few tests. We eventually found we were able to best approximate our local brand of half-and-half by using either ⅔ cup skim milk plus ⅓ cup heavy cream, or ¾ cup whole milk plus ¼ cup heavy cream. Of course, to do this you'll need to have heavy cream on hand. Or, if you don't mind a slightly thinner consistency and lighter flavor, whole milk will work in most recipes.

Matzo Ball Soup with Chicken and Asparagus

Serves 4 to 6

✔ **WHY THIS RECIPE WORKS:** Matzo ball soup is a great comfort food, but traditionally it takes a while to prepare, calling for homemade stock, matzo balls made with chicken fat skimmed from the stock, and 30 minutes to 2 hours for chilling the matzo ball batter. For our weeknight version, we use canned broth and precooked rotisserie chicken, and we then boost the flavor by adding asparagus, carrots, and dill. We found that just 10 minutes is sufficient to hydrate store-bought matzo meal and make the dough easy to handle, and using club soda rather than water gives these matzo balls an extra-light texture. Making our matzo balls smaller than traditional versions saves on cooking time.

2   large eggs, lightly beaten

3   tablespoons vegetable oil

    Salt and pepper

½   cup matzo meal

2   tablespoons club soda

1   onion, chopped fine

2   carrots, peeled and sliced thin

10   cups low-sodium chicken broth

1   pound asparagus, trimmed and
    cut into 1-inch pieces

1   (2½-pound) rotisserie chicken,
    skin and bones discarded, meat
    shredded into bite-size pieces
    (3 cups)

2   tablespoons chopped fresh dill

1. Whisk together eggs, 2 tablespoons oil, 1 teaspoon salt, and ¼ teaspoon pepper in bowl. Stir in matzo meal and club soda. Cover and let sit until mixture thickens, about 10 minutes.

2. Meanwhile, heat remaining 1 tablespoon oil in Dutch oven over medium-high heat until shimmering. Add onion and carrots and cook until softened, about 4 minutes. Stir in broth and bring to boil. Using wet hands, roll teaspoonfuls of matzo mixture into ¾-inch balls, dropping balls immediately into simmering broth. Reduce heat to medium-low and gently simmer, covered, until balls have doubled in size, about 15 minutes.

3. While matzo balls cook, place asparagus in bowl, cover, and microwave until tender and bright green, 2 to 4 minutes.

4. Stir asparagus, chicken, and dill into soup. Simmer, uncovered, until chicken is heated through, about 1 minute. Season with salt and pepper to taste and serve.

SMART SHOPPING MATZO MEAL VS. MATZO BALL MIX
Judging by the ingredient list on the package, matzo ball mix attempts to improve traditional matzo meal (really just wheat flour and water) with a host of additives both basic (garlic) and complex (monocalcium phosphate). We wondered if there was a real difference, so we cooked up several batches of matzo balls to find out. The biggest difference wasn't in flavor or ease of preparation, but in texture: Matzo balls made with the matzo meal alone were fluffy but not overly soft and held together nicely, while those made with the matzo ball mix were relatively loose, ragged-looking, and nearly falling apart. Our verdict? Don't mess with a classic—stick with the meal and leave the mix on the shelf.

Cambodian Chicken Soup

Serves 4

✓ **WHY THIS RECIPE WORKS:** The combination of tart lime, bold ginger, rice stick noodles, and fresh herbs makes this soup distinctly Cambodian, a cuisine that reflects the influence of several countries, including Thailand, Vietnam, and India. We rely on the deep flavors of our aromatic-infused broth to make this soup stand out. We infuse the broth with lime zest, ginger, garlic, and chiles and leave the latter three components in large pieces. This allows them to flavor the broth during the 15-minute simmer, but their size makes them easy to remove before serving (it also simplifies prep). Using a rotisserie chicken saves us time, and shredding the meat allows it to really soak up the flavors in our broth.

8	cups low-sodium chicken broth
1	tablespoon grated lime zest plus 2 tablespoons juice (2 limes)
1	(3-inch) piece ginger, peeled, halved lengthwise, and smashed
6	garlic cloves, peeled and gently smashed
5	jalapeño chiles, stemmed, halved, and seeded
	Salt and pepper
7	ounces (⅜-inch-wide) rice noodles
1	(2½-pound) rotisserie chicken, skin and bones discarded, meat shredded into bite-size pieces (3 cups)
¼	cup chopped fresh cilantro
¼	cup chopped fresh basil
5	scallions, sliced thin on bias

1. Combine broth, zest, ginger, garlic, jalapeños, and 1 teaspoon salt in Dutch oven over medium-high heat and bring to boil. Reduce heat to medium, cover, and simmer until broth is flavorful and fragrant, about 15 minutes. Discard ginger, garlic, and chiles.

2. Meanwhile, bring 3 quarts water to boil in large saucepan over medium-high heat. Add noodles and 1 tablespoon salt and cook until tender, about 8 minutes. Drain and transfer to 4 individual serving bowls.

3. Stir chicken, lime juice, cilantro, basil, and scallions into infused broth. Season with salt and pepper to taste and ladle equal amounts over each bowl of noodles. Serve.

QUICK PREP TIP
SMASHING GINGER
Peel knob of fresh ginger root to expose yellow, fibrous flesh. Using sharp knife, halve ginger lengthwise. Then crush each half with butt end of chef's knife or meat pounder until fibers loosen and spread.

White Chicken Chili

Serves 4

✓ **WHY THIS RECIPE WORKS:** There are numerous interpretations of white chicken chili, ranging from a brothy chicken and bean soup to a thick, stewlike version. We wanted our chili to have a texture somewhere in between, with all the appealing flavors and colors of the Southwest. To get the texture just right, we puree half the soup ingredients, then stir the puree back into the pot. The puree turns the stew an appealing, fresh shade of green (from the poblano and jalapeño chiles) and also lends body. To save time, we rely on canned beans and rotisserie chicken, avoiding rubbery, overcooked meat by adding the chicken just before serving to heat it through. To boost the flavor and visual appeal of this dish even more, we recommend that any number of garnishes be passed at the table: diced onion and tomato, hot sauce, sour cream, lime wedges, cilantro leaves, and diced avocado. If you like a spicier chili, increase the number of jalapeños from two to three.

2	tablespoons vegetable oil
1	onion, chopped
2	poblano chiles, stemmed, seeded, and chopped
2	jalapeño chiles, stemmed, seeded, and chopped fine
4	garlic cloves, minced
2	teaspoons ground cumin
1	(15-ounce) can cannellini beans, rinsed
3	cups low-sodium chicken broth
1	(2½-pound) rotisserie chicken, skin and bones discarded, meat shredded into bite-size pieces (3 cups)
¼	cup lime juice (2 limes)
½	cup chopped fresh cilantro
	Salt and pepper

1. Heat oil in Dutch oven over medium-high heat until shimmering. Add onion, poblanos, and jalapeños and cook until soft, 6 to 8 minutes. Add garlic and cumin and cook until fragrant, about 30 seconds.

2. Stir in beans and broth, then transfer 2 cups mixture to blender and process until smooth, 1 to 2 minutes. Stir processed mixture back into pot and bring to simmer. Cook over medium heat until flavors meld and chiles are tender, about 10 minutes.

3. Stir in chicken, lime juice, and cilantro and cook until heated through, about 2 minutes. Season with salt and pepper to taste and serve.

SMART SHOPPING POBLANOS
Poblano chiles are a medium-size Mexican chile. They taste slightly bitter, similar to green bell peppers but with a spicier finish. They are sold both fresh and dried (the dried are called anchos). If you can't find them, you can substitute 1 medium green bell pepper and 1 to 2 tablespoons minced jalapeño (about ½ chile) per poblano.

Escarole, Linguiça, and White Bean Soup

Serves 4

✓ **WHY THIS RECIPE WORKS:** This dish is loosely based on a Tuscan white bean soup recipe in which cured pork, white beans, and hearty greens are the stars. Linguiça is a style of cured pork sausage from Portugal that is seasoned with garlic and paprika (if you have trouble finding it, use chorizo). Browning the sausage before building the soup in the same pot allows us to incorporate the browned bits left behind, which enrich the flavor of the soup. We save time by using canned beans instead of dried and supermarket chicken broth instead of a homemade stock. Escarole contributes a slightly bitter flavor to the dish—a nice counterpoint to the salty linguiça and creamy beans. The addition of garlic and rosemary lends an authentic taste of Tuscany to this soup. To thicken it and make it taste richer, we puree some of the beans and broth in a blender and then add the mixture back to the pot.

2   **tablespoons olive oil**

8   **ounces linguiça sausage, sliced ¼ inch thick**

1   **onion, chopped fine**

3   **garlic cloves, minced**

2   **teaspoons minced fresh rosemary**

2   **(15-ounce) cans white beans, rinsed**

4   **cups low-sodium chicken broth**

1   **head escarole (1 pound), trimmed and sliced ½ inch thick**

     Salt and pepper

1. Heat oil in Dutch oven over medium-high heat until just smoking. Add linguiça and cook until browned, about 4 minutes. Transfer to paper towel–lined plate.

2. Add onion to now-empty pot and cook until softened, about 3 minutes. Add garlic and rosemary and cook until fragrant, about 30 seconds. Add beans and broth and simmer until flavors have melded, about 10 minutes.

3. Transfer 2 cups soup to blender and process until smooth, 1 to 2 minutes. Return processed soup to pot, stir in linguiça and escarole, and cook until escarole has wilted, about 2 minutes. Season with salt and pepper to taste and serve.

SMART SHOPPING ESCAROLE

Escarole is a versatile green that works well whether added raw to salads or cooked briefly in soups or stews. It one of the three main varieties of endive, the others being Belgian endive and curly endive. Distinguished by its broad, slightly curved, pale green leaves, escarole has a milder flavor than its bitter cousins. Escarole is a green that provides various degrees of flavor as its outer leaves are removed. As layers of leaves are peeled back, those remaining are lighter in both color and flavor. Therefore, it's possible to use different layers of the escarole to achieve different tastes within the same dish. Look for heads that are tightly bunched with a fresh, crisp texture and leaves with no wilted ends. Store in the refrigerator, tightly wrapped, for up to three days.

Smoky Chorizo, Chickpea, and Spinach Soup

Serves 4

✓ **WHY THIS RECIPE WORKS:** Sautéing the onions in the rendered sausage fat helps build flavor for this quick-cooking Spanish-inspired soup. After we brown the chorizo and set it aside, we let the rest of the ingredients (aside from the spinach, which is added at the end) cook until the flavors meld; then we puree a portion of the soup and add it back to the pot. This gives the final soup a thicker consistency and more body without having to cook it for hours. Spanish chorizo, which is dry-cured and seasoned with smoked paprika, is the sausage of choice for this soup, but either fresh chorizo or linguiça is an acceptable substitute. You can substitute 8 cups roughly chopped Swiss chard for the spinach, but keep in mind that the chard will require a longer cooking time. Add it to the soup at the end and let it cook for 10 more minutes, or until it is tender.

2	tablespoons olive oil
8	ounces chorizo sausage, cut into ½-inch pieces
1	onion, chopped fine
3	garlic cloves, minced
2	teaspoons minced fresh thyme
1	teaspoon paprika
1	(14.5-ounce) can diced tomatoes
2	(15-ounce) cans chickpeas, rinsed
4	cups low-sodium chicken broth
5	ounces (5 cups) baby spinach
	Salt and pepper

1. Heat oil in Dutch oven over medium-high heat until just smoking. Add chorizo and cook until browned, about 4 minutes. Transfer to paper towel–lined plate.

2. Add onion to now-empty pot and cook until softened, about 3 minutes. Add garlic, thyme, and paprika and cook until fragrant, about 30 seconds. Add tomatoes, chickpeas, and broth and simmer until flavors have melded and tomatoes are very soft, about 10 minutes.

3. Transfer 2 cups soup to blender and process until smooth, 1 to 2 minutes. Return processed soup to pot. Stir in chorizo and spinach and cook until spinach has wilted, about 2 minutes. Season with salt and pepper to taste. Serve.

QUICK PREP TIP PUREEING SOUPS SAFELY

To prevent getting sprayed or burned by an exploding blender top when pureeing hot soup, fill blender jar as directed, making sure it is never more than two-thirds full, hold lid in place with folded kitchen towel, and pulse rapidly a few times before blending continuously.

Making Better Soups 101

They might seem easy enough to make, but all too often soups turn out watery and bland. To make sure every spoonful of soup is richly flavored, with juicy meat and tender vegetables, follow these tips.

1. SAUTÉ YOUR AROMATICS AND SPICES

The first step for many of our soups is to sauté aromatics, such as onion and garlic, which makes for a more complex, fuller-flavored soup. Cook the aromatics just until they begin to soften; onions will take several minutes, while garlic requires just 30 seconds.

2. USE GOOD BROTH

Whether you're using homemade stock or store-bought broth that's been enhanced with aromatics, starting with a good base is essential. For store-bought broth, our favorite beef broth is Rachael Ray Stock-in-a-Box; our favorite chicken broth is Swanson Certified Organic Free Range Chicken Broth; and our favorite vegetable broth is Swanson Vegetarian Vegetable Broth.

3. SIMMER, DON'T BOIL

It's a fine line between simmering and boiling, and it can make all the difference in soups. A boil refers to a rapidly bubbling and reducing liquid. A simmer is a restrained version of a boil; fewer bubbles break the surface and do so with less vigor. A boil can break down vegetables, toughen meat, and cause fat droplets to become more finely dispersed, making the soup difficult to defat.

4. CUT VEGETABLES PROPERLY AND STAGGER THEIR ADDITION

Improperly cut vegetables can cook unevenly, so make sure to cut them to the size specified. When using a variety of vegetables, staggering their addition accounts for their varying cooking times. Hardy vegetables can usually be added early on, whereas delicate vegetables should be added later.

5. SEASON BEFORE SERVING

Many ingredients, such as store-bought broth, canned tomatoes, and canned beans, are heavily seasoned, so it's best to add salt at the end of cooking, after tasting the finished soup first. We also often reserve some additional flavorings, such as fresh herbs or lemon juice, to add freshness and brightness.

Pick the Right Pot

We like to use a Dutch oven with at least a 6-quart capacity. The pot's bottom should be thick so it conducts heat evenly and prevents food from scorching, and the lid should fit tightly to prevent moisture loss. Our favorites are the Le Creuset French Oven ($269; above) and the All-Clad Stainless 8 Quart Stockpot ($294.95). Our best buy is the Tramontina 6.5 Quart Cast-Iron Dutch Oven, which is just $54.95.

Gazpacho with Avocado and Crab

Serves 4

✔ **WHY THIS RECIPE WORKS:** Making gazpacho the traditional way can be labor-intensive, from mashing garlic and stale bread (the thickener) with a mortar and pestle to cutting all the vegetables into perfect small dice. For this streamlined version, we omit the stale bread (to save time and give our soup a fresher taste), and we use a food processor to quickly chop the vegetables. Mixing the vegetables with tomato juice gives the soup the proper gazpacho consistency, while adding crab makes it a hearty yet light meal. We avoid refrigerating fresh tomatoes since it dulls their taste, but we keep the other ingredients (especially the tomato juice since we use a significant amount) in the refrigerator until we're ready to make the soup to keep them cold. Since gazpacho is typically served chilled, you can refrigerate the finished soup until you are ready to serve it. If you like a little heat in your gazpacho, feel free to add hot sauce to taste.

1 cucumber, peeled, halved lengthwise, seeded, and chopped into large pieces

1 red bell pepper, stemmed, seeded, and chopped into large pieces

1 pound tomatoes, cored and quartered

1 shallot, minced

1 garlic clove, minced

3 tablespoons sherry vinegar

2 cups tomato juice
  Salt and pepper

1 pound lump crabmeat, picked over for shells

1 avocado, halved, pitted, and cut into ½-inch pieces

2 tablespoons extra-virgin olive oil

1. Place 4 serving bowls in refrigerator to chill. Pulse cucumber and bell pepper in food processor until broken down to ¼- to ½-inch pieces, about 12 pulses, and transfer to bowl. Repeat with tomatoes.

2. Add shallot, garlic, vinegar, and tomato juice to bowl with tomatoes, cucumber, and bell pepper and stir until thoroughly combined. Season with salt and pepper to taste.

3. Ladle gazpacho into chilled bowls, top with crabmeat and avocado, then drizzle with oil. Serve.

SMART SHOPPING GRADES OF CRABMEAT

Though preferable, fresh crabmeat can be hard to come by; packaged crabmeat that has been cooked, cleaned, and pasteurized is acceptable. Differences in grade correspond to the part of the crab the meat comes from and the size of the pieces. Jumbo lump is from the two large muscles connected to the swimming legs. The most expensive, it boasts large pieces with a bright white color and delicate flavor. Lump is composed of smaller or broken pieces of jumbo lump, along with other smaller pieces of body meat. It is also white and has a delicate flavor. Backfin is a mix of smaller "flake" pieces of body meat. Backfin is finer textured than lump, but its flavor is similar. Claw meat comes from the swimming fins and claws. Because these are very active muscles (much like dark meat in poultry) the meat is pink or brown, high in fat, and has a much stronger flavor. Its texture is similar to backfin, but it's oilier.

Quick Bouillabaisse

Serves 4

✔ **WHY THIS RECIPE WORKS:** Bouillabaisse is a classic French stew made with an assortment of fish and shellfish, as well as tomatoes, white wine, garlic, saffron, and seasonings. Traditional recipes usually involve making a homemade fish stock and call for varieties of fish that are hard to find and/or expensive, as well as Pernod (or other anise-flavored liqueurs). For our version, we add fennel to provide the anise flavor in lieu of Pernod, and we rely on the simple seafood duo of clams and red snapper. We found that a combination of clam juice and canned tomatoes, bolstered with onion, plenty of garlic, orange zest, and fennel, is an excellent substitute for homemade stock, providing deep flavor in a fraction of the time.

2	tablespoons extra-virgin olive oil
1	onion, chopped fine
1	large fennel bulb, stalks discarded, bulb halved, cored, and sliced thin
6	garlic cloves, minced
6	(4-inch) strips orange zest
1	(28-ounce) can whole tomatoes
2	pounds medium hard-shell clams, scrubbed
4	(8-ounce) bottles clam juice
1	pound skinless red snapper fillets, cut into 2-inch pieces
	Salt and pepper
¼	cup chopped fresh parsley

1. Heat oil in Dutch oven over medium heat until shimmering. Add onion and fennel and cook until softened, about 5 minutes. Add garlic and orange zest and cook until fragrant, about 30 seconds. Increase heat to medium-high and add tomatoes. Simmer until slightly thickened, stirring frequently to break apart tomatoes, about 3 minutes.

2. Add clams, cover, and cook until clams start to open, about 3 minutes, checking pot periodically and transferring clams to plate as soon as they open. Discard any unopened clams.

3. Add clam juice to pot and bring to simmer. Reduce heat to medium, then gently add fish to broth and cook until fish is opaque, about 3 minutes. Remove zest. Season with salt and pepper to taste, return clams to pot, and cook until heated through, about 1 minute. Sprinkle with parsley and serve.

SIMPLE SIDE EASY ROUILLE CROUTONS

Rouille, a fiery red sauce consisting of fresh bread crumbs, garlic, olive oil, saffron, and cayenne, is a traditional accompaniment to seafood dishes such as bouillabaisse. Our version substitutes roasted red peppers for the saffron, giving it a more vibrant red color and a more affordable price. Place 8 thin slices of baguette on a baking sheet and toast in a 350-degree oven until crisp and dry, about 10 minutes. Meanwhile, process 1 cup jarred roasted red peppers, 1 cup baguette cut into 1-inch pieces, 2 minced garlic cloves, and ⅛ teaspoon cayenne pepper in a food processor until smooth. With the processor running, slowly add ¼ cup extra-virgin olive oil. Season the mixture with salt and pepper to taste, then spread it on the toasts and serve with the bouillabaisse. Serves 4.

Shrimp Tortilla Soup

Serves 4 to 6

✓ **WHY THIS RECIPE WORKS:** The inspiration for this recipe comes from Southwestern chicken tortilla soup, but we change things up a bit by substituting shrimp for the chicken. Since we don't want to spend the time making shrimp broth, we keep convenient, canned chicken broth in the lineup. Pureeing the broth with canned tomatoes and hominy gives the soup a nutty and slightly sweet flavor that's perfect for this recipe while also adding body to the broth. The soup can be served with avocado slices if desired.

4   **(6-inch) corn tortillas, cut into ¼-inch-thick strips**

2   **tablespoons vegetable oil**
    Salt and pepper

1   **large onion, chopped**

4   **garlic cloves, minced**

2   **tablespoons minced canned chipotle chile in adobo sauce**

6   **cups low-sodium chicken broth**

2   **(15-ounce) cans hominy, rinsed**

1   **(14.5-ounce) can diced tomatoes**

1½ **pounds medium shrimp (41 to 50 per pound), peeled and deveined**

¼   **cup chopped fresh cilantro**

1   **tablespoon lime juice, plus lime wedges for serving**

1. Adjust oven rack to middle position and heat oven to 425 degrees. Spread tortilla strips on rimmed baking sheet and toss with 1 tablespoon oil. Bake until strips are deep golden brown and crisp, 12 to 14 minutes, tossing strips halfway through baking. Season with salt to taste and transfer to paper towel–lined plate.

2. Meanwhile, heat remaining 1 tablespoon oil in Dutch oven over medium-high heat until shimmering. Add onion and cook until soft, about 4 minutes. Add garlic and chipotle and cook until fragrant, about 30 seconds. Add broth, hominy, and tomatoes and bring to simmer. Reduce heat to low, cover, and simmer until flavors meld, about 15 minutes.

3. Working in batches, process soup in blender until smooth, 1 to 2 minutes. Transfer pureed soup to clean pot and bring to simmer. Add shrimp and cook, stirring occasionally, until opaque in center, about 3 minutes. Stir in cilantro and lime juice and season with salt and pepper to taste. Ladle soup into individual bowls and top with tortilla strips. Serve, passing lime wedges separately.

SMART SHOPPING HOMINY
Hominy is made from dried corn kernels that have been soaked or cooked in an alkaline solution (commonly lime-water or calcium hydroxide) to remove the germ and hull. It has a slightly chewy texture and toasted corn flavor and is widely used in soups, stews, and chilis throughout the Southern United States and South America. It is sold both dried and canned; we prefer the convenience of canned hominy, which only requires a quick rinse before using.

Quick Black Bean Soup

Serves 4

✔ **WHY THIS RECIPE WORKS:** A hearty black bean soup is a meal that satisfies carnivores and vegetarians alike. A staple in Mexican, Cuban, and Caribbean cuisines, black bean soup is usually a long-simmered affair that begins with dried beans. For this recipe, we trade in the dried beans for canned to save time. Traditionally, black bean soups include some kind of pork; to keep this recipe vegetarian and at the same time give it deep flavor, we use plenty of garlic, cumin, and smoky chipotle. Toasting the spices in the skillet before adding any liquid (a technique known as blooming) intensifies their flavor and keeps them from tasting raw in the final soup. We puree some of the beans before adding them to the pot to give the soup extra body; doing this before we start cooking makes the dangerous task of pureeing hot liquids unnecessary. We call for serving this soup with diced avocado and cilantro; cooked white rice, sour cream, lime wedges, and pico de gallo are also great accompaniments.

2	tablespoons olive oil
1	onion, chopped
1	red bell pepper, stemmed, seeded, and chopped
	Salt and pepper
6	garlic cloves, minced
1	teaspoon ground cumin
1	teaspoon minced canned chipotle chile in adobo sauce
4	(15-ounce) cans black beans, rinsed
4	cups vegetable broth
½	cup chopped fresh cilantro
1	avocado, halved, pitted, and cut into ½-inch pieces

1. Heat oil in Dutch oven over medium-high heat until shimmering. Cook onion, bell pepper, and ½ teaspoon salt until lightly browned, 6 to 8 minutes. Add garlic, cumin, and chipotle and cook until fragrant, about 30 seconds.

2. Meanwhile, puree half of beans and 1 cup broth in blender until smooth. Stir pureed beans, remaining whole beans, and remaining broth into pot and bring to simmer. Cook until slightly thickened, about 10 minutes. Stir in cilantro and season with salt and pepper to taste. Serve with diced avocado.

SIMPLE SIDE EASY WHITE RICE
Bring 2 cups rinsed long-grain rice and 2½ cups water to boil in saucepan. Reduce heat to low, cover, and cook until water is just absorbed and small holes appear in surface of rice, about 10 minutes. Remove pot from heat and let sit, covered, until rice is tender, about 15 minutes. Serves 4.

SIMPLE SIDE PICO DE GALLO
Combine 1 pound cored, chopped plum tomatoes, ½ small diced red onion, 1 stemmed, seeded, and minced jalapeño chile, 2 tablespoons chopped fresh cilantro, and 2 teaspoons lime juice in bowl. Season with salt and pepper to taste. Let sit at room temperature for 15 minutes for flavors to meld before serving. Serves 4.

Creamy White Bean Soup with Kale Pesto

Serves 4

✔ **WHY THIS RECIPE WORKS:** A combination of leeks, carrots, garlic, and rosemary lends earthy flavors to our white bean soup, while lemon juice added at the end gives it brightness. We found the perfect complement to our mildly flavored, creamy soup was a kale pesto, a unique alternative to standard basil pesto. It's a bit more assertive and thus gives our bean soup a bolder spark of flavor. Instead of fussing with blanching the kale in water, we microwave it to tame the bitterness. (It's important not to overdo it in the microwave: If the kale is microwaved for too long, it can turn dry and leathery. Leave it slightly damp after washing to help along the wilting.) Then we quickly puree it with walnuts and Parmesan as you would with a classic pesto.

6   ounces kale, stemmed and chopped

5   tablespoons extra-virgin olive oil

1   pound leeks, white and light green parts only, halved lengthwise, sliced ½ inch thick, and washed thoroughly

1   carrot, peeled and chopped fine

1½   teaspoons minced fresh rosemary

4   garlic cloves, minced

4   cups water

4   (15-ounce) cans cannellini beans, rinsed

2   tablespoons lemon juice
    Salt and pepper

¼   cup walnuts, toasted

¼   cup grated Parmesan cheese

1. Place kale in bowl, cover, and microwave until slightly wilted, about 2 minutes. Let cool to room temperature, about 10 minutes.

2. Meanwhile, heat 2 tablespoons oil in Dutch oven over medium-high heat until shimmering. Add leeks and carrot and cook until softened, about 5 minutes. Add rosemary and three-quarters of garlic and cook until fragrant, about 30 seconds. Stir in water and beans and bring to boil. Reduce heat to medium-low and simmer, covered, until flavors have melded, about 10 minutes. Working in batches, process soup in blender until smooth, 1 to 2 minutes. Return to clean pot, stir in lemon juice, and season with salt and pepper to taste.

3. Process kale, remaining garlic, walnuts, Parmesan cheese, and remaining 3 tablespoons oil in blender until smooth. Season with salt and pepper to taste. Ladle soup into bowls, spoon pesto over each portion, and serve.

QUICK PREP TIP
STEMMING GREENS
To remove stems and clean leaves at once, hold each leaf at base of stem over bowl of water. Using sharp knife, slash leafy portion from both sides of thick stem.

Moroccan Sweet Potato Soup

Serves 4

✔ **WHY THIS RECIPE WORKS:** This creamy, silky soup balances the warm spice combination of garam masala (an Indian spice mix) and smoked paprika with the brightness of a lemon-herb pesto. We build a flavorful base for our soup in the Dutch oven with our spices, onion, and plenty of garlic, then add broth and finally the sweet potatoes, which only take 10 minutes to cook through since we cut them into thin pieces. The fragrant lemon-herb pesto made with cilantro, cumin, red pepper flakes, and lemon juice and zest is the ideal finishing touch: It brightens the flavor of the soup while simultaneously reinforcing its Moroccan pedigree. Any orange-fleshed sweet potato can be used in this recipe. Avoid the purple and white varieties—they turn an unappetizing color when blended.

6	tablespoons olive oil
1	onion, chopped
	Salt and pepper
4	garlic cloves, minced
2	teaspoons garam masala
1	teaspoon smoked paprika
5	cups vegetable broth
2	pounds sweet potatoes, peeled, quartered lengthwise, and sliced thin
½	cup chopped fresh cilantro
½	teaspoon ground cumin
⅛	teaspoon red pepper flakes
1	teaspoon grated lemon zest plus 1 tablespoon juice

1. Heat 2 tablespoons oil in Dutch oven over medium-high heat until just shimmering. Add onion and 1 teaspoon salt and cook, stirring frequently, until onion is softened, about 5 minutes. Stir in three-quarters of garlic, garam masala, and ½ teaspoon paprika and cook until fragrant, about 30 seconds.

2. Add broth and sweet potatoes and bring to boil. Reduce heat to medium and cook, partially covered, until sweet potatoes are easily pierced with knife, about 10 minutes.

3. Meanwhile, combine cilantro, remaining garlic, remaining ½ teaspoon paprika, cumin, red pepper flakes, remaining 4 tablespoons oil, and lemon zest and juice in small bowl. Season with salt and pepper to taste.

4. Working in batches, process soup in blender until smooth, 1 to 2 minutes. Return soup to clean pot and season with salt and pepper to taste. Ladle soup into individual bowls, swirl in lemon-herb pesto, and serve.

SMART SHOPPING **VEGETABLE BROTH**

We turn to vegetable broth for vegetarian dishes and for lighter soups or vegetable dishes that might be overwhelmed by the flavor of chicken broth. Often we use a mix of chicken and vegetable broths since vegetable broth can be too sweet used alone. In our search for the best vegetable broth, we tested 10 brands, finding that a hefty amount of salt and the presence of enough vegetable content to be listed on the ingredient list were key. Our favorite was **Swanson Vegetarian Vegetable Broth**.

COCONUT-LIME CHICKEN AND CABBAGE-MANGO SLAW

Salads

28 Blue Cheese Wedge with Maple-Glazed Bacon

29 Cabbage with Kielbasa and Honey-Dijon Dressing

30 Spanish Tapas Salad

32 Southwest Beef Salad with Cornbread Croutons

35 Steak Salad with Creamy Horseradish Dressing

36 Blue Cheese and Walnut Chopped Chicken Salad

37 Italian Cobb Salad

38 Basil-Parmesan Chicken Salad with Apples

40 Moroccan-Style Chicken, Date, and Olive Salad

41 Coconut-Lime Chicken and Cabbage-Mango Slaw

42 Chicken, Goat Cheese, and Cherry Salad

44 Frisée and Fried-Egg Salad with Lentils

45 Tuscan-Style Tuna and White Bean Salad

47 Smoked Trout Salad

48 Lemony Salmon and Roasted Beet Salad

49 Romaine Wedge with Shrimp and Feta Dressing

50 Tropical Shrimp and Rice Salad

Blue Cheese Wedge with Maple-Glazed Bacon

Serves 4

✔ **WHY THIS RECIPE WORKS:** The blue cheese wedge is a diner favorite, but it's usually predictably boring (read: just a wedge of iceberg) and drowning in thick, flavorless dressing. Adding maple-glazed bacon for a hit of sweet smokiness and some meaty heft is our first step toward giving this classic new life. For bacon bits that are both crisp and well glazed, we precook chopped bacon to render as much fat as possible. After letting the cooked bits briefly drain on paper towels, we pour maple syrup into the pan, add the bacon, and let the syrup reduce until it creates the perfect coating. Our other key to success? A homemade dressing. Made with sour cream, mayonnaise, buttermilk, and blue cheese (which we crumble ourselves, rather than buy the stale-tasting precrumbled stuff), it's far fresher and more balanced than the store-bought variety, and it only takes a few minutes to whip up.

3	ounces blue cheese, crumbled (¾ cup)
5	tablespoons buttermilk
5	tablespoons sour cream
3	tablespoons mayonnaise
1	tablespoon cider vinegar
	Salt and pepper
12	ounces bacon, chopped
¼	cup maple syrup
1	head iceberg lettuce (9 ounces), cored and quartered lengthwise
3	tomatoes, cored and cut into wedges

1. Using fork, mash blue cheese and buttermilk together in small bowl until mixture resembles cottage cheese, about 1 minute. Stir in sour cream, mayonnaise, and vinegar and season with salt and pepper to taste.

2. Cook bacon in large skillet over medium heat until crisp, 5 to 7 minutes. Transfer bacon to paper towel–lined plate and pour off fat from skillet. Pour maple syrup into now–empty skillet and add bacon, stirring to coat. Cook over medium heat until syrup is reduced to glazy consistency and bacon is thoroughly coated, about 4 minutes. Transfer to plate, separating bacon pieces to prevent clumping.

3. Arrange lettuce wedges on individual plates. Arrange tomatoes around each wedge, spoon dressing over wedges, and sprinkle with bacon pieces. Serve.

QUICK PREP TIP STORING CHEESE

Storing cheese presents a conundrum: As it sits, it releases moisture. If this moisture evaporates too quickly, the cheese dries out. But if the moisture is trapped on the cheese's surface, it encourages mold. Specialty cheese paper avoids this problem with a two-ply construction that lets cheese breathe without drying out, but it usually requires mail-ordering. For a more accessible method, we found wrapping our cheese with waxed or parchment paper, then loosely wrapping around the parchment with aluminum foil, did the trick. Both papers wick moisture away, while the foil cover traps just enough water to keep the cheese from drying out.

Cabbage with Kielbasa and Honey-Dijon Dressing

Serves 4

☑ **WHY THIS RECIPE WORKS:** We typically call on smoky kielbasa (aka Polish sausage) when we are making slow-cooked dishes such as stews and braises; here we find a creative way to use its bold flavor in a weeknight salad that will satisfy even the heartiest appetite. For the base, we opt for cabbage since it is a traditional side to sausage dishes, and we use the light, sweet napa variety to freshen up things up. Wilting the cabbage quickly on the stovetop adds flavor and gives it a softer texture. For a little extra heartiness, we add creamy white beans to the mix. Kielbasa and mustard are a classic pairing, so we combine Dijon with honey and cider vinegar to make a tangy, sweet dressing that pulls this salad together.

5	tablespoons olive oil
2	tablespoons Dijon mustard
2	tablespoons honey
2	tablespoons cider vinegar
1	pound kielbasa, sliced ½ inch thick on bias
1	red onion, halved and sliced thin
½	teaspoon caraway seeds
1	(15-ounce) can cannellini beans, rinsed
	Salt and pepper
1	small head napa cabbage (1½ pounds), cored and shredded (8¼ cups)
¼	cup chopped fresh dill

1. Whisk together 4 tablespoons oil, mustard, honey, and vinegar in bowl. Cook sausage in 12-inch skillet over medium-high heat until well browned, 3 to 4 minutes per side. Transfer sausage to plate and tent with foil.

2. Add remaining 1 tablespoon oil, onion, and caraway seeds to now-empty skillet, reduce heat to medium, and cook, stirring frequently, until onion is softened and browned, about 12 minutes. Add beans and 2 tablespoons mustard mixture and cook until warmed through, about 1 minute. Season with salt and pepper to taste.

3. Reduce heat to low, add remaining dressing and cabbage to skillet, and toss until warmed through and slightly wilted, about 4 minutes. Off heat, stir in dill and season with salt and pepper to taste. Serve topped with kielbasa and bean mixture.

QUICK PREP TIP REVIVING CRYSTALLIZED HONEY

All honey hardens and crystallizes over time, but it doesn't have to be discarded. To bring honey back to its translucent, liquid state, you can use either simmering water or a microwave. In either case, make sure the honey's container is heatproof or microwave-safe. Place the opened jar of honey in a medium saucepan filled with about 1 inch of water and place the saucepan over low heat, stirring the honey frequently, until the crystals melt. Alternatively, heat the opened jar in the microwave in 10-second increments, stirring intermittently, until liquefied.

Spanish Tapas Salad

Serves 4

✓ **WHY THIS RECIPE WORKS:** Spanish tapas platters offer a lot of appeal since you can enjoy a number of flavors and textures on a single plate. Here we bring together many of the classic tapas components into an easily assembled, dinner-size composed salad. We dress canned chickpeas and pimento-stuffed olives with a garlicky olive oil dressing, and then we toss some baby greens with the remaining dressing. To complete the meal, we add chorizo (which we sauté quickly in a skillet), Manchego cheese, and another tapas favorite known as *pan de tomate*. Though similar to Italian bruschetta, pan de tomate skips the chopped tomato topping and instead rubs the toasted bread with a cut tomato, which gives it just a hint of sweetness and color. Adding the bread to the hot skillet after sautéing the chorizo makes quick work of toasting it.

½   **cup extra-virgin olive oil**

½   **cup pimento-stuffed green olives, sliced, plus 2 tablespoons brine**

2   **garlic cloves, peeled (1 minced, 1 whole)**

1   **(15-ounce) can chickpeas, rinsed**
     Salt and pepper

8   **ounces chorizo sausage, sliced ¼ inch thick**

4   **(¾-inch-thick) slices crusty Italian bread**

1   **tomato, halved**

5   **ounces (5 cups) mesclun greens**

1   **ounce Manchego cheese, cut into 4 slices**

1. Whisk 5 tablespoons oil, olive brine, and minced garlic together in bowl. Toss 2 tablespoons dressing with olives and chickpeas and season with salt and pepper to taste.

2. Heat 1 tablespoon oil in 12-inch skillet over medium-high heat until just smoking. Cook chorizo until lightly browned and crisp, about 2 minutes per side. Transfer chorizo to paper towel–lined plate.

3. Add remaining 2 tablespoons oil to now-empty skillet and heat until shimmering. Lay bread slices in skillet and cook until crisp and golden on both sides, about 1 minute per side. Remove from skillet and rub 1 side of each slice with whole garlic clove and halved tomato.

4. Toss mesclun greens with remaining dressing and season with salt and pepper to taste. Arrange greens, toasted bread, chickpea salad, chorizo, and cheese on platter or individual plates and serve.

QUICK PREP TIP
MAKING PAN DE TOMATE
The method for making the tomato- and garlic-rubbed toasts for this recipe is similar to that for making Italian-style bruschetta. Start by toasting the bread slices on both sides. Then, while they are still warm, rub the slices on one side with the whole garlic clove, followed by the halved tomato.

Southwest Beef Salad with Cornbread Croutons

Serves 4

✓ **WHY THIS RECIPE WORKS:** The beefy flavor of flank steak is the perfect choice for the Southwestern profile of this salad. For a bold yet simple-to-make dressing, we combine cilantro, jalapeño, garlic, and lime juice. Red bell pepper adds sweetness and crunch to the mix, while mild Bibb lettuce allows the strong flavors of the dressing to shine through. Corn is a familiar ingredient in Southwestern cooking, and convenient store-bought cornbread, cut into cubes and toasted to make croutons, incorporates it in a creative, tasty way. To keep this recipe streamlined, we toast the cornbread cubes while we cook our steak and prepare the rest of the salad.

10	ounces store-bought cornbread, cut into ¾-inch cubes
1	(1-pound) flank steak, trimmed
	Salt and pepper
7	tablespoons vegetable oil
½	cup chopped fresh cilantro
¼	cup lime juice (2 limes)
1	jalapeño chile, stemmed, seeded, and chopped
1	garlic clove, minced
2	heads Bibb lettuce (1 pound), leaves separated and torn into bite-size pieces
1	red bell pepper, stemmed, seeded, and sliced thin

1. Adjust oven rack to middle position and heat oven to 375 degrees. Coat rimmed baking sheet with vegetable oil spray and spread cornbread cubes in even layer on sheet. Coat cubes with oil spray and bake until crisp and golden brown, 15 to 18 minutes, rotating sheet and stirring cubes halfway through baking.

2. Meanwhile, pat steak dry with paper towels and season with salt and pepper. Heat 1 tablespoon oil in 12-inch skillet over medium-high heat until just smoking. Cook steak until meat registers 125 degrees (for medium-rare), 3 to 5 minutes per side. Transfer to cutting board, tent with foil, and let rest for 5 minutes.

3. Process remaining 6 tablespoons oil, cilantro, lime juice, jalapeño, garlic, and 1 teaspoon salt in food processor until smooth, 15 seconds. Transfer ⅓ cup dressing to large bowl, toss with lettuce and bell pepper, and season with salt and pepper to taste. Slice steak thin against grain. Transfer lettuce mixture to serving platter or individual plates, top with steak and croutons, and drizzle with remaining dressing. Serve.

QUICK PREP TIP
MAKING CORNBREAD CROUTONS
Cut store-bought cornbread into ¾-inch-wide "logs," then cut logs into roughly equal-size cubes. Place cubes on rimmed baking sheet, spray lightly with vegetable oil spray, and bake in 375-degree oven, stirring halfway through baking time, when some cubes have browned on 1 side.

ALL ABOUT Salad Greens

There's a whole world out there of salad greens, which only seems to complicate things if you are racing through the supermarket and need to get dinner on the table. Here are a few varieties we particularly like to use when putting together a quick weeknight meal, as they offer a good mix of flavors and textures.

Arugula

Arugula has delicate, dark green leaves and a peppery bite. It is sold in bunches, usually with roots attached, or prewashed in cello bags. Arugula bruises easily and can be very sandy, so wash it thoroughly in several changes of water before using.

Bibb Lettuce

Heads of Bibb lettuce are small and compact and pale to medium green in color. The outer leaves are soft and buttery, while the inner leaves have a nice crunch and a sweet, mild flavor that makes it adaptable.

Napa Cabbage

In addition to familiar green and red cabbage, there's also napa or Chinese cabbage (pictured). This variety has pale yellow or light green crinkled leaves, a mild and refreshing flavor and crunch, and is sweeter and more tender than green or red cabbage.

Spinach

All varieties of spinach have a vibrant green color and an earthy flavor; choose tender, deep green flat-leaf or baby spinach (pictured) for salads rather than the tough and fibrous curly-leaf variety, which is better suited to cooking. If purchased loose, spinach must be rinsed thoroughly in several changes of water to remove dirt.

Iceberg Lettuce

Iceberg has been enjoying a renaissance, thanks to its clean, slightly sweet flavor and crisp texture. When shopping, look for heads that are heavy for their size and show no signs of browning at the leaves' edges. Iceberg is the classic choice for wedge salads.

Romaine Lettuce

With long, full heads and stiff, deep green leaves, romaine has a crisp, crunchy texture with a mild earthy flavor that makes it a great all-purpose lettuce. Romaine hearts are also sold in bags, a great choice for weeknight cooks. Tough, dry outer leaves should be discarded.

Frisée

Its feathery white and pale green leaves are a clue that frisée is a member of the chicory family. It is milder in flavor than other chicories, which are typically bitter.

Watercress

Watercress's delicate, dark green leaves have a refreshing mustardlike flavor. If buying watercress in bunches (it's also available prewashed in bags), make sure to wash it thoroughly. Recently we've also come across a related green that goes by names including upland cress, American cress, early yellow rocket, and land cress. It holds up better than watercress, but while we thought its flavor somewhat resembled that of its cousin, tasters felt it actually had more in common with peppery arugula.

Steak Salad with Creamy Horseradish Dressing

Serves 4

✔ **WHY THIS RECIPE WORKS:** Because strip steaks take only a few minutes to cook on the stovetop, they make a great choice for a weeknight meal. But instead of serving a steak dinner, here we slice strip steaks thin to crown a hearty salad. Since horseradish sauce is a classic match for beef, we turn it into a dressing by adding 2 tablespoons of lemon juice to loosen our standard sauce recipe enough to dress our greens. Though unexpected, sweet, earthy beets are a great foil to the richness of the steak and the heat from the horseradish. Since roasting beets until they are tender takes too long for a quick weeknight meal, we grate them and add them to our salad raw. It's an unusual approach that gives this salad just the right fresh, sweet flavor and crunchy texture. Toasted, chopped walnuts make the perfect finishing touch.

2   **(10- to 12-ounce) strip steaks, 1 inch thick, trimmed**

      Salt and pepper

1   **tablespoon vegetable oil**

¼   **cup sour cream**

2   **tablespoons lemon juice**

2   **tablespoons chopped fresh chives**

1   **tablespoon prepared horseradish**

2   **romaine hearts (12 ounces), torn into bite-size pieces**

½   **cup walnuts, toasted and chopped**

1   **beet, trimmed, peeled, and grated**

1. Pat steaks dry with paper towels and season with salt and pepper. Heat oil in 12-inch skillet over medium-high heat until just smoking. Cook steaks until browned on both sides and meat registers 125 degrees (for medium-rare), 3 to 5 minutes per side. Transfer to cutting board, tent with foil, and let rest for 5 minutes.

2. Meanwhile, whisk sour cream, lemon juice, chives, and horseradish together in large bowl.

3. Slice steak thin against grain. Add romaine, walnuts, and beet to bowl with dressing and toss to coat. Season with salt and pepper to taste. Arrange salad on individual plates, top with sliced steak, and serve.

QUICK PREP TIP
GRATING BEETS
Julienning beets is a tedious chore, so we opt to use a box grater to get the job done quickly and easily. For the longest strands, grate the beet on the large holes of the box grater using long, measured strokes from the top of the grater to the bottom.

Blue Cheese and Walnut Chopped Chicken Salad

Serves 4

✓ **WHY THIS RECIPE WORKS:** To avoid a run-of-the-mill chicken salad, we focus on two things: flavor and convenience. To keep things light and fresh, we start by making romaine lettuce, with its slightly bitter taste and unmistakable crunch, the foundation. We then add all of the usual favorite chicken salad ingredients, but with a few twists. Instead of cutting poached chicken into cubes, we shred the meat (from a ready-to-eat rotisserie chicken), which gives our salad better texture and allows the chicken to grab hold of the dressing. We avoid a salad bogged down by a heavy mayonnaise-based dressing by opting for a simple mixture of sherry vinegar, Dijon mustard, and extra-virgin olive oil to pull it all together. Slicing the grapes in half makes for easier eating, and crumbled blue cheese and toasted walnuts add contrasting textures and richness to take this salad to the next level.

3   **tablespoons sherry vinegar**

3   **tablespoons Dijon mustard**

¼   **cup extra-virgin olive oil**
     Salt and pepper

1   **(2½-pound) rotisserie chicken, skin and bones discarded, meat shredded into bite-size pieces (3 cups)**

9   **ounces red grapes, halved (1½ cups)**

1   **cup walnuts, toasted and chopped**

2   **ounces blue cheese, crumbled (½ cup)**

1   **large head romaine lettuce (14 ounces), torn into bite-size pieces**

1. Whisk vinegar and mustard together in medium bowl until thoroughly combined. Drizzle in oil, whisking constantly, until dressing is thick and emulsified. Season with salt and pepper to taste.

2. Combine chicken, grapes, walnuts, cheese, and lettuce in large bowl. Add dressing and gently toss until ingredients are thoroughly coated. Season with salt and pepper to taste. Serve.

QUICK PREP TIP
MAKING A VINAIGRETTE
In this recipe, mustard works as our emulsifying agent. After it's combined with the sherry vinegar, we pour the oil into the mixture in a slow, steady stream, whisking constantly, until a thick and creamy mixture is formed.

Italian Cobb Salad

Serves 4

✔ **WHY THIS RECIPE WORKS:** Cobb salad, a favorite since the 1920s, gets a fresh look in this recipe with an Italian twist. We swap pancetta for the bacon, omit the usual avocado, add basil, and use milder, creamier Italian Gorgonzola rather than the traditional Roquefort. To really drive home the flavor of the cheese, we not only crumble it over the finished salad but also whisk it right into the vinaigrette. Sweet cherry tomatoes get a quick sauté in a hot pan to soften their flesh, blister their skins a bit, and intensify their flavor. While deli turkey breast often appears in diner versions of this salad, we prefer to cook boneless, skinless chicken breasts in the rendered pancetta fat for plenty of flavor, then shred the meat to ensure it soaks up the dressing.

3	ounces thinly sliced pancetta
2	(6-ounce) boneless, skinless chicken breasts, trimmed
	Salt and pepper
5	tablespoons extra-virgin olive oil
12	ounces cherry tomatoes
2	tablespoons red wine vinegar
3	ounces Gorgonzola cheese, crumbled (¾ cup)
3	romaine lettuce hearts (18 ounces), torn into bite-size pieces
½	cup shredded fresh basil
3	large hard-boiled eggs, quartered

1. Cook pancetta in 12-inch skillet over medium-high heat until crisp, about 6 minutes. Transfer to paper towel–lined plate. Pat chicken dry with paper towels and season with salt and pepper. Cook chicken in now-empty skillet until golden brown and cooked through, 7 to 8 minutes per side. Transfer chicken to plate with pancetta. Crumble pancetta, then shred chicken into bite-size pieces using 2 forks.

2. Heat 1 tablespoon oil in now-empty skillet over high heat until shimmering. Add tomatoes and cook, shaking skillet occasionally, until tomatoes char and skins begin to split, 4 to 5 minutes. Season with salt and pepper to taste.

3. Whisk vinegar, remaining ¼ cup oil, and ¼ teaspoon pepper in large bowl, then stir in ½ cup Gorgonzola. Toss lettuce and basil with dressing. Transfer to serving platter or individual plates. Top with chicken, tomatoes, eggs, crumbled pancetta, and remaining ¼ cup Gorgonzola. Serve.

SIMPLE SIDE ROSEMARY-OLIVE FOCACCIA
Adjust oven rack to middle position and heat oven to 400 degrees. Press 1 pound prepared pizza dough into well-oiled 8-inch square baking dish or 10-inch pie plate and dimple surface with fingers. Brush dough liberally with extra-virgin olive oil and sprinkle with ¼ cup chopped kalamata olives, ½ teaspoon minced fresh rosemary, ½ teaspoon kosher salt, and ½ teaspoon pepper. Bake until golden brown, about 30 minutes. Cool on wire rack and serve warm. Serves 4.

Basil-Parmesan Chicken Salad with Apples

Serves 4 to 6

✓ **WHY THIS RECIPE WORKS:** The addition of basil, apples, arugula, and Parmesan makes this chicken salad out of the ordinary, and opting for an already-cooked rotisserie chicken means it's also fast to prepare. The arugula lends peppery notes; the basil brings in sweetness and a slight hint of anise; the apples add tart flavor and crisp texture; and the Parmesan finishes it with just the right salty richness. Shredding the meat (rather than dicing or slicing it into smooth-sided chunks) means there are plenty of nooks and crannies to hold the dressing, giving the whole salad a boost in flavor. Be sure to add the baby arugula just before serving, as the dressing will wilt the greens if left to sit too long.

1	cup mayonnaise
½	cup fresh basil leaves
1	ounce Parmesan cheese, grated (½ cup)
2	tablespoons lemon juice
2	garlic cloves, peeled
1	(2½-pound) rotisserie chicken, skin and bones discarded, meat shredded into bite-size pieces (3 cups)
4	celery ribs, sliced thin
2	Granny Smith apples, cored and cut into ½-inch chunks
4	ounces (4 cups) baby arugula
	Salt and pepper

1. Process mayonnaise, basil, Parmesan, lemon juice, and garlic in food processor until smooth and pale green, about 10 seconds.

2. Combine chicken, celery, apples, and mayonnaise mixture in large bowl. Gently toss arugula into chicken salad and season with salt and pepper to taste. Serve.

QUICK PREP TIP STORING CELERY

To find the best way to keep celery fresh, we tested storing bunches five different ways: in a paper bag, wrapped in aluminum foil, wrapped in plastic wrap, in its original perforated plastic sleeve, and upright in a container holding about 2 inches of water. The foil-wrapped celery came out on top. Why? Harvested celery produces small amounts of the ripening hormone ethylene, and since the foil is not "gas tight," it doesn't cause the vegetable to go limp and spoil faster like the other methods. In a pinch, you can always revive tired celery stalks by cutting off about an inch from both ends and submerging the stalks in a bowl of ice water for 30 minutes. But to prolong freshness, we recommend wrapping celery in foil.

Moroccan-Style Chicken, Date, and Olive Salad

Serves 4

✔ **WHY THIS RECIPE WORKS:** A few well-chosen ingredients—olives, dates, oranges, lemon zest and lemon juice, and cinnamon—give this salad a distinctly Moroccan profile and bold, bright flavor without calling for a lengthy ingredient list. The sweetness of the dates along with the richness of the chicken (we opt for rotisserie for speed and ease) help to keep the flavors in balance, and we create a complexly flavored citrus dressing by simply reducing orange juice with the lemon zest and ½ teaspoon of cinnamon. Salad dressings typically have more oil than acid, but we use equal parts of each here to maintain our salad's distinctive brightness. If pitted green olives are not available, use green olives stuffed with pimentos and remove the red pepper strip when you halve the olives. You can serve this recipe with flatbreads either to wrap around the salad, creating a quick sandwich, or to mop up the last drops of dressing.

4	oranges (2 whole, 2 juiced to yield ⅔ cup)
4	(3-inch) strips lemon zest, sliced into thin strips, plus 4 tablespoons juice (2 lemons)
½	teaspoon ground cinnamon
¼	cup extra-virgin olive oil
3	ounces pitted dates, chopped (½ cup)
8	ounces (8 cups) watercress
1	(2½-pound) rotisserie chicken, skin and bones discarded, meat shredded into bite-size pieces (3 cups)
½	cup pitted green olives, halved
½	small red onion, sliced thin
	Salt and pepper

1. Cut away peel and pith from whole oranges. Over bowl, use paring knife to slice between membranes to release segments; set aside.

2. Combine orange juice, lemon zest, and cinnamon in small saucepan. Bring to boil over medium-high heat, then reduce heat and simmer until reduced by half, about 9 minutes. Transfer to large bowl and whisk in lemon juice, oil, and dates.

3. Add watercress, chicken, olives, orange segments, and onion to bowl with dressing, toss to coat, and season with salt and pepper to taste. Serve.

QUICK PREP TIP
CHOPPING DATES
Dried fruits, especially dates and apricots, very often stick to the knife when you try to chop them. To avoid this problem, coat the blade with a thin film of vegetable oil spray just before you begin chopping the fruit. This helps to keep the fruit from clinging to the blade.

Coconut-Lime Chicken and Cabbage-Mango Slaw

Serves 4

WHY THIS RECIPE WORKS: It takes just a handful of well-chosen ingredients and a brightly flavored dressing to turn chicken breasts into an Asian-style summer salad. We poach the chicken to ensure tender, moist meat, and add fish sauce and Asian chili-garlic sauce to the poaching liquid to infuse the chicken with flavor. Then we simply shred the meat, toss it with a quickly prepared coconut-lime dressing (bolstered with more fish sauce and chili-garlic sauce), and use this same dressing for the shredded cabbage and sliced mango. We like using cilantro in this slaw, but you can substitute basil or mint, if desired. For more heat, use 1 tablespoon Asian chili-garlic sauce. To quickly shred the cabbage, you can use a mandoline or a food processor fitted with a slicing disk.

1	cup water
3	tablespoons fish sauce
2	teaspoons Asian chili-garlic sauce
3	(6-ounce) boneless, skinless chicken breasts, trimmed
5	tablespoons cream of coconut
5	tablespoons lime juice (3 limes)
½	head napa cabbage, halved, cored, and shredded (6 cups)
⅓	cup chopped fresh cilantro
1	mango, peeled, pitted, and sliced thin
½	cup cashews, toasted and chopped

1. Bring water, 1 tablespoon fish sauce, and 1 teaspoon chili-garlic sauce to boil in 12-inch skillet. Add chicken and simmer, covered, over medium-low heat until chicken registers 160 degrees, 10 to 15 minutes, flipping chicken halfway through cooking. Transfer chicken to plate and, using 2 forks, shred into bite-size pieces.

2. Whisk cream of coconut, lime juice, remaining 2 tablespoons fish sauce, and remaining 1 teaspoon chili-garlic sauce in large bowl.

3. Toss chicken with 3 tablespoons dressing in second bowl. Add cabbage, cilantro, and mango to bowl with remaining dressing and toss to combine. Transfer slaw to platter, top with chicken, and sprinkle with cashews. Serve.

SMART SHOPPING CREAM OF COCONUT
Coconut cream, which is a concentrated version of coconut milk, is made by steeping shredded coconut in water. Cream of coconut is coconut cream with added sugar, stabilizers, and emulsifiers to ensure it stays creamy in both drinks and cooking. We tasted five brands plain and in piña colada smoothies. Products from **Goya** and **Coco López** took first and second place, respectively. Both offered the most "authentic" and fresh coconut flavor, and—no surprise—both listed coconut as their first ingredient. Our two least-favorite brands—Roland and Coco Reál—listed sugar as their first ingredient; no wonder tasters found them too sweet and lacking in coconut flavor. Do not substitute coconut milk or coconut cream for cream of coconut.

Chicken, Goat Cheese, and Cherry Salad

Serves 4

✓ **WHY THIS RECIPE WORKS:** When fresh, bright-red cherries hit the summertime market, it's hard to think of any recipe beyond the classic pie. But we wanted something savory, and this salad—which brings together sweet cherries, creamy goat cheese, toasted pecans, and chicken—really hits the mark. A bright vinaigrette of sherry vinegar and orange marmalade pulls it all together. For juicy yet flavorful meat, we use a hybrid sauté/poach cooking method by browning chicken breasts on one side, then flipping them over and adding liquid to the pan. Stirring a little orange marmalade into the poaching water infuses the meat with flavor and carries across the flavors of our dressing.

2	(6-ounce) boneless, skinless chicken breasts, trimmed
	Salt and pepper
5	tablespoons extra-virgin olive oil
½	cup water
2½	tablespoons orange marmalade
2½	tablespoons sherry vinegar
1	small shallot, minced
12	ounces fresh sweet cherries, pitted and halved
5	ounces (5 cups) mesclun greens
½	cup pecans, toasted and chopped coarse
4	ounces goat cheese, crumbled (1 cup)

1. Pat chicken dry with paper towels and season with salt and pepper. Heat 1 tablespoon oil in 10-inch nonstick skillet over medium-high heat until just smoking. Cook chicken until browned on first side, about 3 minutes. Flip chicken, then stir water and 1 tablespoon marmalade into skillet. Reduce heat and simmer, covered, until chicken is cooked through, 5 to 7 minutes. Transfer to cutting board.

2. In large bowl, combine remaining 1½ tablespoons marmalade, vinegar, and shallot. Slowly whisk in remaining ¼ cup oil. Season with salt and pepper to taste. In small bowl, toss cherries with 1 tablespoon dressing.

3. Add mesclun to large bowl with dressing, toss to combine, and divide among individual plates. Top with cherries, pecans, and goat cheese. Slice chicken crosswise and arrange on top of salad. Serve.

QUICK PREP TIP PITTING CHERRIES

A cherry pitter certainly makes the job easier, but it's still not a neat and tidy job given the pits and juice that tend to go flying. For neater cherry pitting, place a large bowl of water in the sink. Add the cherries and use a cherry pitter to pit them at the bottom of the bowl. The pits float to the surface for easy removal, and the cherries are rinsed in the process.

Frisée and Fried-Egg Salad with Lentils

Serves 4

✔ **WHY THIS RECIPE WORKS:** A take on a classic French bistro salad, this elegant yet satisfying recipe tops earthy lentils and frisée with fried eggs. The eggs' runny yolks coat the greens and mingle with the other ingredients to enrich and balance the dressing. Microwaving the lentils shortens their cooking time, while baking soda tenderizes their exteriors. Lentilles du Puy, or French green lentils, have a rich, earthy flavor, and they don't break down like some types of lentils, making them an ideal choice for salads such as this one.

1   cup lentilles du Puy, picked over
     and rinsed
3   cups water
¼   teaspoon baking soda
7   tablespoons extra-virgin olive oil
¼   cup sherry vinegar
2   shallots, minced
2   carrots, peeled and sliced thin
4   large eggs
¼   cup chopped fresh parsley
     Salt and pepper
2   small heads frisée (8 ounces),
     ends trimmed, cut into 1-inch
     pieces

1. Combine lentils, water, and baking soda in bowl, cover, and microwave until lentils are soft, about 20 minutes. Drain and rinse under cold water. Combine ¼ cup oil and vinegar in small bowl.

2. Meanwhile, heat 1 tablespoon oil in 12-inch nonstick skillet over medium-high heat until shimmering. Add shallots and carrots and cook until shallots are beginning to brown and carrots are tender, about 4 minutes. Transfer to large bowl; wipe out skillet with paper towels.

3. Heat remaining 2 tablespoons oil in now-empty skillet over medium-low heat. Crack 2 eggs each into 2 cups or small bowls. Add eggs to skillet simultaneously, pouring each pair into opposite sides of skillet. Cover and cook until whites are set, 2 to 3 minutes.

4. Add lentils, parsley, and half of dressing to bowl with shallot mixture and season with salt and pepper to taste. Toss frisée with remaining dressing in separate bowl and season with salt and pepper to taste. Arrange greens and lentils on individual plates and top each with fried egg. Serve.

QUICK PREP TIP FRYING EGGS

Frying a single egg is simple, but things get tricky when you're trying to fry four in one pan and have them cook through simultaneously; the first egg is usually half cooked by the time the fourth one hits the pan. Another problem is that the first white has a tendency to run all over the place, leaving no cooking surface for the three eggs to follow. Our technique gets around these problems. By pouring the eggs into the pan from two small bowls simultaneously, we ensure even distribution and cooking.

Tuscan-Style Tuna and White Bean Salad

Serves 4

✓ **WHY THIS RECIPE WORKS:** This quick, freshly flavored salad takes its inspiration from Tuscany, where hearty portions of white beans and tuna are lightly dressed with olive oil for an easy summer dinner. Here we toss tuna and cannellini beans—both canned for convenience—with fennel, oil-cured olives, tomatoes, and peppery watercress, then dress it all in a citrusy vinaigrette. While that might sound like a salad with too many flavors going on, it all comes together into perfect balance. The fennel lends its anise flavor to the mix, as well as an appealing crunch. For an appealingly delicate texture, we make very thin, ribbon-like slices, which also lends visual appeal. (A mandoline makes the slicing job both easy and fast.)

4   **(3-inch) strips orange zest, sliced into thin strips, plus ½ cup juice (2 oranges)**

3   **tablespoons lemon juice**

¼   **cup extra-virgin olive oil**

2   **teaspoons chopped fresh thyme**
    Salt and pepper

8   **ounces (8 cups) watercress**

1   **(15-ounce) can cannellini beans, rinsed**

1   **fennel bulb, stalks discarded, bulb halved, cored, and sliced very thin**

½   **cup pitted oil-cured olives, halved**

12   **ounces grape tomatoes, halved**

2   **(12-ounce) cans tuna in water, drained, shredded into bite-size pieces**

1. Combine orange zest, orange juice, and lemon juice in small saucepan and bring to boil over medium-high heat. Reduce heat and simmer until reduced by half, about 4 minutes. Transfer to medium bowl, whisk in oil and thyme, and season with salt and pepper to taste.

2. In large bowl, combine watercress, beans, fennel, olives, and tomatoes. Add dressing, toss to coat, and season with salt and pepper to taste. Arrange on individual plates, divide tuna among each portion, and serve.

SMART SHOPPING A NEW WORLD OF CANNED TUNA
Recently, a few new outfits have joined the "big three" canned-tuna companies (Chicken of the Sea, StarKist, and Bumble Bee), claiming to bring not only higher-quality fish but also better processing methods. We pitted eight brands of solid white albacore tuna against each other: two new brands, two "gourmet" lines from the big three, and four regular samples that we grew up eating. Even in our Classic Tuna Salad, with all its added ingredients, the differences were clear. The tuna from the two newer companies, **Wild Planet** and **American Tuna**, had heartier chunks of fish, and richer, more flavorful meat that made them well worth their higher price tags. Why the difference? They both cook their tuna just once (rather than twice like the bigger companies) and pack the fish in its own juices, not water and broth.

Smoked Trout Salad

Serves 4

✔ **WHY THIS RECIPE WORKS:** We love the idea of a Niçoise salad—with its fresh profile of crisp-tender vegetables, no-prep-required canned tuna, and sliced potatoes that lend heft—so we start there for inspiration, then go on to give it a new, flavorful twist. Trout adds a bold smokiness, while quick-cooking sugar snap peas lend texture and sweet freshness. Potatoes offer a heartiness that is well appreciated here, and we slice them into rounds to speed up the cooking time. Tossing the potatoes with the dressing while still warm ensures they soak up plenty of flavor. Capers and thinly sliced red onion are a natural with smoked fish and fit right into the picture while requiring minimal prep work. And finally, peppery watercress and mint leaves lend spicy and fresh flavors that balance the smoky trout.

⅓ **cup extra-virgin olive oil**

3 **tablespoons lemon juice**

2 **tablespoons capers, rinsed and chopped**

Salt and pepper

1 **pound small red potatoes, sliced ¼ inch thick**

8 **ounces sugar snap peas, strings removed**

8 **ounces (8 cups) watercress**

¼ **cup chopped fresh mint**

½ **small red onion, sliced thin**

8 **ounces smoked trout, flaked**

1. Whisk oil, lemon juice, and capers together in large bowl. Season with salt and pepper to taste.

2. Bring potatoes, 6 cups water, and 1 tablespoon salt to boil in large saucepan. Reduce heat and simmer gently until potatoes are just tender, about 7 minutes. Drain and transfer to large bowl. Add 3 tablespoons dressing to bowl with potatoes, toss to coat, then set aside and let cool.

3. Meanwhile, fill large bowl with ice water. Bring 2 quarts water to boil in medium saucepan, add peas and 1 teaspoon salt, and cook until crisp-tender, 1½ to 2 minutes. Drain peas, shock in ice water, and drain again.

4. Add peas, watercress, mint, and onion to bowl with remaining dressing and toss to coat. Transfer to platter, top with potatoes and trout, and serve.

SMART SHOPPING SMOKED TROUT

We love smoked trout's cool, rich flavor and its flaky yet moist texture, and it's easy to find in your supermarket in a variety of forms. Smoked trout can be found sold whole, in full fillets, in fillet pieces, and canned in water or oil. Vacuum-packed fillets are typically located next to smoked salmon in the deli case. Use whichever type you prefer. Smoked trout fillets are often sold with additional flavorings and spices; make sure to purchase an unflavored, simply smoked variety for this recipe.

Lemony Salmon and Roasted Beet Salad

Serves 4

✔️ **WHY THIS RECIPE WORKS:** We love the sweet, earthy flavor of roasted beets, especially as they are paired here with rich salmon and a bright lemon–caper dressing. But roasting them in the oven takes around an hour (and canned beets are not a worthy substitute). For this recipe, we found a speedy way to cook beets: We peel and dice them, then cook them in the microwave. This cuts their cooking time down to just 4 minutes. Poaching the salmon fillets in barely simmering water ensures their meat is moist and perfectly cooked. Taking time to dress each component of this composed salad is worth the effort, ensuring each is properly seasoned.

3	(6- to 8-ounce) skinless salmon fillets, ¾ to 1 inch thick
	Salt and pepper
1	teaspoon grated lemon zest plus 7 tablespoons juice (3 lemons)
⅓	cup extra-virgin olive oil
1	shallot, minced
2	tablespoons capers, rinsed
3	tablespoons minced fresh dill
2	beets, peeled and cut into ½-inch cubes
6	ounces (6 cups) baby arugula
2	large hard-boiled eggs, grated

1. Season salmon with salt and pepper. Bring 4 cups water to boil in 12-inch skillet. Add ¼ cup lemon juice, reduce heat to simmer, and gently slip salmon into water. Cover and cook until salmon is still slightly pink in middle, 4 to 6 minutes. Transfer salmon to plate. Using 2 forks, break salmon into 1-inch chunks.

2. Meanwhile, whisk lemon zest and remaining 3 tablespoons juice, oil, shallot, capers, and 1 tablespoon dill together in bowl.

3. Season beets with salt and pepper in bowl. Cover and microwave until tender, about 4 minutes. Toss beets with 2 tablespoons dressing and let cool slightly.

4. Toss salmon with 2 tablespoons dressing. Toss arugula with remaining dressing and season with salt and pepper to taste. Arrange arugula on individual plates or platter, top with salmon, beets, grated eggs, and remaining 2 tablespoons dill. Serve.

QUICK PREP TIP
HARD-BOILED EGGS
We hard-boil eggs using residual heat, making them nearly impossible to over-cook. This method will work for up to a dozen eggs. Place the eggs in a large saucepan in a single layer and cover with 1 inch water. Bring to a boil over high heat. Remove the pan from the heat, cover, and let sit for 10 minutes. Pour out the water and shake the pan back and forth to crack

the shells, then transfer the eggs to a bowl of ice water using a slotted spoon and let sit for 5 minutes. Starting at the wider end of each egg, peel away the shell.

Romaine Wedge with Shrimp and Feta Dressing

Serves 4

✔ **WHY THIS RECIPE WORKS:** For a twist on the classic iceberg wedge, we start by swapping in more tender and delicate romaine, then we combine tangy yogurt and feta cheese for a dressing with a Greek twist. Topping the salad with sweet, briny shrimp makes it a meal, and to save time, we purchase precooked shrimp at the supermarket (although if you are not in a rush, you can certainly poach your own; just be sure to chill them thoroughly before serving). You can use either low-fat or full-fat Greek yogurt, but don't swap in regular yogurt since it will make the dressing too thin. This salad is a nice match with warmed or toasted pita.

1   **large head romaine lettuce (14 ounces), quartered lengthwise**

4   **ounces feta cheese, crumbled (1 cup)**

½   **cup plain Greek yogurt**

1   **garlic clove, minced**

2   **tablespoons lemon juice**

2   **tablespoons extra-virgin olive oil**

    Salt and pepper

1   **pound cooked and peeled large shrimp (26 to 30 per pound), chilled and cut into ½-inch chunks**

1   **cucumber, peeled, halved lengthwise, seeded, and chopped**

¾   **cup kalamata olives, pitted and chopped**

1   **pound beefsteak tomatoes, cored, seeded, and chopped**

1. Rinse romaine wedges to remove dirt and grit and pat dry. Drain wedges, then gently shake to remove water and wrap in clean dish towels to dry.

2. Process cheese, yogurt, garlic, lemon juice, and oil in food processor until smooth, about 30 seconds. Transfer to bowl and season with salt and pepper to taste.

3. In separate large bowl, toss shrimp and cucumber with ⅓ cup dressing and season with salt and pepper to taste.

4. Transfer romaine wedges to individual plates. Spoon remaining dressing over wedges and top with shrimp mixture, olives, and tomatoes. Serve.

SMART SHOPPING FETA CHEESE

In 2005, the European Union ruled that only cheese produced in Greece from at least 70 percent sheep's milk can rightfully bear the label "feta." Here in the United States, where these stipulations don't apply, imitators abound. We tasted five brands, both imports and domestic. Tasters preferred the "barnyard" taste of the sheep's- and goat's-milk imports, giving **Mt. Vikos Traditional Feta**, which hails from the mother country, the top spot. Keep feta submerged in the brine in which it was packed. When stored properly, feta can keep for up to three months, though it will become considerably saltier and more pungent over time.

Tropical Shrimp and Rice Salad

Serves 4

✔ **WHY THIS RECIPE WORKS:** A classic picnic and potluck side dish, rice salad is a great option when looking for a dressed-up take on an otherwise simple grain. Here, we incorporate just a few creative add-ins to turn rice salad into a meal, and we give it a tropical spin in the process. The combination of shrimp, peas, and mint lends fresh flavors, while the lime juice–mango chutney dressing, as well as some toasted coconut, go a long way in taking this recipe to the next level without much work. Using a prepared chutney keeps things simple, and its spicy flavor adds complexity and depth to the vinaigrette, which we whip together quickly in a blender. To ensure the dressing maintains its flavorful punch and doesn't become watered down, we spread the cooked rice out on paper towels to thoroughly dry the grains.

1½	**cups long-grain white rice**
	Salt and pepper
½	**cup mango chutney**
⅓	**cup olive oil**
2	**tablespoons lime juice**
1	**pound cooked and peeled medium shrimp (41 to 50 per pound)**
½	**cup frozen peas, thawed**
⅓	**cup chopped fresh mint**
4	**scallions, minced**
¼	**cup unsweetened shredded coconut, lightly toasted**

1. Bring 2 quarts water to boil in large saucepan. Add rice and 1 tablespoon salt and cook over medium heat until just tender, 8 to 10 minutes. Drain rice, rinse under cold water, then transfer to rimmed baking sheet lined with several layers of paper towels.

2. Meanwhile, process chutney, oil, and lime juice in blender until smooth, about 30 seconds.

3. Toss rice with dressing, shrimp, peas, mint, and scallions in bowl. Season with salt and pepper to taste. Top with coconut and serve.

SMART SHOPPING MANGO CHUTNEY

Mango chutney (sometimes called Major Grey's chutney, an uncopyrighted name based on a fictional British character that isn't brand specific and can be used by any bottled chutney) is a welcome accompaniment to curries and roasted meats. In this recipe, it comes in handy to make a flavorful dressing. Classic mango chutney preparations cook unripe green mangos with sugar, vinegar, and aromatic spices. Unfortunately, large amounts of high-fructose corn syrup and food coloring cloud many store-bought brands, and any natural mango flavors are often overshadowed. Many of the supermarket brands we tested were sickeningly sweet, with insipid, weak flavor. However, we found a winner in **Silver Palate Mango Chutney**, which has a balanced sweetness and acidity as well as a tangy boost from lemon juice and peel.

ROAST CHICKEN WITH LIMA BEAN RAGOUT

Poultry

54 Blue Cheese and Walnut-Stuffed Chicken Breasts

56 Wintry Roast Chicken with Honey-Glazed Parsnips

57 Roast Chicken with Lima Bean Ragout

59 Chicken Thighs with Fennel, Orange, and Olives

60 Skillet Glazed Drumsticks

61 Caribbean Chicken Pepper Pot

62 Quick White Wine–Braised Chicken and Potatoes

64 Country Captain Chicken

66 Prosciutto-Wrapped Chicken with Sage Butter

67 Pine Nut and Parmesan–Crusted Chicken

69 Chicken and Mexican Green Rice Skillet Supper

70 Chicken and Artichoke Paella

71 Chicken with Mexican-Style Pumpkin Seed Sauce

72 Skillet Chicken with Spicy Red Beans and Rice

74 Sautéed Chicken with Parsley Sauce and Celery Root Slaw

75 Chicken Cutlets with Ginger-Shiitake Sauce and Chard

77 Quick Southern Fried Chicken Dinner

78 Chicken Francese with Broccoli Rabe

79 Hearty Chicken and Chorizo Skillet Supper

80 Chicken Parmesan Fingers with Marinara Sauce

82 Chicken Tenders with Meaty Green Beans

83 Sweet and Savory Cuban Chicken Pie

85 Curried Chicken Meatballs with Apricot Rice Pilaf

86 Turkey Saltimbocca

87 Mustard-Sage Turkey Cutlets and Barley Salad

88 Spicy Orange Chipotle–Glazed Turkey Tenderloins

89 Spanish-Style Turkey Meatballs

90 Mini Barbecued Turkey Meatloaves

Blue Cheese and Walnut-Stuffed Chicken Breasts

Serves 4

✔ **WHY THIS RECIPE WORKS:** We make a quick yet elegant weeknight meal by stuffing bone-in chicken breasts with blue cheese and walnuts, which we beat together, roll into logs, then place inside a slit we cut in the top of each breast. A fruity grape pan sauce, prepared while the chicken is in the oven, is the perfect balance to the stuffing's richness. Mashing some of the grapes gives the sauce body without requiring additional ingredients.

3   ounces blue cheese, crumbled (¾ cup)

½   cup walnuts, chopped

4   (12-ounce) bone-in split chicken breasts, trimmed
     Salt and pepper

2   tablespoons unsalted butter

2   shallots, minced

9   ounces (2 cups) seedless red grapes

1   cup low-sodium chicken broth

¼   cup chopped fresh parsley

1. Adjust oven rack to upper-middle position and heat oven to 475 degrees. Beat blue cheese and walnuts together with fork until combined.

2. Lay chicken breasts on counter skin side up, pat dry with paper towels, and season with salt and pepper. Cut slit lengthwise down center of each breast, through skin and almost to bone, leaving about 1 inch flesh intact at each end. Roll cheese mixture into 4 logs same length as slit and press 1 log into each slit. Pinch meat up around top of cheese mixture in each chicken breast, closing up slit as much as possible. Transfer chicken to baking sheet and bake until golden brown and chicken registers 160 degrees, about 20 minutes. Transfer chicken to platter and tent loosely with aluminum foil.

3. Meanwhile, melt 1 tablespoon butter in 12-inch skillet over medium-high heat. Add shallots and cook until softened, about 3 minutes. Add grapes and cook until skins blister, 2 to 3 minutes. Reduce heat to medium and cook until grapes break apart, 8 to 10 minutes. Mash half of grapes into skillet with back of spoon. Add chicken broth and reduce by half, 2 to 3 minutes. Off heat, whisk in remaining 1 tablespoon butter and parsley. Season sauce with salt and pepper to taste, pour over chicken, and serve.

Wintry Roast Chicken with Honey-Glazed Parsnips

Serves 4

☑ **WHY THIS RECIPE WORKS:** Achieving a beautifully bronzed roast chicken and vegetable dinner usually requires a few hours. We turn the classic Sunday-supper duo into a weeknight meal by opting for bone-in, skin-on breasts, which we cut in half to further speed things up. We start by browning the chicken on the stovetop, then transfer it to the oven to finish cooking. Parsnips make a great change of pace from the typical carrot side, and roasting them in the skillet with the chicken concentrates their flavor, plus they pick up some of the chicken's released juice. Once the chicken is done, we set it aside so we can quickly glaze the parsnips on the stovetop and finish cooking them through. For the glaze, we opt for honey and rosemary, a combination that adds just the right herbal and sweet finish. You will need an ovensafe skillet for this recipe.

4 **(12-ounce) bone-in split chicken breasts, trimmed and halved crosswise**
Salt and pepper
2 **tablespoons vegetable oil**
2 **pounds parsnips, peeled and cut into 3 by ¾-inch pieces**
3 **tablespoons honey**
1 **tablespoon minced fresh rosemary**

1. Adjust oven rack to middle position and heat oven to 450 degrees. Pat chicken dry with paper towels and season with salt and pepper. Heat oil in 12-inch ovensafe skillet over medium-high heat until just smoking. Cook chicken, skin side down, until well browned and crisp, about 4 minutes. Transfer to plate. Add parsnips to skillet and cook until lightly browned, about 3 minutes.

2. Nestle chicken, skin side up, into parsnips in skillet. Transfer skillet to oven and bake until chicken registers 160 degrees and parsnips are almost tender, about 20 minutes.

3. Transfer chicken to platter and tent loosely with aluminum foil. Using potholder (skillet handle will be hot), return skillet with parsnips to stovetop, add honey and rosemary, and cook until liquid has thickened to glazy consistency, about 3 minutes. Spoon parsnips onto platter with chicken, drizzle with glaze, and serve.

QUICK PREP TIP
TRIMMING AND CUTTING PARSNIPS
Peel parsnips and trim off ends, then cut crosswise into 2- to 3-inch lengths. To ensure even cooking, cut larger end sections into smaller pieces to match size of others. Make sure to cut out bitter core found in very large parsnips.

Roast Chicken with Lima Bean Ragout

Serves 4

✓ **WHY THIS RECIPE WORKS:** Mild lima beans, along with earthy mushrooms and briny olives, make a flavorful match to the simple and delicious roast chicken in this appealingly autumnal meal. Browning the chicken breasts on the stovetop helps keep their oven time short and ensures the meat has time to rest while we finish up the ragout. By transferring the chicken to a baking sheet before it goes in the oven, we can make use of the flavorful fond left in the skillet to add richness and depth to the ragout. We opt for oil-cured olives, which have been dry-cured and then soaked in olive oil, for our ragout since they add a meaty texture and rich flavor.

4   **(12-ounce) bone-in split chicken breasts, trimmed**
    Salt and pepper
1   **tablespoon vegetable oil**
1   **onion, chopped fine**
1   **pound cremini mushrooms, trimmed and quartered**
2   **garlic cloves, minced**
½   **cup dry white wine**
1   **cup low-sodium chicken broth**
2   **cups frozen baby lima beans, thawed**
¼   **cup oil-cured black olives, pitted and halved**

1. Adjust oven rack to middle position and heat oven to 450 degrees. Pat chicken dry with paper towels and season with salt and pepper. Heat oil in 12-inch skillet over medium-high heat until just smoking. Brown chicken, skin side down, until crisp and golden, about 4 minutes. Flip chicken and cook 4 minutes longer. Transfer chicken, skin side up, to rimmed baking sheet and roast in oven until chicken registers 160 degrees, 12 to 16 minutes. Transfer to platter and tent loosely with aluminum foil.

2. Meanwhile, pour off all but 1 tablespoon fat from skillet. Add onion and cook until softened, about 4 minutes. Add mushrooms and cook until moisture has evaporated and mushrooms begin to brown, about 4 minutes. Add garlic and cook until fragrant, about 30 seconds. Add wine and cook until reduced by half, about 2 minutes. Add chicken broth and cook until reduced by half and thickened, about 5 minutes.

3. Add lima beans and olives to skillet and cook until lima beans are bright green and tender, about 4 minutes. Season ragout with salt and pepper to taste, transfer to platter with chicken, and serve.

SMART SHOPPING WHITE WINE FOR COOKING
When a recipe calls for dry white wine, it's tempting to grab whatever open bottle is in the fridge. We have found that only Sauvignon Blanc consistently boils down to a "clean" yet sufficiently acidic flavor that meshes nicely with a variety of ingredients in savory recipes. Vermouth can be an acceptable substitute in certain recipes. Never buy supermarket cooking wine, which has added sodium and a vinegary flavor.

Chicken Thighs with Fennel, Orange, and Olives

Serves 4

☑ **WHY THIS RECIPE WORKS:** Fennel, orange, and olives are a classic Italian combination, but one that's usually presented in a chilled, uncooked salad. Here, we roast the fennel and orange together, then pair them with chicken to make a warm, hearty supper. We brown the chicken thighs on the stovetop, then add them to the fennel and orange partway through the roasting time. By the end of cooking, the orange flavor has infused the whole dish, and the peel has become tender and mellow, worthy of eating along with the rest of the components. Often, we spread out meat in a skillet to ensure even browning, but here we fit the thighs together snugly so the exuded fat stays on the skin and makes it extra-crisp. We love the dense, rich flavor and meaty texture of oil-cured black olives. However, if you can't find them, you can substitute any black olive you like in this recipe.

1   orange
3   fennel bulbs, stalks discarded, bulbs halved, cored, and sliced thin
2   garlic cloves, minced
2   tablespoons plus 2 teaspoons olive oil
1   tablespoon minced fresh thyme
8   (6-ounce) bone-in chicken thighs, trimmed
    Salt and pepper
½   cup chopped oil-cured black olives

1. Adjust oven rack to upper-middle position and heat oven to 475 degrees. Cut orange in half lengthwise, then slice crosswise into thin half moons (do not peel). Toss fennel, orange slices, garlic, 2 tablespoons oil, and thyme together on rimmed baking sheet. Roast until fennel begins to soften, about 15 minutes.

2. Meanwhile, pat chicken dry with paper towels and season with salt and pepper. Heat remaining 2 teaspoons oil in 12-inch skillet over medium-high heat. Add chicken and cook, skin side down, until skin is browned and crisp, 10 to 12 minutes.

3. Stir roasted fennel mixture to recombine, then nestle chicken, skin side up, into mixture on sheet. Return to oven and roast until chicken registers 175 degrees, about 10 minutes. Transfer chicken to platter. Toss fennel mixture with olives, season with salt and pepper to taste, and transfer to platter with chicken. Serve.

SIMPLE SIDE CHEESY POLENTA
Bring 2 cups water and 2 cups milk to boil in large saucepan. Slowly whisk in 1 cup instant polenta. Cook, stirring constantly, until polenta is thickened, about 3 minutes. Stir in ¾ cup grated Parmesan cheese and season with salt and pepper to taste. Serves 4.

Skillet Glazed Drumsticks

Serves 4

✓ **WHY THIS RECIPE WORKS:** Inspired by sticky, spicy chicken wings, we came up with this family-friendly recipe for glazed drumsticks. A simple combination of jalapeño jelly, orange zest and juice, and molasses gives the glaze a sweet and spicy kick. We start by browning the drumsticks on the stovetop, then we coat them with the glaze before moving them to the oven, where they finish cooking through evenly. To make this recipe work within the 30-minute time frame, it is important to have two pans going at once, a skillet to brown the chicken and a saucepan for simmering the glaze. Be careful when working with the glaze, as sugary sauces such as this one get very hot. If you want more spicy heat, you can add 1 teaspoon hot sauce to the glaze in step 1.

3	tablespoons jalapeño jelly
1	teaspoon grated orange zest plus ⅔ cup juice (2 oranges)
1	shallot, minced
2	tablespoons molasses
1	teaspoon cornstarch
8	(6-ounce) chicken drumsticks, trimmed
	Salt and pepper
1	tablespoon vegetable oil

1. Adjust oven rack to middle position and heat oven to 450 degrees. Combine jelly, orange zest and juice, and shallot in small saucepan. Whisk in molasses and cornstarch. Simmer mixture over medium heat until thickened, about 5 minutes.

2. Meanwhile, pat chicken dry with paper towels and season with salt and pepper. Heat oil in 12-inch skillet over medium-high heat until just smoking. Cook chicken until well browned, about 5 minutes. Add glaze, turning chicken until thoroughly coated. Transfer skillet to oven and roast until chicken registers 175 degrees, 20 to 25 minutes, flipping chicken halfway through cooking.

3. Transfer chicken to platter, season glaze with salt and pepper to taste, and pour glaze over chicken. Serve.

SIMPLE SIDE LEMONY STEAMED BROCCOLI
Combine 1 pound broccoli florets and ¼ cup water in large bowl. Cover and microwave until broccoli is bright green and tender, about 4 minutes. Melt 2 tablespoons unsalted butter in small saucepan over medium heat. Whisk in 1 tablespoon lemon juice. Drain broccoli, toss with lemon butter, and season with salt and pepper to taste. Serves 4.

Caribbean Chicken Pepper Pot

Serves 4

✔ **WHY THIS RECIPE WORKS:** If you are tired of even the most creative of roast chicken dinners, this recipe offers a great change of pace. A Caribbean pepper pot is a classic island dish made with beef, mutton, or pork and aggressively flavored with hot peppers, warm spices, and cassava (aka yuca). A Scotch bonnet pepper gives this dish its characteristic heat, while allspice and thyme lend Caribbean authenticity. Using chicken instead of one of the standard, longer-cooking meats turns it into a weeknight option, and the combination of sweet potatoes (a more convenient alternative to cassava), collards, and okra makes it a flavorful and colorful one-pot meal.

8	(3-ounce) boneless, skinless chicken thighs, trimmed and cut into 1-inch pieces
	Salt and pepper
2	tablespoons vegetable oil
1	onion, chopped fine
6	garlic cloves, minced
2	tablespoons tomato paste
1	teaspoon dried thyme
½	teaspoon ground allspice
4	cups low-sodium chicken broth
1	Scotch bonnet pepper, stemmed, seeded, and minced
2¼	pounds sweet potatoes, peeled and cut into 1-inch chunks
1	pound collard greens, stemmed and chopped
1	pound frozen sliced okra, thawed

1. Pat chicken dry with paper towels and season with salt and pepper. Heat oil in Dutch oven over medium-high heat until just smoking. Cook chicken, stirring occasionally, until golden brown, about 6 minutes. Transfer to bowl.

2. Add onion to now-empty Dutch oven and cook until softened, about 4 minutes. Add garlic, tomato paste, thyme, and allspice and cook until fragrant, about 30 seconds. Add chicken broth, Scotch bonnet pepper, sweet potatoes, collard greens, and chicken and any accumulated juices and cook until chicken and sweet potatoes are almost tender, about 10 minutes. Add okra and cook until chicken and potatoes are completely tender, about 5 minutes. Serve.

SMART SHOPPING SCOTCH BONNET PEPPER

The Scotch bonnet pepper—named for its resemblance to the traditional floppy wool Scottish tam o' shanter hat—is among the hottest peppers in the world, having a heat rating in the range of 100,000 to 350,000 Scoville units (most jalapeños have a heat rating of between 2,500 and 8,000 Scoville units). The Scotch bonnet can range widely in color, from green to pumpkin orange to scarlet red. Despite its name, this variety of pepper is grown mainly in the Caribbean islands, Guyana, and the Maldives. Scotch bonnets are commonly used in jerk dishes and other Caribbean fare.

Quick White Wine-Braised Chicken and Potatoes

Serves 4

✔ **WHY THIS RECIPE WORKS:** Braising a chicken typically takes around an hour, but we whip up this French-inspired dish in just 30 minutes. While we often think of coq au vin as the quintessential French chicken braise, the flavors of this hearty cold-weather recipe, with its crème fraîche–enriched white wine sauce, carrots, and leeks, are standard in the northern Alsace region. Instead of breaking down a whole bird, we opt for quicker-cooking boneless, skinless thighs, and we microwave the potatoes to further speed things up.

4	tablespoons unsalted butter
1½	pounds extra-small red potatoes, halved
	Salt and pepper
8	(3-ounce) boneless, skinless chicken thighs, trimmed and halved
1	pound leeks, white and light green parts only, chopped and washed thoroughly
4	carrots, peeled and sliced ½ inch thick
1	cup dry white wine
½	cup crème fraîche or heavy cream
1	tablespoon lemon juice
¼	cup chopped fresh parsley

1. Cut 1 tablespoon butter into 4 pieces and toss with potatoes in bowl. Season with salt and pepper, cover, and microwave until potatoes are tender, 8 to 10 minutes, tossing potatoes halfway through cooking.

2. Meanwhile, pat chicken dry with paper towels and season with salt and pepper. Melt 1 tablespoon butter in 12-inch skillet over medium-high heat. Add half of chicken and cook until lightly browned on 1 side, about 4 minutes. Transfer to plate and tent with aluminum foil. Repeat with 1 tablespoon butter and remaining chicken.

3. Melt remaining 1 tablespoon butter in now-empty skillet, add leeks and carrots, and cook until softened and starting to brown, about 4 minutes. Stir in wine, scraping up any browned bits, then add chicken and any accumulated juices. Reduce heat to medium, cover, and cook until chicken is tender and registers 175 degrees, about 15 minutes. Transfer chicken to plate and tent loosely with foil. Reduce liquid until slightly thickened, about 4 minutes. Off heat, whisk in crème fraîche, lemon juice, and parsley. Season sauce with salt and pepper to taste. Arrange chicken and potatoes on serving platter, pour over sauce, and serve.

SMART SHOPPING CRÈME FRAÎCHE

Crème fraîche is often considered the French equivalent of sour cream, but it has a lighter, more refined flavor that isn't sour or acidic. Because crème fraîche will not curdle, it is often stirred into savory soups or sauces to add a lush finish. If your supermarket doesn't carry crème fraîche, stir 1 tablespoon cultured buttermilk into 1 cup heavy cream, cover, and let sit at room temperature until the mixture has thickened (at least 8 hours or up to 2 days). Homemade crème fraîche will keep, refrigerated, for about 2 weeks.

Country Captain Chicken

Serves 4

✔ WHY THIS RECIPE WORKS: Country captain, an old-fashioned, boldly flavored Southern dish consisting of chicken braised with onion, tomatoes, green pepper, fruit, and curry powder, typically calls for bone-in chicken pieces. Since they can take up to an hour to braise, we substitute boneless chicken thighs, cut in half. We also save on ingredients by swapping out the usual mangos and raisins for mango chutney; it adds just the right amount of sweet-tart tang with minimal work. To intensify the flavor of the braise and ensure that this quick-cooking version has the complexity of the long-simmered original, we bloom the curry powder by cooking it in the tomato paste before adding the liquid. Country captain chicken is traditionally served over rice (see recipe for Easy White Rice, page 22) and garnished with any or all of the following: toasted shredded coconut, sliced toasted almonds, sliced scallions, diced Granny Smith apples, and even diced banana. Feel free to garnish your version as much or as little as you'd like.

1	**tablespoon vegetable oil**
1	**onion, chopped fine**
1	**green bell pepper, stemmed, seeded, and chopped**
5	**tablespoons tomato paste**
2	**tablespoons curry powder**
4	**garlic cloves, minced**
8	**(3-ounce) boneless, skinless chicken thighs, trimmed and halved**
	Salt and pepper
1	**(14.5-ounce) can diced tomatoes**
½	**cup low-sodium chicken broth**
½	**cup mango chutney**

1. Heat oil in Dutch oven over medium-high heat until shimmering. Add onion and bell pepper and cook until softened, about 5 minutes.

2. Lower heat to medium-low, stir in tomato paste, curry powder, and garlic, and cook until fragrant and color deepens, about 2 minutes.

3. Pat chicken dry with paper towels and season with salt and pepper. Add chicken to pot and stir to coat with onion mixture. Stir in diced tomatoes, broth, and chutney and bring to simmer. Cook over medium heat until chicken registers 175 degrees and sauce is slightly thickened, 10 to 12 minutes. Season with salt and pepper to taste and serve.

SMART SHOPPING TOMATO PASTE

Tomato paste is naturally full of glutamates, which stimulate tastebuds just as salt and sugar do, and it brings out subtle flavors and savory notes even in recipes in which tomato flavor isn't at the forefront. We wanted to know if a better-tasting paste would elicit more flavors than a less tasty option. We gathered 10 top-selling brands and sampled each one uncooked, cooked plain, and in marinara sauce. **Goya Tomato Paste** earned top marks in both the uncooked and cooked tastings, and it came in second in our marinara test. Granted, the losers were not far behind top-ranked Goya. Many tomato pastes supply reasonably good concentrated tomato flavor.

ALL ABOUT Spices

Just one or two spices can elevate an everyday dish to the next level. But a jar of spices isn't a pantry staple that stays good forever; all too often home cooks reach for old, stale bottles of spices that essentially have turned into expensive dust. Like many a pantry staple, spices can go rancid or stale. Here are a few tips that can help you get the most from your spice rack.

Buying Tips

Since grinding releases the compounds that give a spice its flavor and aroma, try to buy spices whole and grind them just before using. (That said, there's no denying the convenience of preground spices.) The longer a spice sits, the more its flavor will disappear, so buy spices in small quantities, preferably from places (like spice shops) more likely to have high turnover. And it never hurts to check for an expiration date.

Spice Storage

Don't store spices and herbs on the counter close to the stove since heat, as well as light and moisture, shortens their shelf life. Keep them in a cool, dark, dry place in well-sealed containers.

Bringing Out the Flavor

In the test kitchen, we often like to bloom spices, a technique that removes any raw edge or dustiness from spices and intensifies their flavor. To bloom spices, cook them briefly on the stovetop in a little oil or butter (this also works in the microwave). Many spices are oil- rather than water-soluble, so as they dissolve, their flavorful essential oils are released from a solid state into solution form, where they mix and interact, thereby producing a more complex flavor. Often we will bloom spices in oil along with a few other ingredients at the same time. Of course you have to be careful to avoid burning them.

Checking for Freshness

Grind or finely grate whole spices onto parchment or waxed paper or sprinkle a small amount into the palm of your hand and take a whiff. If the spice releases a lively aroma, it's still good to go. If the aroma and color have faded, it's time to restock. It is helpful to label them with the date opened; whole spices are generally good for two years and ground spices for one year.

Spice Rack Essentials

From arrowroot to mountain pepper to sumac to za'atar, there are hundreds of spices out there to choose from, but in the test kitchen there are only a chosen few we believe are a must in every pantry. We have found we go through chili powder, cinnamon, paprika, and peppercorns (pictured below, left to right) fairly quickly; all others we recommend buying on a need-to-use basis.

Not the Same Old Grind

Everyone should have a good pepper mill in their kitchen, and one-handed pepper mills are (ahem) handy since they free up the other hand to stir a sauce or season raw meat. We put six models priced $50 or less through a range of tests. The **Chef'n Pepper Ball**, $11.95, a manual model that is sturdy and compact, won our hearts. It proved easy to fill and adjust for different grinds (very coarse, coarse, and medium, but not fine). It gave us 1 teaspoon in 45 seconds of easy squeezing.

Prosciutto-Wrapped Chicken with Sage Butter

Serves 4

☑ **WHY THIS RECIPE WORKS:** To infuse simple boneless, skinless chicken breasts with richness, we start by topping them with softened butter blended with sage and olives. Then we wrap the breasts with slices of prosciutto, which add elegance and deep flavor. Browning the prosciutto-wrapped chicken breasts on one side before transferring them to the oven crisps the prosciutto slightly for better texture. While the chicken finishes cooking through in the oven, we prepare an easy garlicky green bean side dish on the stovetop.

4	tablespoons unsalted butter, softened
¼	cup pitted mixed olives, chopped fine
2	tablespoons minced fresh sage
4	(6-ounce) boneless, skinless chicken breasts, trimmed
	Salt and pepper
8	thin slices prosciutto
2	tablespoons olive oil
3	garlic cloves, sliced thin
1	pound green beans, trimmed
¼	cup water

1. Adjust oven rack to upper-middle position and heat oven to 400 degrees. Combine butter, olives, and sage in small bowl and stir with fork until combined.

2. Pat chicken dry with paper towels and season with salt and pepper. Spread butter mixture on top of each chicken breast. Working with 1 breast at a time, lay 2 slices prosciutto on counter, slightly overlapped. Lay chicken, buttered side down, in center of slices, fold prosciutto up and around chicken, then press ends of prosciutto together gently to adhere. Repeat with remaining 6 slices prosciutto and 3 chicken breasts.

3. Heat oil in 12-inch skillet over medium-high heat until just smoking. Add chicken, seam side down, and cook until well browned, about 2 minutes per side. Transfer chicken to baking sheet and bake until chicken registers 160 degrees, about 8 minutes. Transfer to platter and tent loosely with aluminum foil.

4. Reduce heat to medium. Add garlic to skillet and cook until lightly browned, 1 to 2 minutes. Add green beans and toss to combine. Add water and cook, covered, until beans are bright green and tender, 8 to 10 minutes. Uncover and cook until water has evaporated, about 1 minute. Season with salt and pepper to taste and serve with chicken.

Pine Nut and Parmesan-Crusted Chicken

Serves 4

✔ **WHY THIS RECIPE WORKS:** Baked chicken goes from ho-hum to flavor-packed in this recipe inspired by the ingredients you find in a classic basil pesto. To infuse the meat with flavor and keep it moist, we spread a simple basil-flavored mayonnaise on the chicken. This mayonnaise coating also keeps the crunchy panko-bread-crumb, Parmesan, and pine-nut topping in place. While the chicken is in the oven, we prepare a simple side of green beans seasoned with more basil and a little garlic.

⅓   **cup panko bread crumbs**

⅓   **cup pine nuts, toasted and chopped**

⅓   **cup grated Parmesan cheese**

3   **garlic cloves, minced**

3   **tablespoons extra-virgin olive oil**

    Salt and pepper

¼   **cup mayonnaise**

½   **cup chopped fresh basil**

4   **(6-ounce) boneless, skinless chicken breasts, trimmed**

1   **pound green beans, trimmed**

1   **tablespoon lemon juice**

1. Adjust oven rack to upper-middle position and heat oven to 450 degrees. Combine panko, pine nuts, Parmesan, two-thirds of garlic, 2 tablespoons oil, ¼ teaspoon salt, and ¼ teaspoon pepper in bowl. Combine mayonnaise and ¼ cup basil in second bowl.

2. Pat chicken dry with paper towels and transfer to 13 by 9-inch baking dish. Spread mayonnaise mixture evenly over 1 side of chicken breasts. Sprinkle panko mixture over mayonnaise, pressing lightly to adhere. Bake chicken until crumbs are golden brown and chicken registers 160 degrees, 18 to 22 minutes.

3. Meanwhile, bring 2½ quarts water to boil in large saucepan. Add 1 teaspoon salt, green beans, and lemon juice and cook until green beans are tender, about 5 minutes. Drain and transfer to bowl. Toss beans with remaining garlic, remaining 1 tablespoon oil, and remaining ¼ cup basil. Season beans with salt and pepper to taste and serve with chicken.

QUICK PREP TIP MAKING CRISP CHICKEN TOPPING
Pat chicken dry and transfer to 13 by 9-inch baking dish. Spread mayonnaise mixture evenly over 1 side of chicken breasts. Sprinkle panko mixture over mayonnaise and press lightly to adhere.

Chicken and Mexican Green Rice Skillet Supper

Serves 4

✔ **WHY THIS RECIPE WORKS:** There are too many versions of chicken and rice to count; most of them are bland and boring and require more time than we're willing to spend on such a simple dish. Our recipe stands out from the crowd since it is both fast and flavorful. Browning the chicken (we opt for flavorful thighs) in the skillet before adding the other ingredients is a step in the right direction, then we swap out the usual broth for a Mexican-inspired combination of convenient canned green enchilada sauce bolstered with onion, cumin, garlic, and chopped poblanos. Chopped cilantro added right before serving gives the dish a final burst of freshness (and a little more green). Be sure to gently stir the rice and chicken occasionally to prevent the rice from sticking to the bottom of the skillet. For more heat, you can add a minced jalapeño with the onion and poblanos in step 2.

8	**(3-ounce) boneless, skinless chicken thighs, trimmed**
	Salt and pepper
2	**tablespoons vegetable oil**
1	**onion, chopped fine**
2	**poblano chiles, stemmed, seeded, and chopped**
3	**garlic cloves, minced**
1	**teaspoon ground cumin**
1	**(14-ounce) can green enchilada sauce**
1¼	**cups water**
1	**cup long-grain white rice**
½	**cup chopped fresh cilantro**

1. Pat chicken dry with paper towels and season with salt and pepper. Heat 1 tablespoon oil in 12-inch skillet over medium-high heat until just smoking. Cook chicken until well browned on 1 side, about 5 minutes. Transfer to plate.

2. Add onion, poblanos, and remaining 1 tablespoon oil to now-empty skillet and cook until softened, about 5 minutes. Stir in garlic and cumin and cook until fragrant, about 30 seconds. Add enchilada sauce, water, rice, and any accumulated chicken juices and bring to boil, scraping up any browned bits. Nestle chicken into rice, browned side up, cover, and cook over low heat, stirring every 5 minutes, until rice is tender and chicken registers 175 degrees, about 20 minutes.

3. Stir in cilantro, season with salt and pepper to taste, and serve.

SMART SHOPPING LONG-GRAIN WHITE RICE

Higher-quality white rice offers a pleasing al dente texture and a natural, slightly buttery flavor. While most of this subtle variation comes from the variety of rice, processing also affects flavor. All rice starts out brown; to become white, it is milled, a process that removes the husk, bran, and germ. The longer the rice is milled, the whiter it becomes. Many brands of rice are then enriched to replace lost nutrients. Unlike medium- or short-grain white rice, cooked long-grain white rice remains fluffy and separate because it contains less starch. We tasted six national brands of long-grain white rice, plain and in pilaf. **Lundberg Organic Long-Grain White Rice** stood out for its nutty, buttery flavor and distinct, smooth grains.

Chicken and Artichoke Paella

Serves 4

✔ **WHY THIS RECIPE WORKS:** Paella, a Spanish dinner party favorite, typically calls for a laundry list of ingredients and some intensive cooking. Our version limits the proteins to chicken and chorizo, which provide plenty of heft and flavor. Since we cook every component in the same skillet, browning the sausage first infuses the oil in the pan with a meatiness that is carried through into the final dish. Artichokes add the perfect complementary grassy flavor, and parcooking the rice in the microwave while we brown the meat keeps things quick.

2	cups water
1	cup long-grain white rice
	Salt and pepper
2	tablespoons vegetable oil
8	ounces chorizo sausage, sliced ½ inch thick
2	(6-ounce) boneless, skinless chicken breasts, trimmed and cut crosswise into ¼-inch-thick pieces
1	onion, chopped
3	garlic cloves, minced
¼	teaspoon saffron threads, crumbled
1	(14.5-ounce) can diced tomatoes
9	ounces frozen artichoke hearts, thawed
½	cup frozen peas

1. Combine 1½ cups water, rice, and ¾ teaspoon salt in bowl. Cover and microwave until rice is softened and most of liquid is absorbed, 10 to 12 minutes.

2. Meanwhile, heat 1 tablespoon oil in 12-inch nonstick skillet over medium-high heat until just smoking. Add chorizo and cook until lightly browned, about 2 minutes per side. Transfer to plate. Pat chicken dry with paper towels and season with salt and pepper. Cook chicken until lightly browned and no longer pink, about 2 minutes per side. Transfer to plate with chorizo.

3. Add onion and remaining 1 tablespoon oil to now-empty skillet and cook until softened, about 5 minutes. Stir in garlic and saffron and cook until fragrant, about 30 seconds. Stir in tomatoes, rice, and remaining ½ cup water and bring to boil, scraping up any browned bits. Reduce heat to medium and cook until rice is tender and liquid is absorbed, 10 to 12 minutes.

4. Stir in chorizo, chicken and any accumulated juices, artichoke hearts, and peas and cook, stirring frequently, until hot, 2 to 3 minutes. Season with salt and pepper to taste and serve.

SMART SHOPPING SAFFRON
Sometimes known as "red gold," saffron is the world's most expensive spice. Luckily, a little saffron goes a long way, and we have found that brand isn't important, as long as the recipe has other strong flavors, as this one does.

Chicken with Mexican-Style Pumpkin Seed Sauce

Serves 4

✔ **WHY THIS RECIPE WORKS:** The Mexican dish *pollo en pipian verde* brings great flavors to the table by braising chicken pieces in a traditional tomatillo-based sauce that has been enhanced with toasted pumpkin seeds. But between grinding toasted pumpkin seeds with myriad spices, combining the mixture with a from-scratch sauce that's been slowly reduced on the stovetop, and adding precooked chicken to the pan, it's a dish that requires an arsenal of cookware and hours, if not days, to make. We maintain the classic flavor profile and minimize the work by using a food processor to make a simple sauce with tomatillos, garlic, and jalapeños. Toasting a mixture of pumpkin seeds, sesame seeds, and allspice (which has also been run through the food processor) deepens the flavors quickly. Then we simply pour the sauce into a skillet and add boneless, skinless chicken breasts. Poaching the meat in the sauce saves cookware and time and ensures moist, flavorful chicken. Finishing the sauce with lime juice and cilantro adds just the right brightness.

1	**cup pumpkin seeds, toasted**
½	**cup sesame seeds, toasted**
½	**teaspoon ground allspice**
	Salt and pepper
½	**pound fresh tomatillos, husks and stems removed, rinsed well and dried**
3	**garlic cloves, minced**
4	**jalapeño chiles, stemmed, seeded, and chopped**
4	**(6-ounce) boneless, skinless chicken breasts, trimmed**
2	**tablespoons vegetable oil**
1	**cup low-sodium chicken broth**
¾	**cup chopped fresh cilantro**
1	**tablespoon lime juice**

1. Process pumpkin seeds, sesame seeds, allspice, and ½ teaspoon pepper in food processor until finely ground, about 30 seconds. Transfer to bowl. Process tomatillos, garlic, and jalapeños in food processor until coarsely ground, about 30 seconds.

2. Pat chicken dry with paper towels and season with salt and pepper. Heat oil in 12-inch skillet over medium-high heat until shimmering. Add pumpkin-seed mixture and cook, stirring occasionally, until fragrant and golden, about 3 minutes. Add tomatillo mixture, broth, and 1 teaspoon salt and stir to combine. Bring to simmer then arrange chicken breasts in skillet. Reduce heat to medium-low and cook, covered, until chicken registers 160 degrees, 13 to 15 minutes, flipping chicken halfway through cooking. Transfer chicken to serving platter.

3. Reduce sauce until slightly thickened, about 1 minute. Stir in cilantro and lime juice and season with salt and pepper to taste. Serve over chicken.

SIMPLE SIDE CILANTRO RICE
Process 3 cups low-sodium chicken broth and 1½ cups fresh cilantro leaves in blender or food processor until pureed, about 15 seconds. Bring cilantro mixture, 1½ cups long-grain white rice, and 1 teaspoon salt to boil over medium-high heat in large saucepan and cook until no liquid is visible, 5 to 8 minutes. Cover and continue to cook on low heat until rice is tender, about 15 minutes. Serves 4.

Skillet Chicken with Spicy Red Beans and Rice

Serves 4

✔ **WHY THIS RECIPE WORKS:** To liven up an everyday skillet chicken dinner, a side dish of New Orleans–style red beans and rice is just the answer. But the classic version requires some hard-to-find regional ingredients, several varieties of pork, and cooking dried beans. To streamline things, we opt for canned kidney beans and we partially cook the rice in the microwave while the chicken browns. Andouille sausage lends plenty of spice and meaty flavor to this dish, and green bell pepper, garlic, and scallions add authenticity without making our grocery list too long. After browning the chicken, we build the base for the red beans and rice, and once the rice and beans are in the pan, we add broth and the chicken and cook it all through together.

2	cups low-sodium chicken broth
1	cup long-grain white rice
	Salt and pepper
4	(6-ounce) boneless, skinless chicken breasts, trimmed
3	tablespoons vegetable oil
1	green bell pepper, stemmed, seeded, and chopped
8	scallions, white parts minced, green parts sliced thin
8	ounces andouille sausage, halved lengthwise and cut crosswise ½ inch thick
3	garlic cloves, minced
2	teaspoons minced fresh thyme
¼	teaspoon cayenne pepper
1	(15-ounce) can red kidney beans, rinsed

1. Combine 1 cup broth, rice, and ¾ teaspoon salt in bowl. Cover and microwave until liquid is absorbed, 10 to 12 minutes.

2. Meanwhile, pat chicken dry with paper towels and season with salt and pepper. Heat 1 tablespoon oil in 12-inch nonstick skillet over medium-high heat until just smoking. Add chicken and cook until golden brown, about 2 minutes per side. Transfer to plate.

3. Heat remaining 2 tablespoons oil in now-empty skillet over medium-high heat until shimmering. Add bell pepper, scallion whites, and sausage and cook until pepper begins to soften and sausage is lightly browned, about 4 minutes. Add garlic, thyme, cayenne, and ¼ teaspoon pepper and cook until fragrant, about 30 seconds.

4. Stir rice, beans, and remaining 1 cup broth into skillet and bring to boil. Reduce heat to medium-low, nestle chicken into rice, and cook, covered, until liquid is absorbed and chicken registers 160 degrees, about 10 minutes. Scatter scallion greens over chicken and rice and serve.

QUICK PREP TIP **KEEPING SCALLIONS FRESH**
Too often, scallions go limp after just a few days in the fridge. We found that if we stand them in an inch of water in a tall container (covering them loosely with a zipper-lock bag and refreshing the water every three days), our scallions last for well over a week with very little loss in quality.

Chicken with Parsley Sauce and Celery Root Slaw

Serves 4

☑ **WHY THIS RECIPE WORKS:** On a busy weeknight, nothing is easier than sautéing a few chicken breasts in a hot skillet. The challenge is achieving great flavor, plus a side dish, without adding tons of work. For this recipe, we rely on the food processor to help make our slaw and our sauce in minutes. A no-cook sauce of parsley, olive oil, lemon juice, and garlic is easy to make and adds great freshness to the chicken. A simple slaw combining celery root and tart Granny Smith apples is the perfect match to complete this summery meal. The slaw's dressing also incorporates lemon juice and parsley, which helps to keep the ingredient list short, and adding a few tablespoons of horseradish to the mix lends a nice contrast to the tart apple and mild celery root.

1   **large head celery root (1 to 1¼ pounds), peeled and cut into 1½-inch pieces**

½   **cup sour cream**

½   **cup water**

½   **cup chopped fresh parsley plus 1½ cups leaves**

¼   **cup lemon juice (2 lemons)**

2   **tablespoons prepared horseradish**

1   **Granny Smith apple, cored and cut into ¼-inch-thick matchsticks**

    Salt and pepper

¼   **cup olive oil**

1   **garlic clove, minced**

8   **(4-ounce) chicken cutlets, trimmed**

1. Using food processor fitted with shredding disk, shred celery root. In medium bowl, combine sour cream, water, chopped parsley, 1 tablespoon lemon juice, and horseradish. Stir in shredded celery root and apple. Season slaw with salt and pepper to taste.

2. Wipe out food processor workbowl and process parsley leaves, 3 tablespoons oil, remaining 3 tablespoons lemon juice, and garlic until smooth. Season with salt and pepper to taste.

3. Pat chicken dry with paper towels and season with salt and pepper. Heat remaining 1 tablespoon oil in 12-inch skillet over medium-high heat until just smoking. Cook chicken until lightly browned and no longer pink, 3 to 5 minutes per side. Transfer to platter, drizzle with parsley sauce, and serve with celery root slaw.

QUICK PREP TIP CUTTING APPLES INTO MATCHSTICKS
After coring and peeling apple, cut horizontally into ¼-inch-thick planks. Stack planks and cut vertically into matchsticks.

Chicken Cutlets with Ginger-Shiitake Sauce

Serves 4

✔ **WHY THIS RECIPE WORKS:** Chicken cutlets are a fantastic weeknight option since they cook through so quickly, and this gingery shiitake cream sauce takes them to the next level. The shiitakes infuse the sauce with a deep, earthy flavor, and ginger adds a punch that cuts through the richness. For a simple side, we cook chard in minutes in the microwave, then use a spatula to press out its excess liquid in a colander, which ensures the final result isn't watery. This recipe works like clockwork: Microwave the chard, sauté the cutlets, build the sauce, and finally sauté the chard to quickly heat it up. An impressive and flavorful dinner is ready in a surprisingly short amount of time—and with minimal cookware required.

2	pounds Swiss chard, stemmed and leaves chopped
8	(4-ounce) chicken cutlets, trimmed
	Salt and pepper
¼	cup vegetable oil
1	pound shiitake mushrooms, stemmed and sliced thin
3	tablespoons grated fresh ginger
¼	cup rice wine or dry sherry
1	cup low-sodium chicken broth
¼	cup heavy cream
2	tablespoons unsalted butter

1. Place chard and ¼ cup water in large bowl. Cover and microwave until chard is wilted, 3 to 4 minutes. Transfer chard to colander. Use rubber spatula to gently press chard to release liquid. Transfer to cutting board and chop coarse. Return to colander and press again to release any remaining liquid.

2. Pat chicken dry with paper towels and season with salt and pepper. Heat 1 tablespoon oil in 12-inch skillet over medium-high heat until just smoking. Add 4 cutlets and cook until golden brown and cooked through, about 3 minutes per side. Transfer to platter and tent loosely with aluminum foil. Repeat with 1 tablespoon oil and remaining 4 cutlets.

3. Add mushrooms and 1 tablespoon oil to now-empty skillet and cook until starting to brown, about 5 minutes. Add ginger and cook until fragrant, about 30 seconds. Add rice wine and cook until reduced to glaze, about 1 minute. Add broth and cream and cook until thickened, about 6 minutes. Off heat, whisk in butter and season with salt and pepper to taste.

4. Heat remaining 1 tablespoon oil in large saucepan over medium-high heat until shimmering. Add chard and stir to coat. Cook until heated through, about 2 minutes. Season with salt and pepper to taste and serve with chicken and sauce.

Quick Southern Fried Chicken Dinner

Serves 4

✔ **WHY THIS RECIPE WORKS:** For a Southern-style fried chicken dinner without the mess or work of traditional recipes, we use boneless cutlets that can be shallow-fried. Cornmeal provides a crunchy coating that pairs perfectly with our Cajun-seasoned side of okra, tomato, and black-eyed peas. Soaking the chicken in buttermilk for 5 minutes adds tangy, rich flavor to the chicken and keeps it tender. After the cutlets are cooked, the side dish goes into the same skillet and is ready in less than 10 minutes. Don't use coarse-ground cornmeal; it will not adhere to the chicken properly. We prefer to use fresh okra here, but you can substitute frozen.

1 **cup cornmeal**

1 **tablespoon Cajun seasoning**

1 **cup buttermilk**

4 **(4-ounce) chicken cutlets, trimmed**

Salt and pepper

½ **cup plus 1 tablespoon vegetable oil**

1 **pound fresh okra, halved lengthwise**

3 **garlic cloves, minced**

1 **(15-ounce) can black-eyed peas, rinsed**

1 **(14.5-ounce) can diced tomatoes, drained**

1. Mix cornmeal and 1 teaspoon Cajun seasoning in shallow baking dish and pour buttermilk into second shallow dish. Pat chicken dry with paper towels and season with salt and pepper. Place chicken in buttermilk and turn to coat. Let soak for 5 minutes, turning occasionally. Working with 1 cutlet at a time, remove from buttermilk, letting excess drip off, and coat with cornmeal, pressing to adhere.

2. Heat ¼ cup oil in 12-inch nonstick skillet over medium-high heat until shimmering. Add 2 cutlets and cook until golden brown and crisp, about 2 minutes per side. Transfer to paper towel–lined plate. Repeat with ¼ cup oil and remaining 2 cutlets.

3. Heat remaining 1 tablespoon oil in now-empty skillet until shimmering. Add okra and cook, turning occasionally, until lightly browned, about 3 minutes. Add garlic, remaining 2 teaspoons Cajun seasoning, and ½ teaspoon salt and cook until fragrant, about 30 seconds. Stir in black-eyed peas and tomatoes and cook until heated through, about 2 minutes. Serve with chicken.

QUICK PREP TIP

MAKING CHICKEN CUTLETS

Place each chicken breast on cutting board. Place one hand on top of breast to hold it steady and use chef's knife to slice meat in half horizontally. For thinner cutlets, cover each piece with plastic wrap and pound to desired thickness. To make cutting meat easier, you can freeze it until just firm, about 20 minutes.

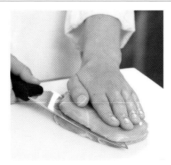

Chicken Francese with Broccoli Rabe

Serves 4

✔ **WHY THIS RECIPE WORKS:** Chicken francese, an Italian-American favorite featuring chicken cutlets in a light, eggy coating and served with a lemony sauce, often falls short. We get the best coating by dipping our cutlets in flour, then egg, then again in flour. We cook the cutlets in two batches, then prepare the wine sauce. Broccoli rabe's bitter flavor is a great match, and we simply microwave it while the sauce reduces.

1	cup plus 1 tablespoon all-purpose flour
2	large eggs
8	(4-ounce) chicken cutlets, trimmed
	Salt and pepper
4	tablespoons unsalted butter
1	onion, chopped fine
2¼	cups low-sodium chicken broth
½	cup dry white wine
⅓	cup lemon juice (2 lemons)
1	pound broccoli rabe, trimmed
¼	cup water

1. Adjust oven rack to middle position, set heatproof serving platter on rack, and heat oven to 200 degrees. Spread 1 cup flour in shallow dish. Beat eggs in second dish. Pat chicken dry with paper towels and season with salt and pepper. Dredge each chicken breast in flour and shake off excess, then dip in eggs to coat, and then return to flour. Coat evenly with flour and shake off any excess.

2. Melt 1 tablespoon butter in 12-inch nonstick skillet over medium-high heat. Add 4 cutlets and cook until golden brown and cooked through, 2 to 3 minutes per side. Transfer cutlets to platter in oven. Wipe out skillet with paper towels and repeat with 1 tablespoon butter and remaining 4 cutlets.

3. Melt 1 tablespoon butter in now-empty skillet, add onion, and cook over medium-high heat until softened, about 5 minutes. Add remaining 1 tablespoon flour and stir until golden brown, about 1 minute. Whisk in broth, wine, and lemon juice and cook until reduced to about 1½ cups, 12 to 15 minutes.

4. Place broccoli rabe and water in bowl, cover, and microwave until tender and bright green, 3 to 5 minutes. Drain, season with salt and pepper to taste, and transfer to platter with cutlets. Whisk remaining 1 tablespoon butter into sauce and season with salt and pepper to taste. Pour sauce over cutlets and serve.

Hearty Chicken and Chorizo Skillet Supper

Serves 4

✓ **WHY THIS RECIPE WORKS:** This homey and hearty dinner comes together quickly, thanks to a few very convenient ingredients. To make this dish as fast and easy as possible, we use quick-cooking chicken tenders, chorizo sausage (which is already cooked), and canned beans. Spanish chorizo, dry-cured and seasoned with smoked paprika, is the sausage of choice here, and adding a teaspoon of smoked paprika to the chicken before cooking helps transport the flavors of the chorizo to the rest of the dish. After browning the chicken, we set it aside while we brown the chorizo and cook the onions. Next, garlic, canned tomatoes, broth, and butter beans go into the pan to cook until slightly thickened. Then all we have to do is add the chicken to this flavorful mixture and take a few minutes to cook it through.

1½	**pounds chicken tenderloins, trimmed**
1	**teaspoon smoked paprika**
	Salt and pepper
2	**tablespoons olive oil**
1	**onion, halved and sliced thin**
8	**ounces Spanish chorizo sausage or linguiça, cut ¼ inch thick**
2	**garlic cloves, minced**
2	**(15-ounce) cans butter beans, rinsed**
1	**(14.5-ounce) can diced tomatoes**
½	**cup low-sodium chicken broth**
2	**tablespoons chopped fresh parsley**

1. Pat chicken dry with paper towels and season with paprika, salt, and pepper. Heat 1 tablespoon oil in 12-inch skillet over medium-high heat until just smoking. Add chicken and cook until lightly browned, about 1½ minutes per side. Transfer to plate.

2. Heat remaining 1 tablespoon oil in now-empty skillet, add onion and chorizo, and cook until onion is soft and chorizo is beginning to brown, about 5 minutes. Add garlic and cook until fragrant, about 1 minute. Add butter beans, tomatoes, and broth and cook until slightly thickened, about 3 minutes.

3. Return chicken and any accumulated juices to skillet and simmer until chicken is cooked through, 3 to 5 minutes. Stir in parsley, season with salt and pepper to taste, and serve.

SMART SHOPPING DICED TOMATOES
Unlike most types of canned produce, which pale in comparison to their fresh counterparts, a great can of diced tomatoes offers flavor almost every bit as intense as ripe, in-season fruit. We gathered 16 widely available styles and brands and tasted them plain and in tomato sauce. To our surprise, nearly half fell short. Factors such as geography and additives played into whether a sample rated highly in our tasting. Our top-ranked tomatoes were grown in California, source of most of the world's tomatoes, where the dry, hot growing season develops sweet, complex flavor. Tasters also overwhelmingly favored those with more salt. In the end, one can, **Hunt's Diced Tomatoes**, stood out from the pack.

Chicken Parmesan Fingers with Marinara Sauce

Serves 4

✔ **WHY THIS RECIPE WORKS:** We took classic Parmesan chicken and gave it a youthful spin by turning it into chicken fingers that we serve with a super-simple, bright marinara dipping sauce. In lieu of the traditional bread-crumb coating, we use ultra-crispy panko, and adding Parmesan to the coating boosts the flavor while keeping the meal finger-food friendly. Rather than make a slow-cooked traditional marinara sauce with fresh tomatoes, we get great results in a fraction of the time by bolstering a can of diced tomatoes with fresh basil and several cloves of garlic, then simmering it all together for less than 10 minutes. To keep this recipe moving, we prepare the chicken fingers while the sauce simmers. You will get the best texture by shredding the Parmesan on the large holes of a box grater.

1	tablespoon plus ½ cup olive oil
4	garlic cloves, minced
1	(14.5-ounce) can diced tomatoes
1	tablespoon shredded fresh basil
	Salt and pepper
½	cup all-purpose flour
2	large eggs
1	cup panko bread crumbs
2	ounces Parmesan cheese, grated (1 cup)
1½	pounds chicken tenderloins, trimmed

1. Heat 1 tablespoon oil in saucepan over medium-high heat until shimmering. Add garlic and cook until fragrant, about 30 seconds. Stir in tomatoes and simmer until slightly thickened, about 7 minutes. Mash mixture until only small chunks of tomato remain. Stir in basil and season with salt and pepper to taste. Cover and keep warm.

2. Spread flour in shallow dish. Beat eggs in second dish. Combine panko and Parmesan in third dish. Pat chicken dry with paper towels and season with salt and pepper. One at a time, dredge tenderloins in flour and shake off excess, dip in eggs, and coat with panko mixture, pressing to adhere.

3. Heat ¼ cup oil in 12-inch nonstick skillet over medium heat until shimmering. Add half of chicken and cook until golden brown, about 3 minutes per side. Transfer to paper towel–lined plate. Wipe out skillet and repeat with remaining ¼ cup oil and remaining chicken. Serve with marinara dipping sauce.

SIMPLE SIDE RANCH SLAW
Whisk ¼ cup mayonnaise, ¼ cup buttermilk, 1 tablespoon white wine vinegar, 2 minced scallions, 1 minced garlic clove, ⅛ teaspoon dried dill, 1 teaspoon salt, and 1 teaspoon pepper together in bowl. Toss dressing with 1 (14-ounce) bag green coleslaw mix. Serves 4.

Chicken Tenders with Meaty Green Beans

Serves 4

✔ **WHY THIS RECIPE WORKS:** This is truly a one-pan meal, with the pancetta (which, along with pine nuts, adds flavor to our vegetable side dish), chicken, and green beans all cooked, in sequence, in the same skillet. Dredging the tenderloins in flour before cooking gives them a light coating without the work of the typical multi-step breading process. Browning the chicken in the fat rendered by the pancetta infuses the meat with great flavor, and using a nonstick skillet ensures the chicken's light coating stays put. Finally, to give the green beans a flavor boost, we steam them with chicken broth instead of the usual water.

2   **tablespoons olive oil**

3   **ounces thinly sliced pancetta**

½   **cup flour**

1½   **pounds chicken tenderloins, trimmed**

      Salt and pepper

1   **pound green beans, trimmed and cut in half on bias**

½   **cup low-sodium chicken broth**

¼   **cup pine nuts, toasted**

1. Heat oil in 12-inch nonstick skillet over medium-high heat, add pancetta, and cook until crisp, about 4 minutes. Transfer to paper towel–lined plate and pour off all but 1 tablespoon fat from skillet, reserving excess. When cool enough to handle, crumble pancetta into bite-size pieces. Meanwhile, spread flour in shallow dish. Pat chicken dry with paper towels and season with salt and pepper. Coat each chicken tenderloin lightly in flour and shake off excess.

2. Heat fat in skillet over medium-high heat until just smoking. Add half of chicken tenderloins and cook until lightly browned, about 3 minutes per side. Transfer to platter and tent loosely with aluminum foil. Repeat with 1 tablespoon reserved fat and remaining chicken.

3. Reduce heat to medium. Add beans and chicken broth to now-empty skillet, cover, and cook until beans are bright green and tender, about 6 minutes. Uncover, increase heat to medium-high, and cook until liquid is reduced to glazy consistency, about 1 minute. Off heat, add pancetta and pine nuts and stir to combine. Season with salt and pepper to taste, and serve with chicken.

SMART SHOPPING CHICKEN TENDERLOINS
The chicken tenderloin is weakly attached to the breast and is easy to remove with a simple tug. They come prepackaged in the meat section of most supermarkets, but if you have trouble finding them, it's simple to create a quick substitute. Just trim an equal amount of boneless, skinless chicken breasts and slice them on the bias into ¾-inch-thick strips.

Sweet and Savory Cuban Chicken Pie

Serves 4

✓ **WHY THIS RECIPE WORKS:** Here a Cuban *picadillo*—a ground meat hash with tomatoes, garlic, onions, cumin, olives, and raisins—meets an American-style chicken pot pie. While the flavors are distinctly Cuban, the topping of crisp wedges of pie dough is a clear nod to the pot pie. We build the sauce in the skillet, then add already-cooked rotisserie chicken meat at the end. By baking the dough for the topping while the filling simmers on the stove, and then placing it on the filling before serving, we keep the crust from turning soggy. Once you've taken the dough out of the oven, give it time to firm up before placing it on the pie.

1	sheet (from 15-ounce box) Pillsbury Pie Crust
2	tablespoons olive oil
1	onion, chopped
5	garlic cloves, minced
1	tablespoon ground cumin
2	(14.5-ounce) cans diced tomatoes
1	cup low-sodium chicken broth
1	cup green olives stuffed with pimento, quartered
½	cup golden raisins
1	(2½-pound) rotisserie chicken, skin and bones discarded, meat shredded into bite-size pieces (3 cups)
	Salt and pepper

1. Adjust oven rack to middle position and heat oven to 400 degrees. Line baking sheet with parchment paper. Place pie dough on prepared baking sheet and cut into 8 wedges. Bake dough until cooked through and golden brown, about 14 minutes. Let cool on baking sheet until firm, about 5 minutes.

2. Meanwhile, heat oil in 12-inch skillet over medium-high heat until shimmering. Add onion and cook until softened, about 4 minutes. Add garlic and cumin and cook until fragrant, about 30 seconds. Stir in tomatoes, broth, olives, and raisins and cook until thickened, about 12 minutes.

3. Stir in chicken and season with salt and pepper to taste. Arrange dough wedges on top of chicken filling and serve.

EASY CUBAN CHICKEN PIE
Cut packaged pie dough into 8 wedges, then bake in 400-degree oven until golden brown. Meanwhile, make filling. Sauté onion, garlic, and cumin in large skillet, then stir in chicken broth, olives, raisins, and tomatoes and simmer. Add chicken, arrange pie crust wedges on top, and serve.

Curried Chicken Meatballs with Apricot Rice Pilaf

Serves 4

✔ **WHY THIS RECIPE WORKS:** Meatballs are another one of our comfort food favorites, so here we give them a new spin by using ground chicken instead of beef and adding the bold flavor of curry and bright freshness of cilantro. Forming small 1-inch meatballs means they cook through quickly just as they finish browning. We then pair the meatballs with an apricot and almond rice pilaf, which provides plenty of complementary flavor to the meal—no sauce necessary. Cooking the rice in a saucepan while we prepare the meatballs ensures this dinner is ready in about 30 minutes.

¼	**cup vegetable oil**
2	**small onions, chopped fine**
1	**cup long-grain white rice**
2	**cups water**
1	**pound ground chicken**
½	**cup panko bread crumbs**
¼	**cup chopped fresh cilantro**
1	**tablespoon curry powder**
	Salt and pepper
½	**cup dried apricots, chopped**
¾	**cup slivered almonds, toasted**

1. Heat 2 tablespoons oil in large saucepan over medium-high heat until shimmering. Add half of onions and cook until softened, about 4 minutes. Add rice and cook until mostly opaque, about 4 minutes. Add water and bring to boil, lower heat to medium-low, cover, and cook until rice is tender, about 20 minutes.

2. Meanwhile, combine chicken, remaining onion, panko, 2 tablespoons cilantro, curry powder, 1 teaspoon salt, and ½ teaspoon pepper in large bowl. Knead mixture with hands until well mixed. Using wet hands, shape into 1-inch meatballs.

3. Heat remaining 2 tablespoons oil in 12-inch nonstick skillet over medium-high heat until just smoking. Add meatballs and cook until browned on all sides, about 6 minutes. Cover and cook through, 4 to 6 additional minutes. Transfer to platter.

4. Add apricots, ½ cup almonds, and remaining 2 tablespoons cilantro to rice and stir until thoroughly incorporated. Season with salt and pepper to taste and sprinkle with remaining ¼ cup almonds. Serve with meatballs.

SIMPLE SIDE EGGPLANT AND GARLIC SAUTÉ
Heat 3 tablespoons olive oil in 12-inch nonstick skillet over medium heat until shimmering. Add 3 minced garlic cloves and cook until fragrant, about 30 seconds. Add 2 eggplants, peeled and cut into 1-inch cubes, cover, and cook until tender, about 10 minutes. Uncover and continue to cook until liquid has reduced by half and eggplant is soft, about 4 minutes. Season with salt and pepper to taste. Serves 4.

Turkey Saltimbocca

Serves 4

✔ **WHY THIS RECIPE WORKS:** Adaptations of this Italian classic overcomplicate the dish with extraneous ingredients and fussy techniques. We wanted a dish that would give cutlets, prosciutto, and sage their due. First, we opt for affordable turkey cutlets instead of the classic veal. While most recipes sauté the cutlets in butter before braising them in wine, we simply brown our prosciutto-topped, sage-seasoned cutlets, then set them aside to make a quick vermouth pan sauce. Crisping whole sage leaves in the skillet doesn't add much work to the recipe and serves as a great garnish to bring the dish together. Make sure to buy prosciutto that is thinly sliced but not shaved; avoid slices that are too thick, since they won't stick to the chicken properly.

6	thin slices prosciutto
½	cup all-purpose flour
	Salt and pepper
6	(4-ounce) turkey cutlets, trimmed
1	tablespoon minced fresh sage plus 8 whole leaves
¼	cup olive oil
1	cup dry vermouth
1	teaspoon lemon juice
2	tablespoons unsalted butter, cut into 4 pieces
1	tablespoon minced fresh parsley

1. Trim prosciutto slices to 5- to 6-inch-long pieces to match turkey cutlets. Combine flour with 1 teaspoon pepper in shallow dish. Pat cutlets dry with paper towels. Dredge turkey in flour and shake off excess, then sprinkle evenly with minced sage. Place 1 prosciutto slice on top of each cutlet, pressing lightly to adhere.

2. Heat 2 tablespoons oil in 12-inch skillet over medium-high heat until shimmering. Add sage leaves and cook until leaves begin to darken and are fragrant, about 30 seconds. Using slotted spoon, transfer leaves to paper towel–lined plate. Add 3 cutlets to skillet, prosciutto side down, and cook until just golden brown, 2 to 3 minutes per side. Transfer to platter and tent loosely with aluminum foil. Repeat with remaining 2 tablespoons oil and remaining 3 cutlets.

3. Pour off excess fat from skillet. Add vermouth, scraping up any browned bits, and simmer until reduced to about 3 tablespoons, 5 to 7 minutes. Stir in lemon juice, then whisk in butter and stir in parsley. Season with salt and pepper to taste. Pour sauce over turkey, garnish with sage leaves, and serve.

SIMPLE SIDE SAUTÉED SPINACH WITH GARLIC CHIPS
Cook 3 tablespoons olive oil and 6 thinly sliced garlic cloves in Dutch oven over medium heat, stirring occasionally, until garlic is golden and very crisp, 10 to 12 minutes. Using slotted spoon, transfer garlic to paper towel–lined plate. Add ¼ teaspoon red pepper flakes to pot and cook until fragrant, about 1 minute. Add 18 ounces baby spinach and stir until spinach is coated in oil. Cover pot, increase heat to medium-high, and cook, stirring occasionally, until spinach is tender and wilted but still bright green, 3 to 5 minutes. Season with salt and pepper to taste and toss with garlic chips. Serves 4.

Mustard-Sage Turkey Cutlets and Barley Salad

Serves 4

✔ **WHY THIS RECIPE WORKS:** For a streamlined recipe that also boasts big flavor, we cook turkey cutlets quickly in a skillet, then set them aside to make a mustard-sage pan sauce that doubles as the base of a dressing for our barley salad. By using quick-cooking barley and the microwave, this rustic, nutty-flavored grain, which usually takes at least 40 minutes to cook, is ready to go in just 10 minutes. Rinsing the grains in cold water halts the cooking quickly, ensuring they have just the right texture for the final salad. Sweet-tart dried cranberries and diced fresh apple round out our side dish.

3	cups low-sodium chicken broth
1½	cups quick-cooking barley
	Salt and pepper
4	(6-ounce) turkey cutlets, trimmed
3	tablespoons olive oil
1	shallot, minced
2	tablespoons Dijon mustard
4	teaspoons chopped fresh sage
1	Granny Smith apple, cored and diced
½	cup dried cranberries
1	tablespoon cider vinegar

1. Combine 2 cups broth, barley, and ½ teaspoon salt in bowl. Cover and microwave until barley is tender and liquid is absorbed, about 10 minutes. Rinse with cold water and return to bowl.

2. Pat cutlets dry with paper towels and season with salt and pepper. Heat 1 tablespoon oil in 12-inch skillet over medium-high heat until just smoking. Cook until golden brown and cooked through, 2 to 4 minutes per side. Transfer to plate and tent loosely with aluminum foil.

3. Heat 1 tablespoon oil in now-empty skillet, add shallot, and cook until soft, about 1 minute. Add remaining 1 cup broth and bring to boil. Whisk in mustard and sage and cook until slightly reduced, 3 to 4 minutes. Add ¼ cup pan sauce to barley along with apple, cranberries, remaining 1 tablespoon oil, and vinegar. Stir to combine and season with salt and pepper to taste.

4. Return turkey and any accumulated juices to skillet and simmer to warm through, about 1 minute. Serve with barley salad.

SMART SHOPPING BARLEY

Barley is a hearty grain with a nutty flavor similar to that of brown rice. It tastes great in soups and salads, prepared risotto-style with a few add-ins, or cooked simply and served as a side dish. Barley is available in multiple forms. Hulled barley, sold with the hull removed and the fiber-rich bran intact, is considered a whole grain. Pearl (or pearled) barley is hulled barley that has been polished to remove the bran. Then there is quick-cooking barley, which has been parcooked. Hulled barley takes a long time to cook and should be soaked before cooking. Pearl barley cooks more quickly, making it a more versatile choice, but better still for weeknight cooking is quick-cooking barley (right); it's ready in just 10 minutes.

Spicy Orange Chipotle-Glazed Turkey Tenderloins

Serves 4

✔ **WHY THIS RECIPE WORKS:** We start by browning the tenderloins in a skillet and then, once they develop nice color on all sides, we add our glaze to the pan. To go beyond a classic syrup- or sugar-based glaze, we add orange and lime juice for brightness, a combination of brown sugar and molasses for sweetness with complexity, and minced canned chipotles for smoky heat and depth. The tenderloins gently simmer while the glaze reduces, and by the time it thickens to the ideal consistency, the turkey is just cooked through. Finishing the glaze with cilantro adds just the freshness it needs.

¾ **cup orange juice (2 oranges)**

¼ **cup lime juice (2 limes)**

¼ **cup packed brown sugar**

1 **tablespoon molasses**

2 **teaspoons minced canned chipotle chile in adobo sauce**

2 **(8- to 12-ounce) turkey tenderloins, trimmed**
 Salt and pepper

1 **tablespoon vegetable oil**

2 **tablespoons chopped fresh cilantro**

1. Stir orange juice, lime juice, brown sugar, molasses, and chipotle in small bowl. Pat tenderloins dry with paper towels and season with salt and pepper.

2. Heat oil in 12-inch nonstick skillet over medium-high heat until just smoking. Cook turkey until browned on all sides, about 5 minutes. Reduce heat to medium. Add orange juice mixture and cook, turning turkey occasionally, until turkey registers 160 degrees, 14 to 17 minutes. Transfer turkey to cutting board, tent loosely with aluminum foil, and let rest for 5 minutes.

3. Simmer glaze until thick and syrupy, 3 to 4 minutes. Cut tenderloins crosswise into ½-inch-thick slices and arrange on platter. Stir cilantro into glaze and season with salt and pepper to taste. Pour glaze over turkey and serve.

SIMPLE SIDE MASHED SWEET POTATOES
In large saucepan, cover 1½ pounds sweet potatoes, peeled and cut into ½-inch pieces, with water by 1 inch and bring to boil. Reduce heat and simmer until potatoes are tender, about 15 minutes. Drain potatoes and return to pot. Add ¼ cup orange juice, 3 tablespoons unsalted butter, and 1 tablespoon molasses and mash until smooth. Season with salt and pepper to taste. Cover to keep warm. Serves 4.

Spanish-Style Turkey Meatballs

Serves 4

✓ **WHY THIS RECIPE WORKS:** This recipe is inspired by the classic Spanish tapas-style meatballs, *albóndigas*. We give them a new spin by using ground turkey instead of beef, and, rather than serving them with a traditional tomato or saffron sauce as you'd find in Spain, we opt for another Spanish favorite, the red pepper and almond–based romesco sauce. Its texture and richness pair perfectly with the meatballs, and it takes only minutes to make in a food processor. Sherry, a quintessential Spanish ingredient, adds depth and subtle sweetness to both the meat and sauce. Avoid extra-lean ground turkey; a moderate fat content will help the meatballs hold together.

3	slices hearty white sandwich bread, torn into pieces
1	cup low-sodium chicken broth
5	tablespoons dry sherry
1½	pounds ground turkey
1½	teaspoons paprika
¼	cup chopped fresh parsley
4	garlic cloves, minced
	Salt and pepper
6	tablespoons slivered almonds, toasted
1½	cups jarred roasted red peppers plus ¼ cup liquid
2	tablespoons extra-virgin olive oil

1. Using fork, mash 2 bread slices with ¼ cup chicken broth and 3 tablespoons sherry in bowl until smooth. Add turkey, paprika, 3 tablespoons parsley, half of garlic, 1 teaspoon salt, and ½ teaspoon pepper and gently stir to combine. Form mixture into 1½-inch meatballs (you should have about 24).

2. Process remaining 1 slice bread and ¼ cup almonds in food processor until nuts are finely ground, 10 to 15 seconds. Add red peppers, remaining garlic, oil, and ½ teaspoon salt and process until smooth, about 20 seconds. With processor running, add remaining ¾ cup chicken broth, remaining 2 tablespoons sherry, and pepper liquid and process until smooth and combined, about 20 seconds. Transfer mixture to 12-inch skillet and bring to simmer over medium-high heat.

3. Carefully arrange meatballs in skillet and return sauce to simmer. Reduce heat, cover, and simmer for 10 minutes, stirring sauce and turning meatballs occasionally. Uncover and continue to simmer until sauce is slightly thickened and meatballs are cooked through, about 5 minutes. Sprinkle with remaining 2 tablespoons almonds and remaining 1 tablespoon parsley and serve.

SIMPLE SIDE SAFFRON RICE
Bring 1½ cups low-sodium chicken broth to boil in medium saucepan. Stir in 1 tablespoon extra-virgin olive oil, 1 teaspoon salt, pinch saffron, and 1 cup long-grain white rice. Cover, reduce heat to medium-low, and simmer until liquid is absorbed, 15 to 20 minutes. Fluff with fork. Serves 4.

Mini Barbecued Turkey Meatloaves

Serves 4

✔ **WHY THIS RECIPE WORKS:** Mini meatloaves make a great weeknight alternative to the standard-size loaf that can take an hour to cook. To start, we brown our single-serving loaves on the stovetop in a skillet, then top them with our sauce and transfer them to the oven to cook through. To boost the flavor of lean ground turkey, we add Italian turkey sausage to the mix, along with a little garlic and parsley. Adding some of the barbecue sauce for the glaze topping to the meat mixture introduces just the right zing. Since a traditional panade of milk and bread would make this already soft mixture too wet to properly brown, we turn to saltines to keep our loaves tender and also help them hold together. Be sure to use a nonstick pan to reduce the chance of the meatloaves sticking or breaking, as the mixture is quite soft. A spatula makes moving the loaves in the skillet during browning easy. You will need a 12-inch ovensafe nonstick skillet for this recipe.

1	cup barbecue sauce
12	ounces 93 percent lean ground turkey
12	ounces sweet Italian turkey sausage, casings removed
17	saltines, crushed fine (⅔ cup)
⅓	cup chopped fresh parsley
1	large egg
3	tablespoons whole milk
2	garlic cloves, minced
	Salt and pepper
2	tablespoons vegetable oil

1. Adjust oven rack to middle position and heat oven to 425 degrees. Cook barbecue sauce in small saucepan over medium heat until slightly thickened, about 6 minutes.

2. Mix ground turkey, turkey sausage, saltines, parsley, egg, milk, 3 tablespoons thickened barbecue sauce, garlic, 1 teaspoon salt, and ¼ teaspoon pepper until combined. Form mixture into four 4 by 3-inch loaves.

3. Heat oil in 12-inch ovensafe nonstick skillet over medium-high heat until shimmering. Cook loaves until well browned, 1 to 2 minutes per side. Spoon 1 tablespoon thickened barbecue sauce over each loaf, transfer skillet to oven, and bake until loaves register 160 degrees, about 20 minutes. Transfer to platter and serve with remaining sauce.

SIMPLE SIDE COLLARD GREENS
Cook 2 slices finely chopped bacon in Dutch oven over medium heat until crisp, 1 to 2 minutes. Add 2 minced garlic cloves and cook until fragrant, about 30 seconds. Stir in 1½ pounds collard greens, stemmed and leaves chopped, and ¼ cup water, cover, and cook until tender, about 20 minutes, stirring occasionally. Remove lid and cook until excess liquid has evaporated, up to 1 minute longer. Season with salt and pepper to taste. Serves 4.

COFFEE-RUBBED RIB EYE WITH CREAMY SLAW

Beef

94   Strip Steaks with Tomato–Ancho Chile Sauce and Buttermilk Mashed Potatoes

95   Strip Steaks with Potato-Artichoke Ragout

97   Steaks with Citrus-Soy Pan Sauce and Edamame-Broccoli Slaw

98   Strip Steaks with Sweet Pepper Ragout

99   Steaks with Boursin and Potato-Cauliflower Mash

101   Pepper-Crusted Steaks with Creamy Leeks

102   Rib-Eye Steaks with Tarragon Smashed Potatoes

105   Coffee-Rubbed Rib Eye with Creamy Slaw

106   Flank Steak with Spicy Peanut Noodles

108   Steak and Zucchini Tostadas

109   Flank Steak with Mustard Sauce and Parsnip-Carrot Mash

111   Spicy Beef Burritos

112   London Broil with Balsamic-Glazed Pearl Onions

113   Balsamic Steak Tips and Tomato Salad

114   Korean-Style Beef and Rice Bowl

116   Southwestern Steak Tips with Refried Beans

117   Quick Beef Wellington

119   Greek Meatballs with Herb and Lemon Orzo

120   Spicy Beef Lettuce Cups

121   Beef Spring Rolls with Spicy Mayo

Strip Steaks with Tomato-Ancho Chile Sauce

Serves 4

✔ **WHY THIS RECIPE WORKS:** To spice up our world of steak sauces, we drew inspiration for this weeknight meal from Mexico. We puree a can of diced tomatoes with some garlic and onion (a sweet Vidalia provides a mellower, more balanced flavor than the standard yellow onion), then give it some warm heat with the help of slightly sweet ancho chile powder (made from dried poblanos) and smoky/spicy minced canned chipotles. Cooking the sauce mixture in the skillet after cooking the steaks adds meaty flavor and reduces it to just the right consistency. A simple side of buttermilk mashed potatoes is all this meal needs, and preparing the sauce and steak while the potatoes simmer ensures that dinner is on the table in minimal time.

1½ **pounds Yukon Gold potatoes, peeled and cut into 1-inch cubes**

½ **cup buttermilk, warmed**

4 **tablespoons unsalted butter, cut into 4 pieces**

Salt and pepper

1 **(14.5-ounce) can diced tomatoes**

1 **Vidalia onion, chopped**

3 **garlic cloves**

1 **tablespoon ancho chile powder**

1 **teaspoon minced canned chipotle chile in adobo sauce**

1 **tablespoon molasses**

3 **(10- to 12-ounce) boneless strip steaks, 1 inch thick, trimmed**

5 **teaspoons vegetable oil**

1. Place potatoes in large saucepan and cover with cold water by 1 inch. Bring to boil over high heat, then reduce heat and simmer gently until potatoes are tender, 10 to 15 minutes. Drain potatoes and return to pot. Add buttermilk and butter and mash with potato masher until smooth. Season with salt and pepper to taste, then cover to keep warm and set aside.

2. Meanwhile, puree tomatoes, onion, garlic, chile powder, chipotle, molasses, ½ teaspoon salt, and ½ teaspoon pepper in blender until smooth.

3. Pat steaks dry with paper towels and season with salt and pepper. Heat 2 teaspoons oil in 12-inch skillet over medium-high heat until just smoking. Cook steaks until well browned and meat registers 120 to 125 degrees (for medium-rare), 3 to 5 minutes per side. Transfer to cutting board and tent with aluminum foil.

4. Add remaining 1 tablespoon oil and tomato mixture to now-empty skillet and cook until sauce has thickened, about 7 minutes. Season with salt and pepper to taste. Slice steaks thin and serve with potatoes and sauce.

SMART SHOPPING SWEET ONIONS

Known for their mild flavor and high moisture and sugar content, sweet onions are grown in temperate climates such as Vidalia, Georgia, and Walla Walla, Washington, places that have given two varieties their names. We like sweet onions raw, grilled, or quickly cooked as they are here. Buy onions with dry skins and no signs of spotting or moistness; avoid those with soft spots. Sweet onions typically spoil faster than other varieties but can sometimes last up to six weeks; just make sure to store them in a cool, dry place with good air circulation. Leftover onions should be tightly wrapped, refrigerated, and used within four days.

Strip Steaks with Potato-Artichoke Ragout

Serves 4

✓ **WHY THIS RECIPE WORKS:** A classic vegetable ragout is a great complement to a hearty steak, but most recipes require a lengthy simmer to develop flavor and make the vegetables tender so they break down to form the sauce. We pulse tomatoes in the food processor to jump-start the process, and we microwave the potatoes and opt for frozen artichoke hearts over fresh. Fresh rosemary, garlic, red wine vinegar, and white wine give our sauce plenty of depth with minimal effort, while parsley adds just the right freshness.

1 large tomato, cored, seeded, and quartered

6 tablespoons olive oil

1 tablespoon red wine vinegar

3 garlic cloves, minced

1½ teaspoons chopped fresh rosemary

Salt and pepper

1 pound Yukon Gold potatoes, peeled and cut into ½-inch half-moons

3 (10- to 12-ounce) boneless strip steaks, 1 inch thick, trimmed

9 ounces frozen artichoke hearts, thawed and patted dry

½ cup white wine

½ cup low-sodium chicken broth

2 tablespoons chopped fresh parsley

1. Pulse tomato in food processor until chopped, about 8 pulses. Remove ½ cup chopped tomato and set aside. Add 3 tablespoons oil, vinegar, 1 teaspoon garlic, and ½ teaspoon rosemary to food processor and pulse to combine, about 4 pulses. Transfer to serving bowl and season with salt and pepper to taste.

2. Combine potatoes and 1 tablespoon oil in bowl and season with salt and pepper. Cover and microwave until potatoes are softened, 4 to 6 minutes. Meanwhile, pat steaks dry with paper towels and season with salt and pepper. Heat 1 tablespoon oil in 12-inch skillet over medium-high heat until just smoking. Add steaks and cook until well browned and meat registers 120 to 125 degrees (for medium-rare), 3 to 5 minutes per side. Transfer to cutting board and tent with aluminum foil.

3. Add remaining 1 tablespoon oil, potatoes, and artichokes to now-empty skillet and cook until artichokes are starting to brown, about 2 minutes. Add remaining garlic and remaining 1 teaspoon rosemary and cook until fragrant, about 30 seconds. Add wine, broth, and reserved tomato and cook until potatoes are tender and liquid has evaporated, about 5 minutes. Stir in parsley and season with salt and pepper to taste. Slice steaks thin. Transfer to platter, drizzle with tomato vinaigrette, and serve with potato-artichoke ragout.

QUICK PREP TIP FREEZING GARLIC

If you go through a lot of garlic, buying prepeeled cloves is an acceptable alternative to fresh. But after about two weeks prepeeled turns yellowish and starts to smell disagreeably strong. Is freezing leftover cloves a solution? We found that freezing mellowed the garlic flavor appreciably. In a pinch, you can use frozen prepeeled garlic as long as you keep in mind that the freezer robs it of its full power.

Steaks with Citrus-Soy Pan Sauce and Slaw

Serves 4

✔ **WHY THIS RECIPE WORKS:** Topping a steak with a pat of butter or pouring over a butter-enriched pan sauce just before serving are classic ways to dress up the meat and add richness. A pan sauce feels decadent but requires surprisingly little work, as it is made in the skillet once the steaks have been cooked and set aside to rest. We give this idea an Asian twist by making an orange–soy sauce pan sauce (likewise enriched with butter). A combination of soy sauce, rice vinegar, ginger, and orange juice and zest gives us a sauce that is bright and flavorful, and swirling several tablespoons of butter into the pan with this mixture mellows the flavors and ensures balance. Reserving a few tablespoons of our pan sauce base, then adding a little sesame oil, creates the dressing for our slaw side dish—a clever trick that keeps the ingredient list to a minimum. Adding edamame to our quick slaw lends texture and carries through the Asian-inspired theme. We like to serve this recipe with Easy White Rice (page 22).

1½	**cups frozen edamame**
5	**tablespoons soy sauce**
1	**tablespoon grated orange zest plus ¼ cup juice**
2	**tablespoons rice vinegar**
1	**tablespoon grated fresh ginger**
2	**tablespoons toasted sesame oil**
1	**(10-ounce) bag broccoli slaw mix**
	Salt and pepper
3	**(10- to 12-ounce) boneless strip steaks, 1 inch thick, trimmed**
1	**tablespoon vegetable oil**
4	**tablespoons unsalted butter, cut into 4 pieces and chilled**

1. Place edamame in bowl, cover, and microwave until tender, 4 to 6 minutes. Let cool for 5 minutes. Whisk soy sauce, orange zest and juice, vinegar, and ginger together in another bowl. Transfer 3 tablespoons of mixture to separate bowl, then whisk in sesame oil. Add broccoli slaw and edamame to bowl with dressing and toss to coat. Season with salt and pepper to taste.

2. Meanwhile, pat steaks dry with paper towels and season with salt and pepper. Heat vegetable oil in 12-inch skillet over medium-high heat until just smoking. Cook steaks until well browned and meat registers 120 to 125 degrees (for medium-rare), 3 to 5 minutes per side. Transfer to cutting board and tent loosely with aluminum foil. Let rest for 5 minutes.

3. Add remaining soy sauce mixture to now-empty skillet and cook until slightly thickened, about 1 minute. Off heat, whisk in butter, 1 piece at a time. Slice steaks thin, drizzle with sauce, and serve with slaw.

SMART SHOPPING EDAMAME
Edamame, aka soybeans, are protein-rich and have a savory, nutty flavor and firm, dense texture. Frozen edamame is sold both in the pod and shelled. Edamame pods that are simply boiled and salted are a classic, familiar starter in Japanese restaurants; the frozen shelled beans can be cooked and served like shelled peas.

Strip Steaks with Sweet Pepper Ragout

Serves 4

✓ **WHY THIS RECIPE WORKS:** Strip steaks are a great weeknight dinner choice; they cook quickly yet have great beefy flavor. Here we balance their richness with a colorful pepper ragout. To streamline things, we cook the steaks and side dish on the stovetop in the same skillet. This ragout, inspired by the sweet-and-sour Italian condiment known as peperonata that combines onion, garlic, bell peppers, and balsamic vinegar, offers a sweet-tart counterpoint to the beef. The steaks are simply seasoned with salt and pepper, cooked, then set aside to rest while we cook the ragout. Cooking the peppers after the steaks picks up the fond left behind, adding a deeper flavor and richness to the pepper mixture and marrying the two components of the dish. We like the look of three colored peppers for our version, but any combination of bell peppers will work if you are after an even simpler shopping list.

3   **(10- to 12-ounce) boneless strip steaks, 1 inch thick, trimmed**

    Salt and pepper

2   **tablespoons vegetable oil**

1   **onion, halved and sliced thin**

1   **red bell pepper, stemmed, seeded, and sliced thin**

1   **yellow bell pepper, stemmed, seeded, and sliced thin**

1   **green bell pepper, stemmed, seeded, and sliced thin**

2   **garlic cloves, minced**

1   **tablespoon balsamic vinegar**

1. Pat steaks dry with paper towels and season with salt and pepper. Heat 1 tablespoon oil in 12-inch skillet over medium-high heat until just smoking. Cook steaks until well browned and meat registers 120 to 125 degrees (for medium-rare), 3 to 5 minutes per side. Transfer to cutting board and tent loosely with aluminum foil.

2. Add remaining 1 tablespoon oil, onion, and bell peppers to now-empty skillet and cook until crisp-tender, 8 to 10 minutes. Add garlic and cook until fragrant, about 30 seconds. Add vinegar and any accumulated steak juices and simmer to meld flavors, about 1 minute. Season with salt and pepper to taste. Slice steaks thin and serve with pepper mixture.

SIMPLE SIDE POTATOES WITH LEMON AND PARSLEY
In large saucepan, simmer 1 pound small red potatoes, 1 tablespoon salt, and enough water to cover potatoes by 1 inch, covered, stirring once or twice, until potatoes are just tender, 10 to 14 minutes. Drain well. Cut potatoes in half, transfer to bowl, and toss with 2 tablespoons extra-virgin olive oil, 2 tablespoons chopped fresh parsley, and 1 teaspoon grated lemon zest. Season with salt and pepper to taste. Serves 4.

Steaks with Boursin and Potato-Cauliflower Mash

Serves 4

✓ **WHY THIS RECIPE WORKS:** We put a new spin on the classic steakhouse pairing of blue cheese and steak by swapping in Boursin for the blue, and we liven up plain old mashed potatoes by adding cauliflower to the mix. The cauliflower not only lightens the potatoes but also adds an appealing nuttiness. We boil the cauliflower in the same pot as the potatoes, then drain the vegetables and return them to the pot to mash. While the vegetables cook, we sauté the steaks in a very hot skillet, which ensures a perfect crust. Dotting the cheese over the steaks while they rest gives it a chance to melt just slightly. Though Boursin comes in several flavors, we prefer the garlic and fine herbs variety in this recipe.

1 **pound Yukon Gold potatoes, peeled and cut into 1-inch chunks**

½ **head cauliflower (1 pound), cored and cut into 1-inch florets**

4 **tablespoons unsalted butter, cut into 4 pieces**

⅓ **cup whole milk, warmed**
   Salt and pepper

3 **(10- to 12-ounce) boneless strip steaks, 1 inch thick, trimmed**

1 **tablespoon vegetable oil**

2 **ounces Boursin cheese, crumbled (½ cup)**

1. Bring potatoes, cauliflower, and enough water to cover by 1 inch to boil in large pot. Reduce heat to medium and simmer until vegetables are tender, about 15 minutes. Drain potatoes and return to pot. Add butter and milk and mash until smooth. Season with salt and pepper to taste. Remove from heat, cover to keep warm, and set aside.

2. Meanwhile, pat steaks dry with paper towels and season with salt and pepper. Heat oil in 12-inch skillet over medium-high heat until just smoking. Cook steaks until well browned and meat registers 120 to 125 degrees (for medium-rare), 3 to 5 minutes per side. Transfer to cutting board, sprinkle cheese on top, tent with aluminum foil, and let rest for 5 minutes. Slice steaks thin and serve with potato-cauliflower mash.

SMART SHOPPING BOURSIN
Boursin is a soft, spreadable cheese that comes in several varieties that are available in every supermarket. It is a versatile cheese that works well as a sandwich spread (try it with roast beef), as a stuffing for chicken breasts, as a topping for steaks, in mashed potatoes, on crackers, in dips, or as part of a cheese plate.

Pepper-Crusted Steaks with Creamy Leeks

Serves 4

✓ **WHY THIS RECIPE WORKS:** Mild leeks braised in a rich, creamy sauce are the perfect match to the big flavor of these pepper-crusted steaks. We get two skillets going at once, one for the steaks and one for the leeks so that entrée and side are ready at once. We transform the leeks' braising liquid into a luxurious sauce by adding white wine, chicken broth, and fresh thyme, while a touch of heavy cream, added toward the end, balances the acidity. When preparing the leeks, it's important to trim only the dangling roots off that end; leaving the interior root intact ensures that your leek halves stay in one piece during browning and braising. If your pepper mill can't grind pepper coarsely, you can also crush the peppercorns with the bottom of a small skillet. You will need both a traditional and a nonstick skillet for this recipe.

3 **(10- to 12-ounce) boneless strip steaks, 1 inch thick, trimmed**
 Salt
1 **tablespoon pepper, coarsely ground**
2 **tablespoons vegetable oil**
2 **tablespoons unsalted butter**
2 **pounds leeks, halved lengthwise and washed thoroughly**
½ **cup dry white wine**
½ **cup low-sodium chicken broth**
1 **tablespoon minced fresh thyme**
2 **tablespoons heavy cream**

1. Pat steaks dry with paper towels and season with salt and pepper. Heat oil in 12-inch skillet over medium-high heat until just smoking. Cook steaks until well browned and meat registers 120 to 125 degrees (for medium-rare), 3 to 5 minutes per side. Transfer to cutting board and tent with aluminum foil.

2. Meanwhile, melt butter in 12-inch nonstick skillet over medium-high heat. Add leeks, cut side down, in single layer. Cook until golden brown, about 5 minutes, adjusting heat as needed if leeks are browning too quickly. Add wine, broth, and thyme to skillet, reduce heat to low, cover, and simmer until leeks turn translucent and are tender, about 10 minutes. Add cream and cook until sauce is slightly thickened, about 2 minutes. Season with salt and pepper to taste.

3. Slice steaks thin. Spoon sauce onto individual plates, top with steak and leeks, and serve.

SIMPLE SIDE MASHED POTATOES
Place 2 pounds russet potatoes, peeled and cut into 1-inch chunks, in large saucepan and cover with water. Bring to boil, then reduce heat and simmer until tender, about 20 minutes. Drain potatoes, wipe saucepan dry, then add potatoes back to pan and mash to uniform consistency. Stir in 8 tablespoons melted butter and ¾ cup warmed half-and-half. Season with salt and pepper to taste. Serves 4.

Rib-Eye Steaks with Tarragon Smashed Potatoes

Serves 4

♥ **WHY THIS RECIPE WORKS:** For a spin on classic steak and potatoes, we top pan-seared rib eyes with a creamy sherry-mushroom sauce and amp up the flavor of potatoes by mashing them with sour cream and tarragon. The sauce is elegant and rich, yet a snap to make. We simply brown the mushrooms in the same skillet used to cook the steaks, then add some sherry and chicken broth to the pan. After a few minutes of simmering we whisk in some cream and butter to give it just the right rich flavor and luxurious texture.

2	pounds red potatoes, cut into 1-inch pieces
	Salt and pepper
¼	cup sour cream
6	tablespoons unsalted butter
2	tablespoons minced fresh tarragon
4	(10-ounce) bone-in rib-eye steaks, 1 inch thick, trimmed
3	tablespoons vegetable oil
1	pound white mushrooms, trimmed and sliced ¼ inch thick
½	cup dry sherry
1	cup low-sodium chicken broth
2	tablespoons heavy cream

1. Place potatoes in large saucepan and cover with cold water by 1 inch. Add 1 tablespoon salt, bring to boil over high heat, then reduce heat and simmer until potatoes are tender, 10 to 15 minutes; drain and return to pot. Add sour cream, 4 tablespoons butter, and tarragon, and mash with potato masher. Season with salt and pepper to taste. Transfer to serving bowl and cover to keep warm.

2. Meanwhile, pat steaks dry with paper towels and season with salt and pepper. Heat 2 tablespoons oil in 12-inch skillet over medium-high heat until just smoking. Cook steaks until well browned and meat registers 120 to 125 degrees (for medium-rare), 4 to 6 minutes per side. Transfer steaks to platter, tent with aluminum foil, and let rest for 5 minutes.

3. Add remaining 1 tablespoon oil and mushrooms to now-empty skillet and cook until mushrooms start to brown, about 8 minutes. Add sherry and cook until reduced to glaze, about 2 minutes. Add chicken broth and cook until reduced by half, about 4 minutes. Off heat, whisk in heavy cream and remaining 2 tablespoons butter until butter is melted and sauce thickens. Season with salt and pepper to taste. Serve steak with potatoes and top with mushroom sauce.

SMART SHOPPING BEEF GRADING
Most meat available is confined to three quality grades assigned by the U.S. Department of Agriculture: prime, choice, and select. Grading is strictly voluntary on the part of the meat packer. Inspectors evaluate color, grain, surface texture, and fat content and its distribution. In our blind tasting, prime ranked first for its tender, buttery texture and rich, beefy flavor. Next came choice, with good meaty flavor and a little more chew. The tough and stringy select steak followed, with flavor that was barely acceptable.

Pan-Searing Steaks 101

Though few foods are as perfect as a grilled steak, pan-searing in a skillet over high heat works particularly well with steaks that are 1 to 1¼ inch thick. Because the bone can prevent bone-in steaks from even contact with the pan, we prefer boneless. Here we use boneless rib eye, but strip steaks are another great option.

1. DRY THE STEAKS
While browning a steak doesn't seal in juices, it does add dramatically to flavor. To ensure proper browning, make sure the meat is dry before it goes into the pan by patting it thoroughly with paper towels. This is especially important with previously frozen meat, which often releases a great deal of water.

2. SEASON THE MEAT
Season both sides of the meat with salt and pepper. It's OK to season ahead of time, but since salt draws juices to the surface, make sure if you are going to let the meat sit more than a couple of minutes that you allow enough time for that liquid to then be reabsorbed (we have found that 40 minutes is sufficient). This will actually flavor the meat more deeply.

3. GET YOUR SKILLET READY
Choose a traditional (not nonstick) skillet large enough to allow at least ¼ inch of space between the steaks; any tighter and the meat will steam instead of browning. Heat 1 tablespoon vegetable oil over medium-high heat until just smoking, then add the steaks. If your pan isn't properly preheated, the steaks will overcook before developing a good crust.

4. COOK THE STEAKS
Add the steaks (in batches if necessary) and brown the first side well (3 to 5 minutes for an 8- to 10-ounce rib eye). Flip the steaks with tongs and cook until the meat registers 120 to 125 degrees (for medium-rare), 3 to 5 minutes longer. (See at right for more on temping steaks.) To ensure a good crust, don't move the steaks during cooking.

5. LET THE STEAKS REST
Transfer the steaks to a cutting board and let them rest, tented loosely with aluminum foil, for 5 minutes to allow the juices to redistribute. Note that the internal temperature will continue to climb about 5 degrees as the steak rests.

Temping Steaks

The most accurate way to judge when meat is done is by using an instant-read thermometer. Hold the meat with tongs and push the thermometer through to the center. To make sure the thermometer is deeply embedded, take the temperature from the side, avoiding the bone, if there is one. Note that the temperature of a steak will continue to climb as it rests. Remove the steak from the heat when it registers 115 to 120 degrees for rare, 120 to 125 degrees for medium-rare, 130 to 135 degrees for medium, 140 to 145 degrees for medium-well, and 150 to 155 degrees for well-done.

Coffee-Rubbed Rib Eye with Creamy Slaw

Serves 4

✔ **WHY THIS RECIPE WORKS:** There's nothing wrong with seasoning a steak with salt and pepper before pan-searing it, but we wanted to take things up a notch. We found that a coffee-and-spice rub works wonders. While recipes for coffee-rubbed steak exist, they are often overwrought, incorporating cocoa powder and a slew of often out-of-place spices that only make for a long shopping list. We opt for the simple combination of instant coffee (its subtle flavor is a better fit here than instant espresso), garlic powder, chili powder, salt, and pepper. Then we add brown sugar, which gives our steaks just the right amount of sweetness and encourages a good crust to form. Cooking the steaks over medium rather than medium-high heat and using a bit more oil than we usually would prevents the spice rub from burning. A creamy coleslaw is the perfect counterpoint to the boldly flavored steaks and comes together quickly with the help of bagged coleslaw mix and just three dressing components.

2	**tablespoons chili powder**
2	**tablespoons instant coffee**
2	**teaspoons paprika**
4	**teaspoons packed dark brown sugar**
½	**teaspoon garlic powder**
	Salt and pepper
½	**cup mayonnaise**
2	**tablespoons cider vinegar**
1	**(14-ounce) bag green coleslaw mix**
1	**tablespoon vegetable oil**
4	**(8- to 10-ounce) boneless rib-eye steaks, 1 inch thick, trimmed**

1. Combine chili powder, instant coffee, paprika, 2 teaspoons sugar, garlic powder, ½ teaspoon salt, and ¼ teaspoon pepper in small bowl. In large bowl, whisk together mayonnaise, vinegar, 2 teaspoons spice mixture, and remaining 2 teaspoons sugar. Add coleslaw mix, toss to combine, and season with salt and pepper to taste.

2. Heat oil in 12-inch nonstick skillet over medium heat until just smoking. Pat steaks dry with paper towels and rub evenly with remaining spice mixture. Lay steaks in skillet and cook until well browned on first side, 3 to 5 minutes.

3. Flip steaks and continue to cook until meat registers 120 to 125 degrees (for medium-rare), 5 to 7 minutes. Transfer steaks to carving board, tent with aluminum foil, and let rest for 5 minutes. Slice steaks thinly against grain and serve with coleslaw.

SMART SHOPPING CHILI POWDER
Chili powder is not itself a single spice but a blend of spices. While there is no established formula, it typically consists of about 80 percent chile pepper blended with garlic powder, oregano, ground cumin seeds, sometimes salt, and occasionally even monosodium glutamate. Some blends also include traces of clove, allspice, anise, and coriander. To find the best, we made a bare-bones version of our favorite chili with various brands of chili powder and rated each for aroma, depth of flavor, and level of spiciness. Tasters concluded that **Spice Islands Chili Powder** was the clear winner.

Flank Steak with Spicy Peanut Noodles

Serves 4

✓ **WHY THIS RECIPE WORKS:** Southeast Asian cuisine brings together a wonderful mix of flavors—salty, sweet, spicy, and sour—but the exotic ingredient lists in such recipes (you will often see kaffir lime leaves and galangal, among others) can quickly cut them from the weeknight-menu running. Yet with a simple, balanced combination of prepared red curry paste, lime juice, sugar, and peanut butter, we bring those flavors to the weeknight table in short order. We cook a straightforwardly seasoned flank steak on the stovetop as the perfect match to our more boldly seasoned Thai-style noodle side dish. Saucing the noodles with light coconut milk as the base instead of regular keeps this meal from being too rich, and upping the typical amount of curry paste ensures a side dish with great punch. We like the flavor of natural peanut butter in this recipe, but any creamy peanut butter will work fine. See page 313 for information about fresh Chinese Noodles.

½ **cup creamy peanut butter**

½ **cup light coconut milk**

¼ **cup lime juice (2 limes)**

3 **tablespoons fish sauce**

4 **teaspoons Thai red curry paste**

3 **garlic cloves, minced**

2 **teaspoons sugar**

1 **(9 ounce) package fresh Chinese noodles**

Salt and pepper

4 **scallions, sliced thin on bias**

1 **(1½-pound) flank steak, trimmed**

1 **tablespoon vegetable oil**

1. Bring 3 quarts water to boil in large pot. Meanwhile, process peanut butter, coconut milk, lime juice, fish sauce, curry paste, garlic, and sugar in blender until smooth, about 15 seconds.

2. Add noodles and 1 tablespoon salt to boiling water and cook until tender. Drain, run under cold water to cool, and drain again. Return noodles to pot, add ½ cup peanut sauce and scallions, and toss to combine. Season with salt and pepper to taste.

3. Pat steak dry with paper towels and season with salt and pepper. Heat oil in 12-inch skillet over medium-high heat until just smoking. Cook steak until well browned and meat registers 120 to 125 degrees (for medium-rare), about 5 minutes per side. Transfer to cutting board, tent loosely with aluminum foil, and let rest for 5 minutes. Slice steak thin against grain and serve with remaining peanut sauce and noodles.

SIMPLE SIDE CUCUMBER SALAD

Whisk ¼ cup chopped fresh mint, 3 tablespoons lime juice, 1 tablespoon fish sauce, 1 tablespoon sugar, and ½ seeded and minced jalapeño together in large bowl. Toss 2 cucumbers, peeled, halved lengthwise, seeded, and sliced thin, and ½ thinly sliced red onion in dressing to combine. Serves 4.

Steak and Zucchini Tostadas

Serves 4

✓ **WHY THIS RECIPE WORKS:** With flank steak, zucchini, cilantro, and feta, these tostadas are a great change from the typical taco dinner. Though unusual in a tostada recipe, zucchini adds appealing texture and bright flavor. Queso fresco, a crumbly, mild Mexican cheese, is a classic choice, but feta is a worthy substitute that lends a tangy flavor boost. We make our own fresh-tasting tostadas in the oven in 10 minutes. While they bake, we cook the steak, then the zucchini. In addition to lime wedges and cilantro, serve these tostadas with Pico de Gallo (page 22).

12   **(6-inch) corn tortillas**
4   **tablespoons vegetable oil**
   Salt and pepper
1   **(1-pound) flank steak, trimmed**
2   **zucchini, halved lengthwise and sliced thin**
2   **ounces feta cheese, crumbled (½ cup)**
½   **cup fresh cilantro leaves**
   Lime wedges

1. Adjust oven racks to lower-middle and upper-middle positions and heat oven to 450 degrees. Brush both sides of tortillas with 2 tablespoons oil and season with salt and pepper to taste. Lay tortillas in single layer on 2 baking sheets. Bake until golden brown and crisp, rotating baking sheets and flipping tortillas halfway through baking, about 10 minutes.

2. Meanwhile, pat steak dry with paper towels and season with salt and pepper. Heat 1 tablespoon oil in 12-inch skillet over medium-high heat until just smoking. Cook steak until well browned and meat registers 120 to 125 degrees (for medium-rare), about 5 minutes per side. Transfer to cutting board and tent loosely with aluminum foil.

3. Add remaining 1 tablespoon oil and zucchini to now-empty skillet and cook until tender, about 4 minutes.

4. Cut steak in half lengthwise, then slice thin crosswise against grain. Divide beef and zucchini among tostadas, top with feta and cilantro, and serve with lime wedges.

QUICK PREP TIP SLICING FLANK STEAK FOR TOSTADAS
Since flank is best when thinly sliced against the grain, we found a simple way to cut the steak into easy-to-eat, bite-size pieces. Once the steak is cooked and rested, cut it in half lengthwise, then slice each piece crosswise into thin pieces.

Flank Steak with Parsnip-Carrot Mash

Serves 4

✔ **WHY THIS RECIPE WORKS:** To keep this recipe moving, we cook the vegetables for the mash in a saucepan while the steak sears in a skillet. Then we whip up a quick, creamy mustard sauce with sour cream, Worcestershire, and whole-grain mustard, a combination that balances the beefiness of the flank steak. Browning the carrots and parsnips in butter before cooking them through in the broth caramelizes them and brings out their natural sweetness.

2	tablespoons unsalted butter
12	ounces carrots, peeled and cut into 2 by ½-inch pieces
12	ounces parsnips, peeled and cut into 2 by ½-inch pieces
1	pound Yukon Gold potatoes, sliced thin
1	cup low-sodium chicken broth
	Salt and pepper
1	(1½-pound) flank steak, trimmed
1	tablespoon vegetable oil
½	cup sour cream
2	tablespoons whole-grain mustard
1	teaspoon Worcestershire sauce

1. Melt butter in large saucepan over medium-high heat. Cook carrots and parsnips, stirring occasionally, until well browned, 8 to 10 minutes. Add potatoes, broth, and ½ teaspoon salt and bring to boil. Reduce heat to low, cover, and simmer, stirring occasionally, until vegetables are tender, 10 to 15 minutes. Gently mash vegetables with potato masher and season with salt and pepper to taste.

2. Meanwhile, pat steak dry with paper towels and season with salt and pepper. Heat oil in 12-inch skillet over medium-high heat until just smoking. Cook steak until well browned and meat registers 120 to 125 degrees (for medium-rare), about 5 minutes per side. Transfer to cutting board and tent loosely with aluminum foil.

3. Whisk sour cream, mustard, and Worcestershire together in bowl and season with salt and pepper to taste. Slice steak thin against grain and serve with sauce and parsnip-carrot mash.

QUICK PREP TIP **STORING LOOSE CARROTS**

We've found that carrots sold with their green tops attached have better flavor than those sold trimmed. But what's the best way to store them once purchased? Since the vegetable will continue to feed the leafy tops in storage, should you remove the tops when you get home from the market? We purchased several bunches, left the tops intact on half, and removed the tops from the other half. We then stored them in the crisper drawer for two weeks. When we examined the samples, those stored with their tops attached were extremely limp, indicating moisture loss. But to our surprise, the trimmed carrots fared only slightly better. We repeated the test, placing both trimmed and untrimmed batches in open zipper-lock bags—a setup that trapped most of their moisture but allowed some to escape. After two weeks, the carrots with their tops on had still softened significantly, while the trimmed ones were just as firm and sweet-tasting as they had been two weeks prior.

Spicy Beef Burritos

Serves 4

✔ **WHY THIS RECIPE WORKS:** Burritos offer appeal to young and old, but it's easy to take shortcuts that result in a meal no better than boring, bland, and heavy fast-food versions. We avoid these pitfalls by starting with flavorful, quick-cooking skirt steak. By cooking the beans with a healthy dose of red pepper flakes and adding a minced jalapeño to a quick pico de gallo, we ensure good heat. With just five ingredients—tomatoes, red onion, jalapeño, lime juice, and cilantro—our quick pico lends a necessary cool, fresh element to our burritos. And by using precooked rice instead of cooking it from scratch, we save at least 20 minutes.

3 tablespoons vegetable oil

4 garlic cloves, minced

1 teaspoon red pepper flakes

1 (15-ounce) can black beans
   Salt and pepper

½ cup chopped fresh cilantro

4 plum tomatoes, cored and
   chopped

½ red onion, minced

1 jalapeño chile, stemmed,
   seeded, and minced

1 tablespoon lime juice

2 (12-ounce) skirt steaks, trimmed

4 (10-inch) flour tortillas

1 (8.8-ounce) package Uncle Ben's
   Original Long Grain Ready Rice,
   cooked according to package
   directions

1. Heat 1 tablespoon oil in large saucepan over medium-high heat until shimmering. Add garlic and red pepper flakes and cook until fragrant, about 30 seconds. Add black beans with their liquid, bring to boil, then reduce heat and simmer, stirring frequently, until mixture thickens, about 12 minutes. Season with salt and pepper to taste. Meanwhile, combine 2 tablespoons cilantro, tomatoes, onion, jalapeño, and lime juice in medium bowl. Season with salt and pepper to taste.

2. Heat remaining 2 tablespoons oil in 12-inch skillet over medium-high heat until just smoking. Cook steaks until well browned and meat registers 120 to 125 degrees (for medium-rare), 4 to 6 minutes per side. Transfer to cutting board, tent loosely with aluminum foil, and let rest for 5 minutes.

3. Slice steaks thin against grain. Place tortillas on individual plates and top each with rice, beans, steak, and pico de gallo. Sprinkle remaining 6 tablespoons cilantro on top and fold tortillas to form burritos. Serve.

EASY BURRITOS

Once the filling is in place, fold the flap nearest to you over the filling. Next, fold the sides of the tortilla inward to form the ends of the burrito (near right) and prevent the filling from falling out. Roll the burrito away from you (far right), keeping it tight, to form a log. Once it is rolled, rest the burrito on its seam so that it does not unravel.

London Broil with Balsamic-Glazed Pearl Onions

Serves 4

✔ **WHY THIS RECIPE WORKS:** Caramelized onions are a great match for steak, but they require a lot of slicing time plus up to 45 minutes of cooking. For a quick alternative, we turn to frozen pearl onions, which we glaze with a brown sugar–balsamic mixture. After we give them a jump start in the microwave, they only need about 10 minutes in the skillet. Cooking the meat in the pan before the onions means the onions pick up the flavor left behind. Sliced almonds, added to the skillet once the onions have properly glazed, lend just the right crunch. Be sure to drain the onions before adding them to the skillet with the brown sugar and vinegar; they release a fair amount of liquid that could alter the consistency and cooking time of the glaze. We typically cook individual steaks over medium-high heat, but because this cut (bottom round) is larger, we opt for medium heat to make sure the outside doesn't burn before the interior cooks through. (If the meat isn't browning adequately, increase the heat to medium-high for the last few minutes of cooking.)

1   **pound frozen pearl onions**
1   **(1½-pound) bottom round steak, trimmed**
    Salt and pepper
1   **tablespoon vegetable oil**
1   **tablespoon packed brown sugar**
3   **tablespoons balsamic vinegar**
½   **cup sliced almonds, toasted**

1. Place onions in bowl, cover, and microwave until onions are tender, 4 to 6 minutes. Drain and set aside.

2. Meanwhile, pat meat dry with paper towels and season with salt and pepper. Heat oil in 12-inch skillet over medium heat until just smoking. Cook steak until well browned and meat registers 120 to 125 degrees (for medium-rare), 5 to 7 minutes per side. Transfer to cutting board, tent loosely with aluminum foil, and let rest for 5 minutes.

3. Add onions, sugar, and vinegar to now-empty skillet and cook until onions are caramelized, about 5 minutes. Stir in almonds and season with salt and pepper to taste. Slice meat thin against grain and serve with onions.

SMART SHOPPING LONDON BROIL

"London broil" doesn't refer to a particular cut but is a generic label used by butchers to sell large, cheap steaks. For a while, flank steak was the most common cut for London broil, but flank's popularity on the grill and in stir-fries bumped its price into the $6.99-a-pound range—a bit too rich for London broil territory. Nowadays, you'll mostly see chuck shoulder steak, top round steak, and bottom round steak labeled London broil. Bottom round is our favorite for London broil because of its appealingly beefy flavor and uniform shape.

SIMPLE SIDE ARUGULA WITH ROQUEFORT VINAIGRETTE

Whisk ¼ cup extra-virgin olive oil, 2 tablespoons red wine vinegar, and ¼ teaspoon pepper together in bowl. Stir in ½ cup crumbled Roquefort cheese. Toss dressing with 6 ounces baby arugula and season with salt and pepper to taste. Serves 4.

Balsamic Steak Tips and Tomato Salad

Serves 4

✅ **WHY THIS RECIPE WORKS:** A colorful fresh tomato, onion, and watercress salad is a summery match to the steak tips in this recipe. To add richness to the tomato side dish without weighing it down, we sprinkle crisped bacon bits and crumbled blue cheese on top just before serving. This recipe is a favorite because it doesn't require much hands-on cooking time and needs just one pan to cook the bacon and the steak tips. Balsamic vinegar, used in the salad dressing and as a glaze for the meat, draws all the elements together and adds a sweet-tart accent. We use a mix of colorful heirloom tomatoes for an eye-catching salad, and we assemble it just before serving to ensure the flavors aren't diluted: Once dressed, the tomatoes begin to release their juices and the watercress will quickly wilt.

4	slices bacon, chopped
5	tablespoons balsamic vinegar
1½	pounds sirloin steak tips, trimmed and cut into 2-inch chunks
	Salt and pepper
1	tablespoon vegetable oil
1½	pounds heirloom tomatoes, cored and cut into 1-inch-thick wedges
½	small red onion, sliced very thin
2	ounces (2 cups) watercress
2	tablespoons extra-virgin olive oil
3	ounces blue cheese, crumbled (¾ cup)

1. Cook bacon in 12-inch skillet over medium heat until crisp, 5 to 7 minutes. Using slotted spoon, transfer bacon to paper towel–lined plate. Pour off fat and wipe out skillet with paper towels. Add 4 tablespoons vinegar and simmer over medium-high heat until syrupy and reduced to about 2 tablespoons, about 4 minutes. Transfer to small bowl. Rinse skillet and wipe dry.

2. Pat steak tips dry with paper towels and season with salt and pepper. Heat vegetable oil in now-empty skillet over medium-high heat until just smoking. Add steak tips and cook until well browned all over, 6 to 8 minutes. Transfer to serving platter and tent loosely with aluminum foil.

3. Combine tomatoes, onion, and watercress in large bowl. Drizzle with olive oil and remaining 1 tablespoon vinegar and toss. Season with salt and pepper to taste. Transfer to serving bowl and sprinkle with blue cheese and bacon.

4. Drizzle balsamic glaze over steak tips and serve with salad.

QUICK PREP TIP **STORING TOMATOES**
Can storing a tomato with its stem end facing down prolong shelf life? To find out, we placed one batch of tomatoes stem end up and another stem end down and kept them at room temperature. A week later, nearly all the stem-down tomatoes remained in perfect condition, while the stem-up tomatoes had shriveled and started to mold. We surmised that the scar left on the tomato skin where the stem once grew provides both an escape for moisture and an entry point for mold and bacteria. Placing a tomato stem end down blocks air from entering and moisture from exiting the scar. To confirm this, we compared tomatoes stored stem end down with another batch stored stem end up, but with a piece of tape sealing off their scars. The taped, stem-end-up tomatoes survived just as well as the stem-end-down batch.

Korean-Style Beef and Rice Bowl

Serves 4

✓ **WHY THIS RECIPE WORKS:** The Korean dish known as *bibimbap*, which tops tender-chewy short-grain rice with sautéed vegetables, beef, and a fried egg (the runny yolk creates a sauce), looks simple and appeals with its mix of textures and flavors. However, bibimbap's ingredient list is traditionally quite long. For the weeknight table, we hit the texture and flavor bulls-eye, and we cook the steak and vegetables in a skillet while the rice cooks. Bibimbap is typically served with kimchi, a Korean pickled vegetable condiment that you can buy at Asian markets as well as many supermarkets; while not essential, it does add nice contrast.

3	cups water
1½	cups short-grain white rice
	Salt and pepper
3	tablespoons soy sauce
1	tablespoon packed brown sugar
1	pound sirloin steak tips, trimmed and sliced thin
¼	cup vegetable oil
8	ounces shiitake mushrooms, stemmed and sliced thin
10	ounces (10 cups) baby spinach
4	large eggs

1. Adjust oven rack to lower-middle position and heat oven to 200 degrees. Bring water, rice, and 1 teaspoon salt to boil in medium saucepan over medium-high heat. Cook until water level drops below surface of rice and small holes form, about 5 minutes. Reduce heat to low, cover, and cook until water is absorbed, about 15 minutes.

2. Meanwhile, whisk 2 tablespoons soy sauce and sugar together in large bowl. Add steak and toss to coat. Heat 1 tablespoon oil in 12-inch nonstick skillet over medium-high heat until just smoking. Cook half of steak until well browned, 1 to 2 minutes per side. Transfer to bowl and tent loosely with aluminum foil. Repeat with 1 tablespoon oil and remaining steak.

3. Add 1 tablespoon oil, mushrooms, and remaining 1 tablespoon soy sauce to now-empty skillet and cook until mushrooms are soft, about 2 minutes. Add spinach and cook until wilted, 2 to 3 minutes. Transfer to bowl and tent with foil. Portion rice into bowls and top with beef and mushroom-spinach mixture. Keep bowls warm in oven.

4. Wipe out skillet and heat remaining 1 tablespoon oil over medium heat until shimmering. Crack eggs into 2 small bowls (2 eggs in each). Add eggs to skillet, pouring each bowl into opposite side of skillet. Season with salt and pepper, cover, and cook until whites are set, 2 to 3 minutes. Remove bowls from oven and top each with 1 egg. Serve.

Southwestern Steak Tips with Refried Beans

Serves 4

✔ **WHY THIS RECIPE WORKS:** Steak tips have a beefy flavor that matches well with the warmly spiced tomato sauce here, and the combination of cumin, chipotle chile powder, lime juice, and cilantro creates a distinctly Southwestern profile. This recipe comes together easily: We first cook the meat, then set it aside and prepare the sauce before returning the meat to the pan toward the end of cooking to meld the flavors. Starting with canned refried beans saves time, and we freshen up their flavor with cilantro and lime juice. Steak tips, aka flap meat, are sold as whole steaks, cubes, and strips. To ensure chunks that will cook evenly, we prefer to purchase a whole steak and cut it ourselves. If you can't find ground chipotle chile powder, substitute 1½ teaspoons minced canned chipotle chiles in adobo. We like to serve this recipe with warm tortillas.

1½ pounds sirloin steak tips, trimmed and cut into 2-inch chunks
Salt and pepper
2 tablespoons vegetable oil
1 onion, chopped fine
1 teaspoon chipotle chile powder
1 teaspoon ground cumin
1 (14.5-ounce) can diced tomatoes
½ cup water
3 tablespoons lime juice (2 limes), plus lime wedges for serving
5 tablespoons chopped fresh cilantro
2 (15-ounce) cans refried beans

1. Pat steak tips dry with paper towels and season with salt and pepper. Heat 1 tablespoon oil in 12-inch skillet over medium-high heat until just smoking. Add steak tips and cook until well browned all over, 6 to 8 minutes. Transfer to serving platter and tent loosely with aluminum foil.

2. Add remaining 1 tablespoon oil, onion, and ¼ teaspoon salt to now-empty skillet. Lower heat to medium and cook until onion softens, about 5 minutes. Add chile powder and cumin and cook until fragrant, about 30 seconds. Add tomatoes and water and cook until sauce has almost thickened, about 5 minutes. Return steak tips and any accumulated juices to skillet. Stir in 1 tablespoon lime juice and 2 tablespoons cilantro and simmer until sauce is thickened, about 1 minute. Season with salt and pepper to taste.

3. Meanwhile, combine refried beans, remaining 2 tablespoons lime juice, and remaining 3 tablespoons cilantro in bowl. Cover and microwave until warmed through, about 4 minutes. Serve with steak tips and lime wedges.

SMART SHOPPING CHIPOTLE CHILE POWDER
The traditional chili powder called for in most, if not all, recipes for chili is a blend of several spices, typically including one or two types of ground red chiles as well as cumin and oregano and sometimes salt, garlic, and/or paprika. Chipotle chile powder (right) is made only from ground smoked-and-dried jalapeños (aka chipotle chiles), with no other ingredients. Chipotle chile powder carries a spicier kick and a richer smoky flavor than the chili powder blends.

Quick Beef Wellington

Serves 4

✓ **WHY THIS RECIPE WORKS:** Indulgent Beef Wellington is difficult and costly to make, and it often ends up as a dry roast covered in soggy pastry and overcooked pâté and duxelles (a mix of mushrooms, shallots, herbs, and butter). This reinvention turns the classic into a 30-minute tart with the help of deli-sliced roast beef, store-bought puff pastry and pâté, and a quick take on duxelles made using the food processor. To thaw frozen puff pastry, allow it to sit either in the refrigerator for 24 hours or on the counter for 30 to 60 minutes.

10 ounces cremini mushrooms, trimmed and broken into rough pieces

2 tablespoons unsalted butter

1 shallot, chopped fine

2 tablespoons dry sherry
    Salt and pepper

2 (9½ by 9-inch) sheets puff pastry, thawed

6 ounces smooth pâté, mashed slightly with fork

8 ounces thinly sliced deli roast beef

1 large egg, lightly beaten

1. Adjust oven rack to middle position and heat oven to 450 degrees. Line baking sheet with parchment paper. Pulse mushrooms in food processor until fine, about 10 pulses. Melt butter in 12-inch skillet over medium-high heat. Add shallot and cook until soft, about 1 minute. Add mushrooms and cook until lightly golden, about 8 minutes. Add sherry and cook until dry, about 1 minute. Season with salt and pepper to taste.

2. Unfold 1 sheet pastry onto lightly floured counter. Using rolling pin, roll sheet out to 13 by 11-inch rectangle and place on prepared baking sheet.

3. Using rubber spatula, spread pâté over puff pastry sheet, leaving 1-inch border on all sides. Top with mushroom mixture, followed by roast beef. Brush border with some of egg.

4. Roll remaining 1 sheet pastry to 13 by 11-inch rectangle and place on top. Using tines of fork, seal edges and prick top of pastry. Brush with remaining egg. Bake until puffed and golden, about 15 minutes. Transfer to cutting board, cut into 8 squares, and serve.

EASY BEEF WELLINGTON

After preparing mushrooms, spread pâté over rolled-out puff pastry sheet, leaving 1-inch border on all sides. Top with mushrooms, then beef. Brush border with egg and top with second puff pastry sheet. Seal edges with tines of fork, prick top several times to vent, then brush with remaining egg. Bake until puffed and golden, about 15 minutes.

Greek Meatballs with Herb and Lemon Orzo

Serves 4

✔ **WHY THIS RECIPE WORKS:** Well-prepared meatballs are usually a hit, and here we give them a new, flavorful spin by seasoning the meat with mint and dill. Our panade—a simple paste made from yogurt and torn pieces of white bread—binds our meatballs, keeps them moist, and lends a slight tangy flavor that carries through the Greek profile (just be sure to use regular yogurt; avoid substituting Greek-style yogurt). Instead of saucing these flavorful meatballs, we simply pair them with a quick lemony orzo pasta side dish. The same herbs added to the meatballs are also tossed with the orzo, which brings the whole dish together and keeps the ingredient list short. A final sprinkling of feta cheese adds a dose of briny, salty goodness.

1⅓	**cups orzo**
	Salt and pepper
1	**teaspoon grated lemon zest plus 1 tablespoon juice**
2	**tablespoons chopped fresh mint**
2	**tablespoons chopped fresh dill**
2	**garlic cloves, minced**
2	**tablespoons plus ¼ cup olive oil**
2	**slices hearty white sandwich bread, torn into pieces**
⅓	**cup plain yogurt**
1½	**pounds 85 percent lean ground beef**
1	**small red onion, grated**
2	**ounces feta cheese, crumbled (½ cup)**

1. Bring 3 quarts water to boil in large saucepan. Add orzo and 1 teaspoon salt and cook over medium heat until just tender, about 10 minutes. Drain and toss with lemon zest and juice, 1 tablespoon mint, 1 tablespoon dill, half of garlic, and 2 tablespoons oil. Season with salt and pepper to taste.

2. Meanwhile, mash bread with yogurt in bowl until smooth. Add beef, onion, remaining garlic, remaining 1 tablespoon mint, remaining 1 tablespoon dill, 1 teaspoon salt, and ½ teaspoon pepper. Form mixture into 1½-inch meatballs (you should have 24).

3. Heat remaining ¼ cup oil in 12-inch nonstick skillet over medium-high heat until just smoking. Add meatballs and cook gently, shaking pan and turning meatballs with tongs, until browned on all sides and cooked through, about 7 minutes. Spoon orzo onto serving platter, top with meatballs, and sprinkle with feta. Serve.

QUICK PREP TIP STORING LEMONS

We tested three methods for storing lemons, both at room temperature and in the refrigerator: in an uncovered container, in a sealed zipper-lock bag, and in a sealed zipper-lock bag with ¼ cup water added. All the lemons stored at room temperature hardened after a week. The refrigerated samples fared much better: The uncovered lemons (which we kept in the crisper drawer) began to lose a small amount of moisture after the first week and 5 percent of their weight in the following weeks; the lemons stored in zipper-lock bags, both with and without water, didn't begin to dehydrate until four weeks had passed. As it turned out, the water wasn't offering any preservation benefits, but the zipper-lock bag did seal in some moisture. For the juiciest, longest-lasting lemons, the best approach is to seal them in a zipper-lock bag and refrigerate.

Spicy Beef Lettuce Cups

Serves 4

✓ **WHY THIS RECIPE WORKS:** This Sichuan-inspired recipe of seasoned ground meat that's spooned into lettuce leaves and eaten like a taco is light and healthy, packed with flavor, and quick to make—in other words, an all-around winner. We season our lean ground beef (which we cook in minutes on the stovetop) with grated ginger and chili-garlic sauce, then toss the meat with a flavorful sherry and oyster sauce mixture. Chopped bell pepper and sliced scallions add color, a touch of sweetness, and appealing texture. We found that topping the beef with a small amount of chopped roasted peanuts adds a welcome crunch and nutty flavor. You can substitute ground chicken or turkey for the ground beef for a still lighter version, or add a minced jalapeño to the filling to make it spicier.

¼	cup water
3	tablespoons oyster sauce
2	tablespoons dry sherry
1	pound 85 percent lean ground beef
1	red bell pepper, stemmed, seeded, and diced
5	scallions, sliced thin
1	tablespoon Asian chili-garlic sauce
1	tablespoon grated fresh ginger
1	head Bibb lettuce (8 ounces), leaves separated
¼	cup chopped roasted peanuts (optional)

1. Whisk water, oyster sauce, and sherry in bowl; set aside. Cook beef in 12-inch nonstick skillet over medium-high heat, stirring to break up clumps, until just cooked through, 3 to 5 minutes. Drain beef, reserving 2 teaspoons rendered fat.

2. Heat reserved fat in now-empty skillet over medium-high heat. Add bell pepper and scallions and cook until bell pepper softens, about 3 minutes. Clear center of skillet, add chili-garlic sauce and ginger, and cook until fragrant, about 30 seconds. Return beef to skillet with oyster sauce mixture and cook until thickened, about 1 minute. Spoon mixture into lettuce leaves, sprinkle with peanuts, if using, and serve.

SIMPLE SIDE SESAME-SCALLION NOODLES
Cook 1 (9-ounce) package fresh Chinese egg noodles in large pot of boiling water until just tender, about 3 minutes, and drain. Melt 1 tablespoon butter in now-empty pot over medium heat. Add 8 sliced scallions and cook until fragrant, about 1 minute. Stir in noodles and 2 tablespoons toasted sesame oil. Season with salt and pepper to taste. Serves 4.

Beef Spring Rolls with Spicy Mayo

Serves 4

✓ **WHY THIS RECIPE WORKS:** Adding ground beef to spring rolls changes them from an appetizer into an entrée, while ingredients like bean sprouts and cilantro maintain the classic fresh profile. Once the beef has cooked, we toss it with sprouts, cilantro, scallions, and a spicy mayonnaise mixture that makes the filling cohesive. Then we top each wrapper with filling, roll it up, and serve with more spicy mayo for dipping. Rice wrappers, which can be found in Asian markets and most supermarkets, require a short soak to make them pliable. Avoid soaking too many wrappers at once (we suggest four) so that they don't stick together.

¾   **cup mayonnaise**

3   **tablespoons soy sauce**

1   **tablespoon sriracha**

1   **(12-ounce) bag bean sprouts**

¾   **cup chopped fresh cilantro**

6   **scallions, white parts minced, green parts sliced thin**

1   **tablespoon vegetable oil**

1   **pound 85 percent lean ground beef**

1   **tablespoon grated fresh ginger**

12   **(9-inch) rice paper wrappers**

1. Combine mayonnaise, 2 teaspoons soy sauce, and sriracha in small bowl. In large bowl, combine sprouts, cilantro, and scallion greens.

2. Heat oil in 12-inch skillet over medium-high heat until just smoking. Add beef and remaining 2 tablespoons plus 1 teaspoon soy sauce and cook until no longer pink, about 5 minutes. Stir in scallion whites and ginger and cook until fragrant, about 1 minute. Transfer beef to bowl with sprouts mixture. Add ¼ cup mayonnaise mixture and toss to combine.

3. Spread clean, damp kitchen towel on counter. Soak 4 wrappers in bowl of warm water until just pliable, about 10 seconds, then spread out on towel. Place ½ cup filling on each wrapper, leaving 2-inch border at bottom. Fold in sides, then carefully but tightly roll wrap up, starting at bottom. Transfer finished roll to platter and cover with second clean, damp towel. Repeat with remaining wrappers and filling. Serve, passing remaining mayonnaise mixture separately.

EASY SPRING ROLLS
Arrange 4 soaked rice wrappers on clean, damp kitchen towel and top each with ½ cup filling, leaving 2-inch border at bottom. Fold in sides, then roll wrap up carefully but tightly, starting at bottom.

CIDER-GLAZED PORK CHOPS WITH WALDORF SALAD

Pork

124   Orange-Ginger Pork Tenderloin and Carrot Salad

126   Port-and-Cherry-Glazed Pork Tenderloin with
Creamy Turnip Puree

127   Quick Pork Jambalaya

129   Skillet Pork Fajitas

130   Cider-Glazed Pork Chops with Waldorf Salad

131   Spicy Pork Chops with Summer Vegetable Sauté

132   Pork Chops with Creamy Roasted Poblanos

134   Apricot-Crusted Pork Chops with Radicchio

135   Pork Chops with Roasted Red Pepper Sauce and Paprika
Roasted Cauliflower

137   Maple-Glazed Pork Chops with Sweet Potato–Bacon Hash

138   Pork Chops with Quick Ginger-Peach Chutney

139   Pork Chops with Chorizo and Spanish Rice

140   Cola-Glazed Pork Chops with Mustard Greens

142   Teriyaki Pork Chops with Baby Bok Choy

143   Hoisin-Glazed Boneless Ribs with Garlicky Broccolini

145   Pork Florentine Casserole

146   Rye-Crusted Pork Schnitzel with Quick Cinnamon Applesauce

147   Parmesan Pork Cutlets with Garlicky Broccoli Rabe

148   Crispy Sesame Pork Cutlets

150   Skillet-Braised Bratwurst and Sauerkraut

151   Thai-Style Pork Patties

153   Pork-and-Sausage-Stuffed Peppers

Orange-Ginger Pork Tenderloin and Carrot Salad

Serves 4 to 6

✔ **WHY THIS RECIPE WORKS:** Carrots have an earthy sweetness that makes them a classic match for pork, and here we put a bright new twist on the average steamed or roasted carrot side dish by making a flavorful shredded carrot salad to go with our pork tenderloins. Since orange is another favorite with pork, we make a simple glaze for the meat with orange juice and orange marmalade plus some freshly grated ginger for balancing heat. To keep things efficient, we use these glaze ingredients to serve as the base for the salad's dressing. All it needs is some cumin and cinnamon for extra warmth, plus cilantro for freshness and color, in addition to the expected olive oil, salt, and pepper. And best of all, there's minimal cooking and cookware involved; just some stovetop time and a skillet to prepare the tenderloins.

¾ **cup orange juice (2 oranges)**

3 **tablespoons orange marmalade**

1 **tablespoon grated fresh ginger**

4 **carrots, peeled and shredded**

2 **tablespoons chopped fresh cilantro**

¼ **teaspoon ground cumin**

⅛ **teaspoon ground cinnamon**

Salt and pepper

3 **tablespoons olive oil**

½ **cup water, plus 1 to 2 tablespoons, if needed**

2 **(12- to 16-ounce) pork tenderloins, trimmed**

1. Combine orange juice, marmalade, and ginger in small bowl. Transfer ¼ cup orange juice mixture to large bowl. Add carrots, cilantro, cumin, cinnamon, ½ teaspoon salt, ½ teaspoon pepper, and 2 tablespoons oil to large bowl and toss to combine. Whisk ½ cup water into remaining orange juice mixture.

2. Pat pork dry with paper towels and season with salt and pepper. Heat remaining 1 tablespoon oil in 12-inch nonstick skillet over medium-high heat until just smoking. Cook tenderloins until well browned all over, 5 to 8 minutes. Reduce heat to medium. Add orange juice mixture and cook, turning tenderloins occasionally, until mixture is thickened and meat registers 145 degrees, about 12 minutes. If sauce sticks to pan, thin it with remaining 1 to 2 tablespoons water.

3. Transfer pork to cutting board, tent loosely with aluminum foil, and let rest for 5 minutes. Slice pork ½ inch thick and transfer to platter. Spoon sauce over pork and serve with carrot salad.

QUICK PREP TIP SHOULD YOU USE OLD GINGER?

We rarely use up an entire knob of fresh ginger in one go, and we routinely store the remainder in the fridge. But after a few weeks, the root tends to shrivel and dry out. Is this an indication that it's no longer suitable for cooking? Two batches of stir-fried broccoli later, we had our answer. Though tasters found both acceptable, the sample made with fresh, plump ginger packed spicy heat and "zing," while the broccoli made with a more wizened specimen turned out "mild" and "flat." Why? As ginger ages, it loses its signature pungency from the compound gingerol, which over time converts into a more mild-flavored compound called zingerone. If possible, buy small pieces of ginger and use it while fresh. And if you're polishing off an older piece, be prepared to use more than the recipe calls for and add it as close as possible to the end of cooking.

Glazed Pork Tenderloin with Creamy Turnip Puree

Serves 4 to 6

☑ **WHY THIS RECIPE WORKS:** We love serving quick-cooking pork tenderloin for a weeknight meal, but its mild flavor can always use a boost. Here we opt for a sweet-tart glaze with the bright flavor of cherries and the warmth of port, while rosemary adds the right herbal depth. By adding the glaze ingredients to the pan after browning the pork, we thicken the glaze, plump the cherries, and gently cook the pork through all at once. A side of creamy turnip puree makes a surprising and appealing change of pace from the typical mashed potato side. After microwaving the turnip pieces while the pork cooks on the stovetop, all we have to do is puree them in the food processor with butter and cream to get a perfect side for this satisfying winter meal.

2	pounds turnips, peeled and cut into ½-inch pieces
½	cup heavy cream
4	tablespoons unsalted butter
	Salt and pepper
2	(12- to 16-ounce) pork tenderloins, trimmed
1	tablespoon vegetable oil
1	cup ruby port
1	cup low-sodium chicken broth
1	cup dried cherries
1	sprig fresh rosemary

1. Place turnips in bowl, cover, and microwave until tender, 7 to 9 minutes, tossing halfway through cooking. Bring cream and butter to simmer in small saucepan over medium heat. Process turnips and butter mixture in food processor until smooth and creamy, about 30 seconds. Transfer puree to bowl and season with salt and pepper to taste. Cover to keep warm.

2. While turnips cook, pat pork dry with paper towels and season with salt and pepper. Heat oil in 12-inch skillet over medium-high heat until just smoking. Cook tenderloins until well browned all over, 5 to 8 minutes. Add port, broth, cherries, and rosemary and cook, turning pork occasionally, until mixture is slightly thickened and meat registers 145 degrees, about 10 minutes. Transfer pork to cutting board, tent loosely with aluminum foil, and let rest for 5 minutes.

3. Reduce sauce mixture until thick and syrupy, about 3 minutes. Discard rosemary and season sauce with salt and pepper to taste. Slice pork and serve with sauce and turnip puree.

SMART SHOPPING TURNIPS AND RUTABAGAS

Although turnips (left) and rutabagas (right) can often be used interchangeably in cooking, they are not the same. Both vegetables belong to the mustard family, but the mild-flavored, yellow-tinged rutabaga (also known as a "Swede" or yellow turnip) is generally larger, sweeter, and starchier. It is thought to have evolved from a cross between a wild cabbage and a turnip. White and purple-topped turnips, however, are all turnip and have a sharper bite. You can substitute rutabagas for the turnips in this particular recipe, though we feel the sweeter flavor of rutabagas doesn't work quite as well here.

Quick Pork Jambalaya

Serves 4

✔ **WHY THIS RECIPE WORKS:** With chicken, shrimp, sausage, rice, tomatoes, and a laundry list of herbs and spices, jambalaya is anything but short on flavor, but a classic recipe is also anything but quick to prepare. To shorten the shopping list, we keep the key flavor elements—onion, celery, red pepper, and thyme—and limit the proteins to pork tenderloin and andouille sausage, which lends its characteristic spiciness and ensures this meal is plenty hearty. To streamline, we microwave the rice and prepare the rest of the ingredients on the stovetop while the rice cooks.

2 **cups low-sodium chicken broth**

1 **cup long-grain white rice**

   Salt and pepper

1 **(1-pound) pork tenderloin, trimmed and sliced crosswise ¾ inch thick**

4 **teaspoons vegetable oil**

8 **ounces andouille sausage, halved lengthwise and sliced thin**

1 **onion, chopped fine**

1 **celery rib, chopped fine**

1 **red bell pepper, stemmed, seeded, and chopped fine**

5 **garlic cloves, minced**

1 **teaspoon minced fresh thyme**

   Hot sauce

1. Combine 1 cup broth, rice, and ¾ teaspoon salt in bowl, cover, and microwave until liquid is absorbed, 10 to 12 minutes.

2. Meanwhile, pat pork dry with paper towels and season with salt and pepper. Heat 2 teaspoons oil in 12-inch nonstick skillet over medium-high heat until just smoking. Add sausage and cook, stirring occasionally, until browned, about 4 minutes. Transfer sausage to plate. Cook tenderloin medallions in sausage fat until browned, about 4 minutes. Transfer to plate with sausage.

3. Add onion, celery, bell pepper, and remaining 2 teaspoons oil to now-empty skillet and cook over medium-high heat until softened, about 5 minutes. Stir in garlic and thyme and cook until fragrant, about 30 seconds. Stir rice, remaining 1 cup broth, and sausage into skillet and bring to boil. Reduce heat to medium-low and cook, covered, until liquid is absorbed, about 10 minutes. Stir in pork. Remove skillet from heat and let sit, covered, until pork is heated through, about 5 minutes. Season with salt and pepper to taste and serve with hot sauce.

SMART SHOPPING ANDOUILLE SAUSAGE

Traditional Louisiana andouille sausage is made from ground pork, salt, garlic, and plenty of black pepper, then smoked over pecan wood and sugarcane for up to 14 hours. Used in a wide range of Louisiana dishes, it lends a characteristic intense smoky, spicy, earthy flavor. We tasted four brands, looking for the right combination of smokiness and heat with a traditional chewy but dry texture.

Of course, a sausage straight from Louisiana won: **Jacob's World Famous Andouille.** Tasters voted these mail-order links with a burgundy tint the smokiest and spiciest in the lineup. Coming in second, Wellshire Andouille Sausage from Whole Foods held its own.

Skillet Pork Fajitas

Serves 4

♥ WHY THIS RECIPE WORKS: Fajitas are a quick-cooking, all-in-one meal by design, making them the perfect choice for a busy evening. Recipes for indoor chicken or beef fajitas are fairly easy to find, so we use pork as the starring protein in this version for something a little different. Slicing pork tenderloin into bite-size pieces before cooking, rather than after, speeds up the cooking process, while the duo of bell pepper and red onion adds just the right texture, color, and sweetness to the meal. A little chili powder, added to the skillet while the vegetables cook, is all that's needed for a flavor boost. Once the vegetables are done, we set them aside and the pork goes into the pan to cook for just a few minutes. Stirring a little lime juice, cilantro, and cumin in with the pork once it's done adds just the right brightness.

1 tablespoon lime juice, plus lime wedges for serving

2 tablespoons minced fresh cilantro

½ teaspoon ground cumin

¼ cup vegetable oil

2 red bell peppers, stemmed, seeded, and sliced thin

1 red onion, halved and sliced thin

1 teaspoon chili powder

Salt and pepper

1 (1-pound) pork tenderloin, trimmed, halved lengthwise, and sliced crosswise ¼ inch thick

12 (6-inch) flour tortillas, warmed

1. Whisk lime juice, cilantro, cumin, and 1 tablespoon oil in bowl.

2. Heat 1 tablespoon oil in 12-inch skillet over medium-high heat until shimmering. Add bell peppers, onion, chili powder, and ½ teaspoon salt to skillet and cook until onion is softened, about 7 minutes. Transfer vegetables to platter and tent loosely with aluminum foil.

3. Pat pork dry with paper towels and season with salt and pepper. Add remaining 2 tablespoons oil to now-empty skillet and heat until just smoking. Add pork and cook, stirring often, until cooked through, about 4 minutes. Off heat, stir lime juice mixture into pork and season with salt and pepper to taste. Transfer to platter with vegetables and serve with tortillas and lime wedges.

SIMPLE SIDE CHUNKY CHIPOTLE GUACAMOLE
Roughly mash 3 halved and pitted ripe avocados with ¼ cup minced fresh cilantro, 2 tablespoons minced red onion, 2 tablespoons lime juice, and 1 to 2 teaspoons minced canned chipotle chile in adobo sauce in medium bowl. Season with salt and pepper to taste. Serves 4.

Cider-Glazed Pork Chops with Waldorf Salad

Serves 4

✓ **WHY THIS RECIPE WORKS:** We put a whole new spin on the favorite seasonal fall pairing of pork and apples by coating pork chops with a quick cider glaze and serving Waldorf salad (an inherently simple dish) on the side. By deeply browning the chops on just one side and then braising them in a cider and honey mixture, we give them visual appeal while keeping them moist and infusing them with flavor. While the meat is gently simmering, the liquid reduces to a thick consistency perfect for glazing the chops. As for the salad, it comes together in a snap, with chunks of apple and celery tossed in a mayonnaise-based dressing. We add pecans and dried cherries to the mix for a punch of flavor, color, and texture, and the cider vinegar and honey play double-duty, used in both the dressing and the glaze. For visual appeal, we recommend using a combination of apples; Granny Smith, Gala, and Braeburn are all good choices.

⅓ **cup dried cherries**

1 **cup apple cider**

¼ **cup mayonnaise**

¼ **cup cider vinegar**

¼ **cup honey**

3 **apples, cored and cut into ½-inch pieces**

1 **celery rib, chopped fine**

⅓ **cup pecans, toasted and chopped**

Salt and pepper

4 **(8- to 10-ounce) bone-in pork rib or center-cut chops, ¾ to 1 inch thick, trimmed**

1 **tablespoon vegetable oil**

1. Combine cherries and ¼ cup cider in bowl, cover, and microwave until cider begins to boil, about 1 minute. Let sit until cherries are soft and liquid is absorbed, about 5 minutes. Set aside to cool.

2. Meanwhile, whisk mayonnaise, 2 tablespoons vinegar, and 1 tablespoon honey together in large bowl. Add apples, celery, pecans, and cherries to bowl and toss to coat. Season with salt and pepper to taste.

3. Cut 2 slits, about 2 inches apart, through outer layer of fat and silverskin on each chop. Pat pork dry with paper towels and season with salt and pepper. Heat oil in 12-inch skillet over medium-high heat until just smoking. Cook pork until well browned on first side, about 5 minutes. Flip and cook until lightly browned on second side, about 1 minute. Reduce heat to medium-low. Add remaining ¾ cup cider and remaining ¾ cup honey and simmer until pork registers 145 degrees, about 8 minutes. Transfer pork to plate and tent loosely with aluminum foil.

4. Continue to simmer glaze until thick and syrupy, about 2 minutes. Stir in remaining 2 tablespoons vinegar and season with salt and pepper to taste. Spoon sauce over pork and serve with salad.

Spicy Pork Chops with Summer Vegetable Sauté

Serves 4

✓ **WHY THIS RECIPE WORKS:** For those who like a hit of spice at suppertime, this is the perfect recipe. A combination of paprika and chili powder gives these pork chops a big boost of flavor without much work, while a medley of squash, corn, and poblano chiles serves as a sweet, smoky, and slightly spicy side dish that nicely complements the pork. We rub the chops with the spices, then cook them over medium heat rather than the usual medium-high to prevent the spices from burning. When the chops come out of the skillet, in go the side dish ingredients, where they pick up any spices and fond the chops left behind. Stirring in a little cilantro adds just the right balancing brightness. You can substitute 1 cup thawed frozen corn for the fresh if necessary, adding it to the vegetable mixture for the last two minutes to heat through.

1 teaspoon paprika

1 teaspoon chili powder

Salt and pepper

4 (8- to 10-ounce) bone-in pork rib or center-cut chops, ¾ to 1 inch thick, trimmed

2 tablespoons vegetable oil

1 small onion, chopped

1 pound summer squash, cut into ½-inch cubes

2 poblano chiles, stemmed, seeded, and sliced thin

2 ears corn, kernels cut from cobs

2 tablespoons chopped fresh cilantro

Lime wedges

1. Combine paprika, chili powder, ½ teaspoon salt, and ½ teaspoon pepper in small bowl. Cut 2 slits, about 2 inches apart, through outer layer of fat and silverskin on each chop. Pat pork chops dry with paper towels and rub with spice mixture.

2. Heat 1 tablespoon oil in 12-inch nonstick skillet over medium heat until just smoking. Add chops and cook until well browned and chops register 145 degrees, about 5 minutes per side. Transfer to serving platter and tent loosely with aluminum foil.

3. Add remaining 1 tablespoon oil, onion, squash, poblanos, and corn to now-empty skillet and cook until vegetables have softened, about 6 minutes. Stir in cilantro and season with salt and pepper to taste. Serve with pork chops and lime wedges.

QUICK PREP TIP CUTTING KERNELS OFF THE COB
Standing ear of corn upright inside large bowl, carefully cut kernels from cob using paring knife.

Pork Chops with Creamy Roasted Poblanos

Serves 4

✓ **WHY THIS RECIPE WORKS:** We liven up the usual ho-hum pork chop dinner by topping these chops with a creamy, zesty sauce inspired by the Mexican dish *poblano rajas*. This combination of roasted poblano chiles, onions, oregano, and cream has multiple uses in Mexican recipes—as a filling, a topping, or a side dish—and makes this meal a sure win. To keep to a short time frame, we broil the poblanos in the oven while we cook the pork on the stovetop in a skillet. After the chiles come out of the oven, we remove their skin, slice them into strips, and stir them (along with some garlic and dried oregano for an authentic touch) into the pan with the sautéed onions. After that, it takes just a minute once the cream is added for the sauce to reach the right consistency.

4	poblano chiles, stemmed, halved, and seeded
4	(8- to 10-ounce) bone-in pork rib or center-cut chops, ¾ to 1 inch thick, trimmed
	Salt and pepper
2	tablespoons vegetable oil
2	onions, halved and sliced thin
2	garlic cloves, minced
½	teaspoon dried oregano
½	cup heavy cream

1. Position oven rack 3 inches from broiler element and heat broiler. Place poblanos on baking sheet cut side down and broil until skins begin to char and blister, 7 to 9 minutes. Transfer chiles to cutting board. When cool enough to handle, remove charred skins from chiles and slice into ½-inch-thick strips.

2. Meanwhile, cut 2 slits, about 2 inches apart, through outer layer of fat and silverskin on each chop. Pat pork dry with paper towels and season with salt and pepper. Heat oil in 12-inch skillet over medium-high heat until just smoking. Add chops and cook until well browned and meat registers 145 degrees, about 5 minutes per side. Transfer to plate and tent loosely with aluminum foil.

3. Add onions to now-empty skillet and cook until softened and beginning to brown, about 7 minutes. Add garlic, oregano, and poblanos and cook until chiles are tender, about 2 minutes. Add cream and cook until slightly thickened, about 1 minute. Season with salt and pepper to taste and serve with pork chops.

SIMPLE SIDE MASHED SWEET POTATOES WITH LIME ZEST
Bring 1½ pounds peeled, diced sweet potatoes and enough water to cover by 1 inch to boil in large saucepan. Reduce to simmer and cook until potatoes are tender, about 15 minutes. Drain potatoes and return to pot. Add ¼ cup heavy cream, 2 tablespoons softened unsalted butter, 1 teaspoon grated lime zest, and 1 tablespoon lime juice and mash until smooth. Season with salt and pepper to taste. Serves 4.

ALL ABOUT Buying Pork

When it comes to buying pork for quick and easy dinners, flavorful roasts like pork butt or pork shoulder are off-limits since they take hours of cooking to become tender. While ground pork is an obvious quick-cooking choice, there are many cuts tailor-made for the weeknight table. The key is to pair these mildly flavored cuts with a boldly flavored side dish or sauce, both of which you'll find in the recipes throughout this chapter. Here are our favorites:

Tenderloin

Pork tenderloin is easy to jazz up with a simple spice rub or glaze. But be careful when cooking tenderloin, as lean, delicate, boneless tenderloin has little marbling so it can dry out faster than fattier cuts. A thin, tough membrane called the silverskin covers part of the tenderloin and is best removed before cooking. Simply slip a knife under the silverskin, angle it slightly upward, and remove using a gentle back-and-forth motion.

Bone-In Rib and Center-Cut Chops

These are our two favorite bone-in pork chops. The rib chops (left), easily identified by the bone that runs along one side, are cut from the rib section of the loin and have a relatively high fat content, making them flavorful and unlikely to dry out. Center-cut chops (right) have a bone that divides the loin meat from the tenderloin. Because the leaner tenderloin section cooks more quickly, these chops are a bit more difficult to cook, and they have less fat than rib chops. However, they still have good flavor.

Boneless Chops

It's hard to deny the convenience of boneless chops; they cook in a jiffy and there's no bone to work around at the dinner table. However, since there's also no bone to help keep the meat juicy or add flavor, it's critical to keep a close eye on the cooking time and to put an emphasis on flavorful pairings.

Cutlets

Thin, lean pork cutlets cook through in the blink of an eye, making them a natural for the weeknight table. They are made by cutting a tenderloin into sections and then pounding each piece until it is ¼ to ½ inch thick. You can buy ready-to-go cutlets from the supermarket or, for evenly sized cutlets just the thickness you want, you can make your own (see page 147 for instructions).

Boneless Country-Style Ribs

These meaty, tender ribs are cut from the upper side of the rib cage from the fatty blade end of the loin. They contain mostly fattier meat and are a favorite for braising or smoking. Butchers usually cut them into individual ribs and package several together.

Enhanced vs. Unenhanced Pork

Because modern pork is remarkably lean and therefore somewhat bland and prone to dryness, a product called "enhanced" pork has overtaken the market. Enhanced pork has been injected with a solution of water, salt, sodium phosphate, sodium lactate, potassium lactate, sodium diacetate, and varying flavor agents to bolster flavor and juiciness, with the total amount of enhancing ingredients adding 7 to 15 percent extra weight. Pork containing additives must be so labeled, with a list of the ingredients. We have found that while enhanced pork is indeed juicier and more tender than unenhanced pork, the latter has more genuine pork flavor and is thus our preference. Enhanced pork can also leach juices that, once reduced, will result in overly salty sauces. If you buy enhanced pork, you shouldn't brine it, as it has essentially already been brined.

Apricot-Crusted Pork Chops with Radicchio

Serves 4

✔ **WHY THIS RECIPE WORKS:** Adding apricots and lemon zest to a buttery bread-crumb mixture is just the ticket to taking breaded chops to the next level. Breading just one side of our chops keeps things simple, and after browning the pork on one side we transfer the skillet to the oven for a hands-off finish. We roast the radicchio side dish in the oven while the chops brown. Cutting the radicchio through the center of the core ensures the wedges hold together, which helps them brown evenly and makes turning them easy.

2   **slices hearty white sandwich bread, torn into quarters**

2   **tablespoons unsalted butter, melted**

1   **tablespoon grated lemon zest**

½   **cup dried apricots, chopped**
    Salt and pepper

5   **tablespoons olive oil**

2   **heads radicchio (20 ounces), cut lengthwise into quarters**

4   **(8- to 10-ounce) bone-in pork rib or center-cut chops, ¾ to 1 inch thick, trimmed**

3   **tablespoons minced fresh chives**

1. Adjust 1 oven rack to lowest position and second rack 8 inches from broiler element. Heat oven to 475 degrees. Pulse bread, butter, and zest in food processor to large crumbs, about 8 pulses. Transfer to small bowl and fold in apricots. Season with salt and pepper to taste.

2. Brush baking sheet with 3 tablespoons oil and arrange radicchio, cut side down, on baking sheet. Season with salt and pepper and transfer to lower oven rack. Roast until golden brown, 8 to 10 minutes per side, then transfer to serving platter.

3. Cut 2 slits, about 2 inches apart, through outer layer of fat and silverskin on each chop. Pat pork dry with paper towels and season with salt and pepper. Heat remaining 2 tablespoons oil in 12-inch skillet over medium-high heat until just smoking. Add pork and cook until well browned on first side, about 2 minutes. Flip chops over and top with bread-crumb mixture, pressing to adhere. Transfer skillet to lower oven rack and bake until pork registers 140 degrees and bread crumbs are starting to brown, about 4 minutes. Move skillet to upper rack and broil until crumbs are golden brown, about 4 minutes. Transfer chops to platter with radicchio, sprinkle with chives, and serve.

SMART SHOPPING DRIED APRICOTS

Dried apricots are a great pantry item to keep handy for adding tart flavor to a variety of recipes, from side dishes to salads to mains. In addition to the typical supermarket dried apricots, which are treated with sulfur dioxide to preserve their sunny color and extend shelf life, you can also find organic, unsulfured dried apricots. In a side-by-side taste test, we found that eaten out of hand, the plump sulfured apricots (near right) had "citrus and honey" flavors. Unsulfured apricots were drier, chewier, and "mud-colored" raw, but revealed bright, true apricot flavor when cooked.

Pork Chops with Roasted Red Pepper Sauce

Serves 4

✔ **WHY THIS RECIPE WORKS:** Inspired by the classic Spanish romesco sauce, we puree roasted red peppers, almonds, garlic, and cayenne together to make a sauce that perks up pork chops. Adding sandwich bread, water, and olive oil to the processor creates a sauce that is surprisingly creamy. Roasting the cauliflower in the oven while the chops cook on the stovetop keeps this recipe efficient.

1 cup jarred roasted red peppers

¼ cup slivered almonds

1 slice hearty white sandwich bread, toasted and torn into pieces

2 tablespoons water

2 garlic cloves, minced

⅛ teaspoon cayenne pepper

7 tablespoons olive oil
Salt and pepper

1 pound cauliflower florets

1 tablespoon paprika

4 (8- to 10-ounce) bone-in pork rib or center-cut chops, ¾ to 1 inch thick, trimmed

1. Adjust oven rack to middle position and heat oven to 425 degrees. Puree peppers, almonds, bread, water, garlic, and cayenne in food processor until smooth, about 15 seconds. With processor running, slowly drizzle in ¼ cup oil until sauce is creamy, about 30 seconds. Transfer to bowl and season with salt and pepper to taste.

2. Toss cauliflower with paprika and 2 tablespoons oil until thoroughly coated, then season with salt and pepper. Transfer to rimmed baking sheet and roast until cauliflower is tender and lightly browned, about 20 minutes. Transfer to serving bowl and tent loosely with aluminum foil.

3. Meanwhile, cut 2 slits, about 2 inches apart, through outer layer of fat and silverskin on each chop. Pat chops dry with paper towels and season with salt and pepper. Heat remaining 1 tablespoon oil in 12-inch skillet over medium-high heat until just smoking. Add chops and cook until well browned and meat registers 145 degrees, about 5 minutes per side. Transfer to serving platter, tent loosely with foil, and let rest for 5 minutes. Serve with red pepper sauce and cauliflower.

SMART SHOPPING ROASTED RED PEPPERS
You can certainly roast your own peppers at home, but jarred peppers are especially convenient. We tasted eight supermarket brands. Our tasters preferred firmer, smokier, sweeter-tasting peppers in strong yet simple brines of salt and water. Peppers packed in brines that contained garlic, vinegar, olive oil, and grape must—characteristic of most of the European peppers—rated second. The extra ingredients provided "interesting" and "lively" flavor profiles, but the vinegar often masked the authentic red pepper flavor and smoky notes that tasters preferred. The blandest peppers were also the slimiest ones, both of which rated dead last. Our winner? The domestically produced **Dunbars Sweet Roasted Peppers**, which lists only red bell peppers, water, salt, and citric acid on its ingredient list.

Maple Pork Chops with Sweet Potato-Bacon Hash

Serves 4

✓ **WHY THIS RECIPE WORKS:** Sweet maple syrup, sharp cider vinegar, and tangy mustard come together to make a simple, balanced, and flavorful glaze for the chops. For a complementary side dish, we parcook sweet potatoes in the microwave while the chops cook, then put them in the pan, along with crisped bacon bits and some thyme, once the chops are done. To boost the flavor of the dish, we cook the bacon in a skillet first so that the chops, and then the potatoes, can cook in the rendered fat.

1¼	pounds sweet potatoes, peeled and cut into ¾-inch chunks
6	slices bacon, chopped fine
4	(8-ounce) bone-in pork rib chops, 1 inch thick, trimmed
	Salt and pepper
2	teaspoons minced fresh thyme
½	cup maple syrup
1	tablespoon cider vinegar
2	teaspoons Dijon mustard

1. Place potatoes in large bowl, cover, and microwave until tender, 4 to 7 minutes. Meanwhile, cook bacon in 12-inch nonstick skillet over medium-high heat until crisp, about 5 minutes. Using slotted spoon, transfer bacon to paper towel–lined plate. Pour off fat, reserving 2 tablespoons.

2. Cut 2 slits, about 2 inches apart, through outer layer of fat and silverskin on each chop. Pat chops dry with paper towels and season with salt and pepper. Heat 1 tablespoon reserved fat in now-empty skillet over medium-high heat until just smoking. Add chops and cook until browned, about 4 minutes per side. Transfer chops to plate and tent loosely with aluminum foil.

3. Add remaining 1 tablespoon reserved fat and potatoes to now-empty skillet and cook, turning occasionally, until browned all over, 5 to 7 minutes. Stir in thyme and bacon. Season with salt and pepper to taste. Transfer to serving bowl.

4. Add maple syrup, vinegar, and mustard to now-empty skillet and cook until thickened, about 2 minutes. Add chops and any accumulated juices and simmer, turning often, until glaze coats chops, about 2 minutes. Serve with potatoes.

QUICK PREP TIP MICROWAVING WITH PLASTIC WRAP
It used to be common practice to cover bowls and dishes with plastic wrap in the microwave. But the chemicals contained in some plastic wraps are potentially harmful if the plastic is heated to the point that it melts or burns. To avoid exposure to these chemicals, the FDA recommends using only wrap (and containers) that are marked "microwave-safe" and leaving several inches of room between the food and the plastic wrap during cooking. Our advice: Use ceramic or glass cookware for microwaving, and instead of plastic wrap, cover food with an overturned microwave-safe bowl or plate, which we've found retains moisture just as well as plastic wrap.

Pork Chops with Quick Ginger-Peach Chutney

Serves 4

✔ **WHY THIS RECIPE WORKS:** Pork is perfect for pairing with sweet fruit, and peaches are a great summertime choice. While jarred chutneys are fine, we use fresh peaches in this recipe to make a full-flavored chutney that is sweet, tangy, and slightly spicy—and best of all, it takes mere minutes to make. This simple recipe requires just one skillet; we cook the pork chops first, then set them aside to make the peach chutney. Mincing the ginger instead of grating it adds a nice textural component to the chutney. Ripe but still firm peaches will hold some of their shape throughout cooking, resulting in an appealingly chunky chutney. Though we like fresh peaches in this recipe, a 1-pound bag of frozen peaches can be substituted.

4	**(8- to 10-ounce) bone-in pork rib or center-cut chops, ¾ to 1 inch thick, trimmed**
	Salt and pepper
2	**tablespoons vegetable oil**
1	**red onion, chopped fine**
1¼	**pounds ripe peaches, peeled, halved, pitted, and chopped**
2	**jalapeño chiles, stemmed, seeded, and chopped fine**
2	**tablespoons minced fresh ginger**
⅓	**cup packed brown sugar**
¼	**cup cider vinegar**
¼	**teaspoon ground cardamom**

1. Cut 2 slits, about 2 inches apart, through outer layer of fat and silverskin on each chop. Pat pork chops dry with paper towels and season with salt and pepper. Heat 1 tablespoon oil in 12-inch nonstick skillet over medium-high heat until just smoking. Add chops and cook until well browned and chops register 145 degrees, about 5 minutes per side. Transfer to platter and tent loosely with aluminum foil.

2. Add remaining 1 tablespoon oil and onion to now-empty skillet and cook over medium heat until softened, 3 to 4 minutes. Add peaches and cook until soft but still intact, about 4 minutes. Add jalapeños and ginger and cook until fragrant, about 1 minute. Stir in sugar, vinegar, and cardamom and simmer until liquid is very thick and syrupy, about 3 minutes. Season with salt and pepper to taste and serve with chops.

SIMPLE SIDE SWISS CHARD WITH ONION AND BACON
Cook 4 slices chopped bacon in 12-inch skillet over medium-high heat until crisp, about 5 minutes. Using slotted spoon, transfer bacon to paper towel-lined plate. Add 1 thinly sliced onion to fat left in skillet and cook until soft, about 5 minutes. Add 1½ pounds coarsely chopped Swiss chard and ½ cup low-sodium chicken broth and cook, stirring occasionally, until chard is tender and liquid has evaporated, about 5 minutes. Stir in bacon and season with salt and pepper to taste. Serves 4.

Pork Chops with Chorizo and Spanish Rice

Serves 4

☑ **WHY THIS RECIPE WORKS:** We make the most of our cookware so that this Spanish-inspired dinner comes together in a flash. We parboil the rice in the microwave while we brown the chorizo and cook aromatics on the stovetop in a saucepan. Using precooked Spanish chorizo, rather than raw Mexican-style chorizo, helps speed things up even more. Then the parcooked rice, saffron, and broth go into the pan to cook through. While the rice cooks, we cook our pork chops in a skillet; a smoked paprika spice rub really boosts their flavor.

2   cups low-sodium chicken broth

1   cup long-grain rice

1   teaspoon plus 2 tablespoons olive oil

8   ounces Spanish chorizo sausage, halved lengthwise and sliced crosswise ¼ inch thick

1   onion, chopped

1   red bell pepper, stemmed, seeded, and chopped
    Pinch saffron

1   teaspoon smoked paprika
    Salt and pepper

4   (8-ounce) bone-in pork rib chops, ¾ inch thick, trimmed

½   cup frozen peas

1. Combine 1½ cups chicken broth and rice in large bowl, cover, and microwave until rice is softened and most of liquid has been absorbed, 10 to 12 minutes.

2. Meanwhile, heat 1 teaspoon oil in medium saucepan over medium heat until simmering. Add chorizo and cook until browned, about 4 minutes. Using slotted spoon transfer chorizo to small bowl; set aside. Add onion and bell pepper to now-empty saucepan and cook until softened, about 4 minutes. Stir in rice, saffron, and remaining ½ cup broth and bring to boil. Reduce heat to medium-low, cover, and cook until rice is tender and liquid is absorbed, about 5 minutes.

3. While the rice cooks, combine paprika, ½ teaspoon salt, and ¼ teaspoon pepper in small bowl. Cut 2 slits, about 2 inches apart, through outer layer of fat and silverskin on each chop. Pat pork chops dry with paper towels and rub both sides with spice mixture. Heat remaining 2 tablespoons oil in 12-inch nonstick skillet over medium heat until just smoking. Cook pork chops until well browned and chops register 145 degrees, 4 to 5 minutes per side. Transfer to serving platter, tent loosely with aluminum foil, and let rest for 5 minutes.

4. Add chorizo and peas to rice and cook, stirring frequently, until hot, about 2 minutes. Season with salt and pepper to taste and serve with chops.

Cola-Glazed Pork Chops with Mustard Greens

Serves 4

✔ **WHY THIS RECIPE WORKS:** Some unexpected complementary ingredients—five-spice powder, cola, and ketchup—make this an all-around appealing meal. Rubbing the chops with the five-spice powder (a mix of spices such as cinnamon, cloves, and star anise) gives them a warm, subtle pungency, while the cola and ketchup, along with brown sugar, create an irresistible glaze. To round out the meal, we prepare a side of mustard greens. Since each component is prepared on the stovetop in a skillet, this recipe stays streamlined.

½ **teaspoon five-spice powder**
   Salt and pepper
4 **(8- to 10-ounce) bone-in pork rib or center-cut chops, 1 inch thick, trimmed**
4 **teaspoons vegetable oil**
2 **pounds mustard greens, stemmed and chopped**
½ **cup low-sodium chicken broth**
3 **garlic cloves, minced**
1 **cup cola**
¼ **cup packed light brown sugar**
¼ **cup ketchup**

1. Combine five-spice powder, ½ teaspoon salt, and ½ teaspoon pepper in small bowl. Cut 2 slits, about 2 inches apart, through outer layer of fat and silverskin on each chop. Pat pork chops dry with paper towels and season with spice mixture. Heat 2 teaspoons oil in 12-inch skillet over medium-high heat until just smoking. Add chops and cook until well browned, about 5 minutes per side. Transfer to plate and tent with aluminum foil.

2. Heat remaining 2 teaspoons oil in now-empty skillet over medium-high heat until shimmering. Add mustard greens, broth, garlic, ¼ teaspoon salt, and ¼ teaspoon pepper. Cover and cook until greens are just tender and wilted, 8 to 10 minutes. Transfer to serving bowl and tent loosely with foil.

3. Whisk cola, brown sugar, and ketchup in medium bowl. Add mixture to now-empty skillet and simmer until slightly thickened, about 3 minutes. Return chops and any accumulated juices to skillet and continue to simmer until glaze coats chops, 1 to 2 minutes. Transfer chops to platter, pour over glaze, and serve with greens.

SMART SHOPPING KETCHUP
Since the 1980s, most ketchup has been made with high-fructose corn syrup (HFCS); manufacturers like this ingredient because it's cheap and easy to mix with other ingredients. But in the past few years, many manufacturers have started offering alternatives, such as ketchup made with white sugar. For our recent taste test of eight national brands, we focused on classic tomato ketchups. Tasters tried each plain and with fries. It was clear they wanted ketchup that tasted the way they remembered it: boldly seasoned, with all the flavor elements—salty, sweet, tangy, and tomatoey. Our top three ketchups were all sweetened with sugar; **Heinz Organic Tomato Ketchup** got the top spot.

Teriyaki Pork Chops with Baby Bok Choy

Serves 4

✔ **WHY THIS RECIPE WORKS:** Maple syrup is a surprisingly tasty and convenient replacement for the sugar-mirin combination typically found in teriyaki sauce. We brown the chops, then add the sauce to the pan so that it reduces and the chops cook through (and stay moist) all at once. While the chops cook, we steam the bok choy in a separate saucepan, then toss it with sesame oil for a hit of flavor.

4	**(5- to 7-ounce) boneless pork chops, trimmed**
	Salt and pepper
⅓	**cup maple syrup**
¼	**cup soy sauce**
1	**teaspoon grated fresh ginger**
1	**garlic clove, minced**
1	**tablespoon vegetable oil**
4	**heads baby bok choy (4 ounces each), halved**
1	**teaspoon toasted sesame oil**

1. Cut 2 slits, about 2 inches apart, through outer layer of fat and silverskin on each chop. Pat pork chops dry with paper towels and season with salt and pepper. Combine maple syrup, soy sauce, ginger, and garlic in medium bowl.

2. Heat vegetable oil in 12-inch nonstick skillet over medium-high heat until just smoking. Cook chops until well browned on 1 side, 4 to 6 minutes. Flip chops and add maple syrup mixture to skillet. Reduce heat to medium-low and cook until chops register 145 degrees, 5 to 8 minutes. Transfer chops to plate and tent loosely with aluminum foil.

3. Meanwhile, fit large saucepan with steamer basket. Add water, keeping level below basket. Bring water to boil and add bok choy. Cover and steam until bok choy is just tender, 4 to 6 minutes. Transfer to bowl and toss with sesame oil.

4. Return any accumulated pork juices to skillet and simmer with maple syrup mixture over medium heat until sauce is thickened and rubber spatula leaves wide trail when pulled through sauce, 2 to 3 minutes. Spoon sauce over chops and serve with bok choy.

QUICK PREP TIP
NO-CURL PORK CHOPS
To prevent chops from curling when cooking, cut 2 slits, about 2 inches apart, through fat and silverskin on each chop.

Hoisin-Glazed Boneless Ribs with Garlicky Broccolini

Serves 4

✔ **WHY THIS RECIPE WORKS:** It's easy to pass over country-style pork ribs when looking for a quick entrée, but they're actually a great choice for a weeknight meal, especially the boneless variety, since they have minimal connective tissue that needs to be broken down. In this recipe, we brown the ribs first on the stovetop in a skillet, then add a glaze, which we give an Asian twist with the help of hoisin sauce, soy sauce, ginger, and rice vinegar. While the ribs cook and the glaze reduces, we cook the broccolini in a separate saucepan. We like to serve this recipe with Easy White Rice (page 22).

3	tablespoons soy sauce
3	tablespoons hoisin sauce
2	tablespoons ketchup
1	tablespoon rice vinegar
3	garlic cloves, minced
1	tablespoon grated fresh ginger
1½	pounds boneless country-style pork ribs, trimmed
	Salt and pepper
3	tablespoons vegetable oil
½	cup water
1	pound broccolini, trimmed

1. Whisk soy sauce, hoisin, ketchup, rice vinegar, half of garlic, and ginger together in bowl.

2. Cut any ribs over 5 inches long crosswise in half. Pat ribs dry with paper towels and season with salt and pepper. Heat 2 tablespoons oil in 12-inch skillet over medium-high heat until just smoking. Cook ribs until browned on both sides, about 3 minutes per side.

3. Add hoisin mixture and cook, flipping ribs occasionally, until sauce is thickened and meat registers 145 degrees, 3 to 5 minutes.

4. Meanwhile, bring water and ½ teaspoon salt to boil in large saucepan. Add broccolini and simmer, covered, over medium-low heat until bright green and tender, about 5 minutes. Remove lid and cook until liquid has evaporated, about 30 seconds. Stir in remaining 1 tablespoon oil and remaining garlic and cook until fragrant, about 30 seconds. Season with salt and pepper to taste, transfer to platter, and serve with ribs.

QUICK PREP TIP
TRIMMING BROCCOLINI
A cross between broccoli and *kai-lan* (Chinese broccoli), broccolini is mild in flavor, and the tender stalks do not need to be peeled. To prepare for cooking, simply remove the leaves from the broccolini and trim off the ends of the stalks.

Pork Florentine Casserole

Serves 4

✔ **WHY THIS RECIPE WORKS:** We change up the usual steak (or eggs) Florentine by using boneless, country-style pork ribs, which are quick-cooking and lend the dish deep, meaty flavor. This recipe comes together like clockwork. We cook the spinach in a skillet in batches, then set it aside, brown the ribs (cooking them in batches ensures plenty of fond is left behind), and then we build the sauce. Once the spinach is stirred in, we nestle the ribs into the mixture, sprinkle it with more cheese, and pop the whole thing under the broiler to cook until bubbling and golden brown. Make sure to use an ovensafe skillet for this recipe.

¼ **cup olive oil**

1½ **pounds baby spinach**

1½ **pounds boneless country-style pork ribs, trimmed and halved lengthwise**

Salt and pepper

2 **shallots, minced**

2 **tablespoons all-purpose flour**

4 **garlic cloves, minced**

2 **cups low-sodium chicken broth**

1 **cup heavy cream**

Pinch ground nutmeg

3 **ounces Parmesan cheese, grated (1½ cups)**

1. Adjust oven rack to middle position and heat oven to 400 degrees. Heat 1 tablespoon oil in 12-inch ovensafe skillet over medium-high heat until shimmering. Add spinach, in 4 additions, to skillet and cook, stirring until all spinach is wilted and decreased in volume by half, about 5 minutes. Transfer spinach to colander and, using wooden spoon or rubber spatula, press to remove excess liquid. Place spinach on cutting board and chop coarse. Transfer to colander and press again.

2. Pat ribs dry with paper towels and season with salt and pepper. Heat 1 tablespoon oil in skillet over medium-high heat until smoking. Cook half of ribs until browned on both sides, about 4 minutes. Transfer to plate. Repeat with 1 tablespoon oil and remaining ribs.

3. Reduce heat to medium, add remaining 1 tablespoon oil and shallots to now-empty skillet, and cook until softened, 1 minute. Add flour and garlic and cook until fragrant, about 30 seconds. Slowly add broth and cream, stirring constantly. Add ¼ teaspoon salt, ¼ teaspoon pepper, and nutmeg and simmer until mixture is thickened, about 5 minutes. Off heat, stir in ½ cup Parmesan and spinach. Nestle ribs into skillet.

4. Spread spinach mixture in even layer over ribs and sprinkle with remaining 1 cup Parmesan. Transfer to oven and cook until bubbling and cheese is golden brown, 10 to 12 minutes. Serve.

Rye-Crusted Pork Schnitzel with Quick Applesauce

Serves 4

✔ **WHY THIS RECIPE WORKS:** Schnitzel is a favorite cold-weather comfort food, and we jazz up the typical coating by adding rye bread. Applesauce is the perfect accompaniment, and nothing beats homemade. Grating the apples first ensures they break down quickly, and once they're soft, we add a bit of water to get the right consistency. Cinnamon, a little brown sugar, and a touch of lemon juice add a great flavor boost.

5	tablespoons unsalted butter
4	Granny Smith apples, cored, peeled, and grated
1	tablespoon packed brown sugar
¼	teaspoon ground cinnamon
2	tablespoons water
1	tablespoon lemon juice
4	slices rye bread, torn into quarters
½	cup all-purpose flour
2	large eggs
6	(3- to 4-ounce) pork cutlets, trimmed
	Salt and pepper

1. Set wire rack in rimmed baking sheet and set aside. Melt 1 tablespoon butter in large saucepan over medium heat. Add apples, sugar, and cinnamon, bring to simmer, then lower heat to medium-low and cook, stirring frequently, until apples start to break down, about 5 minutes. Reduce heat to low, cover, and cook until soft and slightly thickened, 10 to 12 minutes. Off heat, stir in water and lemon juice, transfer to bowl, and tent loosely with aluminum foil.

2. Meanwhile, microwave 2 tablespoons butter in small bowl until melted, about 30 seconds. Pulse bread and melted butter in food processor into crumbs, about 10 pulses. Transfer breadcrumb mixture to shallow dish. Spread flour in second shallow dish. Beat eggs in third shallow dish. Pat cutlets dry with paper towels and season with salt and pepper. Working with 1 cutlet at a time, dredge cutlets in flour, dip in egg, then coat with bread crumbs, pressing gently to adhere.

3. Melt 1 tablespoon butter in 12-inch nonstick skillet over medium heat. Add 3 cutlets and cook until golden brown and crisp, 3 to 4 minutes per side. Transfer to prepared wire rack and tent loosely with foil. Wipe out skillet and repeat with remaining 1 tablespoon butter and remaining 3 cutlets. Serve with applesauce.

SIMPLE SIDE ROASTED BROCCOLI

Adjust oven rack to lowest position and heat oven to 500 degrees. Place foil-lined baking sheet in oven. Cut 1 pound broccoli at juncture of crown and stalk. Peel stalk and cut into ½-inch-thick planks about 3 inches long. Place crown upside down and cut in half through central stalk, then cut each half into 3 or 4 wedges for 3- to 4-inch diameter crown, or into 6 wedges if 4- to 5-inch diameter crown. Toss with 3 tablespoons extra-virgin olive oil and ½ teaspoon sugar, and season with salt and pepper. Place on baking sheet and roast until tender, 14 to 16 minutes. Serves 4.

Parmesan Pork Cutlets with Broccoli Rabe

Serves 4

✔ **WHY THIS RECIPE WORKS:** Adding Parmesan cheese to the classic flour-egg coating makes these chops irresistible. Instead of opting for thin-cut pork chops in this recipe, we make our own tender cutlets by gently pounding slices of pork tenderloin to an even ¼-inch thickness. We use the large holes of a box grater to grate the Parmesan. This method creates bigger pieces of cheese that form a thicker crust on the pork.

1   **pound broccoli rabe, trimmed and cut into 1-inch pieces**
½   **cup plus 2 tablespoons all-purpose flour**
2   **large eggs**
4   **ounces Parmesan cheese, grated (2 cups)**
1   **(1-pound) pork tenderloin, trimmed, cut into 8 pieces, and pounded to ¼-inch thickness**
    Salt and pepper
3   **tablespoons olive oil**
3   **garlic cloves, minced**
    Lemon wedges

1. Adjust oven rack to middle position and heat oven to 200 degrees. Combine broccoli rabe and ¼ cup water in large bowl, cover, and microwave until tender, about 4 minutes. Drain.

2. Set wire rack in rimmed baking sheet. Spread ½ cup flour in shallow dish, beat eggs in second shallow dish, and combine Parmesan and remaining 2 tablespoons flour in third shallow dish.

3. Pat pork dry with paper towels and season with salt and pepper. Working with 1 cutlet at a time, dredge cutlets in flour, dip in eggs, and coat in Parmesan mixture, pressing gently to adhere.

4. Heat 1 tablespoon oil in 12-inch nonstick skillet over medium-high heat until shimmering. Add 4 cutlets, reduce heat to medium, and cook until cheese turns pale golden brown, about 3 minutes per side. Transfer to prepared sheet and place in oven. Repeat with 1 tablespoon oil and remaining 4 cutlets.

5. Heat remaining 1 tablespoon oil in now-empty skillet over medium-high heat until shimmering. Add broccoli rabe and garlic and cook until garlic is fragrant, about 1 minute. Season with salt and pepper to taste. Serve with cutlets and lemon wedges.

QUICK PREP TIP MAKING YOUR OWN PORK CUTLETS
After cutting tenderloin into 8 pieces, sandwich pieces, cut side up, between 2 large pieces of plastic wrap. Using meat pounder, flatten pork to uniform ¼-inch thickness.

Crispy Sesame Pork Cutlets

Serves 4

☑ **WHY THIS RECIPE WORKS:** Toasted sesame seeds add great nutty flavor to the bread-crumb coating on these cutlets. Grinding some of the seeds in a food processor ensures that their flavor gets distributed throughout the coating, but we also leave some of the seeds whole for added texture and visual appeal. Instead of using store-bought bread crumbs, we make our own in seconds by adding a few torn-up bread slices to the food processor with the seeds. To ensure that the sesame seeds don't burn, we cook the cutlets over medium heat. If your cutlets are thicker than ½ inch, it's best to pound them to the right thickness so that the meat cooks through at the same time that the coating is browned and crisped. We prefer peanut oil for frying, but vegetable oil will also work.

¾ **cup sesame seeds, toasted**

3 **slices hearty white sandwich bread, torn into pieces**

½ **cup all-purpose flour**

2 **large eggs**

6 **(3- to 4-ounce) boneless pork cutlets, trimmed**

Salt and pepper

½ **cup peanut or vegetable oil**

1. Process ½ cup sesame seeds in food processor until coarsely ground, about 15 seconds. Add bread and pulse to coarse crumbs, about 6 pulses. Transfer to shallow dish and toss with remaining sesame seeds. Spread flour in second shallow dish. Beat eggs in third shallow dish.

2. Pat pork dry with paper towels and season with salt and pepper. Working with 1 cutlet at a time, dredge cutlets in flour, dip in eggs, then coat with sesame bread crumbs, pressing gently to adhere.

3. Heat ¼ cup oil in 12-inch skillet over medium heat until just smoking. Fry 3 cutlets until golden brown and crisp, 2 to 3 minutes per side. Transfer to paper towel–lined plate. Wipe out skillet and repeat with remaining ¼ cup oil and remaining 3 cutlets. Serve.

SIMPLE SIDE NAPA CABBAGE SALAD
Whisk 3 tablespoons vegetable oil, 2 tablespoons rice vinegar, 1 tablespoon toasted sesame oil, 1 teaspoon grated fresh ginger, and 1 minced garlic clove together in large bowl. Add ½ large head napa cabbage, cored and shredded (8 cups), and 2 peeled and grated carrots and toss to coat. Season with salt and pepper to taste. Serves 4.

Skillet-Braised Bratwurst and Sauerkraut

Serves 4

✔ **WHY THIS RECIPE WORKS:** While seemingly simple, the classic take on this dish traditionally requires a fair amount of time, as recipes usually call for a slow braise for the brats and sauerkraut to achieve full flavor. We turn this dish into a quick skillet supper by trading in the slow braise for a simple sauté. First, we brown the bratwurst; just a minute or two per side intensifies flavor and develops fond in the pan that is stirred into the sauerkraut. While the bratwurst browns, we microwave the sauerkraut with bacon, chicken broth, juniper berries (a traditional inclusion), and bay leaves (note that all but the broth lend flavor and are not meant to be eaten here). We prefer fresh bratwurst versus the precooked variety in this recipe.

2   **pounds sauerkraut, rinsed**

1   **cup low-sodium chicken broth**

2   **slices bacon**

10   **juniper berries**

2   **bay leaves**

2   **tablespoons unsalted butter**

1½   **pounds bratwurst, cut into 3-inch lengths**

1   **onion, halved and sliced thin**

     Salt and pepper

1   **Granny Smith apple, peeled, cored, and grated**

4   **teaspoons packed brown sugar**

1. Combine sauerkraut, broth, bacon, juniper berries, and bay leaves in large bowl. Cover and microwave until sauerkraut is softened, about 10 minutes.

2. Meanwhile, melt butter in 12-inch skillet over medium-high heat. Add bratwurst and cook until lightly browned on all sides, about 3 minutes. Transfer to plate.

3. Add onion and ½ teaspoon salt to now-empty skillet and cook until softened, about 5 minutes. Stir in sauerkraut mixture, apple, and brown sugar and bring to simmer. Nestle bratwurst into sauerkraut, cover, and reduce heat to medium-low. Cook until sausages are no longer pink in center, 10 to 12 minutes. Discard bay leaves and bacon, season with salt and pepper to taste, and serve.

SMART SHOPPING SAUERKRAUT

Briny, salty sauerkraut is an essential component in this recipe, but with all the choices at the market it can be hard to discern which type is best for a recipe. We tasted eight national contenders—in jars, cans, and vacuum-sealed bags—both plain and layered onto a Reuben. Right off the bat, tasters panned the heavily processed (and long-cooked) canned brands as "flaccid and flavorless" and "flat." Jarred and bagged brands are cooked less; these generally had more crunch and flavor. Our winning sauerkraut, **Boar's Head**, is a bagged variety that was praised for its "chewy-crisp" texture and "fresh, vinegary kick." Another brand of bagged sauerkraut, Great Lakes Kraut Co. Krrrrisp Kraut, was our runner-up.

Thai-Style Pork Patties

Serves 4

✔ **WHY THIS RECIPE WORKS:** It only takes a handful of ingredients to give these patties the classic Thai flavor profile, and using a stand mixer gives the patties a delicate texture that lets the flavors shine through. You can combine the meat mixture by hand, but the patties will not be as smooth. Serve the patties with Easy White Rice (page 22), as well as our Spicy Bean-Sprout Salad (below).

1	large egg
2	tablespoons fish sauce
1	tablespoon lime juice
1	tablespoon packed brown sugar
2	slices hearty white sandwich bread, torn into small pieces
1	shallot, minced
1	serrano chile, stemmed, seeded, and minced
1	lemon grass stalk, trimmed to bottom 6 inches and minced
1	pound ground pork
¼	cup minced fresh cilantro
2	tablespoons peanut or vegetable oil

1. Combine egg, fish sauce, lime juice, and brown sugar in small bowl. Mash in bread pieces and set aside. Using stand mixer fitted with paddle, beat shallot, serrano, lemon grass, and ½ cup pork on medium-high speed until mixture is smooth and pale, about 2½ minutes, scraping down bowl as needed. Add remaining pork, bread mixture, and cilantro and mix on medium-low speed until just incorporated, about 30 seconds, scraping bowl as needed. Divide mixture into 8 equal portions and shape into ½-inch-thick patties.

2. Heat 1 tablespoon oil in 12-inch nonstick skillet over medium heat until shimmering. Add 4 patties and cook until well browned and cooked through, 4 to 5 minutes per side. Transfer to plate and tent loosely with aluminum foil. Repeat with remaining 1 tablespoon oil and remaining 4 patties. Let rest for 5 minutes and serve.

SIMPLE SIDE SPICY BEAN-SPROUT SALAD
Combine 3 tablespoons vegetable oil, 1½ tablespoons lime juice, 1 teaspoon packed brown sugar, and 1 teaspoon sriracha. Add 4 cups bean sprouts, 4 thinly sliced scallions, and ½ cup cilantro and toss to coat. Stir in ⅓ cup chopped dry-roasted peanuts. Season with salt and pepper to taste. Serves 4.

QUICK PREP TIP
MINCING LEMON GRASS
Trim and discard all but bottom 6 inches of stalk, then peel off tough outer sheath. Cut stalk in quarters lengthwise, then slice thin crosswise.

Pork-and-Sausage-Stuffed Peppers

Serves 4

✔ **WHY THIS RECIPE WORKS:** We promote rice-stuffed peppers from side dish to main course by adding plenty of ground pork and sweet Italian sausage to the filling. Microwaving the peppers prior to stuffing gives them a head start, then they simply finish cooking under the broiler. While the peppers are parcooking, the other components come together in a single skillet. Pepper Jack cheese lends a little extra character and heat, but Monterey Jack can be substituted in a pinch. For a flavorful finishing touch, we reserve 1 cup of the cheese to sprinkle on top of the stuffed peppers just before we place them under the broiler.

4	red bell peppers, stems left intact, halved lengthwise, and seeded
3	tablespoons vegetable oil
8	ounces ground pork
4	ounces sweet Italian pork sausage, casings removed
1	onion, chopped fine
3	garlic cloves, minced
1	(8.8-ounce) package Uncle Ben's Brown Ready Rice
12	ounces pepper Jack cheese, shredded (3 cups)
¼	cup minced fresh parsley
	Salt and pepper

1. Adjust oven rack 6 inches from broiler element and heat broiler. Place bell peppers in bowl, cover, and microwave until just tender, 3 to 6 minutes.

2. Meanwhile, heat 1 tablespoon oil in 12-inch nonstick skillet over medium-high heat until just smoking. Add pork and sausage and cook, breaking up meat with wooden spoon, until no longer pink, about 5 minutes. Add onion and cook until softened, about 4 minutes. Add garlic and cook until fragrant, about 30 seconds. Stir in rice and cook until heated through, about 2 minutes. Off heat, stir in 2 cups pepper Jack and parsley, and season with salt and pepper.

3. Pat peppers dry with paper towels and season with salt and pepper. Brush baking sheet with remaining 2 tablespoons oil. Place peppers, cut side down, on baking sheet and broil until spotty brown, about 3 minutes. Flip peppers over, fill with pork mixture, then sprinkle with remaining 1 cup pepper Jack. Broil until cheese is spotty brown and melted, 3 to 5 minutes, and serve.

QUICK PREP TIP PREPARING BELL PEPPERS FOR STUFFING
This technique for stuffing peppers is both quicker and easier than scooping out the insides from a hole in the top. First, slice the bell pepper in half through the stem. Then pull out the core and seeds from both sides, removing as much of the ribs as possible. We leave the stem on the pepper halves for a more rustic presentation.

PAN-SEARED SCALLOPS WITH SQUASH PUREE AND SAGE BUTTER

Seafood

156   Spicy Cornmeal-Crusted Flounder and Lemony Slaw

157   Orange-Tarragon Trout with Smoky Green Beans

158   Crisp-Skinned Snapper with Spicy Broccoli and Red Pepper

160   Crab-Stuffed Sole with Lemon-Butter Sauce

161   Thai-Style Fish and Creamy Coconut Rice Packets

162   Cod with Herbed Tomato-Caper Compote

164   Cod Cakes with Garlic-Basil Aïoli

165   Macadamia-Crusted Cod with Mango-Mint Salsa

167   Moroccan Fish and Couscous Packets

168   Pan-Fried Halibut and Potatoes with Lemon-Caper Sauce

169   Tuna with Miso Butter and Sesame Spinach

170   Mediterranean Tuna and White Bean–Fennel Salad

172   Swordfish with Lemon Couscous and Olive Relish

173   Smoked Salmon Scrambled Eggs with Chive Butter

175   Chili-Glazed Salmon with Bok Choy

176   Mustard-Crusted Salmon with Potato-Cabbage Hash

178   Skillet Shrimp and Orzo with Feta

179   Spicy Shrimp with Corn Cakes

180   Sautéed Shrimp with Artichokes and Mushrooms

182   Pan-Seared Scallops with Squash Puree and Sage Butter

183   Pan-Seared Scallops with Bacon Succotash

185   Steamed Mussels with Chorizo and Garlic Crostini

Spicy Cornmeal Flounder and Lemony Slaw

Serves 4

✔ **WHY THIS RECIPE WORKS:** A quick cornmeal coating adds appealing texture to delicate flounder fillets. We give this dish a Southern spin by adding hot sauce to the coating, and we pair the fish with a remoulade that's likewise spiked with hot-sauce heat. We found that using Tabasco sauce, rather than another brand of hot sauce, was key to creating the right appealing, vinegary bite. For a cooling counterpoint, we whip together a quick side of prepared broccoli slaw tossed with a bright lemony dressing and add parsley for freshness.

½ **cup mayonnaise**

½ **cup chopped fresh parsley**

¼ **cup lemon juice (2 lemons)**

1 **celery rib, chopped fine**

4 **scallions, chopped fine**

1 **teaspoon plus 2 tablespoons Tabasco sauce**

Salt and pepper

9 **tablespoons olive oil**

1 **(10-ounce) bag broccoli slaw mix**

1½ **cups cornmeal**

2 **large eggs**

4 **(5- to 7-ounce) skinless flounder fillets**

1. Adjust oven rack to lower-middle position, set heatproof serving platter on rack, and heat oven to 200 degrees. Combine mayonnaise, ¼ cup parsley, 1 tablespoon lemon juice, celery, scallions, and 1 teaspoon Tabasco in bowl. Season remoulade with salt and pepper to taste and set aside.

2. Combine remaining ¼ cup parsley, remaining 3 tablespoons lemon juice, and 3 tablespoons oil in large bowl. Add broccoli slaw and toss to coat. Season with salt and pepper to taste.

3. Spread cornmeal in shallow dish. Beat eggs and remaining 2 tablespoons Tabasco in second shallow dish. Pat fish dry with paper towels and season with salt and pepper. Working with 1 fillet at a time, dip fillets in egg mixture, then in cornmeal, pressing to adhere.

4. Heat 3 tablespoons oil in 12-inch nonstick skillet over medium-high heat until just smoking. Place 2 fillets in skillet and cook until browned and crisp, about 2 minutes per side. Transfer fish to platter in oven. Repeat with remaining 2 tablespoons oil and remaining 2 fillets. Serve with remoulade and broccoli slaw.

QUICK PREP TIP
CORNMEAL-CRUSTED FLOUNDER
Whisk eggs with 2 tablespoons Tabasco in shallow dish and spread cornmeal in second dish. Dip fish in egg mixture, then cornmeal, pressing to adhere. Heat 2 tablespoons oil in 12-inch nonstick skillet over medium-high heat until just smoking. Cook fillets, two at a time, until browned.

Orange-Tarragon Trout with Smoky Green Beans

Serves 4

🗹 WHY THIS RECIPE WORKS: Trout fillets are a great weeknight option since they cook quickly, but we were after a change from the usual trout-bacon pairing. This compound butter, brightly flavored with orange zest and fresh tarragon, is just the answer. A side dish of green beans, cooked quickly in the microwave, gets tossed with some of the butter as well, keeping this dinner simple and streamlined. Smoked almonds, which we toast in the skillet with a little butter before cooking the fish, add texture and another layer of flavor to the green beans, making them a perfect pairing with the trout.

6   **tablespoons unsalted butter, softened**

¼   **cup minced fresh tarragon**

1   **teaspoon grated orange zest**
     Salt and pepper

½   **cup smoked almonds, chopped fine**

1   **pound green beans, trimmed**

¼   **cup water**

¼   **cup all-purpose flour**

8   **(3- to 4-ounce) skin-on rainbow trout fillets**

1. Adjust oven rack to lower-middle position, set heatproof serving platter on rack, and heat oven to 200 degrees. Using fork, mix 3 tablespoons butter, tarragon, and orange zest in bowl until thoroughly combined. Season with salt and pepper to taste and set aside.

2. Melt 1 tablespoon butter in 12-inch skillet over medium-high heat. Add almonds and cook, stirring frequently, until nuts are toasted and fragrant, 1 to 2 minutes. Transfer nuts to small bowl.

3. Combine beans and water in large bowl and microwave, covered, until beans are bright green and tender, about 5 minutes. Drain and toss with 1 tablespoon tarragon butter and almonds. Season with salt and pepper to taste.

4. Meanwhile, spread flour in shallow dish. Pat fish dry with paper towels and season with salt and pepper. Dredge fish in flour, shaking off excess. Wipe out now-empty skillet with paper towels. Melt 1 tablespoon butter over medium-high heat in skillet. Add 4 fillets, skin side down, and cook until skin is crisp, about 3 minutes. Flip and cook until fish flakes apart when gently prodded with paring knife, about 2 minutes. Transfer cooked fillets to platter in oven. Repeat with remaining 1 tablespoon butter and remaining 4 fillets. Top each fillet with remaining tarragon butter and serve.

Snapper with Spicy Broccoli and Red Pepper

Serves 4

✓ **WHY THIS RECIPE WORKS:** The flavors found in bright, spicy Thai cuisine helped us create a saucy broccoli–red pepper topping for mild snapper. We precook the broccoli in the microwave while we cook the fish on the stovetop, then set the fish aside and put together the topping in the skillet. Thinly sliced shallot, lightly browned with the pepper, lends the richness that completes the meal.

3	tablespoons sugar
3	tablespoons white vinegar
1	tablespoon soy sauce
1	tablespoon Asian chili-garlic sauce
1	tablespoon dry sherry
1	tablespoon ketchup
2	teaspoons cornstarch
1½	pounds broccoli, florets cut into 1-inch pieces, stalks peeled and sliced thin
¼	cup water
3	tablespoons vegetable oil
4	(6- to 8-ounce) skin-on red snapper fillets
	Salt and pepper
1	red bell pepper, stemmed, seeded, and cut into ¾-inch pieces
1	large shallot, sliced thin

1. Adjust oven rack to lower-middle position, set heatproof serving platter on rack, and heat oven to 200 degrees. Whisk sugar, vinegar, soy sauce, chili-garlic sauce, sherry, ketchup, and cornstarch together in small bowl; set aside. Combine broccoli and water in large bowl. Microwave, covered, until bright green and tender, about 5 minutes.

2. Meanwhile, heat 1 tablespoon oil in 12-inch nonstick skillet over medium-high heat until just smoking. Pat fish dry with paper towels and season with salt and pepper. Place 2 fillets in skillet, skin side down, and cook until fish flakes apart when gently prodded with paring knife, about 3 minutes per side. Transfer to platter in oven. Repeat with 1 tablespoon oil and remaining 2 fillets.

3. Add bell pepper, shallot, and remaining 1 tablespoon oil to now-empty skillet and cook until shallot is lightly browned, about 3 minutes. Add sauce mixture and broccoli and cook until sauce is thickened and vegetables are well coated, about 1 minute. Season with salt and pepper to taste, spoon mixture over fish, and serve.

QUICK PREP TIP TRIMMING BROCCOLI
Hold broccoli upside down on cutting board and trim florets from stalk, separating larger florets into 1-inch pieces, if necessary. Trim top and bottom from stalk, and use chef's knife or vegetable peeler to remove ⅛ inch of tough outer peel before slicing stalk into thin pieces.

Crab-Stuffed Sole with Lemon-Butter Sauce

Serves 4

👆 **WHY THIS RECIPE WORKS:** For a quick, foolproof, and company-worthy meal, we stuff sole with a crab filling. Using crispy panko bread crumbs ensures this filling doesn't turn soggy, while mayonnaise binds it together. To complement the sole and crab, all the filling needs is lemon, garlic, and chives. To balance the filling's richness, we opt for a bright lemon-butter sauce, which we prepare while the fish is baking. A sprinkling of chives lends a fresh finish. Serve with Steamed Asparagus with Olive Oil and Sea Salt (page 232).

4	tablespoons unsalted butter
8	ounces lump crabmeat, picked over for shells
½	cup mayonnaise
¼	cup panko bread crumbs
3	tablespoons finely chopped fresh chives
2	garlic cloves, minced
2	teaspoons grated lemon zest plus 2 tablespoons juice
	Salt and pepper
8	(3- to 4-ounce) skinless sole fillets

1. Adjust oven rack to middle position and heat oven to 475 degrees. Grease 13 by 9-inch baking dish with 1 tablespoon butter. Stir together crabmeat, mayonnaise, panko, 2 tablespoons chives, garlic, lemon zest, ¼ teaspoon salt, and ⅛ teaspoon pepper in bowl.

2. Pat fish dry with paper towels and season with salt and pepper. Arrange fillets, skinned side up, on cutting board. Place ¼ cup filling in center of each fillet, fold ends over filling to form roll, and transfer, seam side down, to prepared baking dish. Cover fish with aluminum foil and bake until stuffing is heated through and fish flakes apart when gently prodded with paring knife, 12 to 14 minutes.

3. Meanwhile, heat lemon juice in small saucepan over medium heat until just steaming. Add remaining 3 tablespoons butter, whisk constantly until thoroughly melted, and remove from heat. Season with salt and pepper to taste. Remove fish from oven, transfer to platter, pour sauce over fish, and sprinkle with remaining chives. Serve.

QUICK PREP TIP
ASSEMBLING CRAB-STUFFED SOLE
After preparing crab filling, place ¼ cup filling in center of each seasoned sole fillet and wrap ends of fish around filling to create roll. Arrange stuffed fillets, seam side down, in greased baking dish. Prepare lemon-butter sauce while fish bakes for 12 to 14 minutes, then pour sauce over fish.

Thai-Style Fish and Creamy Coconut Rice Packets

Serves 4

✓ **WHY THIS RECIPE WORKS:** Cooking fish *en papillote*, or in a pouch, is a classic French technique. In addition to being incredibly easy, it allows the fish to steam in its own juices and thus emerge moist and flavorful. It's a great option for a simple meal since you can cook a side right along with the entrée in the pouch. Here, we cook the fish fillets on a bed of store-bought precooked rice, and we give the dish a perhaps unexpected Thai spin, in the form of a flavorful sauce. We blend coconut milk, ginger, fish sauce, and rice vinegar, add a little cilantro for a fresh herbal touch, and add red pepper flakes for the slightest hint of heat. The sauce transforms the rice into a rich and creamy dish by the end of cooking and infuses the fish with flavor. Any white fish will work here, but we prefer the thickness and meaty texture of cod or halibut.

⅓ cup rice vinegar

1½ tablespoons sugar

⅛ teaspoon red pepper flakes

½ cup coconut milk

½ cup chopped fresh cilantro

2 tablespoons fish sauce

1 tablespoon grated fresh ginger

3 garlic cloves, minced

4 (6- to 8-ounce) skinless white fish fillets, ¾ to 1 inch thick
   Salt and pepper

2 (8.8-ounce) packages Uncle Ben's Jasmine Ready Rice

1. Adjust oven rack to middle position and heat oven to 400 degrees. Combine vinegar, sugar, and pepper flakes in small saucepan and cook over medium-high heat until sugar dissolves, about 1 minute. Off heat, stir in coconut milk, ¼ cup cilantro, fish sauce, ginger, and garlic.

2. Pat fish dry with paper towels and season with salt and pepper. Lay four 14-inch lengths aluminum foil on counter. Divide rice evenly among foil pieces, mounding it in center of each piece. Place 1 fish fillet on top of each rice mound, spoon sauce over fish, and fold foil over fish and rice, crimping edges to seal.

3. Arrange packets in 1 layer on rimmed baking sheet and bake until fish flakes apart when gently prodded with paring knife and registers 140 degrees, 16 to 19 minutes. Carefully open packets and sprinkle with remaining cilantro. Serve.

SIMPLE SIDE STEAMED BOK CHOY
Fit wide saucepan with steamer basket. Add water to pan, keeping level below basket. Bring water to boil, add 4 heads baby bok choy, cut in half lengthwise, and cover. Steam until bok choy is just tender, 4 to 6 minutes. Transfer to serving bowl, toss with 1 tablespoon unsalted butter, and season with salt and pepper to taste. Serves 4.

Cod with Herbed Tomato-Caper Compote

Serves 4

✔ **WHY THIS RECIPE WORKS:** This bright, summery recipe brings together tomatoes and plenty of fresh herbs to make an appealing one-pot meal. It's also conveniently efficient: We prepare the tomato compote in the skillet, then lay the fish on top of the mixture, put on the lid, and steam the fish until cooked through. Then we set the fish aside (keeping it warm under a tent of foil), and continue to cook the compote until it reduces to just the right consistency. This technique is appealing beyond the efficiency because the fish is infused with the compote's flavor. To balance the natural sweetness of the compote, capers contribute a briny bite. Remember to use care when removing the cod from the skillet, as it becomes tender when cooked and is prone to breaking apart.

3 **tablespoons extra-virgin olive oil**

1 **onion, chopped**

3 **garlic cloves, minced**

1 **pound tomatoes, cored and diced**

3 **tablespoons capers, rinsed**

4 **(6- to 8-ounce) skinless cod fillets, ¾ to 1 inch thick**
   Salt and pepper

3 **tablespoons minced fresh dill**

3 **tablespoons minced fresh parsley**

2 **tablespoons minced fresh tarragon**

1. Heat 1 tablespoon oil in 12-inch skillet over medium-high heat until shimmering. Add onion and cook until softened, about 4 minutes. Add garlic and cook until fragrant, about 30 seconds. Stir in tomatoes and capers and cook until heated through and flavors meld, about 1 minute.

2. Season cod with salt and pepper. Lay cod on top of tomato mixture, cover, and cook until fish flakes apart when gently prodded with paring knife and registers 140 degrees, 6 to 8 minutes. Transfer fish to platter and tent loosely with aluminum foil. Simmer tomato mixture, uncovered, until liquid is reduced by half, about 3 minutes.

3. Stir in herbs and remaining 2 tablespoons oil and season with salt and pepper to taste. Spoon tomato compote over cod and serve.

SIMPLE SIDE GREEN BEAN AND BLACK OLIVE SALAD
Bring 2½ quarts water to boil in large saucepan. Add 1 pound trimmed green beans and 1 tablespoon salt and cook until bright green and tender, about 5 minutes. Drain beans and transfer to large bowl. Toss with ¼ cup chopped pitted black olives, 2 tablespoons chopped fresh basil, 1 tablespoon olive oil, 1 tablespoon lemon juice, and 1 minced garlic clove. Season with salt and pepper to taste. Serves 4.

Cod Cakes with Garlic-Basil Aïoli

Serves 4

☑ **WHY THIS RECIPE WORKS:** Fish cakes are fast to make in the food processor, but many recipes add so much filler that they taste more like bread crumbs than fish. We use fresh cod in this recipe, along with just enough crunchy panko and an egg to hold the cakes together. A light dredging in more panko creates a crisp crust that turns golden once cooked. A quick garlicky *aïoli* dresses up the fish cakes, and we also use a few tablespoons of the aïoli to add a touch more binding power as well as flavor to the cakes. We process the cod in two batches to avoid overworking the fish, which would give the cakes a pasty texture.

½	cup mayonnaise
¼	cup chopped fresh basil
2	tablespoons lemon juice
1	garlic clove, minced
	Salt and pepper
1	pound skinless cod fillets, cut into 1-inch pieces
1½	cups panko bread crumbs
1	large egg, lightly beaten
2	scallions, chopped fine
¼	cup olive oil

1. Process mayonnaise, basil, lemon juice, and garlic in food processor until mixture is smooth and light green, about 20 seconds. Transfer aïoli to bowl and season with salt and pepper to taste.

2. Pulse half of cod in food processor into even mix of finely minced and coarsely chopped pieces, about 4 pulses. Transfer to large bowl and repeat with remaining fish. Mix processed cod with ¾ cup panko, ½ teaspoon salt, ¼ teaspoon pepper, egg, scallions, and 3 tablespoons aïoli. Form mixture into four 3½-inch patties. Place remaining ¾ cup panko in shallow dish and dredge patties in panko, pressing gently to adhere.

3. Heat oil in 12-inch nonstick skillet over medium-high heat until shimmering. Add patties to skillet and cook until golden brown and cooked through, about 4 minutes per side. (Be careful not to let panko crust get too dark before fish cake is cooked through. If bread crumbs are browning too quickly, reduce heat.) Serve with remaining aïoli.

SIMPLE SIDE TOMATO AND OLIVE SALAD
Whisk together 1 tablespoon balsamic vinegar and 3 tablespoons extra-virgin olive oil in large bowl. Add 12 ounces quartered cherry tomatoes, ¼ cup chopped pitted oil-cured black olives, and 3 tablespoons chopped fresh parsley to bowl with dressing and toss to coat. Season with salt and pepper to taste. Serves 4.

Macadamia-Crusted Cod with Mango-Mint Salsa

Serves 4

✔ **WHY THIS RECIPE WORKS:** A nutty-crunchy crust does wonders for lean, mildly flavored cod without requiring a lot of work. By combining meaty macadamia nuts with panko bread crumbs, we create a crust that's both rich-tasting and super crisp. (Hazelnuts or cashews could be used in place of the macadamia nuts.) Mayonnaise is a favorite in the test kitchen for gluing on coatings, and here we add fiery sriracha, an Asian hot chili sauce, to the mayo, making it flavorful as well as functional. While the fish is in the oven, we put together a simple mango salsa featuring mint and lime juice, plus a jalapeño chile for a fresh hit of heat. A side of Easy White Rice (page 22) rounds out the meal.

½   **cup macadamia nuts, chopped**

⅓   **cup panko bread crumbs**

1   **tablespoon olive oil**

3   **tablespoons mayonnaise**

1   **teaspoon sriracha sauce**

1   **teaspoon grated lime zest plus 3 tablespoons juice (2 limes) Salt and pepper**

4   **(6- to 8-ounce) skinless cod fillets, ¾ to 1 inch thick**

2   **large mangos, peeled, pitted, and cut into ¼-inch dice**

1   **jalapeño chile, stemmed, seeded, and minced**

2   **tablespoons minced fresh mint**

1. Adjust oven rack to upper-middle position and heat oven to 450 degrees. Combine nuts, panko, and oil in medium bowl. Whisk mayonnaise, sriracha, lime zest and 1 tablespoon juice, ½ teaspoon salt, and ¼ teaspoon pepper in small bowl.

2. Pat fish dry with paper towels, season with salt and pepper, and arrange in 13 by 9-inch baking dish. Spread mayonnaise mixture evenly over top of each fillet. Sprinkle panko mixture evenly over mayonnaise, pressing lightly to adhere. Bake until fish flakes apart when gently prodded with paring knife and registers 140 degrees, 12 to 15 minutes.

3. Meanwhile, toss mangos, jalapeño, mint, and remaining 2 tablespoons lime juice in medium bowl. Season with salt and pepper to taste and serve with fish.

QUICK PREP TIP
MAKING MACADAMIA-CRUSTED COD
Pat fish dry with paper towels, season with salt and pepper, and arrange in baking dish. Spread prepared mayonnaise mixture over each fillet, then sprinkle panko mixture evenly on top, pressing gently to adhere. Bake until fish flakes apart when gently prodded with paring knife, 12 to 15 minutes.

166 SIMPLE WEEKNIGHT FAVORITES

Moroccan Fish and Couscous Packets

Serves 4

✔ **WHY THIS RECIPE WORKS:** We love cooking quick meals *en papillote,* or in a packet, since it seals in juices and there are myriad combinations of entrée and side you can combine to cook at once. This recipe ventures beyond the everyday by topping fish fillets (we like halibut and cod) with chermoula, a spicy Moroccan condiment combining herbs, ginger, oil, and lemon zest and juice. Steaming the fish with the chermoula ensures it's moist and infused with flavor, and adding quick-cooking couscous to the packet makes it a meal.

1	cup minced fresh cilantro
3	tablespoons extra-virgin olive oil
2	tablespoons smoked paprika
2	tablespoons grated ginger
4	garlic cloves, minced
1	tablespoon grated lemon zest plus 2 tablespoons juice
1	tablespoon ground cumin
½	teaspoon red pepper flakes
	Salt and pepper
1	(10-ounce) box couscous (about 1½ cups)
2	cups boiling water
4	(6- to 8-ounce) skinless white fish fillets, ¾ to 1 inch thick
	Lemon wedges

1. Adjust oven rack to middle position and heat oven to 400 degrees. Combine 6 tablespoons cilantro, oil, paprika, ginger, garlic, lemon zest and juice, cumin, and pepper flakes in small bowl. Season with salt and pepper to taste.

2. Place couscous in medium bowl. Pour boiling water over couscous. Immediately cover with plastic wrap and let sit until liquid is absorbed and couscous is tender, about 5 minutes. Fluff couscous with fork and season with salt and pepper to taste.

3. Pat fish dry with paper towels and season with salt and pepper. Lay four 14-inch lengths of aluminum foil on counter. Divide couscous evenly among center of foil pieces, then place fish fillets on top. Spread 1 tablespoon sauce over top of each piece of fish. Fold foil over fish and couscous, crimping edges to seal.

4. Arrange packets in single layer on rimmed baking sheet and bake until fish flakes apart when gently prodded with paring knife and registers 140 degrees, 14 to 18 minutes. Carefully open packets and sprinkle with remaining cilantro. Serve with remaining sauce and lemon wedges.

EASY MOROCCAN FISH PACKETS
Place mound of prepared couscous in center of each piece of foil, then place fish on top. Spread prepared sauce over fish, then crimp edges to seal packet. Place on rimmed baking sheet and bake at 400 degrees for 14 to 18 minutes, until fish is just cooked through. Open packets, sprinkle fish with remaining cilantro, and serve with remaining sauce.

Halibut and Potatoes with Lemon-Caper Sauce

Serves 4

☑ **WHY THIS RECIPE WORKS:** Every component is made in one skillet in stages. We cook the halibut, then hold it in the oven while we make side then sauce. After parcooking potatoes in the microwave while the fish cooks, we brown them in the skillet once the fish is done. Lastly, we make our pan sauce with lemon and capers.

1½ pounds Yukon Gold potatoes, cut into 1-inch chunks

5 tablespoons olive oil
   Salt and pepper

4 (6- to 8-ounce) skinless halibut fillets, 1 inch thick

4 (3-inch) strips lemon zest, sliced into matchsticks, plus 3 tablespoons juice

1 tablespoon minced fresh rosemary

1 cup low-sodium chicken broth

3 tablespoons capers, rinsed

2 tablespoons unsalted butter

1. Adjust oven rack to lower-middle position, set heatproof serving platter on rack, and heat oven to 200 degrees. Combine potatoes, 1 tablespoon oil, ½ teaspoon salt, and ¼ teaspoon pepper in bowl. Microwave, covered, until potatoes begin to soften, 4 to 7 minutes. Drain potatoes.

2. Meanwhile, pat fish dry with paper towels and season with salt and pepper. Heat 2 tablespoons oil in 12-inch nonstick skillet over medium-high heat until just smoking. Cook fish until golden brown, flakes apart when gently prodded with paring knife, and registers 140 degrees, about 3 minutes per side. Transfer fish to platter in oven.

3. Add remaining 2 tablespoons oil and potatoes to now-empty skillet and cook until potatoes are well browned, about 10 minutes. Transfer potatoes to platter with fish.

4. Add lemon zest strips and rosemary to now-empty skillet and cook until fragrant, about 30 seconds. Add chicken broth, lemon juice, and capers and cook until reduced by about one third and slightly thickened, about 4 minutes. Off heat, stir in butter and season with salt and pepper to taste. Pour sauce over fish and potatoes and serve.

QUICK PREP TIP
MAKING LEMON ZEST STRIPS
We typically call for grated zest, but in this recipe it would burn before the rosemary has a chance to bloom, so we make bigger strips. Using a vegetable peeler, cut the peel off in 3-inch lengths. After scraping away any pith that you may have cut off with the zest, cut each piece into ⅛-inch-wide matchsticks.

Tuna with Miso Butter and Sesame Spinach

Serves 4

☑ **WHY THIS RECIPE WORKS:** This dish takes inspiration from classic Japanese miso-glazed fish, but instead of marinating the fish in a miso-sake mixture for several days, we pan-sear it, then top it with a miso-scallion butter. A side of spinach is quick to make and adds freshness to the meal. For efficiency, and to draw out excess liquid, we microwave the spinach until wilted, then drain it, chop it, and drain it again. Using sesame oil to sauté the spinach pulls the whole meal together. If you don't have a microwave-safe bowl large enough to accommodate all the spinach, cook it in two batches with 2 tablespoons water per batch for 1½ minutes.

3   tablespoons unsalted butter, softened

3   tablespoons white miso

4   teaspoons rice vinegar

2   scallions, minced
    Salt and pepper

18 ounces (18 cups) baby spinach

2   tablespoons toasted sesame oil

1   tablespoon sesame seeds, toasted

4   (6- to 8-ounce) tuna steaks, about 1 inch thick

1   tablespoon vegetable oil

1. Mix butter, miso, 2 teaspoons vinegar, scallions, ¼ teaspoon salt, and ¼ teaspoon pepper in small bowl.

2. Place spinach and ¼ cup water in large bowl. Microwave, covered, until spinach is wilted and volume has decreased by half, 3 to 4 minutes. Transfer spinach to colander and, using rubber spatula, gently press spinach to release liquid. Transfer spinach to cutting board and chop coarse. Transfer back to colander and press again to release any remaining liquid.

3. Heat sesame oil in 12-inch nonstick skillet over medium heat until shimmering. Add spinach and stir to coat with oil. Off heat, stir in remaining 2 teaspoons vinegar and sesame seeds. Season with salt and pepper to taste, transfer to serving platter, and tent loosely with aluminum foil.

4. Pat tuna dry with paper towels and season with salt and pepper. Heat vegetable oil in now-empty skillet over medium-high heat until just smoking. Add tuna to skillet and cook until opaque at perimeter and translucent red at center when checked with tip of paring knife and fish registers 110 degrees (for rare), about 2 minutes per side. Transfer to platter with spinach. Top tuna with miso butter and tent loosely with foil. Let sit until butter just begins to melt, 2 to 3 minutes, before serving.

Mediterranean Tuna and White Bean–Fennel Salad

Serves 4

✔ **WHY THIS RECIPE WORKS:** Puttanesca, a classic Italian pasta sauce, has a zesty flavor profile that is a fantastic match for perfectly cooked, rare tuna steaks. So we combine a few of the sauce's basic ingredients—capers, tomatoes, olives, and garlic—with white beans and fennel to create an accompanying salad for simply cooked pan-seared tuna steaks. The salad comes together quickly in the skillet after we've cooked the tuna, and a tablespoon of extra-virgin olive oil, added at the end, contributes to the Mediterranean flavor of the meal.

2	(10- to 12-ounce) tuna steaks, 1 to 1¼ inches thick
	Salt and pepper
3	tablespoons extra-virgin olive oil
1	onion, chopped
1	fennel bulb, stalks discarded, bulb halved, cored, and cut into ½-inch pieces
3	garlic cloves, minced
1	(15-ounce) can cannellini beans, rinsed
12	ounces cherry tomatoes, quartered
½	cup pitted black olives, minced
2	tablespoons capers, rinsed
¼	cup chopped fresh parsley

1. Pat tuna dry with paper towels and season with salt and pepper. Heat 1 tablespoon oil in 12-inch skillet over medium-high heat until just smoking. Add fish and cook until opaque at perimeter and translucent red at center when checked with tip of paring knife and tuna registers 110 degrees (for rare), about 2 minutes per side. Transfer to cutting board.

2. Add 1 tablespoon oil, onion, and fennel to now-empty skillet and cook until vegetables begin to soften, about 4 minutes. Add garlic and cook until fragrant, about 30 seconds. Add beans, tomatoes, olives, and capers and cook until heated through, 3 to 5 minutes. Off heat, stir in parsley and remaining 1 tablespoon oil and season with salt and pepper to taste.

3. Slice tuna steaks into ½-inch-thick pieces and divide among individual plates. Serve with white bean salad.

QUICK PREP TIP
TRIMMING AND CORING FENNEL
After cutting off stems and feathery fronds, cut off very thin slice from base of bulb. Remove any tough or blemished outer layers and cut bulb in half through base. Using small, sharp knife, remove pyramid-shaped core, then cut each half into strips with chef's knife and chop strips crosswise according to recipe.

Swordfish with Lemon Couscous and Olive Relish

Serves 4

✔ **WHY THIS RECIPE WORKS:** A simple olive relish, whipped together in the food processor, dresses up these swordfish steaks. We start by building a base for our relish with mustard, lemon zest, lemon juice, and olive oil, reserving a portion to double as a dressing for the couscous side dish. Olives, anchovy fillets, garlic, and capers round out the relish. To make good use of every minute, we pan-sear the fish while the couscous steeps to the perfect fluffy texture, then all we have to do is toss the couscous with the reserved dressing and top the fish with the relish. You can substitute any firm-fleshed fish, such as halibut or tuna, for the swordfish.

½	**cup plus 1 tablespoon extra-virgin olive oil**
1	**tablespoon Dijon mustard**
1	**teaspoon grated lemon zest plus 2 tablespoons juice**
1	**cup pimento-stuffed green olives**
3	**tablespoons capers, rinsed**
3	**garlic cloves, minced**
2	**anchovy fillets, rinsed**
1	**(10-ounce) box couscous (about 1½ cups)**
	Salt and pepper
2	**cups boiling water**
½	**cup minced fresh parsley**
4	**(6- to 8-ounce) swordfish steaks, 1¼ inches thick**

1. Whisk ½ cup oil, mustard, and lemon zest and juice together in small bowl. Reserve half of dressing. Pulse remaining dressing with olives, capers, garlic, and anchovies in food processor until coarsely chopped, about 10 pulses.

2. Combine couscous and 1 teaspoon salt in medium bowl. Pour boiling water over couscous. Immediately cover with plastic wrap and let sit until liquid is absorbed and couscous is tender, about 5 minutes. Fluff couscous with fork and stir in reserved lemon dressing and parsley. Season with salt and pepper to taste.

3. Meanwhile, pat fish dry with paper towels and season with salt and pepper. Heat remaining 1 tablespoon oil in 12-inch nonstick skillet over medium-high heat until just smoking. Add fish and cook until golden brown and flakes apart when gently prodded with paring knife and fish registers 140 degrees, 4 to 6 minutes per side. Serve fish with couscous and olive relish.

SMART SHOPPING COUSCOUS
Although couscous looks like a grain, it is technically a pasta. This starch is made from durum semolina, a high-protein wheat flour that is also used to make Italian pasta. Traditional Moroccan couscous is made by rubbing coarse-ground durum semolina and water between the hands to form small, coarse granules. The couscous is then dried and cooked over a simmering stew in a steamer called a *couscoussière*, which is essentially a stockpot fitted with a small-holed colander. The couscous sits in the colander and plumps in the steam produced by the pot's contents. (It could be stock, soup, or stew.) The boxed couscous found in most supermarkets is a precooked version of traditional couscous. About the size of bread crumbs, the precooked couscous needs only a few minutes of steeping in hot liquid to be fully cooked.

Smoked Salmon Scrambled Eggs with Chive Butter

Serves 4

✓ **WHY THIS RECIPE WORKS:** Breakfast for dinner is always a convenient option, but a basic fried egg or scramble doesn't quite cut it. We take scrambled eggs to the next level in this hearty supper by pairing eggs with leeks and smoked salmon and serving it all on top of thick slices of buttery toast. All you need for cookware is a single skillet. We toast the bread in the skillet with butter, then set it aside and add the leeks to cook until softened. The eggs, enriched with half-and-half, then go into the pan. Just as they're done, we fold in the leeks, spoon the eggs over the toast, and top with the salmon and chives and serve.

8	large eggs
¼	cup half-and-half
	Salt and pepper
4	tablespoons unsalted butter
4	(1-inch-thick) slices rustic white bread
1	pound leeks, white and light green parts only, halved lengthwise, sliced thin, and washed thoroughly
8	ounces sliced smoked salmon
¼	cup minced fresh chives

1. Whisk eggs, half-and-half, ¾ teaspoon salt, and ¼ teaspoon pepper in large bowl.

2. Melt 2 tablespoons butter in 12-inch nonstick skillet over medium heat. Add bread and cook until golden on both sides, 2 to 3 minutes per side. Transfer to plate and tent loosely with aluminum foil. Melt 1 tablespoon butter in now-empty skillet over medium heat. Add leeks and cook until softened, about 5 minutes. Transfer to medium bowl and tent loosely with foil.

3. Melt remaining 1 tablespoon butter in now-empty skillet over medium-high heat. Add egg mixture and cook, using rubber spatula to fold eggs while gently scraping bottom of skillet, until large curds begin to form, 3 to 5 minutes. Off heat, fold in leeks.

4. Spoon eggs over toast. Lay salmon slices over eggs and sprinkle with chives. Serve.

QUICK PREP TIP
SCRAMBLING EGGS
After adding eggs to skillet with melted butter, gently push, lift, and fold eggs from 1 side of skillet to other, using rubber spatula, until large, airy curds have formed.

Chili-Glazed Salmon with Bok Choy

Serves 4

✔ **WHY THIS RECIPE WORKS:** This foolproof recipe brings pan-seared salmon, a restaurant favorite for its irresistible crust and rich flavor, home. We match it with an Asian-inspired glaze and bok choy for a complete meal, which we make using a single skillet. After whisking together our glaze, we brown the bok choy to deepen its flavor and add visual appeal, then set it aside and cook the salmon. Next the glaze goes into the pan and coats the fish. Returning the bok choy to the skillet after setting the fish aside to rest quickly cooks it through and coats it with the remaining sauce. If using farmed salmon, which is fattier than wild, you will likely have to discard excess rendered fat from the pan before making the sauce.

¼ cup Asian sweet chili sauce
 (see page 310)

2 tablespoons fish sauce

1 tablespoon grated fresh ginger

½ teaspoon cornstarch

3 tablespoons vegetable oil

4 heads baby bok choy
 (4 ounces each), halved
 lengthwise

4 (6- to 8-ounce) skinless salmon
 fillets, 1¼ inches thick
 Salt and pepper
 Lime wedges

1. Whisk chili sauce, fish sauce, ginger, and cornstarch together in small bowl. Heat 2 tablespoons oil in 12-inch nonstick skillet over high heat until shimmering. Cook bok choy, cut side down, until lightly browned, 2 to 3 minutes. Turn and continue to cook until lightly browned on second side, about 1 minute. Transfer to platter.

2. Pat salmon dry with paper towels and season with salt and pepper. Add remaining 1 tablespoon oil to now-empty skillet and heat over medium-high heat until just smoking. Cook salmon until browned on both sides and center is still translucent when checked with tip of paring knife and fish registers 125 degrees (for medium-rare), 3 to 4 minutes per side. Pour off any rendered fat in skillet. Add chili sauce mixture to skillet with salmon and flip fish once or twice to coat. Transfer fish to platter.

3. Add bok choy to skillet with glaze and stir until coated. Serve with salmon and lime wedges.

QUICK PREP TIP
CLEANING BABY BOK CHOY
Submerge halved baby bok choy in cold water and then agitate heads to remove any dirt and grit.

Mustard Salmon with Potato-Cabbage Hash

Serves 4

✔ **WHY THIS RECIPE WORKS:** Hash may sound ho-hum, but pairing it with salmon makes this dinner anything but ordinary. Since the hash takes some time to cook, midway through its cooking we put the salmon in the oven to ensure perfect timing. Using shredded cabbage and grated potatoes also speeds the hash along. Topping the salmon with panko (Japanese-style extra-crunchy bread crumbs, available at the supermarket) adds texture, and using whole-grain mustard to bind the panko to the fish contributes a tangy hit of flavor.

3 **tablespoons vegetable oil**

4 **slices bacon, chopped**

1 **onion, chopped**

½ **head green cabbage, cored and shredded (6 cups)**

1 **pound russet potatoes, peeled and grated coarse**
   Salt and pepper

4 **(6- to 8-ounce) skinless salmon fillets, 1¼ inches thick**

¼ **cup whole-grain mustard**

½ **cup panko bread crumbs**

1. Adjust oven rack to upper-middle position and heat oven to 450 degrees. Line rimmed baking sheet with aluminum foil and brush with 2 tablespoons oil; set aside.

2. Cook bacon in 12-inch nonstick skillet over medium-high heat until just beginning to crisp, about 4 minutes. Stir in onion and cook until softened and starting to brown, about 4 minutes. Add cabbage and cook until wilted and starting to brown, about 6 minutes. Add potatoes and remaining 1 tablespoon oil and cook, stirring occasionally, until potatoes are tender and hash is lightly browned, 8 to 12 minutes. Season with salt and pepper to taste, then transfer hash to serving platter.

3. Meanwhile, arrange salmon fillets on prepared baking sheet, skinned side down, and brush tops with mustard. Sprinkle panko over mustard, pressing gently to adhere, then transfer to oven. Bake until crust is golden brown and salmon is still translucent at center when checked with tip of paring knife and fish registers 125 degrees (for medium-rare), about 15 minutes. Transfer salmon to platter with hash and serve.

QUICK PREP TIP HOMEMADE PANKO
For the adventurous cook, or if you can't make it to the store, here's how to make panko at home. Feed crustless white sandwich bread through the largest grating disk of a food processor, then bake the crumbs on a rimmed baking sheet at 300 degrees until dry but not toasted, about 6 minutes. Four slices of bread will make 1⅓ cups panko.

ALL ABOUT Salmon

Wild vs. Farmed Salmon

In season, we've always preferred the more pronounced flavor of wild-caught salmon to farmed Atlantic salmon, traditionally the main farm-raised variety in this country. But with more wild and farmed species now available, we decided to reevaluate. We tasted three kinds of wild Pacific salmon and two farmed. We love the generally stronger flavor of wild-caught fish. But if you're going to spend the extra money, make sure it looks and smells fresh, and realize that high quality is available only from late spring through the end of summer.

Salmon and Gray Matter

You might notice that some salmon fillets have a thin layer of gray matter between the skin and the flesh. This layer is a fatty deposit rich in omega-3 fatty acids and low in the natural pink pigments found in the flesh. To get a handle on how the gray area affects flavor, we oven-roasted several salmon fillets, then removed the gray portion from half of them and left it intact on the others. Only a few discerning tasters noted that the samples with the gray substance had an ever-so-slightly fishier flavor; most couldn't tell the difference. It's easy enough to remove the gray stuff by peeling off the skin of the cooked salmon and then scraping it away with the back of a knife, but the flavor difference is so minor that we don't think it's worth the hassle.

Ensuring Evenly Cooked Salmon Fillets

There are several cuts of salmon available: thin, tail-piece fillets; thicker fillets cut from the head end or center of the fish; bone-in steaks; and boneless steaks. We most often go for the thicker fillets, since they are thick enough to sear nicely without overcooking, and they're easy to skin. You can buy proportioned fillets, but if you have just a minute or two extra to spare, it's best to buy one large salmon fillet and cut it into equal-size pieces yourself, which will ensure even cooking. To serve four, buy a fillet that is 1½ to 2 pounds and about 1½ inches at the thickest part.

Skinning Salmon

Using the tip of a sharp knife, begin to cut the skin away from the fish at the corner of the fillet. Grasp the exposed skin firmly with a piece of paper towel, hold it taut, and carefully slice the flesh off of the skin.

Removing Pinbones

Even if you are buying skinned fillets, there is still a chance that a few pinbones, the small white bones that run through the center of the fillet, have been left behind. Run your fingers gently over the surface to locate any bones (they will feel like tiny bumps). Grasp the bone with a pair of clean needle-nose pliers or tweezers, then pull gently to remove.

Skillet Shrimp and Orzo with Feta

Serves 4

✔ **WHY THIS RECIPE WORKS:** With shrimp cooked in an ouzo-spiked tomato sauce and topped with feta and fresh dill, this recipe gets its inspiration from the classic Greek dish known as shrimp saganaki. By adding orzo to the pan, we turn this classic into a complete skillet meal. It all comes together quickly. We cook the orzo like a quick risotto, using a skillet and no extra pot of boiling water so it's done with minimal fuss in less than 15 minutes. First we cook aromatics, then add orzo to the pan. Allowing the orzo to cook in the tomato sauce ensures efficiency and nicely melded flavors. Once the orzo is al dente, we add the shrimp and cheese and finish the recipe under the broiler. Look for sheep's- or goat's-milk feta for this recipe to ensure the best flavor. You will need an ovensafe skillet for this recipe.

1½	pounds jumbo shrimp (16 to 20 per pound), peeled and deveined
3	tablespoons extra-virgin olive oil
3	tablespoons ouzo
5	garlic cloves, minced
	Salt and pepper
1	onion, chopped
½	teaspoon red pepper flakes
1½	cups orzo
1	(28-ounce) can diced tomatoes
1½	cups water
4	ounces feta cheese, crumbled (1 cup)
2	tablespoons chopped fresh dill

1. Position oven rack 5 inches from broiler element and heat broiler. Toss shrimp, 1 tablespoon oil, 1 tablespoon ouzo, 1 teaspoon garlic, ¼ teaspoon salt, and ⅛ teaspoon pepper in bowl.

2. Heat remaining 2 tablespoons oil in 12-inch ovensafe skillet over medium-high heat until shimmering. Add onion and cook until softened, about 4 minutes. Add remaining garlic and pepper flakes and cook until fragrant, about 30 seconds. Add orzo and cook, stirring occasionally, until golden brown, about 2 minutes. Add remaining 2 tablespoons ouzo and cook until evaporated, about 30 seconds. Stir in tomatoes and water and cook, stirring frequently, until liquid is absorbed and orzo is al dente, 10 to 12 minutes. Season with salt and pepper to taste.

3. Scatter shrimp and cheese over orzo. Transfer skillet to oven and broil until shrimp are cooked and cheese is melted, 4 to 6 minutes. Sprinkle with dill and serve.

SMART SHOPPING OUZO

Ouzo, the popular anise-flavored spirit of Greece, lends shrimp saganaki, the inspiration for this 30-minute recipe, a nuanced anise flavor that adds depth to the dish. But since ouzo is not a bottle that everyone keeps stocked in their liquor cabinet, we found a few alternatives that will work just fine in this recipe. Our testing showed that, though slightly sweeter than ouzo, the French anise-flavored liqueur known as Pernod is the next best thing. We found that you can also substitute 1 tablespoon vodka plus a large pinch of anise seeds for the ouzo in the marinade, and 2 tablespoons vodka plus ¼ teaspoon anise seeds for the ouzo in the sauce. But note that because of the whole anise seeds, some bites of this recipe will be more anise-packed than others.

Spicy Shrimp with Corn Cakes

Serves 4

✔ **WHY THIS RECIPE WORKS:** When you tire of boiling, roasting, or grilling your fresh summer corn, this Southwestern-inspired recipe pairing savory, rustic corn cakes with chili-spiced shrimp is a great option. The cakes are easy to make: We stir together a simple batter using fresh corn kernels, egg, buttermilk, flour, and cornmeal (which reinforces the fresh corn's flavor and adds texture), plus a hint of chili powder and baking soda for lift. The batter cooks in minutes in a skillet just like pancakes. Once the corn cakes are done, the shrimp, spiced with more chili powder plus cumin, goes into the skillet. Finally, a few tablespoons of lime juice add brightness that takes this dish to the next level.

¾   **cup all-purpose flour**

½   **cup cornmeal**

2½   **teaspoons chili powder**

½   **teaspoon baking soda**

    Salt and pepper

1¼   **cups buttermilk**

1   **large egg**

2   **ears corn, kernels cut from cobs**

1½   **pounds extra-large shrimp (21 to 25 per pound), peeled and deveined**

5   **tablespoons olive oil**

1   **teaspoon ground cumin**

2   **tablespoons lime juice**

1. Adjust oven rack to middle position, place rimmed baking sheet on rack, and heat oven to 200 degrees. Whisk flour, cornmeal, ½ teaspoon chili powder, baking soda, ¾ teaspoon salt, and ¼ teaspoon pepper in medium bowl. Whisk buttermilk and egg in another bowl. Stir wet ingredients into dry until just combined. Stir in corn.

2. Pat shrimp dry with paper towels and toss with 2 tablespoons oil, remaining 2 teaspoons chili powder, cumin, ½ teaspoon salt, and ¼ teaspoon pepper.

3. Heat 1 tablespoon oil in 12-inch nonstick skillet over medium heat until shimmering. Pour four ¼-cup portions batter into skillet and cook until cakes are lightly browned on both sides, about 3 minutes per side. Transfer cakes to oven. Repeat with 1 tablespoon oil and remaining batter.

4. In now-empty skillet, heat remaining 1 tablespoon oil over medium-high heat until just smoking. Add shrimp and cook until browned in spots and opaque throughout, 40 to 60 seconds per side. Stir in lime juice. Serve shrimp with corn cakes.

SIMPLE SIDE TOMATILLO SALSA

Bring 2 quarts water to boil in large saucepan. Add 2 teaspoons salt and 1 pound tomatillos and cook until tender but not mushy, about 8 minutes. Meanwhile, fill large bowl with ice water. Drain tomatillos, transfer to bowl with ice water, and let cool for 5 minutes. Drain tomatillos and transfer to food processor. Add ½ cup chopped onion, ½ cup fresh cilantro leaves, 1 stemmed, seeded, and chopped jalapeño chile, 1 tablespoon lime juice, 1 clove minced garlic, and ½ teaspoon salt and pulse until coarsely chopped, about 7 pulses. Serves 4.

Sautéed Shrimp with Artichokes and Mushrooms

Serves 4

✔ **WHY THIS RECIPE WORKS:** Matching grassy artichokes and briny shrimp is a great start for this stream-lined one-dish meal, while adding mushrooms to the mix lends heartiness. To give the shrimp a flavor boost, we marinate them with garlic and pepper flakes before pan-searing them. We brown the mushrooms in a hot skillet, followed by the artichokes, then set the vegetables aside to cook the shrimp. Once the shrimp are done, we enrich white wine, reduced in the skillet for concentrated flavor, with a few pats of butter. Finally we stir the shrimp and vegetables into the sauce. We like to serve this meal over Easy White Rice (page 22).

2	pounds extra-large shrimp (21 to 25 per pound), peeled, deveined, and tails removed
	Salt and pepper
¼	cup olive oil
3	garlic cloves, minced
½	teaspoon red pepper flakes
10	ounces white or cremini mushrooms, trimmed and quartered
9	ounces frozen artichoke hearts, thawed
½	cup dry white wine
3	tablespoons unsalted butter, cut into 3 pieces
2	tablespoons minced fresh parsley

1. Pat shrimp dry with paper towels and season with salt and pepper. Combine shrimp, 1 tablespoon oil, garlic, and pepper flakes in medium bowl. Cover and refrigerate for 15 minutes.

2. Meanwhile, heat 1 tablespoon oil in 12-inch nonstick skillet over medium-high heat until shimmering. Add mushrooms and cook until browned, 6 to 8 minutes. Add artichokes and cook until lightly browned, about 3 minutes. Transfer vegetables to medium bowl and tent loosely with aluminum foil.

3. Heat 1 tablespoon oil in now-empty skillet over medium-high heat until just smoking. Add half of shrimp and cook, without moving, until spotty brown on first side, about 1 minute. Transfer shrimp to bowl with vegetables. Repeat with remaining 1 tablespoon oil and remaining shrimp. Add wine to now-empty skillet and simmer until reduced to ⅓ cup, 1 to 2 minutes. Whisk in butter until smooth. Stir in vegetable-shrimp mixture and parsley and simmer until shrimp are opaque throughout, 1 to 2 minutes. Serve.

SMART SHOPPING WHITE VS. BROWN MUSHROOMS
Though slightly different in appearance, white (near right) and cremini (far right) mushrooms belong to the same species. But does the loss of color mean a loss of flavor? To find out, we sautéed white and cremini mushrooms and tasted them in risotto and on pizza. The flavor of the cremini was notice-ably deeper and more complex. This difference in taste was also apparent, though less obvious, when we compared both types sprinkled raw over salads. If bolder mushroom flavor is what you're after, it's worth shelling out a little extra for cremini.

Seared Scallops with Squash Puree and Sage Butter

Serves 4

✓ **WHY THIS RECIPE WORKS:** It doesn't take long to pan-sear a batch of scallops; the success of this recipe lies in the accompaniments. Butternut squash, which we simply microwave and puree with a little half-and-half, butter, and seasoning, is a side that brings out the sweet flavor of the scallops. Once we make the squash puree, we pan-sear the scallops (in two batches to ensure perfect browning), then make a quick shallot-sage browned butter sauce in the same pan.

2	pounds butternut squash, peeled, seeded, and cut into 1-inch chunks (5½ cups)
1	tablespoon half-and-half
4	tablespoons unsalted butter
	Salt and pepper
⅛	teaspoon cayenne pepper
1½	pounds large sea scallops, tendons removed
2	tablespoons vegetable oil
1	shallot, minced
2	teaspoons minced fresh sage plus 8 whole sage leaves
1	tablespoon lemon juice

1. Place squash in bowl, cover, and microwave until tender, 8 to 12 minutes, stirring halfway through cooking. Drain, then transfer to food processor. Add half-and-half, 1 tablespoon butter, ½ teaspoon salt, and cayenne and process until smooth, about 20 seconds. Return to bowl and cover to keep warm.

2. Pat scallops dry with paper towels and season with salt and pepper. Heat 1 tablespoon oil in 12-inch nonstick skillet over high heat until just smoking. Add half of scallops and cook, without moving, until well browned, 1½ to 2 minutes. Flip scallops and cook until sides are firm and centers are opaque, 30 to 90 seconds. Transfer to plate and tent loosely with aluminum foil. Wipe out skillet with paper towels and repeat with remaining 1 tablespoon oil and remaining scallops. Transfer to plate with first batch.

3. Heat remaining 3 tablespoons butter over medium heat, swirling skillet constantly, until butter is starting to brown and has nutty aroma, about 1 minute. Add shallot, minced sage, and sage leaves and cook until fragrant, about 1 minute. Off heat, stir in lemon juice and season with salt and pepper to taste. Pour sauce over scallops and serve with butternut squash.

SMART SHOPPING BUTTERNUT SQUASH

Sure, it saves prep time to buy precut, peeled butternut squash, but we had to wonder: How does the flavor and texture of this time-saving squash stand up to a whole squash we cut up ourselves? Whole squash you peel and cube yourself can't be beat in terms of flavor and texture. That said, when you are trying to make the most of every minute, the peeled, halved squash is acceptable, and we found that it performed admirably in test recipes. However, avoid precut chunks; our tasters agree they are dry and stringy, with barely any squash flavor.

Pan-Seared Scallops with Bacon Succotash

Serves 4

✓ **WHY THIS RECIPE WORKS:** Matching pan-seared scallops with a bacon-infused succotash gives this recipe a Southern flair. The recipe comes together quickly; you cook the bacon, then the scallops, and finally the succotash all in one skillet. Browning the scallops in the rendered bacon fat is a clever yet easy way to enrich the dish and unify the flavors, and the combination of fresh plum tomatoes and corn just off the cob, plus a finish of fresh snipped chives, make this a truly summery recipe. The lima beans lend a Southern feel here, but you can use peas if preferred. We like fresh corn in this recipe, but you can substitute 2 cups frozen corn for the fresh.

4	slices bacon, chopped
1½	pounds large sea scallops, tendons removed
	Salt and pepper
1	onion, chopped fine
3	garlic cloves, minced
4	ears corn, kernels cut from cobs
1	cup frozen lima beans, thawed
2	plum tomatoes, seeded and diced
2	tablespoons unsalted butter
¼	cup chopped fresh chives

1. Cook bacon in 12-inch nonstick skillet over medium-high heat until crisp, about 5 minutes. Transfer bacon to paper towel–lined plate and pour off all but 2 tablespoons fat from skillet.

2. Pat scallops dry with paper towels and season with salt and pepper. Cook scallops in fat left in skillet over high heat until deep golden brown, 1½ to 2 minutes. Flip scallops and cook until sides are firm and centers are opaque, 30 to 90 seconds. Transfer to serving platter and tent loosely with aluminum foil.

3. Add onion and garlic to now-empty skillet and cook until softened, about 3 minutes. Add corn, lima beans, and tomatoes and cook until heated through, stirring frequently, 3 to 5 minutes. Add butter and any accumulated juices from scallops and stir until butter is just melted. Off heat, stir in chives and bacon and season with salt and pepper to taste. Serve with scallops.

SMART SHOPPING SCALLOPS

You may have noticed scallops labeled as "dry," but what exactly does this mean? Some scallops are dipped in a phosphate-water mixture to extend their shelf life; these are known as "wet" scallops. Dry scallops taste fresher and develop a better crust when browned since they aren't pumped full of water, so they're always our top choice. When you are at the market, remember that unprocessed (dry) scallops have a natural ivory or pinkish hue rather than the stark white of wet scallops.

Steamed Mussels with Chorizo and Garlic Crostini

Serves 4

✔ **WHY THIS RECIPE WORKS:** Mussels are a bistro favorite that cook in minutes, and in this recipe we give them a hearty Spanish twist with the help of saffron and spicy chorizo sausage. Leeks, tomatoes, wine, and parsley combine to add fresh flavors and a well-rounded brightness. We really deepen the flavor of the mussels' cooking liquid with two simple tricks. First, we brown the chorizo in the pan before adding the liquid, then set the sausage aside to use as a garnish and cook the aromatics in the rendered fat. Second, we simmer the liquid for a few minutes to concentrate the flavors before adding the mussels.

1 (6-inch) piece baguette, sliced ½ inch thick

3 garlic cloves, peeled (1 whole, 2 minced)

2 tablespoons olive oil

½ pound Spanish chorizo sausage, sliced ½ inch thick

1 pound leeks, white and light green parts only, chopped and washed thoroughly

½ teaspoon red pepper flakes

½ teaspoon saffron

¾ cup dry white wine

2 (14.5-ounce) cans diced tomatoes

4 pounds mussels, scrubbed and debearded

¼ cup chopped fresh parsley

1. Adjust oven rack to middle position and heat oven to 400 degrees. Arrange bread slices on baking sheet. Bake until bread is dry and crisp, 10 to 12 minutes, flipping slices halfway through baking. While still warm, rub 1 side of each toast with peeled garlic clove, then drizzle with 1 tablespoon oil.

2. Meanwhile, heat remaining 1 tablespoon oil in Dutch oven over medium-high heat until shimmering. Add chorizo and cook until crisp and browned, about 4 minutes. Using slotted spoon, transfer chorizo to paper towel-lined plate. Add leeks to pot and cook until softened, about 3 minutes. Add minced garlic, pepper flakes, and saffron and cook until fragrant, about 30 seconds. Add wine and simmer until reduced by half, 3 to 5 minutes. Add tomatoes, reduce heat to medium, cover, and simmer until tomatoes are soft, about 4 minutes.

3. Add mussels to pot and cook, covered and stirring occasionally, until mussels open, 4 to 8 minutes. Using slotted spoon, transfer mussels to individual serving bowls. Stir parsley into broth in pot and pour over mussels. Top each serving with crisped chorizo and serve with crostini.

SMART SHOPPING CHORIZO

There are several styles of chorizo sausage, the two most common being Spanish and Mexican. Spanish (top) is generally sold cured and cooked. Its smoky flavor comes from smoked paprika, and it can be sweet or hot. Mexican chorizo (bottom) is almost always sold raw. Chili powder gives it a spicy, coffeelike flavor. The two styles are not interchangeable; Spanish chorizo is eaten as is or stirred into dishes like paella or *tortilla española,* while Mexican chorizo is typically removed from its casing and cooked like ground meat.

TOFU PARMESAN

Vegetarian Entrées

188   Tofu Parmesan

189   Glazed Caribbean Tofu with Rice and Pigeon Peas

191   Vegetable Tagine with Chickpeas and Olives

193   Crispy Potato Pierogi with Mushroom Ragout

194   Jasmine Rice Cakes with Vegetable Thai Green Curry

195   Couscous Patties with Beet-Yogurt Sauce

196   Couscous-Stuffed Acorn Squash

198   Butternut, Poblano, and Cheese Quesadillas

199   Skillet Summer Vegetable Tamale Pie

200   Cheesy Skillet Polenta and Eggplant Bake

202   Ricotta, Basil, and Summer Squash Frittata

203   Spicy Tomato and Pepper Sauce–Poached Eggs

205   Parmesan French Toast with Tomato-Basil Topping

206   Fennel, Olive, and Goat Cheese Tarts

207   White Bean Panzanella

Tofu Parmesan

Serves 4

✔ **WHY THIS RECIPE WORKS:** This dish puts a creative, vegetarian spin on Chicken Parmesan. Draining the tofu first ensures the coating won't turn soggy. For the coating, plenty of Parmesan and ground black pepper give it a flavor boost, and panko guarantees it's extra-crisp. It only takes a few minutes in the skillet for the coating to crisp and the tofu to warm through. While the tofu drains we make our sauce, then after cooking the coated tofu we top each piece with sauce and cheese and run it quickly under the broiler. Serve with Broccoli with Balsamic Vinaigrette (page 237).

2 **(14-ounce) blocks extra-firm tofu, each cut crosswise into 8 planks**

1 **tablespoon plus ½ cup vegetable oil**

4 **garlic cloves, minced**

1 **(14.5-ounce) can diced tomatoes**

¼ **cup shredded fresh basil**
Salt and pepper

2 **large eggs**

1 **cup panko bread crumbs**

2 **ounces Parmesan cheese, grated (1 cup)**

4 **ounces mozzarella cheese, shredded (1 cup)**

1. Adjust oven rack 5 inches from broiler element and heat broiler. Set wire rack in rimmed baking sheet; set aside. Lay tofu slices in single layer on top of several layers of paper towels, cover with several more layers, and top with rimmed baking sheet. Set heavy skillet or Dutch oven on baking sheet and let tofu drain for 10 minutes.

2. Meanwhile, heat 1 tablespoon oil in medium saucepan over medium-high heat until shimmering. Add garlic and cook until fragrant, about 30 seconds. Stir in tomatoes and simmer until slightly thickened, about 7 minutes. Mash mixture with potato masher until only small chunks of tomato remain. Stir in basil and season with salt and pepper to taste. Cover to keep warm; set aside.

3. Beat eggs in shallow dish. Combine panko, Parmesan, and ½ teaspoon pepper in second shallow dish. Season tofu with salt. Working with 1 piece of tofu at a time, dip into egg, then coat with panko mixture, pressing gently to adhere.

4. Heat ¼ cup oil in 12-inch ovensafe nonstick skillet over medium heat until shimmering. Add half of tofu to skillet and cook until golden brown, 2 to 3 minutes per side. Transfer to prepared wire rack. Wipe out skillet and repeat with remaining ¼ cup oil and remaining tofu. Top each tofu slice with 1 tablespoon tomato sauce and 1 tablespoon mozzarella, then transfer to oven and broil until cheese is melted and spotty brown, about 2 minutes. Serve.

Glazed Caribbean Tofu with Rice and Pigeon Peas

Serves 4

☑ **WHY THIS RECIPE WORKS:** A glaze made with curry and pineapple preserves, brightened with a little lime juice, ensures this tofu is anything but mild mannered, and it takes just minutes to cook on the stovetop. While the tofu drains, we get our rice side dish going in a saucepan. Enriching the rice's cooking liquid with coconut milk makes it a creamy, rich companion for the spicy-sweet tofu, and adding onion, jalapeño, and pigeon peas lends complementary flavor, texture, and heartiness. Kidney beans or black-eyed peas can be substituted for the pigeon peas.

2   **(14-ounce) blocks firm tofu, cut lengthwise in half, and each half cut crosswise into 6 pieces**
    Salt and pepper
1   **tablespoon curry powder**
¼   **cup vegetable oil**
1   **onion, diced**
2   **jalapeño chiles, stemmed, seeded, and chopped**
1½ **cups long-grain rice**
1   **(15-ounce) can pigeon peas, rinsed**
1   **(14-ounce) can coconut milk**
1   **cup plus 3 tablespoons water**
½   **cup pineapple preserves**
2   **tablespoons lime juice**
¼   **teaspoon red pepper flakes**

1. Lay tofu pieces in single layer on top of several layers of paper towels, cover with several more layers, and top with rimmed baking sheet. Set heavy skillet or Dutch oven on baking sheet and let tofu drain for 10 minutes. Gently press tofu dry with paper towels, season with salt and pepper, and sprinkle with curry powder.

2. Meanwhile, heat 2 tablespoons oil in large saucepan over medium-high heat, add onion and jalapeños and cook until softened, about 3 minutes. Add rice and cook until opaque, about 1 minute. Stir in peas, coconut milk, 1 cup water, and 1 teaspoon salt. Bring to boil, cover, and cook over low heat until rice is tender, about 20 minutes. Season with salt and pepper to taste.

3. Place preserves in medium bowl and microwave until bubbling, about 1 minute. Whisk in remaining 3 tablespoons water, lime juice, and red pepper flakes.

4. Heat 1 tablespoon oil in 12-inch nonstick skillet over medium-high heat until just smoking. Add half of tofu and cook, turning occasionally, until golden, about 6 minutes. Transfer tofu to plate and tent loosely with aluminum foil. Repeat with remaining 1 tablespoon oil and remaining tofu. Return first batch to skillet, add glaze, and toss to coat. Simmer until glaze has thickened, about 1 minute. Serve with rice.

SMART SHOPPING PIGEON PEAS
These legumes, the size of a standard garden pea, are native to Africa, making them a good fit for this Caribbean-inspired recipe. Pigeon peas, which are also popular in the American South, can be found dried, fresh, frozen, and canned in most supermarkets, and you'll also find them in Latin American and Indian markets.

ALL ABOUT Canned Beans

As an affordable meatless source of lean protein, beans have long been a staple on the vegetarian shopping list. While we believe dried beans offer superior flavor and texture, they require presoaking and long cooking times—not a good option for the weeknight table. Canned beans are the convenient alternative, and we've had plenty of success using them in a variety of recipes. However, flavor and texture can vary widely from brand to brand, so for the best results, stick with our favorite staple varieties, as listed here, when possible.

Black Beans

Most canned black beans have three main ingredients: beans, water, and salt. Still, we found when we sampled six national brands that taste can vary wildly. Our tasters had a strong preference for well-seasoned beans, but texture was important, too. The "clean," "mild," and "slightly earthy" flavor of **Bush's Best Black Beans**, along with their "firm," "almost al dente" texture made them our winner.

White Beans

Whether labeled cannellini, great Northern, or navy, white beans are versatile and always good to have on hand. We found nationally available varieties ranged from sweet to bland and chalky to mushy. Our favorite was **Westbrae Natural Organic Great Northern Beans** (left), which won for their earthy flavor and creamy texture. **Progresso Cannellini Beans** (right) took second; tasters liked their "plump shape" and "sweet, slightly salty" flavor.

Kidney Beans

These firm, full-flavored beans are a classic in chili and are often found in variations on red beans and rice. Tasting them straight from the can and in chili, we noticed substantial differences in texture and flavor among brands. While some tasted mushy, chalky, and bland, **Goya Dark Kidney Beans** were described as beautiful and plump with a sweet, strong bean flavor.

Refried Beans

Traditional *frijoles refritos* start with dried pinto beans that are cooked, "fried well" in lard, then mashed. While making them isn't hard, it is time-consuming. We sampled six brands of canned refried beans to determine if any were worth buying. In the end, none could replace homemade, but we recommend **Taco Bell Home Originals Refried Beans** with reservations, acceptable to use when pressed for time.

Chickpeas

Popular particularly in Mediterranean, Middle Eastern, and Indian cuisines, canned chickpeas are a favorite among canned beans in the test kitchen since they hold up well to cooking. Our tasters found that many brands are bland or have bitter and metallic flavors. They preferred those that were well seasoned and had a creamy yet "al dente" texture. **Pastene Chickpeas** came out on top.

Why We Rinse Canned Beans

Canned beans are made by pressure-cooking dried beans directly in the can with water, salt, and preservatives. As the beans cook, starches and proteins leach into the liquid, thickening it. To find out if rinsing the beans is really necessary, we used canned beans in two recipes: chickpeas for hummus and red kidney beans for chili. Tasters found no difference in the chili; there are so many bold flavors and contrasting textures in this dish that rinsing the beans didn't matter. However, we detected notable differences in the hummus. Most tasters thought the version with rinsed beans was brighter in flavor and less pasty than the version with unrinsed beans. So while rinsing the beans may not be necessary for a robust dish like chili, a thick, salty bean liquid does have the potential to throw a simpler recipe off-kilter. And rinsing beans takes only a few seconds, so there's no excuse not to do it.

Vegetable Tagine with Chickpeas and Olives

Serves 4

✔ **WHY THIS RECIPE WORKS:** Traditional North African tagines—fragrant, spiced stews of vegetables, beans, dried fruits, and slowly braised meats—are long-simmered affairs with myriad ingredients. Making a vegetarian tagine means there isn't a tough cut of meat that needs to be slowly cooked, making this an inherently faster take on the dish. Microwaving the potatoes and carrots before adding them to the pot further streamlines the process. Some tagines call for a laundry list of spices; we use garam masala, a convenient and readily available blend of several spices, plus paprika. Adding olives and lemon zest and juice rounds out the Moroccan flavors.

1   **pound red potatoes, cut into ½-inch pieces**

1   **pound carrots, peeled and cut into ½-inch pieces**

¼   **cup extra-virgin olive oil**
     Salt and pepper

1   **onion, halved and sliced thin**

6   **(2-inch-long) strips lemon zest, cut into matchsticks, plus 2 tablespoons juice**

5   **garlic cloves, minced**

4   **teaspoons paprika**

2   **teaspoons garam masala**

3   **cups vegetable broth**

2   **(15-ounce) cans chickpeas, rinsed**

1   **cup Greek cracked green olives, pitted and halved**

1. Combine potatoes, carrots, 2 tablespoons oil, 1 teaspoon salt, and ½ teaspoon pepper in large bowl. Cover and microwave until vegetables begin to soften, about 10 minutes.

2. Meanwhile, heat remaining 2 tablespoons oil in Dutch oven over medium-high heat until shimmering. Add onion and lemon zest and cook, stirring occasionally, until onion begins to brown around edges, 5 to 7 minutes. Add garlic, paprika, and garam masala and cook until fragrant, about 1 minute.

3. Add potatoes and carrots to pot and stir to coat with spice mixture. Stir in broth, chickpeas, and olives and bring to simmer. Reduce heat to medium, cover, and cook for 10 minutes. Remove lid and cook until vegetables are tender and sauce is slightly thickened, 6 to 8 minutes. Stir in lemon juice, season with salt and pepper to taste, and serve.

SIMPLE SIDE APRICOT-CILANTRO COUSCOUS
Combine one 10-ounce box plain couscous (about 1½ cups), ⅓ cup chopped dried apricots, and 1 teaspoon salt in medium bowl. Pour 2 cups boiling water over mixture, add 1 tablespoon extra-virgin olive oil, and stir to combine. Cover bowl tightly with plastic wrap and let sit until liquid is absorbed and couscous is tender, about 5 minutes. Fluff couscous with fork, stir in ½ cup chopped fresh cilantro, and season with salt and pepper to taste. Serves 4.

Crispy Potato Pierogi with Mushroom Ragout

Serves 4

✔ **WHY THIS RECIPE WORKS:** Frozen pierogi are a convenient alternative to making homemade, a laborious endeavor few of us have time to take on. Instead of boiling the pierogi and then pan-frying them as most recipes direct, we save time by baking them in the oven while we make a hearty mushroom ragout on the stovetop to serve with them. Brushing the pierogi with butter first encourages browning and gives them flavor. For a heady ragout that doesn't require a lot of time (or a meat product like bacon), we use both fresh and dried mushrooms, and we use the liquid exuded by the cremini to rehydrate the porcini so no flavor is lost. We microwave the cremini and the porcini in two stages, then they go into a skillet with thyme, shallots, and Marsala, followed by cream for richness and chives for a fresh finish.

2 tablespoons unsalted butter, plus 2 tablespoons melted

2 (16-ounce) packages frozen potato-onion pierogi

2 pounds cremini mushrooms, trimmed and sliced thin

½ cup dried porcini mushrooms, rinsed

2 shallots, minced

1 tablespoon minced fresh thyme
   Salt and pepper

½ cup dry Marsala

½ cup sour cream

⅓ cup chopped fresh chives

1. Adjust oven rack to middle position and heat oven to 500 degrees. Brush rimmed baking sheet with 1 tablespoon melted butter and arrange pierogi in single layer. Brush pierogi with remaining 1 tablespoon melted butter and bake, flipping halfway through baking, until spotty golden brown, about 15 minutes.

2. Meanwhile, place cremini mushrooms in bowl, cover, and microwave until mushrooms have exuded their liquid, about 5 minutes. Drain cremini, reserving liquid in measuring cup. Add water to reserved liquid to make 1 cup total, then return liquid to now-empty bowl. Add porcini mushrooms, cover, and microwave until rehydrated, about 3 minutes. Line fine-mesh strainer with paper towels and strain porcini, reserving liquid, then chop porcini.

3. Melt 2 tablespoons butter in 12-inch skillet over medium-high heat, add cremini and chopped porcini mushrooms, distribute in single layer, and cook, stirring once halfway through cooking, until deep golden, about 6 minutes. Add shallots, thyme, ½ teaspoon salt, and ¼ teaspoon pepper to skillet and cook until softened, about 1 minute. Add reserved mushroom liquid and Marsala, increase heat to high, and simmer, scraping up any browned bits, until liquid is thickened, about 5 minutes. Off heat, stir in sour cream and half of chives and season with salt and pepper to taste. Toss pierogi with remaining chives and serve over mushroom ragout.

Jasmine Rice Cakes with Vegetable Thai Green Curry

Serves 4

✓ **WHY THIS RECIPE WORKS:** Rice graduates from side dish to starring role in this fresh, summery recipe. We turn precooked jasmine rice from the supermarket into cakes by combining it with egg, flour, and seasoning. Pulsing half of the rice in the food processor first helps these cakes hold together without turning them pasty, and browning them in a hot skillet gives them great textural contrast. Once they are cooked and set aside, we use the same skillet to make a light, flavorful coconut curry sauce featuring peas and zucchini. It's critical for the rice to be hot before you form it into patties. Otherwise, it will be too dry to hold shape.

2	(8.8-ounce) packages Uncle Ben's Jasmine Ready Rice
1	large egg
2	tablespoons all-purpose flour
¾	teaspoon salt
½	teaspoon pepper
2	tablespoons vegetable oil
1	(14-ounce) can coconut milk
3	tablespoons Thai green curry paste
2	tablespoons fish sauce
1	tablespoon packed brown sugar
2	zucchini, cut into ¾-inch pieces
1	cup frozen peas
4	teaspoons lime juice
	Chopped fresh basil, mint, and/or cilantro

1. Cut slits in rice package and microwave until rice is hot, about 90 seconds. Pulse 1 package microwaved rice in food processor until coarsely ground, about 12 pulses. Transfer to bowl and mix with remaining rice, egg, flour, salt, and pepper. With wet hands, form mixture into 4 patties.

2. Heat oil in 12-inch nonstick skillet over medium-high heat until shimmering. Add patties and cook until golden brown and crisp, about 3 minutes per side. Transfer to plate and tent loosely with aluminum foil.

3. Whisk coconut milk, curry paste, fish sauce, and sugar in now-empty skillet and bring to simmer over medium heat. Add zucchini and peas and cook until vegetables are tender and sauce is thickened, about 6 minutes. Off heat, stir in lime juice. Serve curry with rice cakes garnished with chopped herbs.

SMART SHOPPING THAI GREEN CURRY PASTE
Curry paste, which can be either green or red depending on the type of chile peppers used, is key for adding deep flavor to Thai curries. It's a lot of work to make from scratch since it uses a number of hard-to-find ingredients like lemon grass, kaffir lime leaves, and shrimp paste. We've found that store-bought curry paste does a fine job and saves significant shopping and prep time. It is usually sold in small jars next to other Thai ingredients at the supermarket. Be aware that these pastes can vary in spiciness depending on the brand, so use more or less as desired.

Couscous Patties with Beet-Yogurt Sauce

Serves 4

✔ **WHY THIS RECIPE WORKS:** To create a light yet satisfying spring dinner, we flavor couscous with herbs, stir in crushed peas, and form the mixture into patties. Then we fry the patties until they're crisp and golden on the outside and delicate and moist on the inside. A tangy, colorful no-cook sauce made with Greek yogurt, garlic, beets, and plenty of fresh mint and dill adds contrast in terms of color and flavor. Grating the beets for the sauce adds texture and avoids the need to cook them first. Thick, Greek-style yogurt is a must to ensure the sauce has the proper consistency; do not try to substitute regular yogurt or the sauce will be too thin.

1	cup couscous
	Salt and pepper
1¼	cups boiling water
1	cup plain Greek yogurt
1	small beet, peeled and grated on large holes of box grater
2	garlic cloves, minced
2	tablespoons chopped fresh mint
2	tablespoons chopped fresh dill
1	cup frozen peas, thawed
1	large egg plus 1 large yolk
2	tablespoons all-purpose flour
¼	cup olive oil

1. Combine couscous and 1 teaspoon salt in small bowl, pour boiling water over couscous, cover, and let sit for 5 minutes. Meanwhile, mix yogurt, beet, garlic, 1 tablespoon mint, and 1 tablespoon dill in medium bowl. Season with salt and pepper to taste.

2. Using potato masher, coarsely mash peas in large bowl. Mix in remaining 1 tablespoon mint, remaining 1 tablespoon dill, egg and yolk, flour, couscous, and ¼ teaspoon pepper.

3. Pack ⅓-cup measure with couscous mixture, smooth top, then invert measuring cup onto baking sheet. Repeat with remaining couscous mixture to make 7 more patties. Heat 2 tablespoons oil in 12-inch nonstick skillet over medium-high heat until shimmering. Transfer 4 patties to skillet and, using spatula, gently flatten to ¾-inch thickness. Cook until golden brown and crisp, about 3 minutes per side, and transfer to serving platter (if couscous is browning too quickly, lower heat). Repeat with remaining 2 tablespoons oil and remaining 4 patties. Serve with beet-yogurt sauce.

QUICK PREP TIP
MAKING COUSCOUS PATTIES
Invert ⅓-cup measure of couscous mixture onto baking sheet. Repeat to make 8 patties total. Heat 2 tablespoons oil in 12-inch nonstick skillet over medium-high heat until shimmering. Add patties to skillet and, using spatula, gently flatten patties until they are ¾ inch thick. Cook until golden and crisp, about 3 minutes per side.

Couscous-Stuffed Acorn Squash

Serves 4

✓ **WHY THIS RECIPE WORKS:** Buttery, dense acorn squash is perfect for a hearty stuffed vegetable entrée. Microwaving the squash before stuffing means once stuffed, they just need a quick run under the broiler to brown. Preparing the couscous filling while the squash are in the microwave keeps this recipe on track.

2	acorn squash (1½ pounds each), halved pole to pole and seeded
3	tablespoons olive oil
	Salt and pepper
1	cup couscous
½	cup golden raisins
1	cup boiling water
1	onion, chopped fine
4	garlic cloves, minced
6	ounces (6 cups) baby spinach
½	cup pine nuts, toasted
1½	ounces Pecorino Romano cheese, grated (¾ cup)

1. Position oven rack about 8 inches from broiler element and heat broiler. Coat cut sides of squash with 1 tablespoon oil, season with salt and pepper, and place flesh side down on large plate. Cover and microwave until flesh is softened, 12 to 16 minutes.

2. Meanwhile, combine couscous, raisins, and 1 teaspoon salt in medium bowl. Pour boiling water over couscous, add 1 tablespoon oil, and stir to combine. Cover tightly with plastic wrap and let sit until liquid is absorbed and couscous is tender, about 5 minutes. Fluff couscous with fork and set aside.

3. Heat remaining 1 tablespoon oil in 12-inch skillet over medium-high heat until shimmering. Add onion and cook until softened, about 5 minutes. Add garlic and cook until fragrant, about 30 seconds. Add spinach and cook until wilted and most of liquid has evaporated, about 2 minutes. Off heat, stir in couscous mixture, pine nuts, and ½ cup Pecorino. Season with salt and pepper to taste.

4. Transfer squash, cut side up, to rimmed baking sheet. Mound couscous mixture into squash halves and pack down lightly with palm. Top with remaining ¼ cup Pecorino and broil until lightly browned, 4 to 5 minutes. Serve.

EASY STUFFED ACORN SQUASH
After combining couscous, raisins, and salt with oil and water and letting it sit until tender, cook onion, garlic, and spinach on stovetop until spinach is wilted. Stir in couscous mixture, pine nuts, and ½ cup Pecorino. Mound couscous mixture into squash halves and pack with your palm. Top with remaining ¼ cup Pecorino and broil until lightly browned.

Butternut, Poblano, and Cheese Quesadillas

Serves 4

✓ **WHY THIS RECIPE WORKS:** We were after a fresher, more novel vegetarian quesadilla than the usual bean-based versions. A combination of poblano chiles and sweet butternut squash was just the ticket. Pepper Jack cheese adds the right gooey appeal, while feta lends a briny flavor that sets these quesadillas apart. Cool the quesadillas before cutting and serving them; straight from the skillet, the cheese is molten and will ooze out.

4   **poblano chiles, stemmed, halved lengthwise, and seeded**

1   **pound butternut squash, peeled, seeded, and cut into ½-inch pieces (4 cups)**

1   **tablespoon olive oil**

¼   **cup chopped fresh cilantro**
    Salt and pepper

3   **ounces pepper Jack cheese, shredded (¾ cup)**

3   **ounces feta cheese, crumbled (¾ cup)**

4   **(8-inch) flour tortillas**
    Sour cream

1. Position oven rack 3 inches from broiler element and heat broiler. Place poblanos on baking sheet skin side up and broil until skins begin to char and blister, 7 to 9 minutes. Transfer chiles to cutting board. When cool enough to handle, remove charred skins from poblanos and cut chiles into ½-inch strips.

2. Meanwhile, place squash in bowl, cover, and microwave until almost tender, 7 to 9 minutes, stirring halfway through cooking. Drain.

3. Heat oil in 12-inch nonstick skillet over medium-high heat until shimmering. Cook squash until tender and browned in spots, about 3 minutes. Stir in roasted chiles and cilantro and season with salt and pepper to taste. Transfer mixture to bowl and wipe out skillet with paper towels.

4. Combine pepper Jack and feta cheese, then divide evenly over one-half of each tortilla, leaving ½-inch border around edge. Top cheese with squash mixture. Fold tortillas over filling and press down firmly. Place 2 quesadillas in now-empty skillet and cook over medium-high heat until golden and crisp, 1 to 2 minutes. Using spatula, flip quesadillas and cook until golden and cheese is melted, 1 to 2 minutes. Transfer to cutting board and repeat with remaining 2 quesadillas. Cut into wedges and serve with sour cream.

SIMPLE SIDE SLAW WITH CUMIN-HONEY DRESSING
Whisk together 1 teaspoon lime zest, 2 tablespoons lime juice, 1 tablespoon honey, and 1 teaspoon ground cumin in medium bowl. Whisking constantly, drizzle in 3 tablespoons vegetable oil. Add one 14-ounce bag green coleslaw mix and toss to coat. Season with salt and pepper to taste. Serves 4.

Skillet Summer Vegetable Tamale Pie

Serves 4

✓ **WHY THIS RECIPE WORKS:** With zucchini, fresh corn, poblano chiles, and onion all bound in a cheesy, tomatoey sauce, this vegetarian skillet dinner is as comforting and satisfying as the more familiar meat-based versions of the dish. The chiles plus pepper Jack cheese and chili powder are all that is needed to achieve the right Southwestern flavor profile, and store-bought cornbread mix makes quick work of the topping. Adding a teaspoon of chili powder to the cornbread mix helps to counterbalance its sweetness. Once the filling is prepared on the stovetop, we spread over the topping and bake until golden. Two cups of frozen corn can be substituted for the fresh corn, but it should be added with the tomatoes rather than the zucchini.

¼ **cup olive oil**

1 **onion, chopped**

2 **poblano chiles, stemmed, seeded, and cut into ½-inch pieces**

Salt and pepper

3 **ears corn, kernels cut from cobs**

2 **zucchini, cut into ½-inch cubes**

1 **tablespoon plus 1 teaspoon chili powder**

1 **(14.5-ounce) can diced tomatoes**

4 **ounces pepper Jack cheese, shredded (1 cup)**

¼ **cup chopped fresh cilantro**

1 **(6.5-ounce) package cornbread mix**

½ **cup milk**

1 **large egg, lightly beaten**

1. Adjust oven rack to middle position and heat oven to 450 degrees. Heat 2 tablespoons oil in 12-inch ovensafe skillet over medium-high heat until shimmering. Add onion, poblanos, and ½ teaspoon salt, and cook until soft, about 5 minutes. Add corn and zucchini and cook until just tender, about 4 minutes. Add 1 tablespoon chili powder and cook until fragrant, about 30 seconds.

2. Stir in tomatoes and bring to simmer. Stir in pepper Jack and cilantro and season with salt and pepper.

3. Meanwhile, whisk cornbread mix and remaining 1 teaspoon chili powder together in medium bowl. Add milk, egg, and remaining 2 tablespoons oil and stir until smooth. Spread batter evenly over filling and bake until cornbread is golden and cooked through, 12 to 15 minutes. Serve.

SMART SHOPPING CORNBREAD MIX

Making cornbread from scratch is not difficult, but with all the mixes on the market we wondered if we could get from-scratch quality out of a packaged mix. We gathered several brands, prepared them according to the package directions, and held a blind tasting to find out. Tasters chose **Betty Crocker Cornbread & Muffin Mix** as their favorite. No mix offered the light texture and moistness of from-scratch cornbread, but for use in a speedy weeknight meal like our tamale pie, this convenient option works just fine.

Cheesy Skillet Polenta and Eggplant Bake

Serves 4

✓ **WHY THIS RECIPE WORKS:** Polenta in its soft, silky form is a great match for everything from braised meats to ragout. We top it with a hearty eggplant-tomato mixture and fontina for a vegetarian meal with lots of comfort-food appeal. Traditional polenta takes at least 30 minutes to cook; using quick-cooking polenta speeds up the process. To keep this recipe moving, we sauté the vegetables before setting them aside to make the polenta, then add the vegetables back to the pan, top them with cheese, and put it in the oven to finish.

¼	cup olive oil
1	pound eggplant, cut into ¾-inch pieces
3	garlic cloves, minced
1	(14.5-ounce) can diced tomatoes
	Salt and pepper
4	cups water
1	cup instant polenta
1½	ounces Parmesan cheese, grated (¾ cup)
4	ounces fontina cheese, shredded (1 cup)
⅓	cup chopped fresh basil

1. Adjust oven rack 6 inches from broiler element and heat broiler. Heat oil in 12-inch ovensafe nonstick skillet over medium-high heat until shimmering. Add eggplant and cook, without stirring, until eggplant begins to brown, about 4 minutes. Reduce heat to medium and cook, stirring occasionally, until eggplant is tender and lightly browned all over, about 4 minutes. Stir in garlic and cook until fragrant, about 30 seconds. Add tomatoes and simmer until slightly thickened, about 3 minutes. Season with salt and pepper to taste. Transfer to bowl.

2. Add water to now-empty skillet and bring to boil. Gradually whisk in polenta and ½ teaspoon salt. Cook over medium heat, whisking until very thick, about 5 minutes. Off heat, stir in Parmesan and season with salt and pepper to taste.

3. Spread polenta evenly in skillet and partially up sides. Spread eggplant mixture evenly over polenta, leaving 1-inch border around edge. Top with fontina. Broil until cheese is melted and beginning to brown, about 6 minutes. Sprinkle basil on top and serve.

EASY POLENTA BAKE

After cooking eggplant topping, bring water to boil in 12-inch ovensafe nonstick skillet. Slowly whisk in polenta and cook until thickened. Stir in Parmesan, season with salt and pepper, and spread polenta evenly over skillet bottom and partially up sides. Top with eggplant mixture and fontina. Broil until the cheese begins to brown, then top with basil and serve.

Ricotta, Basil, and Summer Squash Frittata

Serves 4

✔ **WHY THIS RECIPE WORKS:** Frittatas make an appealing dinner option because they can be on the table quickly and rely on a simple base ingredient list of eggs and half-and-half. And unlike most egg dishes, they are equally good served room temperature, so timing isn't as critical. Squash, basil, and ricotta give this version an Italian-inspired profile, and the addition of potatoes makes it plenty hearty. Parcooking the potatoes in the microwave minimizes their cooking time, then we brown them in the skillet for flavor and texture. Similarly, parcooking the squash before combining them with the eggs ensures they're perfectly cooked. A quick run under the broiler melts the ricotta and after a five-minute rest, the eggs are just cooked through.

10 **large eggs**

3 **tablespoons half-and-half**

½ **cup chopped fresh basil**
   Salt and pepper

12 **ounces Yukon Gold potatoes, peeled and sliced ¼ inch thick**

¼ **cup olive oil**

2 **summer squash, halved lengthwise and sliced ¼ inch thick**

4 **ounces (½ cup) whole-milk ricotta cheese**

1. Position oven rack 5 inches from broiler element and heat broiler. Whisk eggs, half-and-half, basil, ½ teaspoon salt, and ¼ teaspoon pepper together in bowl until combined. Toss potatoes with 1 tablespoon oil in another bowl, cover, and microwave until tender, about 5 minutes.

2. Meanwhile, heat 1 tablespoon oil in 12-inch ovensafe non-stick skillet over medium-high heat until shimmering. Add squash and cook until golden brown and tender, 3 to 5 minutes. Transfer to plate. Add remaining 2 tablespoons oil and potatoes to skillet and cook until golden brown, about 5 minutes. Add egg mixture and squash and cook, stirring occasionally, until large curds form but eggs are still very wet, about 2 minutes. Shake skillet to distribute eggs evenly and cook, without stirring, until bottom is set, about 30 seconds. Dollop heaping teaspoons of ricotta on top.

3. Transfer skillet to oven and broil until ricotta is hot and melted and surface of frittata is spotty brown, 3 to 4 minutes (eggs should still be slightly wet). Remove from oven and let sit for 5 minutes. Using rubber spatula, loosen edges of frittata from sides of skillet. Slide loosened frittata onto platter, cut into wedges, and serve.

SIMPLE SIDE ARUGULA SALAD WITH BALSAMIC-MUSTARD VINAIGRETTE
Whisk 2 tablespoons balsamic vinegar, 1½ teaspoons Dijon mustard, ½ teaspoon finely minced shallot, ⅛ teaspoon salt, and pinch pepper together in large bowl. Whisking constantly, drizzle in 2 tablespoons extra-virgin olive oil. Add 6 ounces (6 cups) baby arugula and toss to combine. Serves 4.

Spicy Tomato and Pepper Sauce-Poached Eggs

Serves 4

✔ **WHY THIS RECIPE WORKS:** This dish, a quick version of a popular Mediterranean recipe called *shakshuka,* puts a whole new twist on eggs for dinner. We start by whipping up a simple savory tomato and pepper sauce with jalapeños, garlic, paprika, and cumin. Once the sauce has simmered and thickened and its flavors have melded, we make wells in the sauce for the eggs to poach. This method is not only efficient and minimizes cookware but also allows the eggs to soak up flavor. To make it easier to add the eggs to the simmering sauce, we break each one into a teacup first and then carefully slide it into the sauce. A sprinkling of feta added before serving provides a creamy counterpoint that, along with some parsley, is the perfect finish. We like the taste of sheep's milk feta cheese in this recipe, but any creamy feta cheese will work.

3	tablespoons olive oil
2	jalapeño chiles, stemmed, seeded, and chopped fine
1	red bell pepper, stemmed, seeded, and sliced thin
1	onion, chopped
4	garlic cloves, minced
1	tablespoon paprika
½	teaspoon ground cumin
1	(28-ounce) can diced tomatoes
	Salt and pepper
4	large eggs
2	ounces feta cheese, crumbled (½ cup)
2	tablespoons chopped fresh parsley

1. Heat oil in 12-inch skillet over medium-high heat until shimmering. Add jalapeños, bell pepper, and onion and cook, stirring occasionally, until soft and golden brown, about 6 minutes. Add garlic, paprika, and cumin and cook until fragrant, about 30 seconds.

2. Add tomatoes and reduce heat to medium. Simmer, stirring occasionally, until thickened slightly, about 10 minutes. Season with salt and pepper to taste.

3. Make 4 shallow wells (each about 2 inches wide) in surface of sauce. Crack each egg into individual cup, then slide 1 egg into each indentation. Season eggs with salt and pepper. Reduce heat to medium-low, cover, and cook until eggs are just set, about 5 minutes. Scoop pepper mixture and eggs into individual serving bowls, sprinkle each with feta and parsley, and serve.

QUICK PREP TIP POACHING EGGS
After sauce has slightly thickened, make 4 shallow wells in surface of sauce. Crack each egg into individual cup, then slide 1 egg into each indentation. Season eggs with salt and pepper, then reduce heat to medium-low, cover, and cook until eggs are just set, about 5 minutes.

Parmesan French Toast with Tomato-Basil Topping

Serves 4

✅ **WHY THIS RECIPE WORKS:** To take French toast from the breakfast nook to the dinner table, we add Parmesan and a bright roasted tomato topping. The toast gets a double dose of Parmesan: We add some to the custard mixture for soaking the bread, and we coat each slice in large shreds that melt into a cheesy crust. We use supermarket Italian bread since it holds up and soaks up the right amount of custard. Oven-roasting the tomatoes makes the topping hands off, and their caramelized flavor makes them an ideal match for the toast.

1¼   **pounds grape tomatoes, halved**

6   **garlic cloves, sliced thin**

6   **tablespoons olive oil**

    Salt and pepper

2   **tablespoons chopped fresh basil**

3   **large eggs**

2   **cups whole milk**

¼   **cup all-purpose flour**

¼   **cup finely grated Parmesan cheese plus 2 cups shredded on large holes of box grater**

8   **(¾-inch-thick) slices supermarket Italian bread**

1. Adjust oven rack to middle position and heat oven to 450 degrees. Toss tomatoes and garlic with 2 tablespoons oil in bowl and season with salt and pepper. Arrange tomatoes cut side up on rimmed baking sheet. Roast until skins begin to brown on bottom, about 20 minutes. Transfer tomatoes to bowl and toss with basil.

2. Meanwhile, whisk eggs in shallow dish with milk, flour, grated Parmesan, ¼ teaspoon salt, and ¼ teaspoon pepper. Place shredded Parmesan in second shallow dish. Soak bread, 4 slices at a time, in milk mixture for 5 minutes, flipping bread halfway through soaking. One at a time, remove bread slices from milk mixture, then dredge in shredded Parmesan, pressing gently to adhere. Repeat with remaining bread.

3. Heat 2 tablespoons oil in 12-inch nonstick skillet over medium heat until shimmering. Cook 4 slices bread until golden and crisp, 2 to 3 minutes per side. Transfer to platter and tent loosely with foil. Repeat with remaining 2 tablespoons oil and remaining 4 slices bread. Serve topped with roasted tomatoes.

QUICK PREP TIP
MAKING PARMESAN FRENCH TOAST
Soak bread in mixture of eggs, milk, finely grated Parmesan, flour, salt, and pepper for 5 minutes, flipping bread halfway through. Working with 1 slice at a time, remove bread from milk mixture and dredge in shredded Parmesan, pressing gently to adhere. Cook soaked bread, 4 slices at a time, in 2 tablespoons oil over medium heat.

Fennel, Olive, and Goat Cheese Tarts

Serves 4

✓ **WHY THIS RECIPE WORKS:** This elegant dish is surprisingly simple. Allow the frozen pastry to sit in the refrigerator for 24 hours or on the counter for 30 minutes to 1 hour. Serve with Steamed Asparagus (page 232).

1   (9½ by 9-inch) sheet puff pastry, thawed and cut crosswise into 2 rectangles

8   ounces goat cheese, softened

½   cup chopped fresh basil

3   tablespoons extra-virgin olive oil

1   teaspoon grated lemon zest plus 1 tablespoon juice
    Salt and pepper

1   large fennel bulb, stalks discarded, bulb halved, cored, and sliced thin

3   garlic cloves, minced

½   cup dry white wine

½   cup oil-cured pitted black olives, chopped

1. Adjust oven rack to middle position and heat oven to 425 degrees. Lay pastry rectangles on parchment paper–lined baking sheet, poke all over with fork, and bake until puffed and golden brown, about 15 minutes, rotating baking sheet halfway through baking. Using tip of paring knife, cut border around perimeter ½ inch from edge of pastry shells. Press down center of each shell with fingertips.

2. While pastry bakes, beat goat cheese with ¼ cup basil, 2 tablespoons oil, lemon zest, and ¼ teaspoon pepper in small bowl. Heat remaining 1 tablespoon oil in 12-inch skillet over medium-high heat until shimmering. Add fennel and cook, stirring occasionally, until softened and brown in places, 10 to 12 minutes. Add garlic and cook until fragrant, 30 seconds. Add wine, cover, and cook for 5 minutes. Uncover and continue to cook until liquid has evaporated and fennel is very soft, 3 to 5 minutes longer. Stir in olives and lemon juice and remove from heat.

3. Spread goat cheese mixture evenly in center of shells, leaving raised edges clean. Spoon fennel mixture evenly over cheese layer. Transfer filled tarts to oven and bake until cheese is heated through and crust is deep golden brown, about 5 minutes. Remove from oven, sprinkle with remaining ¼ cup basil, season with salt and pepper to taste, and serve.

QUICK PREP TIP MAKING TART SHELLS
Lay pastry rectangles on a parchment-lined baking sheet and poke all over with fork. Bake until shells are puffed and golden, about 15 minutes, rotating halfway through baking. Using tip of paring knife, cut border around perimeter of shells, ½ inch from edge. Press center down with fingertips so it rests about ¼ inch lower than edge to create bed for filling.

White Bean Panzanella

Serves 6

✓ **WHY THIS RECIPE WORKS:** With its colorful mix of tomatoes, arugula, red onion, and white beans all tossed in a bright dressing with chunks of rustic bread, this take on the classic Italian dish known as panzanella is not only visually appealing and healthy, but also plenty satisfying. Panzanella traditionally relies on day-old bread since it can stand up to the dressing better than fresh. We "stale" fresh bread fast by cutting our loaf into pieces, lightly spraying them with olive oil, and baking them until golden. While the bread toasts, we whisk together our dressing, then we add our vegetables and beans to the bowl and let it sit so the flavors can meld. As soon as the bread cubes have cooled slightly, our dressing/vegetable mixture is ready to go. All that's left is tossing it all together along with more fresh herbs and a sprinkling of Parmesan. It's essential to use high-quality rustic Italian bread here; avoid sliced white sandwich bread or airy supermarket Italian bread—both will turn to mush.

12	ounces rustic Italian bread, cut or torn into 1-inch cubes (about 4 cups)
	Olive oil spray
¼	cup extra-virgin olive oil
3	tablespoons red wine vinegar
	Salt and pepper
1½	pounds ripe tomatoes, cored and chopped medium, seeds and juice reserved
1	(15-ounce) can cannellini beans, rinsed
1	small red onion, halved and sliced very thin
3	tablespoons chopped fresh basil
2	tablespoons minced fresh oregano
3	ounces (3 cups) baby arugula
2	ounces Parmesan cheese, shaved (½ cup)

1. Adjust oven rack to middle position and heat oven to 350 degrees. Lightly spray bread cubes with oil spray and spread out over rimmed baking sheet. Bake, stirring occasionally, until just lightly golden brown, 15 to 20 minutes. Let croutons cool to room temperature.

2. Meanwhile, whisk olive oil, vinegar, and ¼ teaspoon salt together in large bowl until well combined. Stir in tomatoes with their seeds and juice, beans, onion, 1½ tablespoons basil, and 1 tablespoon oregano. Let sit at room temperature to allow flavors to meld, about 20 minutes.

3. Stir in cooled croutons, remaining 1½ tablespoons basil, and remaining 1 tablespoon oregano. Gently fold in arugula and season with salt and pepper to taste. Sprinkle with Parmesan and serve.

SMART SHOPPING RED WINE VINEGAR
The number of red wine vinegars has exploded in the past decade. To find the best, tasters sampled 10 brands plain, in a vinaigrette, and in pickled onions. For an everyday option, our winner, **Laurent du Clos Red Wine Vinegar**, is hard to beat. At 35 cents per ounce, it's not the least expensive brand we tried, but the price is reasonable for a vinegar that doesn't compromise on flavor.

CHICKEN MARSALA PASTA

Pasta & Risotto

210 Farfalle with Bacon, Endive, and Peas

211 Easy Spaghetti Amatriciana with Pancetta Crisps

212 Quick Sausage Ragu with Gemelli

214 Penne with Arugula, Chorizo, and Pecorino

215 Chicken Marsala Pasta

217 Tarragon Chicken and Egg Noodles

218 Pasta with Lemony Chicken and Asparagus

219 Farfalle with Beets, Arugula, and Blue Cheese

222 Mixed-Herb Pesto Pasta with Summer Squash

224 Skillet Tortellini Supper with Sundried Tomatoes and Prosciutto

225 Orecchiette with Broccoli, Currants, and Pine Nuts

227 Spanish-Style Fideos with Swiss Chard

228 Linguine with Cauliflower and Sage Browned Butter

229 Whole-Wheat Pasta with Winter Greens, Walnuts, and Ricotta Salata

230 Pasta with Roasted Tomatoes and Porcini-Wine Sauce

232 Penne alla Vodka with Shrimp

233 Scallops and Angel Hair with Lemon Cream Sauce

235 Spaghetti with Spicy White Fresh Clam Sauce

236 Spring Farfalle with Salmon, Leeks, and Asparagus

237 Skillet Macaroni and Cheese with Bacon

238 Easy Garlicky Risotto with Broccolini

240 Baked Risotto with Shrimp and Zucchini

241 Cheesy Gnocchi and Cauliflower Gratin

243 Gnocchi with Spinach, Ham, and Gorgonzola

244 Sopa Seca

245 Three-Cheese Pesto Lasagna Stacks

Farfalle with Bacon, Endive, and Peas

Serves 4

✓ **WHY THIS RECIPE WORKS:** A combination of Belgian endive, peas, and mint gives this pasta dish plenty of fresh springtime flavor, while bacon adds some heft and appealing smokiness. Cooking the endive in the skillet after the bacon ensures none of the meaty, smoky flavor goes to waste. Cutting the endive in half for the first step of cooking allows it to brown and pick up flavor on the exterior yet remain tender inside; only after it has browned do we cut it into bite-size pieces. Then it goes back in the pan with the peas and some broth. We don't waste time thawing the peas; adding them frozen means they'll be ready just when it's time to pour the sauce over the pasta. To finish, we add a little lemon juice for brightness and Parmesan and sour cream for richness.

8	slices bacon, chopped
4	heads Belgian endive (1 pound), halved lengthwise
2	cups frozen peas
1	cup low-sodium chicken broth
1	pound farfalle
	Salt and pepper
2	ounces Parmesan cheese, grated (1 cup)
¼	cup chopped fresh mint
¼	cup sour cream
2	tablespoons lemon juice

1. Bring 4 quarts water to boil in large pot. Cook bacon in 12-inch nonstick skillet over medium-high heat until crisp, about 5 minutes. Using slotted spoon, transfer to paper towel–lined plate. Add endive to skillet, cut side down, and cook until golden brown and softened, about 4 minutes per side. Remove from skillet and cut into 1-inch pieces. Return endive to skillet, add peas and broth, and bring to simmer. Cook until peas are tender and bright green, 2 to 4 minutes.

2. Meanwhile, add farfalle and 1 tablespoon salt to boiling water and cook, stirring often, until al dente. Reserve ½ cup cooking water, then drain farfalle and return it to pot over medium heat. Add bacon, endive mixture, Parmesan, mint, sour cream, and lemon juice, and toss to combine. Season with salt and pepper to taste, and add reserved cooking water as needed to adjust consistency. Serve.

QUICK PREP TIP BROWNING ENDIVE
Halve each endive lengthwise. After cooking bacon in skillet and setting it aside, add endive halves, cut side down, and cook until browned on first side, about 4 minutes. Flip them and continue to cook until outer sides are browned, about 4 minutes. Remove from skillet and cut into 1-inch pieces.

Easy Spaghetti Amatriciana with Pancetta Crisps

Serves 4

✓ **WHY THIS RECIPE WORKS:** We turn *pasta all'amatriciana*, a lusty Roman pasta dish of tomatoes, pork cheek, onion, and dried chile, into a weeknight meal by substituting pancetta for the pork cheek and using canned tomatoes instead of fresh. Crisping some pancetta for a garnish and adding several more chopped slices to the sauce ensures lots of meaty flavor. While the pancetta crisps in the oven, we prepare the sauce and pasta.

6	ounces thinly sliced pancetta
1	onion, chopped fine
3	garlic cloves, minced
½	teaspoon red pepper flakes
1	(14.5-ounce) can diced tomatoes
1	pound spaghetti
	Salt and pepper
⅓	cup chopped fresh parsley
1	ounce Pecorino Romano cheese, grated (½ cup), plus extra for serving

1. Adjust oven rack to upper-middle position and heat oven to 425 degrees. Bring 4 quarts water to boil in large pot. Line rimmed baking sheet with parchment paper and arrange half of pancetta in single layer on parchment. Top with second sheet of parchment and place second rimmed baking sheet on top. Transfer to oven and cook until pancetta is lightly browned and crisp, about 17 minutes.

2. Chop remaining pancetta and cook in 12-inch skillet over medium heat until almost crisp, 3 to 5 minutes. Add onion and cook until softened, about 3 minutes. Add garlic and red pepper flakes and cook until fragrant, about 30 seconds. Stir in tomatoes and cook until thickened, about 5 minutes.

3. While sauce cooks, add spaghetti and 1 tablespoon salt to boiling water and cook, stirring often, until al dente. Reserve 1 cup cooking water, then drain spaghetti and return it to pot. Add sauce, parsley, and Pecorino and toss to combine. Season with salt and pepper to taste, and add reserved cooking water as needed to adjust consistency. Top with crisped pancetta and serve with extra Pecorino.

QUICK PREP TIP
MAKING PANCETTA CRISPS
Arrange half of pancetta in single layer on parchment-lined rimmed baking sheet. Top with second sheet of parchment, then place second baking sheet on top of parchment to keep slices flat. Transfer to oven and bake until pancetta slices are lightly browned and crisp, about 17 minutes.

Quick Sausage Ragu with Gemelli

Serves 4

✔ **WHY THIS RECIPE WORKS:** Full-bodied, traditional Italian ragus are just what you want on a cold day, but they typically have to simmer on the stovetop for hours. We make a similarly rich but much speedier sauce by bolstering canned tomatoes with wine, garlic, onion, basil, and Parmesan. For the meat component, we keep things simple but flavorful, relying on Italian sausage (rather than the usual ground beef) that we remove from its casings. We love the twisted pasta shape called gemelli in this recipe because it catches the meaty sauce well, but any tubular or molded pasta, such as ziti, penne, or fusilli, will work.

1 tablespoon olive oil

1 onion, chopped fine

3 garlic cloves, minced

1 pound Italian sausage, casings removed

½ cup dry white wine

1 (28-ounce) can diced tomatoes

1 pound gemelli
  Salt and pepper

¼ cup shredded fresh basil

1 ounce Parmesan cheese, grated (½ cup), plus extra for serving

1. Bring 4 quarts water to boil in large pot. Heat oil in 12-inch skillet over medium–high heat until shimmering. Add onion and cook until softened, about 3 minutes. Add garlic and cook until fragrant, about 30 seconds. Add sausage and cook, breaking into small pieces with wooden spoon, until just cooked through, about 3 minutes.

2. Add wine and cook until evaporated, about 1 minute. Add tomatoes and bring to simmer. Cook until sauce has thickened, 6 to 8 minutes.

3. While sauce cooks, add gemelli and 1 tablespoon salt to boiling water and cook, stirring often, until al dente. Reserve ½ cup cooking water, drain gemelli, then return it to pot.

4. Add sauce, basil, and Parmesan to pasta and toss to combine. Season with salt and pepper to taste, and add reserved cooking water as needed to adjust consistency. Serve with extra Parmesan.

SIMPLE SIDE QUICK CHEESY BREADSTICKS
Adjust oven rack to middle position and heat oven to 400 degrees. Roll 1 pound pizza dough into ½-inch-thick rectangle. Cut dough into 1-inch-wide strips and arrange on well-oiled baking sheet. Brush with 2 tablespoons olive oil and sprinkle with ½ cup grated Parmesan cheese, ½ teaspoon kosher salt, and ½ teaspoon pepper. Bake until golden brown, about 15 minutes. Let cool briefly on wire rack; serve warm. Serves 4.

Penne with Arugula, Chorizo, and Pecorino

Serves 4

✔ **WHY THIS RECIPE WORKS:** Hearty chorizo, peppery arugula, and sharp Pecorino Romano cheese come together in this recipe that's as visually appealing as it is tasty. The key to both speed and big flavor is building the recipe in our skillet in stages. We start by browning the chorizo, then set it aside and cook the aromatics in the rendered fat left behind, which ensures the chorizo's flavor is carried throughout. Next, we pour in white wine and let it reduce to concentrate its flavor, then add chicken broth, which lends body and the proper saucy consistency once it's slightly reduced. After boiling and draining the penne, we return it to the pot, add the sauce and browned chorizo, and fold in the baby arugula just until wilted. A cup of grated Pecorino Romano is the final piece; it brings a tangy bite that completes the dish.

1	tablespoon extra-virgin olive oil
8	ounces chorizo, sliced thin
3	shallots, chopped fine
5	garlic cloves, minced
½	cup dry white wine
1	cup low-sodium chicken broth
1	pound penne
	Salt and pepper
2	ounces Pecorino Romano cheese, grated (1 cup)
5	ounces (5 cups) baby arugula

1. Bring 4 quarts water to boil in large pot. Heat oil in 12-inch nonstick skillet over medium heat until shimmering. Add chorizo and cook until golden brown, 2 to 3 minutes per side. Using slotted spoon, transfer chorizo to paper towel–lined plate.

2. Add shallots to fat left in skillet and cook until softened, about 5 minutes. Add garlic and cook until fragrant, about 30 seconds. Add wine and cook until reduced by half, about 1 minute. Add chicken broth and cook until sauce thickens, about 3 minutes.

3. While sauce cooks, add penne and 1 tablespoon salt to boiling water and cook, stirring often, until al dente. Reserve ½ cup cooking water, then drain penne and return it to pot. Add sauce, chorizo, Pecorino, and arugula to pasta and toss until arugula is wilted, about 1 minute. Season with salt and pepper to taste, and add reserved cooking water as needed to adjust consistency. Serve.

SMART SHOPPING PECORINO CHEESE
Pecorino, a firm sheep's milk cheese from Italy (pecorino comes from the Italian word for sheep), has a salty, piquant flavor that makes it a great choice for adding zip to pasta dishes. While Pecorino Romano is probably the best-known variety, each region in Italy has its own distinct style. However, the flavor and texture is similar for all variants, so if you can't find Pecorino Romano when it is specified in a recipe, another type of pecorino can be substituted. Note that as pecorino ages, it gets more pungent and chalky.

Chicken Marsala Pasta

Serves 4

✓ **WHY THIS RECIPE WORKS:** Here we rework the basic components of classic chicken Marsala—chicken, Marsala, and mushrooms—into a simple pasta dish. Cutting chicken breasts into smaller pieces means a shorter cooking time, and we cook them in batches with butter to ensure nice browning and rich flavor. Simmering the pasta in the sauce for a minute allows it to absorb some of the liquid, and in turn the noodles provide starch to thicken the sauce. Lemon juice adds the requisite brightness, while tarragon lends herbal depth.

2	**(6-ounce) boneless, skinless chicken breasts, trimmed and sliced crosswise ¼ inch thick**
	Salt and pepper
5	**tablespoons unsalted butter**
1	**pound white mushrooms, trimmed and quartered**
4	**garlic cloves, minced**
¾	**cup sweet Marsala**
½	**cup low-sodium chicken broth**
2	**tablespoons lemon juice**
4	**teaspoons chopped fresh tarragon**
1	**pound rigatoni**
1	**ounce Parmesan cheese, grated (½ cup), plus extra for serving**

1. Bring 4 quarts water to boil in large pot. Pat chicken dry with paper towels and season with salt and pepper. Melt 1 tablespoon butter in 12-inch skillet over medium-high heat. Add half of chicken and cook until lightly browned, about 3 minutes. Transfer to plate. Repeat with 1 tablespoon butter and remaining chicken.

2. Melt 1 tablespoon butter in now-empty skillet over medium-high heat. Add mushrooms and cook until browned, about 5 minutes. Add garlic and cook until fragrant, about 30 seconds. Add Marsala and broth and bring to boil. Lower heat and simmer until sauce is slightly thickened, about 5 minutes. Off heat, stir in remaining 2 tablespoons butter, lemon juice, and tarragon.

3. While sauce cooks, add rigatoni and 1 tablespoon salt to boiling water and cook, stirring often, until al dente. Reserve ½ cup cooking water, then drain rigatoni and return it to pot. Add mushroom sauce, chicken, and Parmesan to pasta and cook until pasta has absorbed some sauce and chicken is warmed through, about 1 minute, adding reserved cooking water as needed to adjust consistency. Season with salt and pepper to taste. Serve with extra Parmesan.

SMART SHOPPING MARSALA
Marsala, which originally hails from Sicily, is like vermouth or sherry in that it starts with table wine and is then fortified with extra alcohol (often brandy) to increase its shelf life. Marsala offers a rich, smoky flavor that comes from the aging process. An open bottle of Marsala will keep in the pantry for several months, if not longer, making it a great cooking option when using only small quantities. Marsala comes in sweet and dry varieties. Dry (*secco*) is often served as an apéritif, while the semisweet (*semisecco*) and sweet (*dolce*) styles are typically brought out as dessert wines. All varieties are used for cooking.

Tarragon Chicken and Egg Noodles

Serves 4

✔ **WHY THIS RECIPE WORKS:** This company-worthy dinner requires just a handful of ingredients and comes together in a single skillet. First, we cut the chicken into strips, sauté it in butter, and set it aside. Then we briefly sauté a little shallot and use some white wine to deglaze the pan, picking up the fond left behind to ensure all that flavor makes its way into the final dish. Once we've cooked the wine mixture down, the noodles and broth go into the pan, and we cook the noodles right in the sauce. For this dish we opt to use plain egg noodles, rather than a more exotic variety of pasta, because their wide shape and fluffy texture lend themselves to quick cooking in shallow liquid. The anise flavor of tarragon is a classic match for chicken that works well here, while a few tablespoons of cream add a sweet richness.

3	(6- to 8-ounce) boneless, skinless chicken breasts, trimmed and sliced crosswise ¼ inch thick
	Salt and pepper
2	tablespoons unsalted butter
2	shallots, sliced thin
½	cup dry white wine
4	cups low-sodium chicken broth
8	ounces egg noodles
3	tablespoons heavy cream
2	tablespoons minced fresh tarragon

1. Pat chicken dry with paper towels and season with salt and pepper. Melt butter in 12-inch skillet over medium-high heat. Add chicken and cook until lightly browned, about 3 minutes. Transfer chicken to plate and tent loosely with aluminum foil.

2. Add shallots to now-empty skillet and cook until softened, about 2 minutes. Stir in wine and cook, scraping up any browned bits, until pan is nearly dry, about 3 minutes. Add broth and noodles and cook, stirring occasionally, until noodles are tender and liquid has been absorbed, 8 to 10 minutes.

3. Stir in cream, tarragon, and chicken, along with any accumulated juices, and cook until heated through, about 1 minute. Season with salt and pepper to taste, and serve.

SMART SHOPPING SHALLOTS VS. ONIONS

Although both are members of the allium family and are commonly substituted for one another, shallots and onions have clear differences that are worth taking note of before swapping in one for the other in recipes. Shallots—which resemble garlic in that they are small and grow in heads composed of cloves—have a unique flavor that is milder than that of onions. When shallots and onions are cooked, the differences between them are even clearer. A finely minced shallot will melt into a sauce and its flavor will permeate, and in a vinaigrette or salsa, it will add gentle heat. An onion will have a much clearer presence in terms of both flavor and texture. No matter how finely you mince an onion, it's not going to disappear into an otherwise silky sauce, and it needs a much longer cooking time before its flavor will mellow. Bottom line: You can substitute shallots and onions for each other if necessary, but don't expect identical results.

Pasta with Lemony Chicken and Asparagus

Serves 4

☑ **WHY THIS RECIPE WORKS:** Two classic roast chicken dishes—garlic chicken and lemon chicken—inspired this recipe, which relies on a good dose of lemon juice for zing plus eight cloves of minced garlic for bite. Grassy asparagus is the perfect complement and makes this a one-dish meal. To ensure each component is perfectly cooked, we sauté the chicken first, followed by the asparagus and garlic. Then, once the pasta is cooked, we toss them all together, along with lemon juice for brightness, Parmesan for richness, and parsley for a fresh finish.

4	**(6-ounce) boneless, skinless chicken breasts, trimmed and sliced crosswise ¼ inch thick**
	Salt and pepper
4	**tablespoons unsalted butter**
1	**pound asparagus, trimmed and cut into 1-inch pieces**
8	**garlic cloves, minced**
8	**ounces campanelle**
2	**ounces Parmesan cheese, grated (1 cup)**
¼	**cup lemon juice (2 lemons)**
¼	**cup chopped fresh parsley**

1. Bring 4 quarts water to boil in large pot. Pat chicken dry with paper towels and season with salt and pepper. Melt 1 tablespoon butter in 12-inch nonstick skillet over medium heat. Add half of chicken and cook until lightly browned, about 3 minutes. Transfer to bowl. Repeat with 1 tablespoon butter and remaining chicken.

2. Add 1 tablespoon butter and asparagus to now-empty skillet and cook until asparagus is just tender, about 5 minutes. Add garlic and cook until fragrant, about 30 seconds. Transfer to bowl with chicken and cover.

3. While asparagus cooks, add campanelle and 1 tablespoon salt to boiling water and cook, stirring often, until al dente. Reserve ½ cup cooking water, then drain pasta and return it to pot. Add remaining 1 tablespoon butter, chicken, asparagus, Parmesan, lemon juice, and parsley and toss to combine. Season with salt and pepper to taste, and add reserved pasta water as needed to adjust consistency. Serve.

SMART SHOPPING SALTED VS. UNSALTED BUTTER

Though we like salted butter for spreading on bread or topping vegetables just before serving, we generally advise against substituting salted butter for unsalted (even if you reduce salt called for), for three reasons: The amount of salt varies from brand to brand; salt masks some of butter's flavor nuances; and salted butter almost always contains more water than unsalted butter does, which can affect the final recipe (especially in baking). Our favorite unsalted butter is a pricey European-style butter from **Plugra** ($9.98 per pound), but at about half the price, **Land O'Lakes** is a solid performer and our best buy.

Farfalle with Beets, Arugula, and Blue Cheese

Serves 4 to 6

✓ **WHY THIS RECIPE WORKS:** We have fun with the beets' bold color in this recipe by combining farfalle with matchstick-size beets, which gives the pasta a vibrant pink color. We precook the beets, along with a little onion, in a skillet while the pasta boils so that the meal takes minutes to come together. Arugula, which we fold in along with Gorgonzola cheese at the end, adds a peppery bite and a contrasting texture and color, while the Gorgonzola contributes a slightly pungent flavor and creamy body. Just before serving, we garnish our pasta with chopped toasted walnuts for crunch and a final sprinkling of Gorgonzola to pull it together.

1	pound beets, peeled and cut into matchsticks
1	red onion, halved lengthwise and sliced crosswise ¼ inch thick
3	tablespoons extra-virgin olive oil
	Salt and pepper
⅓	cup water
2	tablespoons lemon juice
1	pound farfalle
5	ounces (5 cups) baby arugula
6	ounces Gorgonzola cheese, crumbled (1½ cups)
1	cup walnuts, toasted and chopped

1. Bring 4 quarts water to boil in large pot. Combine beets, red onion, oil, ¼ teaspoon salt, and ¼ teaspoon pepper in 12-inch nonstick skillet set over high heat. Add water, bring to boil, then cover and reduce heat to medium-high. Cook for 10 minutes, then remove lid and continue to cook, uncovered and stirring occasionally, until beets are tender, about 15 minutes. Stir in 1 tablespoon lemon juice and season with salt and pepper to taste.

2. While beets cook, add farfalle and 1 tablespoon salt to boiling water and cook, stirring often, until al dente. Reserve ½ cup cooking water, then drain farfalle and return it to pot. Stir in beets, remaining 1 tablespoon lemon juice, and reserved cooking water as needed to adjust consistency. Season with salt and pepper to taste. Fold in arugula and ¾ cup Gorgonzola. Top with walnuts and remaining ¾ cup Gorgonzola and serve.

QUICK PREP TIP AVOIDING BEET STAINS

Prepping beets always leaves our cutting boards with dark stains that discolors other foods we put on it. Instead of stopping to wash the board, we found that simply giving its surface a light coat of vegetable oil spray before chopping does the trick. This thin coating adds no discernible slickness and allows you to quickly wipe the board clean with a paper towel before proceeding with the next task.

ALL ABOUT Matching Pasta Shapes and Sauces

Pairing a pasta shape with the right sauce might be an art form in Italy, but we think there's only one basic rule to follow: Thick, chunky sauces go with short pastas, and thin, smooth, or light sauces with strand pasta. (Of course, there are a few exceptions—but that's where the art comes in.) Although we specify pasta shapes for every recipe in this book, you should feel free to substitute other pasta shapes as long as you're following this one basic rule. Here are the pasta shapes we use most often, along with translations or alternate names, plus some measuring tips.

Short Pastas

Short tubular or molded pasta shapes do an excellent job of trapping and holding on to chunky sauces. Sauces with very large chunks are best with rigatoni or other large tubes. Sauces with small chunks make more sense with fusilli or penne.

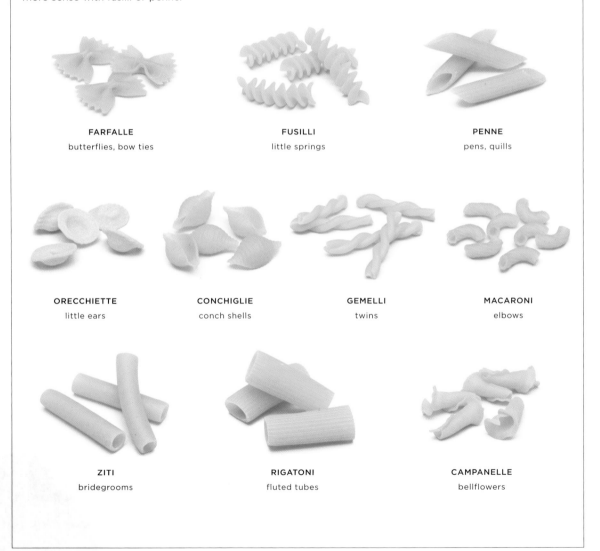

FARFALLE

butterflies, bow ties

FUSILLI

little springs

PENNE

pens, quills

ORECCHIETTE

little ears

CONCHIGLIE

conch shells

GEMELLI

twins

MACARONI

elbows

ZITI

bridegrooms

RIGATONI

fluted tubes

CAMPANELLE

bellflowers

Strand Pastas

Long strands are best with smooth sauces or sauces with very small chunks. In general, wider noodles, such as pappardelle and fettuccine, can support slightly chunkier sauces, like a classic Bolognese.

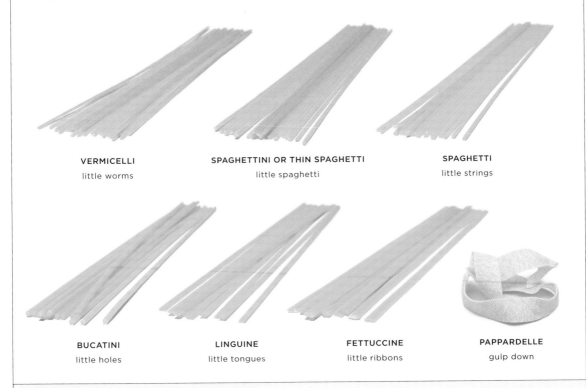

VERMICELLI	SPAGHETTINI OR THIN SPAGHETTI	SPAGHETTI
little worms	little spaghetti	little strings

BUCATINI	LINGUINE	FETTUCCINE	PAPPARDELLE
little holes	little tongues	little ribbons	gulp down

Measuring Less Than a Pound of Pasta

It's easy enough to measure out a pound of pasta, as most packages are sold in this quantity. But in this chapter we've included some recipes that call for less than 1 pound of pasta. Obviously, you can weigh out partial pounds of pasta using a scale or judge by how full the box is, but we think it's easier to measure short pasta shapes using a dry measuring cup, and strand pasta by determining the diameter.

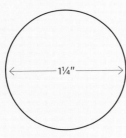

1¼"

When 8 ounces of uncooked strand pasta are bunched together into a tight circle, the diameter measures about 1¼ inches.

PASTA TYPE*	8 OUNCES	12 OUNCES
Elbow Macaroni and Small Shells	2 cups	3 cups
Orecchiette	2¼ cups	3⅓ cups
Penne, Ziti, and Campanelle	2½ cups	3¾ cups
Rigatoni, Fusilli, Medium Shells, Wagon Wheels, Wide Egg Noodles	3 cups	4½ cups
Farfalle	3¼ cups	4¾ cups

*These amounts do not apply to whole-wheat pasta.

Mixed-Herb Pesto Pasta with Squash

Serves 4

✔ **WHY THIS RECIPE WORKS:** We put a new spin on traditional pesto by swapping out the usual basil in favor of a combination of parsley and marjoram, a Mediterranean herb with a sweet, floral aroma and a flavor similar to oregano. Matching the marjoram with parsley mellows its flavor and gives the pesto just the right herbal balance. A nontraditional ingredient, ricotta cheese, turns our pesto into a creamy yet light sauce, as does adding a bit of the reserved pasta cooking water. We break away further from the usual formula by using walnuts instead of pine nuts and Asiago cheese instead of Parmesan. The food processor helps us make quick work of preparing our sauce. The addition of summer squash, which we slice into long ribbons to play off the strands of fettuccine, lends visual appeal and welcome texture and is the perfect match for the brightly flavored pesto sauce.

2	ounces (¼ cup) whole-milk ricotta cheese
¾	cup fresh parsley leaves
½	cup walnuts, toasted
¼	cup fresh marjoram leaves
¼	cup grated Asiago cheese
1	garlic clove, minced
1	teaspoon grated lemon zest plus 2 tablespoons juice
	Salt and pepper
3	tablespoons extra-virgin olive oil
1	pound fettuccine
4	summer squash, sliced lengthwise into ⅛-inch-thick ribbons

1. Bring 4 quarts water to boil in large pot. Process ricotta in food processor until smooth, about 15 seconds. Add parsley, walnuts, marjoram, Asiago, garlic, lemon zest and juice, ½ teaspoon salt, and ½ teaspoon pepper. Process until smooth, about 20 seconds, scraping down bowl once or twice as needed. With processor running, add oil and process mixture until combined, 10 seconds.

2. Meanwhile, add fettuccine and 1 tablespoon salt to boiling water and cook, stirring often, until al dente. Reserve ¾ cup cooking water, then drain fettuccine and return it to pot. Add squash ribbons and pesto and toss to combine. Season with salt and pepper to taste, and add reserved cooking water as needed to adjust consistency. Serve.

QUICK PREP TIP
CUTTING SQUASH INTO RIBBONS
To cut squash into ribbons, we prefer using a mandoline fitted with a slicing blade, but you can also use a vegetable peeler. Run the squash down the length of the mandoline or run the peeler down the length of the squash. Repeat the process until you reach the seeds in the middle, then turn the squash and repeat on the other sides.

Skillet Tortellini Supper

Serves 4 to 6

✔ **WHY THIS RECIPE WORKS:** With crisp, salty prosciutto, cheesy tortellini, peppery arugula, and richly flavored sun-dried tomatoes, this meal has an appealing mix of textures and flavors that make it a sure win. After cooking our tortellini until al dente and crisping the prosciutto and setting it aside, we combine the pasta with the tomatoes and garlic in the skillet. Next, we fold in the arugula and finish with the prosciutto and a sprinkling of salty Parmesan cheese. A little lemon juice lends zing and lightens the dish just enough.

¼ cup extra-virgin olive oil

4 ounces prosciutto, sliced crosswise into thin strips

4 garlic cloves, minced

¾ cup oil-packed sun-dried tomatoes, sliced thin

1¼ pounds dried cheese tortellini

Salt and pepper

5 ounces (5 cups) baby arugula

2 teaspoons lemon juice

1 ounce Parmesan cheese, grated (½ cup)

1. Bring 4 quarts water to boil in large pot. Heat oil in 12-inch nonstick skillet over medium-high heat until just shimmering. Add prosciutto and cook, stirring frequently, until crisped and brown, 4 to 7 minutes. Transfer to paper towel–lined plate. Reduce heat to medium, add garlic, and cook until fragrant, about 30 seconds. Stir in tomatoes and cook until warmed through, about 1 minute.

2. Meanwhile, add tortellini and 1 tablespoon salt to boiling water and cook, stirring often, until al dente. Reserve ½ cup cooking water, then drain tortellini and add to skillet with tomato mixture. Toss to combine.

3. Off heat, fold in arugula and stir until leaves become glossy and begin to wilt. Season generously with pepper, drizzle with lemon juice, and top with crisp prosciutto and Parmesan cheese. Before serving, add reserved cooking water as needed to adjust consistency.

SMART SHOPPING NEW SCHOOL OLIVE OILS
California growers have spent the last two decades developing extra-virgin olive oils that might rival the best of Europe's, which is good news to us since the quality of olive oil degrades over time and the benefit of buying domestically is built in. After running 10 California olive oils through several taste tests against our favorite from abroad, Columela, the imported oil won out again—but by a mere half point. **California Olive Ranch Arbequina** won raves for its fresh, sweet, fruity flavor and pleasing bitterness.

Orecchiette with Broccoli, Currants, and Pine Nuts

Serves 4

✔ **WHY THIS RECIPE WORKS:** Long-cooked broccoli is a classic Italian side dish that relies on cooking the vegetable until it breaks down, a technique that gives it a deep, nutty flavor. Though we rarely think of cooking broccoli to that point, we realized it would be a great way to create a thick, flavorful pasta sauce. To save time, we add the broccoli to the pasta and cook it until the florets start to break apart.. While the pasta and broccoli cook, we plump the currants in chicken broth (along with pine nuts and a generous amount of garlic), and let the broth reduce slightly. After we've combined the pasta, broccoli, and sauce, we add lemon juice for balance and a good dose of Parmesan to bring it all together.

2	**tablespoons extra-virgin olive oil**
½	**red onion, sliced thin**
½	**cup pine nuts, toasted**
4	**garlic cloves, minced**
1	**cup low-sodium chicken broth**
½	**cup dried currants**
1	**pound orecchiette**
	Salt and pepper
1	**pound broccoli florets**
2	**ounces Parmesan cheese, grated (1 cup)**
2	**tablespoons lemon juice**

1. Bring 4 quarts water to boil in large pot. Heat oil in 12-inch skillet over medium-high heat until shimmering. Add onion and cook until softened, about 1 minute. Add pine nuts and garlic and cook until garlic is fragrant, about 30 seconds. Add broth and currants and simmer until slightly reduced and flavors meld, about 4 minutes.

2. While sauce cooks, add orecchiette and 1 tablespoon salt to boiling water and cook for 6 minutes. Add broccoli and cook until pasta is al dente, broccoli is bright green, and florets start to break down, about 5 minutes. Reserve ½ cup cooking water, then drain pasta and broccoli and return them to pot.

3. Add sauce to pasta and toss to combine, allowing broccoli to break up into bits. Stir in Parmesan and lemon juice. Season with salt and pepper to taste, and add reserved cooking water as needed to adjust consistency. Serve.

QUICK PREP TIP
TOASTING PINE NUTS
To toast nuts quickly, using a skillet and the stovetop is easiest. Toast them in a skillet with no oil over medium heat, shaking the pan occasionally to prevent scorching. The nuts should be toasted for 3 to 5 minutes, until they darken slightly.

Spanish-Style Fideos with Swiss Chard

Serves 4

✔️ **WHY THIS RECIPE WORKS:** We combine toasted thin capellini noodles with saffron-infused cream and wine sauce for our spin on fideos, a classic toasted strand pasta dish from Spain. (In Spain, *fideos* actually refers to any noodle.) Toasting the noodles deepens their flavor, and by toasting them in the oven, we can focus on building the sauce on the stovetop. Swiss chard, which we cook in the sauce before adding the pasta, adds color and makes this a one-dish meal. Garlic, onion, and roasted red pepper add complexity and continue the Spanish theme. Once the toasted noodles get added to the pot, it takes just a few minutes of stirring for the noodles to become coated with the sauce and soften.

12	ounces capellini, broken into 3-inch pieces
2	tablespoons extra-virgin olive oil
1	onion, chopped
5	garlic cloves, minced
1	cup dry white wine
½	teaspoon saffron threads, crumbled
2	cups water
1½	cups heavy cream
12	ounces Swiss chard, stemmed and chopped
	Salt and pepper
1	cup jarred roasted red peppers, sliced thin

1. Adjust oven rack to upper-middle position and heat oven to 375 degrees. Arrange pasta in even layer on rimmed baking sheet. Bake pasta until golden brown, 8 to 9 minutes, stirring once or twice during baking.

2. Meanwhile, heat oil in Dutch oven over medium-high heat until shimmering. Cook onion until softened, about 4 minutes. Add garlic and cook until fragrant, about 30 seconds. Add wine and saffron and cook until liquid has evaporated, about 3 minutes.

3. Add water, cream, Swiss chard, and ½ teaspoon salt and cook until greens begin to wilt, about 3 minutes. Add pasta and simmer over medium heat, stirring often, until pasta is tender and sauce is thick and creamy, about 6 minutes. Stir in red peppers and season with salt and pepper to taste. Serve.

QUICK PREP TIP **CHOPPING ONIONS IN ADVANCE**

On busy, scattered weeknights, we always appreciate a little flexibility, so it's nice if we can do some of the prep work for dinner in advance. We already know that for recipes featuring raw onions, it is best to chop them immediately before you need them. Given a little time, sulfurous compounds form and give onions an "old onion" smell that can unpleasantly dominate. To find out if this applies to onions intended for cooking, we ran a few tests. When onions chopped and stored for several days were cooked simply, most of our tasters were able to distinguish the fresher onions from the older ones. However, when they were incorporated into a more complexly flavored dish—braised green beans with tomatoes—very few tasters could identify the older onions. So, if onions are a mere accent in your dish, feel free to prep them in advance. If they're a focal point, chop them right before using.

Linguine with Cauliflower and Sage Browned Butter

Serves 4

✔ **WHY THIS RECIPE WORKS:** Using nutty, rich browned butter for this sauce's base makes the meal irresistible, while cauliflower, which we brown before cooking it through with some broth, reinforces the flavor and lends texture. Sage and shallot lend depth, while a little cider vinegar cuts the richness.

2 slices hearty white sandwich bread, torn into 1-inch pieces

8 tablespoons unsalted butter, cut into 8 pieces

   Salt and pepper

3 garlic cloves, minced

2 tablespoons chopped fresh sage

1 shallot, minced

1 head cauliflower (2 pounds), cored and cut into 1-inch florets

½ cup low-sodium chicken broth

1 teaspoon cider vinegar

1 pound linguine

1 ounce Parmesan cheese, grated (½ cup)

1. Bring 4 quarts water to boil in large pot. Pulse bread in food processor to coarse crumbs, about 6 pulses. Melt 1 tablespoon butter in 12-inch skillet over medium heat. Add bread crumbs and ½ teaspoon salt and cook, stirring frequently, until golden brown, about 4 minutes. Add garlic and continue to cook for 1 minute. Transfer to bowl.

2. Add 5 tablespoons butter to now-empty skillet. Cook over medium heat, swirling pan, until butter is browned and gives off toasted aroma, about 5 minutes. Off heat, add sage and shallot and stir to combine. Transfer to bowl.

3. Melt remaining 2 tablespoons butter in now-empty skillet over medium-high heat. Add cauliflower and cook until spotted brown, about 5 minutes. Add broth, ½ teaspoon salt, and ¼ teaspoon pepper. Reduce heat to medium-low and cook, covered, until cauliflower is tender, 5 to 7 minutes. Add browned butter and vinegar and stir to combine.

4. Meanwhile, add linguine and 1 tablespoon salt to boiling water and cook, stirring often, until al dente. Drain pasta and return it to pot. Add cauliflower mixture and Parmesan and toss to combine. Top with bread crumbs and serve.

QUICK PREP TIP MAKING BROWNED BUTTER
When making browned butter, it is important to use a skillet with a light-colored interior; the dark color of nonstick or anodized aluminum cookware makes it difficult to judge the color of the butter as it browns. Use medium to medium-high heat, and stir or swirl the butter occasionally so that the milk solids brown evenly. Make sure to transfer the browned butter to a bowl immediately; if left in the skillet, the butter will continue cooking because of the residual heat, and it can go from browned to burnt all too quickly.

Whole-Wheat Pasta with Winter Greens

Serves 4

✔ **WHY THIS RECIPE WORKS:** We love the nutty flavor of whole-wheat pasta, and it's a perfect match for earthy, hearty winter greens. Here, we match whole-wheat spaghetti with kale and we rely on a broth-based sauce to keep the flavors pure and simple. Adding the greens in two batches ensures we can get plenty of greens into the final dish. We finish the pasta by simmering it right in the sauce, which not only keeps things streamlined but also unifies the flavors. The combination of garlic, red pepper flakes, and anchovies, which we add to the skillet just before the greens, helps give our dish a distinctly rustic Italian flair. A sprinkling of walnuts and mildly briny ricotta salata cheese (a semifirm salty sheep's milk cheese) add just the right texture and richness to finish this dish. Though ricotta salata is most often compared to feta, we think in this case Pecorino Romano is the best substitute.

2   tablespoons olive oil

2   onions, halved and sliced thin

6   garlic cloves, minced

¼   teaspoon red pepper flakes

4   anchovy fillets, minced

1½   pounds kale, stemmed and
       chopped

2   cups low-sodium chicken broth
       Salt and pepper

1   pound whole-wheat spaghetti

1   cup walnuts, toasted and
       chopped coarse

2   ounces ricotta salata cheese,
       shaved

1. Bring 4 quarts water to boil in large pot. Heat oil in 12-inch skillet over medium-high heat until shimmering. Add onions and cook until starting to brown, about 5 minutes. Add garlic, red pepper flakes, and anchovies and cook until fragrant, about 30 seconds.

2. Add half of greens to skillet and cook, tossing occasionally, until starting to wilt, about 2 minutes. Add remaining greens, broth, and ¾ teaspoon salt. Cover and cook, tossing occasionally, until greens are tender, about 15 minutes.

3. While greens cook, add spaghetti and 1 tablespoon salt to boiling water and cook, stirring occasionally, until al dente. Reserve ½ cup cooking water, then drain spaghetti and return it to pot. Add sauce to pasta and toss to combine. Simmer until sauce has thickened, about 2 minutes. Season with salt and pepper to taste, and add reserved cooking water as needed to adjust consistency. Transfer to serving bowl. Sprinkle with walnuts and cheese and serve.

SMART SHOPPING WHOLE-WHEAT PASTA

While most of its whole-grain brethren landed toward the bottom of our pasta rankings for their "sour" taste and "gritty" texture, one brand boasted the same "firm" bite as the pastas with few or no whole grains. Tasters lauded **Bionaturae Organic 100% Whole Wheat Spaghetti** for being "heartier than white pasta, without being too wheaty."

Pasta with Roasted Tomatoes and Porcini Sauce

Serves 4

☑ **WHY THIS RECIPE WORKS:** Roasting tomatoes does wonders to concentrate their sweetness, making them a perfect flavor match for the earthy mushrooms in this pasta dish. This recipe comes together like clockwork: While the tomatoes roast, we rehydrate the porcini with broth, then set them aside and build our sauce. White mushrooms, in addition to the porcini, boost the earthy flavor of the sauce, while flour helps it achieve the right consistency. Once all the components come together, a little lemon juice adds a balancing tartness to complete the dish.

4	tablespoons unsalted butter
1½	pounds grape tomatoes, halved
	Salt and pepper
1	cup low-sodium chicken broth
¾	ounce dried porcini mushrooms, rinsed
3	shallots, minced
1	pound white or cremini mushrooms, trimmed and sliced ¼ inch thick
4	garlic cloves, minced
1	tablespoon chopped fresh thyme
2	tablespoons all-purpose flour
½	cup dry white wine
1	pound campanelle
3	tablespoons lemon juice

1. Adjust oven rack to middle position and heat oven to 450 degrees. Bring 4 quarts water to boil in large pot. Microwave 2 tablespoons butter in medium bowl until melted, about 30 seconds. Add tomatoes and toss to coat. Season tomatoes with salt and pepper, then arrange cut side up on rimmed baking sheet. Roast until skins begin to brown on bottom, about 20 minutes. Return to bowl.

2. While tomatoes roast, bring chicken broth to boil in small saucepan over medium-high heat. Off heat, add porcini, cover, and steep for 5 minutes. Transfer porcini to cutting board, reserving cooking liquid, and mince.

3. Melt remaining 2 tablespoons butter in 12-inch skillet over medium-high heat, add shallots, and cook until soft, about 2 minutes. Add white mushrooms and cook until browned, about 8 minutes. Add garlic and thyme and cook until fragrant, about 30 seconds. Sprinkle flour over mixture and stir with rubber spatula until thoroughly incorporated, about 1 minute. Pour wine and reserved porcini cooking liquid into skillet and whisk constantly until no lumps remain and liquid has thickened, about 3 minutes.

4. While sauce cooks, add campanelle and 1 tablespoon salt to boiling water and cook, stirring often, until al dente. Reserve 1 cup cooking water, then drain campanelle and return it to pot. Add sauce, porcini, tomatoes, and lemon juice and toss to combine. Season with salt and pepper to taste, and add reserved cooking water as needed to adjust consistency. Serve.

Penne alla Vodka with Shrimp

Serves 4

✔ **WHY THIS RECIPE WORKS:** Vodka sauce, a classic pairing with penne, takes advantage of the neutral, colorless spirit's ability to pack zing into every bite, and in this recipe we add shrimp to make it a heartier meal. But instead of sautéing the shrimp separately, we speed things up by gently cooking them right in the simmering sauce, which we then combine with the pasta before serving. This step also prevents the shrimp from overcooking and infuses both shrimp and sauce with more flavor. While most penne alla vodka recipes call for canned tomatoes, here we combine fresh tomatoes with a generous dose of tomato paste for the right depth and brightness.

1½	pounds plum tomatoes, cored and chopped
	Salt and pepper
2	tablespoons olive oil
2	tablespoons tomato paste
2	garlic cloves, minced
½	teaspoon red pepper flakes
⅓	cup vodka
1	pound large shrimp (26 to 30 per pound), peeled and deveined
½	cup heavy cream
1	pound penne

1. Bring 4 quarts water to boil in large pot. Toss tomatoes with 1½ teaspoons salt and let drain in colander set over bowl for 5 minutes.

2. Heat oil in 12-inch nonstick skillet over medium heat until shimmering. Add tomato paste, garlic, and red pepper flakes and cook until fragrant, about 30 seconds. Stir in tomatoes and vodka and cook until slightly thickened, about 5 minutes.

3. Season shrimp with salt and pepper, add to skillet, and cook until just opaque, about 3 minutes, stirring halfway through cooking. Add cream and cook until heated through, about 1 minute.

4. Meanwhile, add penne and 1 tablespoon salt to boiling water and cook, stirring often, until al dente. Reserve 1 cup cooking water, then drain pasta and return it to pot. Stir in shrimp and sauce and ½ cup reserved cooking water. Simmer over medium heat, stirring until liquid is thickened and mostly absorbed, about 1 minute. Season with salt and pepper to taste, and add more reserved cooking water as needed to adjust consistency. Serve.

SIMPLE SIDE STEAMED ASPARAGUS WITH OLIVE OIL AND SEA SALT
Cut 1 pound trimmed asparagus on bias into 2-inch lengths. Fit wide saucepan with steamer basket. Add water to pan, keeping level below basket. Bring water to boil, add asparagus, cover, and steam until asparagus is just tender, 3 to 5 minutes. Transfer asparagus to large bowl and toss with 1 tablespoon extra-virgin olive oil and sea salt to taste. Serves 4.

Scallops and Angel Hair with Lemon Cream Sauce

Serves 4

✔ **WHY THIS RECIPE WORKS:** Briny, sweet scallops are the perfect match to this rich cream sauce, which we brighten with plenty of herbs as well as lemon zest and juice. This elegant recipe is also streamlined and simple: We cook the scallops in our skillet first, then set them aside and build the base of the sauce by simmering the cream and lemon zest and juice together for just a few minutes until it thickens to the right consistency. Folding the herbs—chives, basil, and parsley—in at the end ensures they stay fresh and bright.

1	pound large sea scallops, tendons removed
	Salt and pepper
3	tablespoons olive oil
1	onion, chopped fine
3	garlic cloves, minced
1	cup heavy cream
2	teaspoons grated lemon zest plus ¼ cup juice (2 lemons)
1	pound angel hair
½	cup finely chopped fresh parsley
¼	cup finely chopped fresh chives
¼	cup finely chopped fresh basil

1. Bring 4 quarts water to boil in large pot. Pat scallops dry with paper towels and season with salt and pepper. Heat 2 tablespoons oil in 12-inch nonstick skillet over high heat until just smoking. Add scallops and cook, without moving, until well browned, 1½ to 2 minutes. Flip scallops and cook until sides are firm and centers are just opaque, 30 to 90 seconds. Transfer to plate and tent loosely with aluminum foil.

2. Add remaining 1 tablespoon oil and onion to now-empty skillet and cook until softened, about 4 minutes. Add garlic and cook until fragrant, about 30 seconds. Add heavy cream and lemon zest and juice and bring to simmer. Cook until sauce is slightly thickened, about 2 minutes.

3. While sauce cooks, add angel hair and 1 tablespoon salt to boiling water and cook, stirring often, until al dente. Reserve 1 cup cooking water, then drain angel hair and return it to pot. Add sauce, parsley, chives, and basil to pasta and toss to combine. Season with salt and pepper to taste, and add reserved cooking water as needed to adjust consistency. Serve with scallops.

QUICK PREP TIP CHOPPING BASIL

Freshly chopped basil can quickly turn black through a process called oxidation. The change in color doesn't lessen its flavor; but is there a way to preserve the color appeal without sacrificing flavor? We tried several tricks we had come across to find out. Dropping basil into boiling water, then transferring it to ice water to stop the cooking and "fix" the color was too much trouble. Coating the basil in oil just before chopping it made it slippery and difficult to chop, and barely helped. Coating just-chopped basil in oil did slow the color change, but it also made the basil a little oily—OK in some, but not all, preparations. Our conclusion? All those "tricks" aren't worth the fuss. For the best flavor and easiest prep, chop basil just before you need it.

Spaghetti with Spicy White Fresh Clam Sauce

Serves 4

☑ **WHY THIS RECIPE WORKS:** Linguine with white clam sauce is an Italian classic, but these days most versions are subpar because they rely on canned clams. Going back to the dish's roots, we use fresh clams here, which means this dish is still plenty quick but also full of appealing flavor. We cook the clams with garlic, shallots, and wine while the pasta cooks in a separate pot, then we combine the two and add butter for richness, as well as a good dose of hot sauce and parsley. We prefer Tabasco in this recipe because it produces a bright heat and distinctive flavor. When shopping for clams, choose the smallest ones you can find (typically littlenecks). Larger clams will work, but allow a few extra minutes for their shells to open. Because clams are naturally salty, be careful when seasoning the pasta before serving.

2	tablespoons extra-virgin olive oil
2	shallots, minced
3	garlic cloves, minced
2	pounds littleneck clams, scrubbed
½	cup dry white wine
1	pound spaghetti
	Salt and pepper
4	tablespoons unsalted butter
2	tablespoons Tabasco
¼	cup chopped fresh parsley

1. Bring 4 quarts water to boil in large pot. Heat oil in 12-inch skillet over medium-high heat until shimmering. Add shallots and cook until softened, about 2 minutes. Stir in garlic and cook until fragrant, about 30 seconds. Reduce heat to medium, stir in clams and wine, cover, and simmer, shaking pan occasionally, until clams begin to open, about 6 minutes. Uncover skillet and continue to simmer until all clams have opened (discard any that do not open), about 2 minutes.

2. Meanwhile, add spaghetti and 1 tablespoon salt to boiling water and cook, stirring often, until al dente. Reserve ½ cup cooking water, then drain spaghetti and return it to pot. Add clam sauce and toss to coat. Add butter, Tabasco, and parsley, stirring constantly until butter is thoroughly melted. Season with salt and pepper to taste, and add reserved cooking water as needed to adjust consistency. Serve.

SMART SHOPPING SPAGHETTI

Spaghetti makes a versatile partner for just about any type of sauce. Plus, it promises a cheap dinner—or, at least, it used to. When we recently checked out brands at the supermarket, we saw a few boxes priced around a dollar, while others cost four times that. We recently sampled eight brands of spaghetti to find out if we had to spend more money for great pasta. After cooking and tasting six Italian imports and two domestic brands dressed simply with olive oil and tossed with a tomato sauce, we found our winner. Our favorite spaghetti—and also one of the two cheapest brands we tasted (less than $2 a pound)—was an Italian import. Tasters preferred **DeCecco Spaghetti no. 12** for its "clean wheat flavor" and "firm" strands with "good chew."

Spring Farfalle with Salmon, Leeks, and Asparagus

Serves 4

✓ **WHY THIS RECIPE WORKS:** The combination of fresh leeks and asparagus makes this a recipe perfect for springtime. We complement the two vegetables by making a wine-and-cream sauce and adding salmon, which lends just the rich flavor the dish needs. Although there are several components here, we minimize the cookware needed by cooking the leeks, salmon, and sauce together in our skillet, and we cook the asparagus and pasta together in a Dutch oven. (If added to the pan with the sauce, the asparagus would turn brown because of the wine's acidity.) Then all we have to do is combine the two components just before serving.

1	tablespoon unsalted butter
2	leeks, white and light green parts only, halved lengthwise, sliced thin, and washed thoroughly
2	(6- to 8-ounce) skinless salmon fillets, 1¼ inches thick
	Salt and pepper
1	cup dry white wine
¾	cup heavy cream
1	pound farfalle
1	pound asparagus, trimmed and cut on bias into 1½-inch lengths
¼	cup chopped fresh parsley
1	tablespoon lemon juice

1. Bring 4 quarts water to boil in large pot. Melt butter in 12-inch nonstick skillet over medium-high heat. Add leeks and cook until tender, about 4 minutes. Season salmon with salt and pepper. Add wine followed by salmon to skillet and cook, covered, until fish is just cooked through, about 6 minutes. Transfer salmon to plate and tent loosely with aluminum foil. Add cream to skillet and cook until sauce has thickened, about 2 minutes. When cool enough to handle, break salmon into bite-size pieces, then re-cover with foil.

2. While salmon cooks, add farfalle and 1 tablespoon salt to boiling water and cook for 10 minutes. Add asparagus and continue cooking until farfalle is al dente and asparagus is tender, about 3 minutes. Reserve ½ cup cooking water, then drain farfalle and asparagus and return them to pot. Add sauce, parsley, and lemon juice to pasta and toss to combine. Gently fold in fish. Season with salt and pepper to taste, and add reserved cooking water as needed to adjust consistency. Serve.

QUICK PREP TIP CLEANING LEEKS
After trimming and discarding root end and dark green leaves of each leek, slice leek in half lengthwise, then cut crosswise into small pieces. Rinse leeks in bowl of water, letting any dirt and sand settle to bottom.

Skillet Macaroni and Cheese with Bacon

Serves 4

✓ **WHY THIS RECIPE WORKS:** Mac and cheese with various add-ins is all the rage these days; here we give it our own spin by using a duo of cheeses—extra-sharp cheddar for flavor and Monterey Jack for gooey appeal—plus crisped bacon for heartiness. Scallions and a bread-crumb topping complete the picture. Best of all, this satisfying meal is made entirely in a skillet. After cooking the bacon, we toast the bread crumbs in the rendered bacon fat to give them great flavor. Next, we cook the pasta in the skillet, using the base ingredients for the sauce (water and evaporated milk) as the pasta cooking liquid. Additional evaporated milk, thickened with a quick cornstarch slurry, stands in for the roux traditionally used to thicken mac and cheese. After the sauce thickens, we stir in the cheese, then scallion whites, and sprinkle the bread crumbs on top.

2	slices hearty white sandwich bread, torn into 1-inch pieces
6	slices bacon, chopped
	Salt and pepper
4	scallions, white parts sliced thin, green parts minced
3¾	cups water, plus more as needed
1	(12-ounce) can evaporated milk
12	ounces (3 cups) elbow macaroni
1	teaspoon cornstarch
12	ounces extra-sharp cheddar cheese, shredded (3 cups)
8	ounces Monterey Jack cheese, shredded (2 cups)

1. Pulse bread in food processor to coarse crumbs, about 6 pulses. Cook bacon in 12-inch nonstick skillet over medium-high heat until crisp, about 5 minutes. Using slotted spoon, transfer bacon to paper towel–lined plate. Pour off all but 1 tablespoon fat from skillet. Add bread crumbs and ¼ teaspoon pepper to skillet and cook, stirring frequently, until deep golden brown, about 4 minutes. Stir in scallion greens, then transfer to bowl and wipe out skillet.

2. Bring water, 1¼ cups evaporated milk, and ½ teaspoon salt to simmer in now-empty skillet over medium-high heat. Add macaroni and cook, stirring often, until macaroni is al dente. Whisk together remaining ¼ cup evaporated milk and cornstarch, then stir into skillet. Simmer until slightly thickened, about 1 minute.

3. Off heat, stir in cheddar and Monterey Jack, 1 handful at a time, adding water as needed to adjust consistency. Stir in bacon and scallion whites, then sprinkle with bread-crumb mixture. Serve.

SIMPLE SIDE BROCCOLI WITH BALSAMIC VINAIGRETTE
Place 1 pound broccoli florets and ¼ cup water in large bowl. Cover and microwave until tender, about 4 minutes; drain. In small bowl, whisk ¼ cup extra-virgin olive oil, 4 teaspoons balsamic vinegar, 1 tablespoon chopped fresh basil, 1 small minced shallot, and 1 small minced garlic clove. Season dressing with salt and pepper to taste and toss with broccoli. Serves 4.

Easy Garlicky Risotto with Broccolini

Serves 4

✔ **WHY THIS RECIPE WORKS:** The classic cooking method for risotto—adding liquid to the pot in small increments while stirring for half an hour—is a deal-breaker for a quick weeknight meal. To speed things up, we start the rice in the microwave and finish it on the stovetop with about five minutes of stirring. And to minimize the cookware, we cook the broccolini along with the rice. Garlic plays triple duty here: Several cloves sliced and fried lend a slightly sweet flavor; the garlic oil from frying is added to the rice before microwaving and used to sauté the aromatics; and three minced cloves are cooked with the rice on the stovetop.

¼	cup extra-virgin olive oil
12	garlic cloves (9 sliced thin, 3 minced)
5	cups low-sodium chicken broth, plus extra as needed
1½	cups Arborio rice
1	onion, chopped fine
½	cup dry white wine
1	pound broccolini, trimmed and cut into 2-inch pieces
1½	ounces Parmesan cheese, grated (¾ cup), plus extra for serving
	Salt and pepper

1. Heat oil and sliced garlic in Dutch oven over medium-high heat. Cook garlic, turning frequently, until light golden brown, 4 to 6 minutes. Using slotted spoon, transfer garlic chips to paper towel–lined plate and transfer oil to bowl.

2. Combine 3½ cups broth, rice, and 2 tablespoons reserved garlic oil in large bowl. Cover and microwave until rice is softened and most of liquid has been absorbed, 10 to 12 minutes.

3. Heat remaining garlic oil in now-empty Dutch oven over medium-high heat until shimmering. Stir in onion and cook until softened, about 3 minutes. Add minced garlic and cook until fragrant, about 30 seconds. Add wine and cook until reduced by half, about 2 minutes. Add rice, remaining 1½ cups broth, and broccolini and simmer, stirring constantly, until rice and vegetables are tender, 5 to 7 minutes. Stir in Parmesan, season with salt and pepper to taste, and add extra broth as needed to adjust consistency. Sprinkle with garlic chips and serve with extra Parmesan.

SMART SHOPPING THE BROCCOLI FAMILY

Between the broccoli, broccolini, and broccoli rabe at the supermarket, it's hard to keep them all straight. So what sets each one apart? We're all pretty familiar with broccoli (left), the cruciferous vegetable that's a relative of cabbage. Broccolini (middle) is a cross between broccoli and Chinese broccoli. It has an elongated stem with tender broccoli shoots and a sweet, slightly mineral taste (see page 143 for information about prepping broccolini). Broccoli rabe (right), also known as rapini, has long leafy stems with green buds similar to broccoli flowers. It is considered part of the broccoli family even though it is also in the same subspecies as the turnip.

Baked Risotto with Shrimp and Zucchini

Serves 4

✔ **WHY THIS RECIPE WORKS:** This is a great weeknight recipe since baking risotto is conveniently hands-off. We choose a simple, classic flavor profile with onion, garlic, and white wine, then we give it fresh flavor and color by topping it with sautéed zucchini and shrimp. After getting the risotto started on the stovetop in a Dutch oven, we transfer it to the oven to cook through, then stir in the Parmesan and parsley at the end. While the risotto bakes, we cook our zucchini on the stovetop. We use already cooked and peeled shrimp to save even more time, so all we have to do is heat it through.

3	cups low-sodium chicken broth
5	tablespoons unsalted butter
1	onion, chopped
1½	cups Arborio rice
2	garlic cloves, minced
½	cup dry white wine
3	ounces Parmesan cheese, grated (1½ cups)
¼	cup chopped fresh parsley
	Salt and pepper
2	large zucchini, halved lengthwise and cut into ¼-inch pieces
20	cooked and peeled large shrimp (26 to 30 per pound), tails removed

1. Adjust oven rack to middle position and heat oven to 400 degrees. Bring broth to simmer in medium saucepan over medium-high heat. Cover and keep warm.

2. Meanwhile, melt 3 tablespoons butter in Dutch oven over medium heat. Add onion and cook until softened, about 4 minutes. Add rice and stir until edges begin to turn translucent, about 2 minutes. Add garlic and cook until fragrant, about 30 seconds. Add wine and cook, stirring until completely absorbed, about 1 minute. Pour broth over rice mixture, cover, and transfer to oven. Bake until rice is tender and liquid is absorbed, about 15 minutes. Stir in Parmesan and parsley and season with salt and pepper to taste.

3. Melt remaining 2 tablespoons butter in 12-inch nonstick skillet over medium heat. Add zucchini and cook until lightly browned and tender, about 8 minutes. Add shrimp and cook until heated through, about 1 minute. Season with salt and pepper to taste, and serve over risotto.

SMART SHOPPING ARBORIO RICE

The stubby, milky grains of Arborio rice, once grown exclusively in Italy, are valued for their high starch content and the creaminess they bring to risotto. But does the best Arborio have to come from Italy? To find out, we cooked up batches of Parmesan risotto with two domestically grown brands of Arborio rice and four Italian imports. To our surprise, the winning rice, **RiceSelect Arborio Rice**, hailed not from the Boot, but from the Lone Star State. Its "creamy, smooth" grains won over tasters with their "good bite." There really isn't a substitute for Arborio rice that will deliver the same results, but our tasters found that batches of risotto made with medium- and short-grain rice were acceptably creamy; they just lacked the signature firmness of the Arborio grains.

Cheesy Gnocchi and Cauliflower Gratin

Serves 4 to 6

✓ **WHY THIS RECIPE WORKS:** Not all comfort food has to take all day to make. This rich gratin is the perfect dinner to warm you through on a cold evening, and it only requires a handful of ingredients and minimal cooking time since we start with store-bought gnocchi. While some gratins call for a cheese topping, we opt for a bread-crumb topping here and employ cheese to help create a sauce. To ensure each component is perfectly cooked, we boil the gnocchi in a pot and prepare the cauliflower and sauce in our skillet. Then we combine the two, top them with bread crumbs (which we make quickly in the food processor), and transfer the gratin to the oven just long enough to brown the crumbs.

2   slices hearty white sandwich bread, torn into 1-inch pieces

2   tablespoons unsalted butter, plus 2 tablespoons melted and cooled

     Salt and pepper

1   pound vacuum-packed gnocchi

1   large head cauliflower (3 pounds), cored and cut into 1-inch florets

¾   cup heavy cream

4   teaspoons dry sherry

1   tablespoon fresh thyme leaves

4   ounces Gorgonzola cheese, crumbled (1 cup)

1. Bring 4 quarts water to boil in large pot. Position oven rack 5 inches from heating element and heat broiler. Pulse bread, melted butter, ¼ teaspoon salt, and ⅛ teaspoon pepper in food processor to coarse crumbs, about 6 pulses.

2. Add gnocchi and 1 tablespoon salt to boiling water and cook, stirring often, until tender and floating, about 4 minutes. Drain gnocchi and transfer to plate.

3. Meanwhile, melt remaining 2 tablespoons butter in 12-inch skillet over medium-high heat. Add cauliflower and cook until lightly browned, about 5 minutes. Add cream, sherry, thyme, then Gorgonzola and cook until cheese is melted and sauce is thickened, about 5 minutes. Stir in gnocchi and simmer until gnocchi is heated through, about 1 minute. Season with salt and pepper to taste.

4. Transfer gnocchi and cauliflower to 3-quart broiler-safe baking dish. Sprinkle bread crumbs evenly on top and broil until bread crumbs are lightly browned, 3 to 5 minutes. Serve.

SIMPLE SIDE SKILLET GREEN BEANS
Heat 1 tablespoon olive oil in 12-inch skillet over medium heat until shimmering. Add 1 minced shallot and cook until lightly browned, about 4 minutes. Stir in ½ teaspoon minced fresh thyme and ¾ cup low-sodium chicken broth. Add 1 pound trimmed green beans, cover, reduce heat to low, and simmer until beans are tender, 15 to 20 minutes. Season with salt and pepper to taste. Serves 4 to 6.

Gnocchi with Spinach, Ham, and Gorgonzola

Serves 4

WHY THIS RECIPE WORKS: Homemade gnocchi is hard to beat, but it's too labor-intensive for a week-night meal so we focus on adding flavor to store-bought. Lightly browning just one side of the gnocchi after cooking it like traditional pasta boosts its flavor and adds texture; we found that drying the gnocchi on paper towels is key to getting good browning. (Pay careful attention when adding the gnocchi to the pan; any excess moisture on the gnocchi will splatter when it meets the hot oil.) We rely on deli ham, which we brown in the skillet after the gnocchi, to add just the right meaty component, while Gorgonzola melts into the dish to create a luxuriously creamy, flavorful sauce. Spinach adds color and a nice balancing mineral flavor, and we wait to add it until the last few minutes of cooking to avoid drab, mushy leaves in the finished dish. Lastly, pine nuts lend just the right texture.

1 pound vacuum-packed gnocchi
  Salt and pepper
2 tablespoons extra-virgin olive oil
6 ounces sliced deli ham, cut into ¼-inch strips
2 garlic cloves, minced
¼ cup pine nuts, toasted
3 ounces Gorgonzola cheese, crumbled (¾ cup)
1 teaspoon lemon juice
2 ounces (2 cups) baby spinach

1. Bring 4 quarts water to boil in large pot. Add gnocchi and 1 tablespoon salt to boiling water and cook, stirring often, until tender and floating, about 4 minutes. Reserve ½ cup cooking water, then drain gnocchi and transfer it to paper towel–lined plate.

2. Heat oil in 12-inch nonstick skillet over medium-high heat until shimmering. Add gnocchi and cook, without stirring, until browned, about 4 minutes. Stir in ham and cook until it begins to brown, 2 to 4 minutes. Add garlic and cook until fragrant, about 30 seconds.

3. Add reserved cooking water, pine nuts, cheese, and lemon juice to skillet and stir until cheese starts to melt and sauce becomes creamy. Add spinach and stir until just wilted, 1 to 2 minutes. Season with salt and pepper to taste. Serve.

SMART SHOPPING **SUPERMARKET POTATO GNOCCHI**
Fresh homemade gnocchi is more tender and delicately flavorful than any store-bought option, but there isn't always time to make your own. When time is short, is it worth buying vacuum-packed, shelf-stable gnocchi, which can be ready in less than five minutes? We recently tasted four nationally available brands, sampling them plain, sautéed in browned butter, and baked into a gratin. Plain and in browned butter, all brands had a distinct acidic "sourdough" flavor due to preservatives that help keep the product shelf-stable. However, when covered in sauce and cheese in the gratin, this flavor was less noticeable in three of the brands and disappeared altogether in our winner, **Gia Russa Gnocchi with Potato.** This brand was praised for having the best flavor and texture of the bunch.

Sopa Seca

Serves 4

✔ **WHY THIS RECIPE WORKS:** The classic Mexican dish *sopa seca*, literally "dry soup," gets its name from its cooking process. Noodles are simmered in a broth that reduces and thickens as the noodles cook. With its flavorful broth and topping of melted cheese, the dish ends up more like a comforting noodle casserole than soup. For this version, we toast vermicelli noodles in a Dutch oven to deepen their flavor, then we cook them with tomatoes, chicken broth, and aromatics. Along with garlic and onion, chili powder and oregano help give this recipe a Mexican flavor profile, and using precooked rotisserie chicken minimizes the work—the meat just gets stirred in at the end. After cooking the noodles and broth together, all we have to do is add the cheese and transfer the casserole to the oven for a few minutes so the cheese can melt.

3 tablespoons olive oil

1 pound vermicelli, broken into 3-inch pieces

1 onion, chopped

5 garlic cloves, minced

1 tablespoon chili powder

2 teaspoons dried oregano

1 (14.5-ounce) can diced tomatoes

1¾ cups low-sodium chicken broth

1 (2½-pound) rotisserie chicken, skin and bones discarded, meat shredded into bite-size pieces (3 cups)

Salt and pepper

8 ounces Monterey Jack cheese, shredded (2 cups)

Sour cream

1. Adjust oven rack to middle position and heat oven to 400 degrees. Grease 13 by 9-inch baking dish. Heat 2 tablespoons oil in Dutch oven over medium heat until shimmering. Add vermicelli and cook until toasted, 3 to 5 minutes. Transfer to plate. Add remaining 1 tablespoon oil and onion to Dutch oven and cook until onion is softened, about 4 minutes. Add garlic, chili powder, and oregano and cook until fragrant, about 30 seconds.

2. Add tomatoes, chicken broth, and toasted noodles and toss to combine. Cover and simmer, stirring occasionally, until noodles are tender and broth has been mostly absorbed, about 15 minutes. Stir in chicken and season with salt and pepper to taste.

3. Transfer noodle mixture to prepared baking dish. Sprinkle with Monterey Jack, transfer to oven, and bake until cheese melts, about 4 minutes. Serve with sour cream.

QUICK PREP TIP SHREDDING SEMISOFT CHEESE
Semisoft cheeses like Monterey Jack can be messy to grate. To keep the holes of the grater from clogging, lightly coat that side of the box grater with vegetable oil spray before shredding the cheese.

Three-Cheese Pesto Lasagna Stacks

Serves 4

✓ **WHY THIS RECIPE WORKS:** This recipe makes lasagna an easy weeknight option by baking four smaller stacks of lasagna for just 10 minutes, then cutting the stacks in half and arranging one half on top of the other to make a multilayered lasagna with impressive height. We use prepared pesto from the supermarket refrigerated section but you can certainly make your own if you have time.

1	tablespoon vegetable oil
12	no-boil lasagna noodles
6	ounces (6 cups) baby arugula
1	pound (2 cups) whole-milk ricotta cheese
1½	ounces Parmesan cheese, grated (¾ cup)
1	large egg, lightly beaten
1	teaspoon grated lemon zest
	Salt and pepper
1	(7- ounce) container basil pesto (⅔ cup)
8	ounces mozzarella cheese, shredded (2 cups)

1. Adjust oven rack to upper-middle position and heat oven to 450 degrees. Brush oil over bottom of baking sheet; set aside. Place noodles in large baking dish and cover with boiling water. Let soak for 10 minutes, agitating noodles occasionally.

2. While noodles soak, place arugula in bowl, cover, and microwave until wilted, 2 to 4 minutes. Drain and chop coarse. Combine ricotta, ½ cup Parmesan, egg, lemon zest, chopped arugula, ½ teaspoon salt, and ¼ teaspoon pepper in bowl.

3. Remove noodles from water and place in single layer on kitchen towel. Arrange 4 noodles on oiled baking sheet. Spread 1 tablespoon pesto over each noodle. Spread ¼ cup ricotta mixture evenly over pesto, followed by 2 heaping tablespoons mozzarella. Repeat with 1 more layer of noodles, remaining pesto, remaining ricotta, and 2 heaping tablespoons mozzarella on each stack. Finish with remaining noodles, remaining mozzarella, and remaining Parmesan. Bake stacks until cheese is bubbly and beginning to brown and filling is heated through, about 10 minutes. Cut each stack in half crosswise, then, using spatula, stack 2 halves on top of each other and repeat to create 4 stacks. Serve.

EASY LASAGNA STACKS

Spread the pesto over the noodles, the ricotta over the pesto, then the mozzarella over the ricotta. Repeat with 1 more layer of noodles, and then pesto, ricotta, and mozzarella. Finish with noodles, mozzarella, and Parmesan. Bake until filling is heated through. Cut each stack in half and place each half stack on top of its other half.

GRILLED BEEF TENDERLOIN WITH WATERCRESS SALAD

Fire Up the Grill

248   Grilled Dijon Steak with Potato–Green Bean Salad

250   Grilled Beef Tenderloin with Watercress Salad

251   Grilled T-Bone Steaks with Radicchio and Endive

253   Grilled Beef Kebabs with Napa Cabbage Slaw

254   Grilled Flank Steak with Thai Pesto Noodles

256   Grilled Indian-Spiced Chicken with Mango Relish

258   Grilled Chicken with Lemon-Thyme Potato Salad

259   Greek-Style Grilled Chicken Pita Sandwiches

261   Grilled Breaded Chicken with Tomato Salad

262   Grilled Thai Turkey Sliders

263   Spice-Rubbed Grilled Pork Tenderloins

264   Mojo Grilled Pork Chops with Orange-Jícama Salad

266   Grilled Andouille Burgers with Spicy Mayonnaise

267   Grilled Garlic Sausages with Lentil Salad

269   Vietnamese-Style Grilled Pork Sandwiches

270   Grilled Glazed Tofu with Warm Cabbage Slaw

271   Grilled Salmon Sandwiches with Broccoli Slaw

272   Grilled Spicy Shrimp Masala

Grilled Dijon Steak with Potato-Green Bean Salad

Serves 4

✔ **WHY THIS RECIPE WORKS:** Simply brushing flank steak with Dijon mustard before putting it on the grill does an impressive job of adding flavor to this beefy, quick-cooking, and affordable cut. Plus, the mustard not only acts as a flavor enhancer for the steak in this recipe, but it also serves as the base, in combination with lemon juice, for the dressing in our potato and green bean salad side dish. While the water for cooking the vegetables is coming to a boil, we prepare the dressing, then the potatoes and beans go into the pot. Tossing the cooked vegetables with the dressing while they're still warm allows them to better soak up the flavors. We recommend cooking the flank steak only to medium-rare or it will become tough and stringy.

½   cup extra-virgin olive oil

5   tablespoons Dijon mustard

3   tablespoons lemon juice
    Salt and pepper

1   pound red potatoes, cut into
    1-inch pieces

8   ounces green beans, trimmed
    and cut into 1½-inch lengths

2   tablespoons chopped fresh dill

1   (1½-pound) flank steak,
    trimmed

1. Bring 4 quarts water to boil in large pot. Whisk oil, 2 tablespoons mustard, and lemon juice together in large bowl and season with salt and pepper. Add potatoes, beans, and 1 tablespoon salt to boiling water and cook until potatoes are tender and beans are bright green, 5 to 7 minutes. Drain vegetables and transfer to bowl with dressing. Add dill and toss to coat. Season with salt and pepper to taste.

2A. FOR A CHARCOAL GRILL: Open bottom vent completely. Light large chimney starter filled with charcoal briquettes (6 quarts). When top coals are partially covered with ash, pour evenly over grill. Set cooking grate in place, cover, and open lid vent completely. Heat grill until hot, about 5 minutes.

2B. FOR A GAS GRILL: Turn all burners to high, cover, and heat grill until hot, about 15 minutes.

3. Pat steak dry with paper towels and brush with remaining 3 tablespoons mustard. Clean and oil cooking grate. Place steak on grill and cook (covered if using gas) until well browned and meat registers 120 to 125 degrees (for medium-rare), 4 to 6 minutes per side. Transfer to platter, tent loosely with aluminum foil, and let rest for 5 minutes. Slice steak thin against grain and arrange on platter. Serve with potato and green bean salad.

Grilled Beef Tenderloin with Watercress Salad

Serves 4

✓ **WHY THIS RECIPE WORKS:** We match mild beef tenderloin with a salad that boasts tons of texture and flavor to give this dinner a big boost. Endive and watercress provide crunch plus a slight bitterness, while blue cheese serves as a creamy, salty counterpoint, and pear and grilled onion give it a hint of sweetness. Grilling raw onion slices can lead to blackened, crunchy onions. To ensure they are cooked through perfectly, we start them in the microwave. Once they're softened, we grill them until they're tender and have a slight char (it's easiest to simply empty the microwaved onions straight from the bowl onto the grill grate into a pile, then spread them into a single layer). Since endive leaves tend to discolor when cut in advance of serving, it's best to wait to cut them until you're ready to toss the salad.

3	tablespoons extra-virgin olive oil
2	tablespoons balsamic vinegar
1	red onion, sliced into ¼-inch-thick rings
4	(6- to 8-ounce) center-cut beef tenderloin steaks, 1 inch thick, trimmed
	Salt and pepper
8	ounces (8 cups) watercress, trimmed
1	head Belgian endive (4 ounces), leaves separated and halved lengthwise
3	ounces blue cheese, crumbled (¾ cup)
1	Bosc pear, halved, cored, and sliced thin

1. Whisk 2 tablespoons oil and vinegar together in large bowl. Toss onion rings with remaining 1 tablespoon oil in second bowl. Cover and microwave on high until rings are almost tender, about 3 minutes. Transfer to plate.

2A. FOR A CHARCOAL GRILL: Open bottom vent completely. Light large chimney starter filled with charcoal briquettes (6 quarts). When top coals are partially covered with ash, pour evenly over grill. Set cooking grate in place, cover, and open lid vent completely. Heat grill until hot, about 5 minutes.

2B. FOR A GAS GRILL: Turn all burners to high, cover, and heat grill until hot, about 15 minutes.

3. Pat steaks dry with paper towels and season steaks and onion with salt and pepper. Clean and oil cooking grate. Place steaks on grill and cook (covered if using gas) until steaks register 120 to 125 degrees (for medium-rare), about 5 minutes per side. Transfer to platter and tent loosely with aluminum foil. Meanwhile, place onion rings on grill and cook until lightly charred and tender, 3 to 5 minutes. Transfer to bowl with vinaigrette.

4. Add watercress, endive, blue cheese, and pear to bowl with onions and toss until thoroughly combined and coated evenly with dressing. Serve with steak.

Grilled T-Bone Steaks with Radicchio and Endive

Serves 4

✔ **WHY THIS RECIPE WORKS:** Grilled T-bone steaks require little more than proper seasoning and a nice side dish. We opt for an elegant duo of endive and radicchio, and we grill the vegetables (while the steaks rest to save time) to add smokiness and lessen their bitterness. For complexity, we toss them in a balsamic-and-honey dressing before putting them on the grill, then finish with another drizzle of the dressing before serving.

½ cup extra-virgin olive oil

3 tablespoons balsamic vinegar

1 tablespoon honey

1 garlic clove, minced
   Salt and pepper

4 heads Belgian endive (1 pound), halved lengthwise

2 heads radicchio (1¼ pounds), cut into quarters through core

2 (1¼-pound) T-bone or porterhouse steaks, 1½ inches thick, trimmed

1. Whisk oil, vinegar, honey, and garlic together in large bowl. Season with salt and pepper to taste. Reserve 2 tablespoons dressing, then add endive and radicchio to bowl with remaining dressing and toss to coat.

2A. FOR A CHARCOAL GRILL: Open bottom vent completely. Light large chimney starter filled with charcoal briquettes (6 quarts). When top coals are partially covered with ash, pour evenly over grill. Set cooking grate in place, cover, and open lid vent completely. Heat grill until hot, about 5 minutes.

2B. FOR A GAS GRILL: Turn all burners to high, cover, and heat grill until hot, about 15 minutes.

3. Season steaks with salt and pepper. Clean and oil cooking grate. Place steaks on grill and cook (covered if using gas) until charred on both sides and meat registers 120 to 125 degrees (for medium-rare), 5 to 8 minutes per side. Transfer steaks to cutting board, tent loosely with aluminum foil, and let rest 5 minutes. Cut both sections of meat (the tenderloin and the strip) off bone for each steak. Slice each piece crosswise ½ inch thick.

4. While steaks rest, place endive and radicchio on grill and cook until charred and tender on both sides, 3 to 4 minutes per side. Drizzle reserved dressing over vegetables and serve with steak.

SMART SHOPPING RADICCHIO AND ENDIVE
Radicchio (left), a member of the chicory family, boasts an assertive flavor, a peppery bitterness, and unmistakable dark red leaves. Its botanical cousin, Belgian endive (right), has crisp, spear-shaped leaves that are refreshingly bitter. Both of these bitter greens lend themselves to grilling. When shopping, look for heads that are tight and firm.

Grilled Beef Kebabs with Napa Cabbage Slaw

Serves 4

✔ **WHY THIS RECIPE WORKS:** Kebabs are a great all-in-one meal, but it takes a little know-how to ensure every component cooks through just right. Marinating steak tips in lemon juice, soy sauce, and garlic gives them a rich flavor that is nicely balanced by the sweetness and slight acidity of the pineapple, while pearl onions add mild bite and texture. Frozen pearl onions are a great choice for weeknight skewers since they require no prep. To make sure the onions finish cooking at the same time as the meat and the pineapple, we microwave them for about three minutes before putting them on the skewer. A slaw with an Asian-inspired dressing—we call on rice vinegar, ginger, and soy sauce—is quick to toss together.

20	frozen pearl onions
5	tablespoons vegetable oil
	Salt and pepper
⅓	cup plus 2 tablespoons soy sauce
2	tablespoons lemon juice
4	garlic cloves, minced
1½	pounds sirloin steak tips, trimmed and cut into 1-inch chunks
2	tablespoons rice vinegar
2	teaspoons grated fresh ginger
½	head napa cabbage, shredded (3 cups)
1	pineapple, peeled, cored, and cut into 1-inch pieces (4 cups)

1. Combine pearl onions and 1 tablespoon oil in large bowl. Season with salt and pepper, cover, and microwave until onions are tender, about 3 minutes.

2. Meanwhile, combine ⅓ cup soy sauce, 2 tablespoons oil, lemon juice, and garlic in large bowl. Add meat and toss to coat. In another bowl, whisk together rice vinegar, remaining 2 tablespoons soy sauce, remaining 2 tablespoons oil, and ginger. Add napa cabbage to bowl with dressing and toss to coat.

3. Thread meat, onions, and pineapple onto six 14-inch metal skewers.

4A. FOR A CHARCOAL GRILL: Open bottom vent completely. Light large chimney starter filled with charcoal briquettes (6 quarts). When top coals are partially covered with ash, pour evenly over grill. Set cooking grate in place, cover, and open lid vent completely. Heat grill until hot, about 5 minutes.

4B. FOR A GAS GRILL: Turn all burners to high, cover, and heat grill until hot, about 15 minutes.

5. Clean and oil cooking grate. Place kebabs on grill and cook (covered if using gas) until meat is lightly charred and cooked through, about 8 minutes, turning every 2 minutes. Transfer to platter and serve with slaw.

Grilled Flank Steak with Thai Pesto Noodles

Serves 4

✔ **WHY THIS RECIPE WORKS:** We love affordable flank steak because it cooks quickly and has great beefy flavor. Here, we pair it with rice noodles that are tossed in a Thai-inspired pesto. The recipe keeps within a quick-cooking weeknight time frame since we can cook the noodles and prepare the pesto all while the grill preheats. Traditionally, rice noodles are soaked in hot water to soften them. However, the usual 20-minute soak takes too long for this recipe, so we cook them like traditional pasta, then rinse them after cooking to keep them from turning starchy and gluey.

8	ounces (¼-inch-wide) rice noodles
	Salt and pepper
1	cup fresh cilantro leaves
1	cup fresh mint leaves
⅔	cup dry-roasted peanuts
2	tablespoons lime juice
2	tablespoons fish sauce
½	jalapeño chile, stemmed, seeded, and chopped
2	garlic cloves, minced
½	cup coconut milk
1	(1½-pound) flank steak, trimmed

1. Bring 3 quarts water to boil in large saucepan. Add rice noodles and 1 teaspoon salt to boiling water and cook until noodles are al dente, 6 to 8 minutes. Drain noodles and rinse under cold water.

2. Meanwhile, process cilantro, mint, peanuts, lime juice, fish sauce, jalapeño, and garlic in food processor until finely ground, 20 to 30 seconds. With processor running, add coconut milk and process until mixture is smooth and creamy, about 20 seconds. Toss noodles with sauce and season with salt and pepper to taste.

3A. FOR A CHARCOAL GRILL: Open bottom vent completely. Light large chimney starter filled with charcoal briquettes (6 quarts). When top coals are partially covered with ash, pour evenly over grill. Set cooking grate in place, cover, and open lid vent completely. Heat grill until hot, about 5 minutes.

3B. FOR A GAS GRILL: Turn all burners to high, cover, and heat grill until hot, about 15 minutes.

4. Season steak with salt and pepper. Clean and oil cooking grate. Place steak on grill and cook (covered if using gas) until well browned and steak registers 120 to 125 degrees (for medium-rare), 4 to 6 minutes per side. Transfer steak to cutting board, tent loosely with foil, and let rest for 5 minutes. Slice steak thin against grain and serve with pesto noodles.

ALL ABOUT Setting Up Your Grill

Lighting Charcoal with a Chimney Starter

We prefer to start a charcoal fire with a chimney starter, or flue starter. Fill the starter's bottom section with crumpled newspaper, set it on the grill grate, and fill the top with charcoal. When you light the newspaper, the charcoal easily ignites. Once the coals are coated with an even layer of fine gray ash, turn them out into the grill.

Lighting Charcoal without a Starter

If you don't have a chimney starter, use the following technique:

1. Place enough sheets of crumpled newspaper beneath charcoal grate to fill space loosely, about 8 sheets.

2. With bottom vents open, pile charcoal on grate and light paper. After about 20 minutes, coals should be covered with gray ash and ready to arrange for cooking.

Lighting a Gas Grill

Follow the directions in your owner's manual regarding the order in which the burners must be lit. An electric igniter lights the burners on most grills, but these can fail; most models have a hole for lighting the burners with a match. Be sure to wait several minutes (or as directed) between lighting attempts to allow excess gas to dissipate. Make sure to check the propane level in your tank before starting. For tanks without a gauge, we do this by bringing a cup or so of water to a boil in a small saucepan or kettle and pouring the water over the side of the tank. Where the water has succeeded in warming the tank, the tank is empty; where the tank remains cool to the touch, there is propane inside.

Is Your Fire Hot Enough?

Whether we're cooking with gas or charcoal, we rely on the same test to determine the heat level of our fire (true, gas grills usually come with a temperature display, but over the years we've found them inconsistent and unreliable). After initially heating up the grill, hold your hand 5 inches above the cooking grate and count how long you can comfortably keep it there. (We preheat gas grills on high heat for 15 minutes with the lid down and charcoal for 5 minutes with the lid on.)

Hot Fire	2 seconds
Medium-Hot Fire	3 to 4 seconds
Medium Fire	5 to 6 seconds
Medium-Low Fire	7 seconds

Cleaning and Oiling the Grate

Just before placing food on the grill, scrape the cooking grate clean with a grill brush to remove any residue. Then dip a large wad of paper towels in vegetable oil, grab it with tongs, and wipe the grate thoroughly to lubricate it and prevent food from sticking.

Grilled Indian-Spiced Chicken with Mango Relish

Serves 4

✓ **WHY THIS RECIPE WORKS:** Authentic versions of tandoori chicken usually require a 24-hour marinade and a tandoor oven. In this recipe, the grill does a nice job of standing in for the tandoor. To make the most of a limited marinating time, we remove the skin and score the chicken for better flavor absorption and use plenty of curry in our marinade. Cutting the chicken breasts in half also helps speed up the cooking. The mango and mint relish, though not an authentically Indian accompaniment, uses many of the same ingredients as the chicken's spice mixture and offers balanced hits of sweetness and freshness. Serve with Easy White Rice (page 22) and naan bread.

½   **cup plain yogurt**

2   **tablespoons vegetable oil**

4   **teaspoons grated fresh ginger**

4   **teaspoons lime juice**

1   **tablespoon curry powder**

1   **jalapeño, stemmed, seeded, and minced**

2   **garlic cloves, minced**
    Salt and pepper

4   **(12-ounce) bone-in split chicken breasts, skin removed, trimmed, and halved crosswise**

2   **mangos, peeled, pitted, and diced**

2   **tablespoons chopped fresh mint**

1. Combine yogurt, oil, 1 tablespoon ginger, 2 teaspoons lime juice, curry powder, half of jalapeño, and garlic in large bowl and season with salt and pepper to taste.

2. Score each piece of chicken twice with sharp knife. Season chicken with salt and pepper, then toss with yogurt mixture.

3A. FOR A CHARCOAL GRILL: Open bottom vent completely. Light large chimney starter three-quarters filled with charcoal briquettes (4½ quarts). When top coals are partially covered with ash, pour evenly over grill. Set cooking grate in place, cover, and open lid vent completely. Heat grill until hot, about 5 minutes.

3B. FOR A GAS GRILL: Turn all burners to high, cover, and heat grill until hot, about 15 minutes. Turn all burners to medium-high.

4. Clean and oil cooking grate. Place chicken on grill and cook (covered if using gas) until lightly charred and chicken registers 160 degrees, 6 to 8 minutes per side.

5. Meanwhile, combine mangos and mint with remaining 1 teaspoon ginger, remaining 2 teaspoons lime juice, and remaining jalapeño in bowl and season with salt and pepper to taste. Serve relish with chicken.

Grilled Chicken with Lemon-Thyme Potato Salad

Serves 4

✔ **WHY THIS RECIPE WORKS:** Oil, garlic, thyme, and lemon juice pull triple duty here. Those four ingredients (plus a little mayonnaise) serve as the potato salad's dressing, and they also flavor the chicken before grilling. A drizzle of the mixture also gives the chicken a fresh hit of flavor before serving. Microwaving the garlic with oil mellows its harshness and infuses the oil with flavor.

½   **cup extra-virgin olive oil**

3   **garlic cloves, minced**

⅓   **cup lemon juice (2 lemons)**

1   **tablespoon minced fresh thyme**
    Salt and pepper

3   **tablespoons mayonnaise**

1½ **pounds fingerling potatoes, halved lengthwise**

8   **(3-ounce) chicken cutlets, trimmed**

3   **ounces (3 cups) baby arugula**

1. Combine oil and garlic in bowl and microwave until bubbling, about 30 seconds. Whisk in lemon juice and thyme and season with salt and pepper to taste. Transfer 3 tablespoons dressing to large bowl and whisk in mayonnaise.

2. Place potatoes in large saucepan and cover with cold water by 1 inch. Bring to boil, add 1 teaspoon salt, then reduce heat and simmer until potatoes are tender, about 8 minutes. Drain potatoes and toss in bowl with mayonnaise mixture. Season with salt and pepper to taste. Season chicken with salt and pepper and toss in bowl with 3 tablespoons dressing.

3A. FOR A CHARCOAL GRILL: Open bottom vent completely. Light large chimney starter filled with charcoal briquettes (6 quarts). When top coals are partially covered with ash, pour evenly over grill. Set cooking grate in place, cover, and open lid vent completely. Heat grill until hot, about 5 minutes.

3B. FOR A GAS GRILL: Turn all burners to high, cover, and heat grill until hot, about 15 minutes.

4. Clean and oil cooking grate. Place chicken on grill and cook (covered if using gas) until lightly charred and chicken registers 160 degrees, 2 to 3 minutes per side. Transfer chicken to platter and drizzle with remaining dressing. Add arugula to bowl with potatoes and toss to combine. Serve immediately with chicken.

SMART SHOPPING FINGERLING POTATOES
Potatoes generally fall into three groups: high-, medium-, and low-starch. These can drastically affect a potato's cooking properties. The fingerling potato (right), called for in this recipe, is a medium-starch potato, as is the Yukon Gold, which is thus a fine substitute. However, we like the unique visual appeal of the fingerling's oblong shape and small size.

Greek-Style Grilled Chicken Pita Sandwiches

Serves 4

☑ **WHY THIS RECIPE WORKS:** Inspired by the Greek gyro, we turn the classic street food into a more accessible weeknight meal by swapping in chicken for the usual lamb. We grill the chicken on kebabs for quicker cooking, and use dark-meat chicken thighs to ensure the meat stays moist. We also toss the chicken pieces in a blend of yogurt, olive oil, garlic, lemon juice, and herbs before grilling for a flavor boost. A simple tzatziki sauce brightens up these sandwiches. We drain the cucumbers to ensure the sauce doesn't get watered down, then toss them with some of the yogurt mixture.

2 cucumbers, peeled, halved lengthwise, seeded, and shredded
   Salt and pepper
1½ cups plain Greek yogurt
¼ cup extra-virgin olive oil
3 tablespoons lemon juice
4 garlic cloves, minced
1 teaspoon dried oregano
¼ teaspoon cayenne pepper
8 (3-ounce) boneless, skinless chicken thighs, trimmed and cut into 1½-inch pieces
2 red onions, cut into 1-inch chunks
4 (8-inch) pita breads

1. Toss cucumbers with ¼ teaspoon salt and let drain in fine-mesh strainer set over bowl for 15 minutes.

2. Meanwhile, whisk yogurt, 2 tablespoons oil, lemon juice, garlic, 1 teaspoon salt, and ¼ teaspoon pepper in bowl. Toss oregano, cayenne, and chicken with half of yogurt mixture. Thread four 12-inch skewers with chicken and onions.

3A. FOR A CHARCOAL GRILL: Open bottom vent completely. Light large chimney starter filled with charcoal briquettes (6 quarts). When top coals are partially covered with ash, pour evenly over grill. Set cooking grate in place, cover, and open lid vent completely. Heat grill until hot, about 5 minutes.

3B. FOR A GAS GRILL: Turn all burners to high, cover, and heat grill until hot, about 15 minutes.

4. Clean and oil cooking grate. Place kebabs on grill and cook (covered if using gas), turning kebabs every 2 minutes, until onions and chicken are charred around edges and chicken registers 175 degrees, about 12 minutes. Transfer skewers to platter, tent loosely with aluminum foil, and let rest for 5 minutes. While chicken rests, brush both sides of pita breads with remaining 2 tablespoons oil and grill until lightly charred and warm, about 1 minute. Transfer to platter with chicken.

5. Place cucumbers on clean dish towel and wring out excess liquid. Toss cucumbers with remaining yogurt mixture. Season with salt and pepper to taste. Spread portion of the yogurt mixture on one side of each pita, top with chicken, and serve.

Grilled Breaded Chicken with Tomato Salad

Serves 4

✔ **WHY THIS RECIPE WORKS:** Most breaded chicken recipes call for sautéing or pan-frying, but here we make the unusual move of taking it out to the grill. Grilling not only turns the bread-crumb coating golden and crisp, but it also gives it a great toasted flavor you couldn't achieve on the stovetop. Using 3-ounce boneless chicken thighs means that the meat stays moist and cooks quickly, before the bread crumbs have a chance to burn. Adding garlic, basil, and red pepper flakes to the coating gives it an Italian flair, making the chicken a perfect match for our easy tomato salad. A colorful variety of heirloom tomatoes gives this dish great visual appeal, but you can use beefsteak if you can't find heirloom. To make sure the coating properly adheres, avoid moving the chicken once it's on the grill until it's time to flip the pieces over.

5   slices hearty white sandwich bread, torn into 1-inch pieces

½   cup chopped fresh basil

6   tablespoons extra-virgin olive oil

6   garlic cloves, minced

¼   teaspoon red pepper flakes
     Salt and pepper

8   (3-ounce) boneless, skinless chicken thighs, trimmed

1   pound large heirloom or beefsteak tomatoes, cored and sliced into 1-inch-thick wedges

12   ounces cherry tomatoes, halved

1. Process bread, ¼ cup basil, ¼ cup oil, two-thirds garlic, red pepper flakes, ½ teaspoon salt, and ¼ teaspoon pepper in food processor to fine crumbs, 10 to 15 seconds. Transfer bread crumbs to shallow dish. Season chicken with salt and pepper, then dredge in bread crumbs, pressing to adhere.

2A. FOR A CHARCOAL GRILL: Open bottom vent completely. Light large chimney starter half filled with charcoal briquettes (3 quarts). When top coals are partially covered with ash, pour evenly over grill. Set cooking grate in place, cover, and open lid vent completely. Heat grill until hot, about 5 minutes.

2B. FOR A GAS GRILL: Turn all burners to high, cover, and heat grill until hot, about 15 minutes. Adjust all burners to medium.

3. Clean and oil cooking grate. Place chicken on grill and cook (covered if using gas) until chicken registers 175 degrees and coating is browned and crisp, about 3 minutes per side (avoid moving chicken except when flipping it to second side). Transfer to platter.

4. Meanwhile, toss tomatoes with remaining garlic, remaining ¼ cup basil, and remaining 2 tablespoons oil. Season with salt and pepper to taste and serve with chicken.

Grilled Thai Turkey Sliders

Serves 4

✔ **WHY THIS RECIPE WORKS:** These mini turkey burgers, topped with peanut sauce and cucumber salad, bring new life to the typical hamburger. A combination of chili-garlic sauce, fish sauce, lime juice, and brown sugar adds Thai flavors to ground turkey, and using many of the same ingredients in the sauce and salad dressing minimizes the shopping. Plenty of scallions and cilantro also go into the turkey mixture for a good hit of freshness. You can substitute 93 percent lean ground turkey for regular ground turkey, but the burgers will be drier. These burgers shrink as they cook, so make the patties slightly larger than the bun.

1½	pounds ground turkey
4	scallions, chopped fine
¼	cup chopped fresh cilantro
1	teaspoon grated lime zest plus 5 tablespoons juice (3 limes)
1	tablespoon Asian chili-garlic sauce
	Salt and pepper
¼	cup creamy peanut butter
2	tablespoons fish sauce
5	teaspoons packed brown sugar
½	seedless English cucumber, sliced into thin rounds
½	red onion, sliced thin
8	slider buns or mini sandwich buns

1. Place turkey, scallions, cilantro, lime zest, chili-garlic sauce, and ½ teaspoon salt in medium bowl and mix until combined. Form mixture into eight ¾-inch-thick patties.

2. Whisk peanut butter, 4 teaspoons fish sauce, 3 tablespoons lime juice, and 1 tablespoon brown sugar together in another bowl until smooth. (Sauce should have consistency of ketchup; if too thick, add water as needed.) Combine cucumber, red onion, remaining 2 tablespoons lime juice, remaining 2 teaspoons fish sauce, and remaining 2 teaspoons brown sugar together in another bowl and season with salt and pepper to taste.

3A. FOR A CHARCOAL GRILL: Open bottom vent completely. Light large chimney starter filled with charcoal briquettes (6 quarts). When top coals are partially covered with ash, pour evenly over grill. Set cooking grate in place, cover, and open lid vent completely. Heat grill until hot, about 5 minutes.

3B. FOR A GAS GRILL: Turn all burners to high, cover, and heat grill until hot, about 15 minutes.

4. Clean and oil cooking grate. Place patties on grill and cook (covered if using gas) until lightly charred and burgers register 160 degrees, 5 to 7 minutes per side. Place burgers on buns, top with peanut sauce and cucumber salad, and serve.

Spice-Rubbed Grilled Pork Tenderloins

Serves 4

✔ **WHY THIS RECIPE WORKS:** Grilling pork tenderloin gives the mild lean meat a good smoky boost, and we take it up a notch further by coating these tenderloins with a flavorful spice rub of brown sugar, sweet paprika, smoked paprika, cinnamon, and allspice before we cook them. Not only does this rub add flavor, but once cooked, the spices form a crust that provides a nice contrasting texture. To make it a meal, we whip together a simple side salad of fingerling potatoes (which we can boil while the grill preheats), pecans, red peppers, and scallions. Setting aside some of the spice rub to include in the salad's vinaigrette ties the whole meal together.

2	pounds fingerling potatoes
4	teaspoons packed brown sugar
	Salt and pepper
2½	teaspoons paprika
1¼	teaspoons smoked paprika
¼	teaspoon ground cinnamon
⅛	teaspoon ground allspice
2	(1-pound) pork tenderloins, trimmed and patted dry
3	tablespoons vegetable oil
2	tablespoons white balsamic vinegar
1	cup jarred roasted red peppers, sliced thin
½	cup pecans, toasted and chopped
2	scallions, sliced thin on bias

1. Combine potatoes and ¼ cup water in large bowl, cover, and microwave until potatoes are just tender, about 5 minutes. Drain potatoes.

2. Meanwhile, combine brown sugar, 1 tablespoon salt, 1 teaspoon pepper, paprika, smoked paprika, cinnamon, and allspice in large bowl. Reserve 1 teaspoon spice rub, then coat tenderloins evenly with remaining rub.

3A. FOR A CHARCOAL GRILL: Open bottom vent completely. Light large chimney starter filled with charcoal briquettes (6 quarts). When top coals are partially covered with ash, pour evenly over grill. Set cooking grate in place, cover, and open lid vent completely. Heat grill until hot, about 5 minutes.

3B. FOR A GAS GRILL: Turn all burners to high, cover, and heat grill until hot, about 15 minutes.

4. Clean and oil cooking grate. Grill tenderloins until browned all over and pork registers 145 degrees, about 3 minutes per side. Transfer tenderloins to platter, tent loosely with aluminum foil, and let rest for 5 minutes.

5. In small bowl, whisk together oil, vinegar, and reserved spice rub. Cut potatoes in half lengthwise and toss in large bowl with red peppers, pecans, scallions, and dressing. Season with salt and pepper to taste. Slice pork and serve with potato salad.

Mojo Grilled Pork Chops with Orange-Jícama Salad

Serves 4

✔ **WHY THIS RECIPE WORKS:** Mojo ("MO-ho"), a garlicky, citrusy sauce often found in Cuban recipes, pulls triple duty in this recipe to ensure simple shopping and cooking. For the chops, it works as both a marinade and sauce, and we also employ it as a dressing for our summery, salad of crisp, refreshing jícama, orange segments, and cilantro. By adding a little brown sugar to this mojo, we promote browning for the chops, and because thin-cut chops cook so fast, we brown just one side for all the flavor and visual appeal they need. If you have time, you can let the pork marinate for 15 to 30 minutes.

⅓ cup extra-virgin olive oil

4 garlic cloves, minced

1 teaspoon ground cumin

¼ cup orange juice plus
2 whole oranges

¼ cup lime juice (2 limes)

1 tablespoon packed brown sugar

½ jícama, peeled and cut into
2 by ¼-inch pieces

2 tablespoons minced fresh
cilantro
Salt and pepper

8 (4-ounce) bone-in pork chops,
½ inch thick, trimmed

1. Heat oil in small saucepan over medium heat. Add garlic and cumin and cook until fragrant but not browned, about 30 seconds. Transfer to bowl and whisk in orange juice, lime juice, and brown sugar. Let cool slightly, about 5 minutes.

2. Slice ½-inch piece from top and bottom of 1 orange. With orange resting on 1 trimmed end, use paring knife to slice off rind and white pith. Slip knife blade between 1 membrane and 1 section of fruit and slice to center. Then turn blade so it is facing out and slide from center out along membrane to free section. Repeat with remaining segments and second orange. Combine orange segments, jícama, cilantro, and ¼ cup dressing in second bowl. Season with salt and pepper to taste. Toss pork chops with ¼ cup dressing and season with salt and pepper.

3A. FOR A CHARCOAL GRILL: Open bottom vent completely. Light large chimney starter filled with charcoal briquettes (6 quarts). When top coals are partially covered with ash, pour evenly over grill. Set cooking grate in place, cover, and open lid vent completely. Heat grill until hot, about 5 minutes.

3B. FOR A GAS GRILL: Turn all burners to high, cover, and heat grill until hot, about 15 minutes.

4. Clean and oil cooking grate. Place chops on grill and cook (covered if using gas) until lightly charred and tops begin to turn opaque, about 2 minutes. Flip chops and grill until just cooked through, about 30 seconds. Transfer to platter, drizzle with remaining dressing, tent loosely with aluminum foil, and let rest for 5 minutes. Serve with jícama salad.

Grilled Andouille Burgers with Spicy Mayonnaise

Serves 4

✔ **WHY THIS RECIPE WORKS:** Andouille sausage is the secret weapon in these rich and flavorful burgers. We start by swapping out the typical ground beef in favor of ground pork, then add finely diced andouille, mustard, and hot sauce to really ramp up the flavor. We top the burgers with sharp cheddar, red onions (which we grill alongside the burgers), and finally, a tangy mayo spiked with more mustard and hot sauce.

1	pound ground pork
8	ounces andouille sausage, chopped fine
¼	cup whole-grain mustard
1	tablespoon hot sauce
	Salt and pepper
¼	cup mayonnaise
1	red onion, sliced into ½-inch-thick rings
1	tablespoon vegetable oil
4	slices deli sharp cheddar cheese
4	onion rolls

1. Place pork, sausage, 2 tablespoons mustard, 2 teaspoons hot sauce, ¼ teaspoon salt, and ½ teaspoon pepper in large bowl and gently mix until combined. Form mixture into four ¾-inch-thick patties.

2. Whisk remaining 2 tablespoons mustard, remaining 1 teaspoon hot sauce, and mayonnaise together in small bowl and season with salt and pepper to taste.

3A. FOR A CHARCOAL GRILL: Open bottom vent completely. Light large chimney starter filled with charcoal briquettes (6 quarts). When top coals are partially covered with ash, pour evenly over grill. Set cooking grate in place, cover, and open lid vent completely. Heat grill until hot, about 5 minutes.

3B. FOR A GAS GRILL: Turn all burners to high, cover, and heat grill until hot, about 15 minutes.

4. Brush onion rounds on both sides with vegetable oil. Clean and oil cooking grate. Place onions on grill and cook (covered if using gas) until lightly charred on both sides, 2 to 3 minutes per side. Place burgers on grill and cook (covered if using gas) until browned on both sides and meat registers 145 degrees, 5 to 6 minutes per side, topping with cheese during last 2 minutes of cooking. Arrange burgers on rolls and top with onions and mustard sauce. Serve.

SIMPLE SIDE MACARONI SALAD
Add 1½ cups dried elbow macaroni and 1 tablespoon salt to 4 quarts boiling water and cook, stirring often, until al dente. Drain and rinse under cold water, then transfer to large bowl. Add 1 small diced red onion, 1 diced green bell pepper, 1 diced celery rib, ⅓ cup mayonnaise, 1 tablespoon cider vinegar, 1 tablespoon Dijon mustard, and 1 tablespoon sugar and stir to combine. Season with salt and pepper to taste. Serves 4.

Grilled Garlic Sausages with Lentil Salad

Serves 4

✔ **WHY THIS RECIPE WORKS:** Pairing an earthy lentil salad with smoky grilled garlic sausages makes for a satisfying meal. Lentils can take more than 30 minutes to cook, but we found the addition of baking soda cuts this time down considerably, and cooking them in the microwave shaves off a few more minutes—and keeps it all hands-off. That frees us up to cook the sausages and prepare a dressing. Tossing the lentils in a red wine vinegar and Dijon dressing and adding creamy goat cheese and walnuts lends texture, richness, and elegance to our side dish. You can substitute sweet Italian sausages for the garlic sausages, if desired.

3	**cups water**
1	**cup lentilles du Puy, picked over and rinsed**
¼	**teaspoon baking soda**
1½	**pounds garlic sausages**
5	**tablespoons extra-virgin olive oil**
2	**tablespoons red wine vinegar**
2	**teaspoons Dijon mustard**
1	**shallot, minced**
½	**cup walnuts, toasted and chopped**
¼	**cup chopped fresh parsley**
	Salt and pepper
2	**ounces goat cheese, crumbled (½ cup)**

1. Place water, lentils, and baking soda in large bowl, cover, and microwave until lentils are soft, about 20 minutes. Drain, then rinse under cold water.

2A. FOR A CHARCOAL GRILL: Open bottom vent completely. Light large chimney starter half filled with charcoal briquettes (3 quarts). When top coals are partially covered with ash, pour evenly over grill. Set cooking grate in place, cover, and open lid vent completely. Heat grill until hot, about 5 minutes.

2B. FOR A GAS GRILL: Turn all burners to high, cover, and heat grill until hot, about 15 minutes. Adjust all burners to medium.

3. Clean and oil cooking grate. Place sausages on grill and cook, turning frequently, until browned on all sides and cooked through, 7 to 9 minutes.

4. Whisk olive oil, vinegar, mustard, and shallot together in bowl. Toss lentils, walnuts, and parsley with dressing and season with salt and pepper to taste. Top salad with crumbled goat cheese and serve with sausages.

SMART SHOPPING LENTILS
Lentils come in dozens of sizes and colors, each with varying flavor and texture. Brown and green lentils have a mild yet light and earthy flavor. They hold their shape when cooked and are tender inside. These are all-purpose lentils, great in soups and salads or simmered and tossed with oil and herbs. Lentilles du Puy, or French green lentils, are smaller than the common brown and green varieties. They are a dark olive green—almost black—and also keep their shape well. They have a rich, earthy, complex flavor and firm yet tender texture. Red and yellow lentils are split and skinless and thus completely disintegrate when cooked. If you want a lentil that will break down into a thick puree, these are the varieties to use.

Vietnamese-Style Grilled Pork Sandwiches

Serves 4

✔ **WHY THIS RECIPE WORKS:** The flavor-packed, fresh-tasting Vietnamese baguette sandwich known as *bánh mi* typically features a protein such as pork topped with pickled vegetables and fresh herbs. In this streamlined version, five-spice powder is a simple way to give our grilled pork tenderloin authentic flavor. For a quick, easy pickled topping, we give carrot and daikon (an Asian variety of radish) a sweet, salty, and spicy hit of flavor with the help of rice vinegar, sugar, sriracha, and fish sauce. Mayonnaise spiked with more sriracha and fish sauce pulls it all together. You can substitute six regular radishes for the daikon if necessary.

½ cup rice vinegar

3 tablespoons sugar

¼ cup fish sauce

2 tablespoons sriracha (see page 310)

1 (6-inch) piece daikon radish, peeled and cut into 2-inch-long matchsticks

1 carrot, peeled and cut into 2-inch-long matchsticks

¾ cup mayonnaise

1 (1-pound) pork tenderloin, trimmed

2 teaspoons five-spice powder

1 (24-inch) baguette, cut into 4 pieces and split partially open lengthwise

1 cup fresh cilantro leaves

1. Combine vinegar and sugar in medium bowl and microwave until sugar has dissolved, about 1½ minutes. Add 2 tablespoons fish sauce, 1 tablespoon sriracha, daikon, and carrot to bowl and toss to combine. Set aside for 15 minutes, then drain and set aside.

2. Meanwhile, whisk mayonnaise, remaining 2 tablespoons fish sauce, and remaining 1 tablespoon sriracha together in second bowl.

3A. FOR A CHARCOAL GRILL: Open bottom vent completely. Light large chimney starter filled with charcoal briquettes (6 quarts). When top coals are partially covered with ash, pour evenly over grill. Set cooking grate in place, cover, and open lid vent completely. Heat grill until hot, about 5 minutes.

3B. FOR A GAS GRILL: Turn all burners to high, cover, and heat grill until hot, about 15 minutes.

4. Rub pork with five-spice powder. Clean and oil cooking grate. Place tenderloin on grill and cook (covered if using gas) until browned on all sides and pork registers 145 degrees, 12 to 14 minutes. Transfer to cutting board, tent loosely with aluminum foil, and let rest for 5 minutes. While pork rests, grill bread until lightly toasted, about 1 minute.

5. Slice pork crosswise into thin slices. Spread mayonnaise on cut sides of bread. Arrange slices of pork on top of mayonnaise and top with vegetables and cilantro. Serve.

Grilled Glazed Tofu with Warm Cabbage Slaw

Serves 4

✔ **WHY THIS RECIPE WORKS:** Grilled tofu gets its due in this flavorful Asian-inspired vegetarian recipe. Brushing the tofu while it cooks with a mixture of mirin, ginger, chili-garlic sauce, hoisin, and sesame oil gives it an irresistible glazed appearance. Most of these ingredients also serve as a dressing for our slaw, and grilling the cabbage imbues it with a subtle smokiness. Serve with Easy White Rice (page 22).

2 **(14-ounce) blocks firm tofu, halved horizontally**

¼ **cup soy sauce**

3 **tablespoons mirin**

2 **tablespoons toasted sesame oil**

1 **tablespoon grated fresh ginger**

1 **tablespoon Asian chili-garlic sauce**

2 **tablespoons hoisin sauce**

1 **head napa cabbage (2 pounds), quartered lengthwise through core**

5 **tablespoons vegetable oil**

1. Lay tofu slices in single layer on top of several layers of paper towels, cover with several more layers, and top with rimmed baking sheet. Set heavy skillet or Dutch oven on baking sheet and let tofu drain for 10 minutes. Meanwhile, combine soy sauce, mirin, sesame oil, ginger, and chili-garlic sauce in bowl. Transfer 3 tablespoons dressing to large bowl and set aside. Whisk hoisin sauce into remaining dressing.

2A. FOR A CHARCOAL GRILL: Open bottom vent completely. Light large chimney starter filled with charcoal briquettes (6 quarts). When top coals are partially covered with ash, pour evenly over grill. Set cooking grate in place, cover, and open lid vent completely. Heat grill until hot, about 5 minutes.

2B. FOR A GAS GRILL: Turn all burners to high, cover, and heat grill until hot, about 15 minutes.

3. Brush cabbage with 3 tablespoons vegetable oil. Clean and oil cooking grate. Place cabbage on grill and cook until slightly wilted and browned on all sides, 3 to 4 minutes per side. Transfer to plate and tent loosely with aluminum foil.

4. Brush tofu with remaining 2 tablespoons vegetable oil. Place tofu on grill and cook, without moving, until browned, 3 to 4 minutes per side. Brush both sides of tofu with half of hoisin mixture and continue to grill until glossy, about 2 minutes per side. Brush both sides with remaining hoisin mixture and grill until both sides are caramelized, about 1 minute per side.

5. Cut cabbage crosswise into thin strips, discarding core. Transfer cabbage to bowl with reserved dressing and toss to combine. Serve with tofu.

Grilled Salmon Sandwiches with Broccoli Slaw

Serves 4

✔ **WHY THIS RECIPE WORKS:** Grilling thick salmon fillets and serving them on toasty rolls makes for an inspired sandwich. The mayonnaise, capers, lemon zest and juice, and parsley do double duty, not only flavoring the sandwich but also serving as a dressing for the slaw. We use prepared broccoli slaw for a change of pace from the usual cabbage. Look for pieces of salmon that are roughly the same shape as the rolls.

1   cup mayonnaise
2   tablespoons drained capers, minced
1   teaspoon grated lemon zest plus 2 tablespoons juice
¼   cup minced fresh parsley
    Salt and pepper
1   (12-ounce) bag broccoli slaw mix
4   (6- to 8-ounce) skinless salmon fillets, 1¼ inches thick
3   tablespoons vegetable oil
4   (6-inch) sub or hoagie rolls, halved lengthwise
4   large Bibb lettuce leaves

1. Combine mayonnaise, capers, and lemon zest and juice in small bowl, then stir in parsley and season with salt and pepper to taste. In another bowl, combine ⅓ cup mayonnaise mixture and broccoli slaw and season with salt and pepper to taste.

2A. FOR A CHARCOAL GRILL: Open bottom vent completely. Light large chimney starter filled with charcoal briquettes (6 quarts). When top coals are partially covered with ash, pour evenly over grill. Set cooking grate in place, cover, and open lid vent completely. Heat grill until hot, about 5 minutes.

2B. FOR A GAS GRILL: Turn all burners to high, cover, and heat grill until hot, about 15 minutes.

3. Season fish with salt and pepper and brush both sides with oil. Clean and oil cooking grate. Place fish on grill and cook (covered if using gas) until lightly charred but center is still translucent when checked with tip of paring knife and fish registers 125 degrees (for medium-rare), 4 to 5 minutes per side. Transfer to cutting board and tent loosely with aluminum foil. Grill rolls, cut side down, until toasted, 1 to 2 minutes.

4. Spread remaining mayonnaise mixture evenly on rolls. Arrange 1 lettuce leaf and salmon fillet on top of mayonnaise. Serve sandwiches with slaw.

SMART SHOPPING CAPERS
An ideal caper has the perfect balance of saltiness, sweetness, acidity, and crunch. These sun-dried, pickled flower buds have a strong flavor that develops as they are cured, either immersed in a salty brine or packed in salt. From previous tastings we knew we preferred the compact size and slight crunch of tiny nonpareil capers, so we tasted six nationally available supermarket brands, evaluating them on their sharpness, saltiness, and overall appeal. The winner, **Reese Non-Pareil Capers**, had every component of the ideal.

Grilled Spicy Shrimp Masala

Serves 4

✔ **WHY THIS RECIPE WORKS:** Shrimp are a great weeknight meal because they are so quick-cooking, and grilling them after they have been coated in an Indian-inspired spice paste made with garam masala, chili powder, sweet paprika, ginger, and garlic results in big flavor. We add both lemon juice and zest to the spice paste to give it a welcome touch of acidity and brightness. Meanwhile, an easy-to-make yogurt dipping sauce serves as a cooling counterpoint to the boldly spiced shrimp. To reinforce the Indian flavors, we add some of the spice paste to the dipping sauce.

1	teaspoon grated lemon zest plus 2 tablespoons juice
2	tablespoons garam masala
1	tablespoon paprika
3	garlic cloves, minced
1	tablespoon grated fresh ginger
2	teaspoons chili powder
1	teaspoon salt
½	cup plain Greek yogurt
¼	cup vegetable oil
1½	pounds extra-large shrimp (21 to 25 per pound), peeled and deveined
2	naan breads

1. In large bowl, combine lemon zest and juice, garam masala, paprika, garlic, ginger, chili powder, and salt to make paste. In another bowl, stir together ½ teaspoon spice paste and yogurt until combined.

2. Add oil to remaining spice paste and stir to combine, breaking up any clumps. Add shrimp to bowl with spice paste and toss to coat. Thread shrimp onto four 14-inch metal skewers.

3A. FOR A CHARCOAL GRILL: Open bottom vent completely. Light large chimney starter filled with charcoal briquettes (6 quarts). When top coals are partially covered with ash, pour evenly over grill. Set cooking grate in place, cover, and open lid vent completely. Heat grill until hot, about 5 minutes.

3B. FOR A GAS GRILL: Turn all burners to high, cover, and heat grill until hot, about 15 minutes.

4. Clean and oil cooking grate. Place shrimp on grill and cook until lightly charred and opaque throughout, 2 to 3 minutes per side. Place naan on grill and cook until heated through, about 1 minute per side. Serve shrimp with naan and yogurt sauce.

SIMPLE SIDE FRAGRANT BASMATI RICE

Heat 1 tablespoon vegetable oil in medium saucepan over high heat until just shimmering. Add 1 cinnamon stick and 2 green cardamom pods, and cook, stirring until pods pop. Add ½ cup thinly sliced onion and cook, stirring until lightly browned, about 2 minutes. Stir in 1 cup basmati rice and 1 teaspoon salt and cook, stirring until fragrant, about 1 minute. Add 1½ cups water and bring to boil. Reduce heat to simmer and cook until water has absorbed and rice is tender, about 17 minutes. Let sit, covered, for 10 minutes, then fluff with fork. Serves 4.

INDIVIDUAL TEX-MEX CHICKEN PIZZAS

Pizzas & Sandwiches

276   Buffalo Chicken Lavash Pizza

277   Individual Tex-Mex Chicken Pizzas

278   Squash, Gorgonzola, and Pancetta Pizza

280   Antipasto Pizza with Arugula Salad

281   Clam, Bacon, and Onion Pizza

282   Arugula Pesto and Potato Pizza with Fennel Salad

284   Sausage and Broccoli Rabe Calzones

285   Curried Chicken Sandwiches with Apple Raita

287   Asian Chicken Salad Sandwiches

288   Steak Sandwiches with Onion Jam and Wasabi Mayo

289   Prosciutto Panini with Artichoke-Lemon Aïoli

290   Pork Burgers with Quick Pickled Peaches

292   Spicy Shrimp-and-Herb-Salad Wraps

294   Salmon Burgers with Tomato Chutney

295   Portobello Sandwiches with Pesto Mayonnaise

297   Gouda and Apple Panini with Tangy Cabbage Slaw

Buffalo Chicken Lavash Pizza

Serves 4

✔ **WHY THIS RECIPE WORKS:** We transform Buffalo wings from a football fan's finger food into a quick and delicious dinner by incorporating the key ingredients in this pizza. Poaching chicken breasts for our topping ensures the meat stays moist, and we give the chicken that Buffalo-wing zing by shredding the meat and tossing it in a mixture of butter and hot sauce. Slices of celery and scallion also play into the classic Buffalo-wing profile, and in lieu of the dipping sauce that accompanies wings, we top our pizza with crumbled blue cheese. Adding some mozzarella to the mix ensures our pizza has the right gooey appeal. We put the cheeses on the crust first so they can act like a glue to hold the chicken, celery, and scallions in place. As for our crust, using lavash—a flatbread often used in Middle Eastern dishes—gives our pizza a crisp base with a minimum of work. Because lavash varies in size, you may need to trim the bread before making this pizza.

¼　**cup hot sauce**

4　**tablespoons unsalted butter, melted and cooled**

1　**teaspoon salt**

4　**(6-ounce) boneless, skinless chicken breasts, trimmed**

2　**tablespoons vegetable oil**

2　**(11 by 8-inch) pieces lavash bread**

2　**ounces blue cheese, crumbled (½ cup)**

4　**ounces mozzarella cheese, shredded (1 cup)**

2　**celery ribs, sliced ¼ inch thick on bias**

4　**scallions, sliced thin on bias**

1. Adjust oven rack to middle position and heat oven to 425 degrees. Combine hot sauce and butter in large bowl. Bring 2 cups water and salt to boil in medium saucepan. Add chicken and simmer, covered, until chicken registers 160 degrees, 10 to 15 minutes, flipping chicken halfway through cooking. Transfer chicken to plate and, using 2 forks, shred meat into bite-size pieces. Add chicken to bowl with hot sauce mixture and toss to coat.

2. Meanwhile, brush oil over both sides of lavash, then arrange on rimmed baking sheet and bake until browned and crisp, about 3 minutes per side.

3. Scatter cheeses evenly over lavash. Top with chicken mixture, celery, and scallions and bake until cheeses are melted and topping is hot, 6 to 8 minutes. Cut into squares and serve.

SMART SHOPPING LAVASH
Lavash, a flatbread commonly used in Middle Eastern cuisine, is made with a simple combination of flour, water, and salt. Though flexible like a tortilla when fresh, lavash quickly becomes brittle and crisp when heated, making it the perfect base for our pizza. Lavash can be found near the tortillas in most supermarkets.

Individual Tex-Mex Chicken Pizzas

Serves 4

✓ **WHY THIS RECIPE WORKS:** Tortillas are a great quick option to use as a pizza base because they crisp up beautifully and are the perfect size for making personal pizzas. All we have to do is brush the tortillas with a little oil and crisp them in the oven while we prep our toppings. We keep with a Tex-Mex theme in this recipe by topping our pizzas with creamy refried beans, shredded chicken, spicy pepper Jack cheese, and pickled jalapeños. Dolloping sour cream on the pizzas before serving adds just the right cooling, creamy counterpoint. We easily boost the flavor of canned refried beans with the help of a little lime juice and chili powder, and we dress up the sour cream by stirring in some cilantro and lime juice.

½ cup sour cream
⅓ cup chopped fresh cilantro
2 tablespoons lime juice
   Salt and pepper
1 (15-ounce) can refried beans
1 teaspoon chili powder
4 (8-inch) flour tortillas
8 teaspoons vegetable oil
2 cups shredded rotisserie chicken
4 ounces pepper Jack cheese, shredded (1 cup)
½ cup chopped pickled jalapeños

1. Adjust oven racks to upper-middle and lower-middle positions and heat oven to 475 degrees. Whisk sour cream, ¼ cup cilantro, and 1 tablespoon lime juice together in bowl. Season with salt and pepper to taste. Stir beans with remaining 1 tablespoon lime juice and chili powder in second bowl.

2. Brush tortillas with oil on both sides, using 1 teaspoon per side. Arrange on 2 rimmed baking sheets and bake until golden, about 5 minutes, flipping tortillas halfway through cooking.

3. Spread ¼ cup bean mixture over each tortilla, leaving ½-inch border around outside edge. Top each with ½ cup chicken, followed by ¼ cup pepper Jack and 2 tablespoons jalapeños. Bake until cheese is melted and all ingredients are heated through, 6 to 8 minutes. Cut each pizza into quarters, dollop each slice with heaping teaspoon sour cream mixture, and sprinkle with remaining cilantro. Serve.

EASY TEX-MEX PIZZA
Brush both sides of tortillas with oil and bake in 475-degree oven until golden, about 5 minutes, flipping tortillas halfway through. Spread each tortilla with ¼ cup prepared refried bean mixture, leaving ½-inch border around edge. Top with ½ cup shredded chicken, ¼ cup pepper Jack cheese, and 2 tablespoons pickled jalapeños. Bake until cheese is melted, 6 to 8 minutes.

Squash, Gorgonzola, and Pancetta Pizza

Serves 4

✔ **WHY THIS RECIPE WORKS:** This creative, rich pizza gets a distinctly fall feel from the butternut squash. While the pancetta and onion are precooking in our skillet, we microwave the squash. For an extra-crisp crust, we use store-bought dough, roll it into two rounds, and parcook them in a skillet before topping and baking.

1 **pound butternut squash, peeled, seeded, and cut into ½-inch pieces (2⅔ cups)**

6 **tablespoons olive oil**

6 **ounces pancetta, diced**

2 **onions, halved and sliced thin**

1 **tablespoon minced fresh rosemary**

¼ **teaspoon red pepper flakes**
  Salt and pepper

1 **pound pizza dough**

4 **ounces Gorgonzola cheese, crumbled (1 cup)**

1. Adjust oven rack to upper-middle position, place rimmed baking sheet on rack, and heat oven to 500 degrees. Place squash in bowl, cover, and microwave until almost tender, 7 to 9 minutes, stirring halfway through cooking. Drain.

2. Meanwhile, heat 2 tablespoons oil in 12-inch nonstick skillet over medium-high heat until shimmering. Add pancetta and onions and cook until onions are softened and pancetta is browned, about 7 minutes. Add rosemary, red pepper flakes, and squash and cook until squash is tender, about 2 minutes. Season with salt and pepper to taste, transfer to bowl, and wipe out skillet.

3. Divide dough into 2 equal pieces. On lightly floured counter, roll each piece of dough into 10-inch circle. Heat 2 tablespoons oil in now-empty skillet over medium-high heat until shimmering. Add 1 dough round to skillet, reduce heat to medium, and cook until golden brown and crisp, 1 to 2 minutes per side. Transfer to wire rack and repeat with remaining 2 tablespoons oil and remaining dough.

4. Spread squash mixture evenly over each crust and top with Gorgonzola. Transfer pizzas to preheated baking sheet and bake until crust is cooked through and cheese is melted, 6 to 8 minutes. Serve.

SMART SHOPPING **PIZZA DOUGH**

While pizza dough is nothing more than bread dough with oil added, minor changes can yield very different results. We think homemade dough is worth the effort, but prepared dough can be a great timesaving option for a weeknight pizza that still beats takeout. Many supermarkets and pizzerias sell dough for just a few dollars a pound. We found that store-bought dough and refrigerated pop-up canisters of pizza dough (Pillsbury brand) all worked well and tasted fine, but we recommend buying dough from a pizzeria, where it is likely to be fresh. Supermarket pizza dough is frequently unlabeled, so there's no way to know how long the dough has been sitting in the case, or how much dough is in the bag.

Antipasto Pizza with Arugula Salad

Serves 4

✔ **WHY THIS RECIPE WORKS:** This pizza turns bistro fare into an easy weeknight option for the home cook. A topping combining prosciutto, salami, roasted red peppers, and olives offers big flavor without requiring any precooking. Pesto (we use prepared pesto from the supermarket refrigerated section to save time) and pepperoncini lend brightness, while fresh mozzarella adds the right cheesy appeal with an upscale feel. We parcook the dough in a skillet while the oven preheats, which keeps things moving and ensures our crust will stay crisp under the toppings. Once the topped pizza is cooked, we add some lightly dressed arugula for a fresh finish, serving extra arugula salad on the side to make it a complete meal.

¾ **cup pepperoncini, stemmed and sliced into rings**

½ **cup pitted kalamata olives, chopped**

6 **tablespoons extra-virgin olive oil**

1 **pound pizza dough**

6 **tablespoons basil pesto**

8 **ounces fresh mozzarella, quartered, sliced ¼ inch thick, and patted dry with paper towels**

2 **ounces thinly sliced prosciutto, cut into ½-inch pieces**

2 **ounces thinly sliced salami, cut into ½-inch pieces**

½ **cup jarred roasted red peppers, rinsed, patted dry, and chopped**

5 **ounces (5 cups) baby arugula**

1. Adjust oven rack to upper-middle position, place rimmed baking sheet on rack, and heat oven to 500 degrees. Combine pepperoncini, olives, and 2 tablespoons oil in large bowl and set aside.

2. Divide dough into 2 equal pieces. On lightly floured counter, roll each piece of dough into 10-inch circle. Heat 2 tablespoons oil in 12-inch nonstick skillet over medium-high heat until shimmering. Add 1 dough round to skillet, reduce heat to medium, and cook until golden brown and crisp, 1 to 2 minutes per side. Transfer to wire rack and repeat with remaining 2 tablespoons oil and remaining dough.

3. Spread 3 tablespoons pesto over each crust, then top evenly with mozzarella, followed by prosciutto, salami, roasted red peppers, and half of olive mixture. Transfer pizzas to preheated baking sheet and bake until dough is cooked through and mozzarella is melted, 6 to 8 minutes. Meanwhile, add arugula to bowl with remaining olive mixture and toss to coat. Top each pizza with 1 cup arugula mixture, slice, and serve with remaining arugula on side.

SMART SHOPPING FRESH MOZZARELLA
Most supermarket mozzarella can be divided into two categories: high moisture (or fresh) and low moisture. Fresh mozzarella, which is usually packed in brine, has a soft texture and milky flavor best appreciated within a day or two of purchase, as it can quickly sour. Low-moisture mozzarella typically comes shrink-wrapped in a block or preshredded in a resealable bag. We prefer the cleaner flavor of fresh mozzarella on this pizza. If you have any left over, store it in its brine in an airtight container and use within a day or two.

Clam, Bacon, and Onion Pizza

Serves 4

✔ **WHY THIS RECIPE WORKS:** Clam pizza is said to have originated in Connecticut, but the wide availability of canned clams means you can make this recipe whether you live in New Hampshire or New Mexico. For a rich, satisfying topping, we cook bacon, caramelize onions in the rendered bacon fat, and follow with garlic, thyme, wine, and clams. Parbaking the crust in the skillet on the stovetop crisps it in record time. All that's left to do is put the topping on the crusts and slide them in the oven to heat through.

6	slices bacon, cut into 1½-inch pieces
1	onion, halved and sliced thin
2	tablespoons minced fresh thyme
3	garlic cloves, minced
4	(6.5-ounce) cans minced clams, drained
3	tablespoons dry white wine
	Salt and pepper
1	pound pizza dough
¼	cup extra-virgin olive oil

1. Adjust oven rack to upper-middle position, place rimmed baking sheet on rack, and heat oven to 500 degrees. Cook bacon over medium heat in 12-inch nonstick skillet until fat is rendered but bacon is still soft, about 3 minutes. Using slotted spoon, transfer bacon to paper towel–lined plate, then pour off all but 2 tablespoons rendered fat from skillet.

2. Cook onion in fat left in skillet until onion begins to brown, 4 to 6 minutes. Add thyme and garlic and cook until fragrant, about 30 seconds. Add clams and wine and cook until liquid has almost evaporated but mixture is moist, 1 to 2 minutes. Transfer mixture to bowl and season with salt and pepper to taste. Wipe out skillet with paper towels.

3. Divide dough into 2 equal pieces. On lightly floured counter, roll each piece of dough into 10-inch circle. Heat 2 tablespoons oil in now-empty skillet over medium-high heat until shimmering. Add 1 dough round to skillet, reduce heat to medium, and cook until golden brown and crisp, 1 to 2 minutes per side. Transfer to wire rack and repeat with remaining 2 tablespoons oil and remaining dough.

4. Spread clam topping evenly over each crust and top with bacon. Transfer pizzas to preheated baking sheet and bake until dough is cooked through and bacon is sizzling, 6 to 8 minutes. Serve.

Arugula Pesto and Potato Pizza with Fennel Salad

Serves 4

✔ **WHY THIS RECIPE WORKS:** Pesto can serve as a flavorful pizza topping, and here we make our own, swapping out the usual basil for peppery arugula. Thinly sliced potatoes add the right starchy, creamy balance, while some shaved Parmesan complements the pesto and adds the requisite cheese component. While the potatoes are parcooking in the microwave, our pesto comes together quickly in the food processor. A side salad featuring fennel and arugula in a bright lemon and olive oil dressing is a snap to put together. You can use a mandoline or a food processor fitted with a slicing disk to prep the potatoes and fennel quickly.

1	pound small red potatoes, sliced ⅛ inch thick
½	cup plus 1 tablespoon extra-virgin olive oil
5	ounces (5 cups) baby arugula
¼	cup pine nuts, toasted
1	garlic clove, minced
1½	ounces Parmesan cheese, grated (¾ cup), plus 2 ounces shaved into long curls
	Salt and pepper
1	pound pizza dough
1	tablespoon lemon juice
1	fennel bulb, stalks discarded, bulb halved, cored, and sliced thin

1. Adjust oven rack to upper-middle position and heat oven to 500 degrees. Toss potatoes with 1 tablespoon oil in bowl, cover, and microwave until potatoes are just tender, 3 to 7 minutes.

2. Meanwhile, process 2 cups arugula, ¼ cup oil, pine nuts, and garlic in food processor until smooth, 30 to 60 seconds. Transfer to bowl, stir in grated Parmesan, and season with salt and pepper to taste.

3. Brush 1 tablespoon oil over rimmed baking sheet. On lightly floured counter, roll dough into 16 by 9-inch oval and transfer to prepared baking sheet. Spread pesto over dough, leaving ½-inch border around edge. Shingle potatoes over dough, then top with shaved Parmesan. Season with salt and pepper and bake until edges of pizza are well browned, about 15 minutes.

4. While pizza bakes, whisk lemon juice with remaining 3 tablespoons oil in large bowl. Add remaining 3 cups arugula and fennel and toss to coat. Season with salt and pepper to taste. Slice pizza into wedges and serve with salad.

QUICK PREP TIP
SHAVING PARMESAN
Run vegetable peeler over block of cheese, making sure to use light touch to ensure thin shavings.

Sausage and Broccoli Rabe Calzones

Serves 4 to 6

✔ **WHY THIS RECIPE WORKS:** Sandwiching a filling between rounds of store-bought pizza dough is a simple way to put a new and satisfying twist on pizza night. In this all-in-one meal, the richness of Italian sausage is nicely balanced by plenty of earthy, bitter broccoli rabe. Using a combination of ricotta and provolone creates cheesy appeal without making our calzone overly rich or heavy, and a single egg yolk helps bind it all together. We cook the broccoli rabe in the microwave while we cook the sausage in the skillet, then all we have to do is roll out the dough, assemble our calzones, and pop them in the oven for about 15 minutes.

4	teaspoons olive oil
1	pound (2 cups) whole-milk ricotta cheese
4	ounces provolone cheese, shredded (1 cup)
1	large egg yolk
	Salt and pepper
1	pound broccoli rabe, trimmed and cut into 1-inch pieces
2	tablespoons water
12	ounces hot Italian sausage, casings removed
3	garlic cloves, minced
2	pounds pizza dough

1. Adjust oven racks to upper-middle and lower-middle positions and heat oven to 475 degrees. Brush 2 baking sheets with 2 teaspoons oil each. In large bowl, stir together ricotta, provolone, egg yolk, ¼ teaspoon salt, and ¼ teaspoon pepper until combined. Combine broccoli rabe, water, and ⅛ teaspoon salt in another bowl, cover, and microwave until tender, about 4 minutes. Drain.

2. While broccoli rabe cooks, add sausage to 12-inch nonstick skillet and cook over medium-high heat, stirring constantly and breaking sausage into ½-inch pieces with wooden spoon, until no longer pink, about 4 minutes. Stir in garlic and cook until fragrant, about 30 seconds. Stir in broccoli rabe and cook until liquid in skillet has evaporated, about 1 minute.

3. On lightly floured counter, divide dough into 2 pieces and roll each piece into 12-inch round. Transfer rounds to prepared sheets, placing 1 round on each sheet. Working with 1 dough round at a time, mound half of cheese mixture over half of dough, leaving 1-inch border around edge. Spread half of sausage mixture on top of cheese, brush edge of dough round with water, then fold dough over filling and crimp edge to seal. Repeat with second dough round. Cut five 1-inch slits in top of each calzone. Bake until golden, 15 to 20 minutes. Let sit for 5 minutes and serve.

Curried Chicken Sandwiches with Apple Raita

Serves 4

✓ **WHY THIS RECIPE WORKS:** Chicken cutlets go beyond the expected in this Indian-inspired naan sandwich. Dredging the cutlets in flour promotes crispness, and adding curry and cayenne to the flour boosts the flavor. With grated apple, ginger, mint, and jalapeño, our take on the Indian condiment raita adds freshness, spiciness, and sweetness. To ensure our raita isn't watered down, we salt the apple before adding it to the yogurt. Letting it drain while we toast the naan and cook the chicken keeps this recipe efficient.

1   **Granny Smith apple, peeled and grated on large holes of box grater**
    Salt and pepper
4   **naan breads**
½   **cup all-purpose flour**
2   **tablespoons curry powder**
¼   **teaspoon cayenne pepper**
4   **(3- to 4-ounce) chicken cutlets, trimmed**
3   **tablespoons vegetable oil**
1   **cup plain Greek yogurt**
1   **jalapeño chile, stemmed, seeded, and minced**
2   **tablespoons chopped fresh mint**
1   **teaspoon grated fresh ginger**

1. Adjust oven rack to middle position and heat oven to 400 degrees. Toss apple with ¼ teaspoon salt, then transfer to colander set over bowl. Let drain for 10 minutes, then press with back of wooden spoon to release as much liquid as possible.

2. Meanwhile, place naan on baking sheet and bake until light golden brown and beginning to crisp, about 10 minutes. Combine flour, curry powder, cayenne, 1 teaspoon salt, and ½ teaspoon pepper in shallow dish. Dredge cutlets in flour mixture, shaking off excess.

3. Heat oil in 12-inch nonstick skillet over medium-high heat until just smoking. Add cutlets to skillet and cook until golden brown, 2 to 3 minutes per side. Transfer to cutting board, tent loosely with aluminum foil, and let rest for 5 minutes. Slice chicken on bias, crosswise, into ½-inch pieces.

4. Stir together yogurt, drained apple, jalapeño, mint, and ginger and season with salt and pepper to taste. Cut each naan in half crosswise. Divide chicken among 4 naan halves, then top with apple raita and remaining 4 naan halves. Serve.

SMART SHOPPING NAAN
Flatbreads, defined simply by their flatness, can be leavened or unleavened, made from any grain, and shaped by rolling or stretching. Naan is a flattened round of yeast-leavened dough cooked against the walls of a tandoor oven so it puffs slightly and browns on one side. You can buy it in many supermarkets (fresh or frozen), farmers' markets, and specialty food stores.

Asian Chicken Salad Sandwiches

Serves 4

✓ **WHY THIS RECIPE WORKS:** For a quick meal with a little more flair than the diner-counter staple, we give our chicken salad sandwiches an Asian twist. We start by adding soy sauce, sesame oil, and ginger to the basic mayonnaise base, and in lieu of the usual grapes, celery, and/or pecans as add-ins, we stir in scallions and sesame seeds with the shredded chicken (we use a rotisserie chicken to minimize the work). To balance the rich flavors of the chicken salad and lend some texture, we add some quick pickles to our sandwiches. We start with an English cucumber since it has fewer seeds and doesn't require peeling, slice it into thin half-moons, then toss it with a mixture of cider vinegar and sugar that we quickly heat up in the microwave. A round loaf of crusty bread, such as a boule, provides the perfect sturdy slices needed for this hearty sandwich.

½ **cup cider vinegar**

3 **tablespoons sugar**

1 **English cucumber, halved, seeded, and sliced thin**

⅔ **cup mayonnaise**

2 **tablespoons soy sauce**

1 **tablespoon toasted sesame oil**

1 **tablespoon grated fresh ginger**

1 **(2½-pound) rotisserie chicken, skin and bones discarded, meat shredded into bite-size pieces (3 cups)**

6 **scallions, sliced thin**

2 **teaspoons sesame seeds**
 Salt and pepper

8 **(½-inch-thick) slices rustic white bread, lightly toasted**

1. Combine vinegar and sugar in medium bowl and microwave until sugar dissolves, about 90 seconds. Add cucumber slices to bowl and toss to combine.

2. Whisk mayonnaise, soy sauce, sesame oil, and ginger together in large bowl until combined. Add chicken, scallions, and sesame seeds to bowl with mayonnaise mixture and toss to combine. Season with salt and pepper to taste.

3. Top 4 slices bread with chicken salad, followed by cucumbers, then remaining 4 slices bread. Serve.

SMART SHOPPING CIDER VINEGAR
To see whether cider vinegar varies from brand to brand, we rounded up 10 vinegars—domestic as well as a couple from France and Canada—and it was immediately clear they were not identical. They ranged in color from pale straw to deep gold, in flavor from sweet to puckeringly tart, and in appearance from crystal clear to clouded with particulate matter. After tasting the vinegars straight, in a vinaigrette, in a cooked sauce, and in a vinegar-based barbecue sauce, one thing was clear: Sweet vinegars stole the show. Our favorite, French-produced **Maille Apple Cider Vinegar** (left), won raves for its "deep, warm" flavor profile and complexity. California-made **Spectrum Naturals Organic Apple Cider Vinegar** (right) came in a close second.

Steak Sandwiches with Onion Jam and Wasabi Mayo

Serves 4

✔ **WHY THIS RECIPE WORKS:** A sweet red onion jam and a zingy wasabi-spiked mayo make these flavor-packed steak sandwiches hard to resist. We make quick work of the jam by cooking the sliced onion until it begins to brown and soften, then we add brown sugar and red wine vinegar and turn up the heat to caramelize the onion and get the right consistency. While the onion cooks, we make our mayo, then cook our steaks. Because fresh wasabi root is hard to find, we use wasabi powder, available at most supermarkets.

5   teaspoons olive oil

1   large red onion, halved
    and sliced thin

¼   cup red wine vinegar

2   tablespoons packed brown sugar
    Salt and pepper

½   cup mayonnaise

4   teaspoons wasabi powder

1   teaspoon soy sauce

2   (10- to 12-ounce) strip steaks,
    1 inch thick, trimmed

8   (1-inch-thick) slices rustic
    white bread

1. Adjust oven rack 6 inches from broiler element and heat broiler. Heat 1 tablespoon oil in large saucepan over medium heat until just shimmering. Add onion and cook until soft and translucent, 10 to 12 minutes. Add vinegar and sugar, increase heat to medium-high, and cook until liquid is reduced to thick, syrupy glaze and onion is caramelized, about 5 minutes. Season with salt and pepper.

2. Meanwhile, mix mayonnaise, wasabi powder, and soy sauce together in small bowl. Cover with plastic wrap and chill until flavors blend, at least 10 minutes.

3. Pat steaks dry with paper towels and season with salt and pepper. Heat remaining 2 teaspoons oil in 12-inch skillet over medium-high heat until just smoking. Cook steaks until well browned and register 120 to 125 degrees, 3 to 5 minutes per side. Transfer steaks to cutting board, tent loosely with aluminum foil, and let rest for 5 minutes. Slice steaks thin.

4. While steaks cook, arrange bread in single layer on rimmed baking sheet and toast until golden brown and crisp, 1 to 2 minutes per side. Spread mayonnaise mixture evenly over 1 side of each slice bread. Divide meat evenly among 4 slices bread, top with caramelized onions, then remaining 4 slices bread, mayonnaise side down. Cut each sandwich in half and serve.

SIMPLE SIDE CUCUMBER AND YOGURT SALAD
Whisk 1 cup plain yogurt with ¼ cup chopped fresh mint, 2 tablespoons extra-virgin olive oil, and 2 minced garlic cloves. Peel, halve lengthwise, seed, and thinly slice 3 cucumbers. Toss cucumbers with yogurt mixture and season with salt and pepper to taste. Serves 4.

Prosciutto Panini with Artichoke-Lemon Aïoli

Serves 4

✔ **WHY THIS RECIPE WORKS:** With salty prosciutto, nutty Italian fontina, and mildly bitter, crunchy radicchio, these panini offer great flavor and texture. To really set them apart, we use a bright artichoke spread made by adding artichoke hearts to a classic *aïoli* (lemon, garlic, and mayonnaise). Making it in the food processor is quick and easy. To ensure the aïoli doesn't become watered down, we squeeze excess liquid from the thawed frozen artichokes using a clean dish towel. And to give our sandwiches the signature marks and texture you would get from a panini press, we cook our sandwiches on a nonstick grill pan and weight the sandwiches with a Dutch oven (you can use a 12-inch nonstick skillet if you don't own a grill pan). Avoid Swedish or Danish fontina; both are inexpensive fontinas coated in red wax that have a generic, unremarkable flavor.

9	ounces frozen artichoke hearts, thawed and patted dry
½	cup mayonnaise
1	teaspoon grated lemon zest plus 1 tablespoon juice
2	garlic cloves, minced
	Salt and pepper
8	(½-inch-thick) slices rustic white bread
8	ounces fontina cheese, shredded (2 cups)
8	ounces thinly sliced prosciutto
½	head radicchio (5 ounces), cored and sliced thin
2	tablespoons olive oil

1. Adjust oven rack to middle position and heat oven to 200 degrees. Set wire rack in rimmed baking sheet. Process artichoke hearts, mayonnaise, lemon zest and juice, and garlic in food processor until smooth, 30 to 60 seconds. Season with salt and pepper to taste.

2. Spread artichoke mixture evenly on 1 side of each bread slice. Layer 1 cup fontina on top of artichoke mixture on 4 slices bread, then top with prosciutto, radicchio, and remaining 1 cup fontina. Place remaining 4 slices bread, artichoke–mixture side down, on top of cheese to make sandwiches.

3. Heat 12-inch nonstick grill pan over medium heat for 1 minute. Brush outside of sandwiches lightly with oil. Place 2 sandwiches in pan and weight with Dutch oven. Cook sandwiches until bread is golden brown and crisp and cheese is melted, 4 to 6 minutes per side. Transfer sandwiches to prepared wire rack and keep warm in oven while cooking remaining 2 sandwiches. Serve.

SIMPLE SIDE SWEET POTATO SALAD
Place rimmed baking sheet on lower rack of oven and heat oven to 450 degrees. Quarter 2 pounds sweet potatoes lengthwise, then slice crosswise into ½-inch cubes. Toss potatoes in large bowl with ⅓ cup vegetable oil, ½ teaspoon salt, and ¼ teaspoon pepper. Spread potatoes on preheated baking sheet and roast, shaking pan occasionally, until potatoes are browned in spots, about 20 minutes. Transfer potatoes to bowl, toss with ½ cup chopped jarred roasted red peppers, 2 chopped scallions, 2 teaspoons cider vinegar, and 1 teaspoon whole-grain mustard. Season with salt and pepper to taste. Serves 4.

Pork Burgers with Quick Pickled Peaches

Serves 4

✔ **WHY THIS RECIPE WORKS:** When you need a change of pace from classic beef burgers, these creative pork-based burgers are just the answer, and since they are cooked in a skillet you don't have to wait for perfect grilling weather to enjoy them. In the test kitchen, we often use a panade (a paste made with bread and milk) to keep our burgers and meatloaves moist, but here we opt for a simpler ingredient that adds not just moisture but also an unusual, yet incredibly appealing, flavor: peanut butter. Since fruit and pork are a natural pairing, we whip up a quick batch of pickled peaches to top our burgers. Soaking the sliced peaches in a warmed mixture of cider vinegar, sugar, cumin seeds, and salt gives them just the right tangy, spicy flavor to balance the richness of the pork. And in lieu of the usual mayo, mustard, or ketchup, we opt for a little salty, rich hoisin sauce on each bun to bring it all together.

2	large ripe peaches, pitted and cut into ¼-inch wedges
½	cup cider vinegar
½	cup sugar
1	tablespoon cumin seeds
2½	teaspoons salt
1½	pounds ground pork
3	tablespoons creamy peanut butter
1	tablespoon vegetable oil
4	teaspoons hoisin sauce
⅔	cup fresh basil leaves
4	whole-wheat hamburger rolls

1. Spread peaches evenly over bottom of large shallow bowl. Bring vinegar, sugar, cumin, and 1 teaspoon salt to simmer in small saucepan. Stir until sugar and salt dissolve, then remove from heat. Pour mixture over peaches and transfer to refrigerator.

2. Place pork, peanut butter, and remaining 1½ teaspoons salt in medium bowl and gently mix until combined. Gently form mixture into four ½-inch-thick patties. Heat oil in 12-inch nonstick skillet over medium-high heat until just smoking. Add patties to skillet and cook until golden brown on both sides and meat registers 145 degrees, 4 to 5 minutes per side.

3. Spread 1 teaspoon hoisin sauce on 1 side of each bun. Place burgers on bottom halves of hamburger rolls. Drain peaches, then divide evenly among burgers. Top peaches with basil leaves, then with other side of rolls, and serve.

QUICK PREP TIP STORING PEACHES

While it may seem like a good idea to put your just-purchased peaches in the refrigerator to prolong their life, can doing so come at a price? To find out, we divided a case of peaches into two batches, allowing one batch to ripen immediately without refrigeration and storing the other for a week in the fridge before allowing it to finish ripening for a couple of days at room temperature. Both sets of peaches were placed in containers sealed with plastic wrap to prevent moisture from evaporating. Our tasters found that despite being soft and ripe to the touch, the peaches that had spent time in the fridge were significantly mealier than those kept at room temperature. The moral of the story? Don't refrigerate your peaches unless you're sure they're ripe. You may prolong their shelf life, but the loss of quality isn't worth it.

For burgers with a great crust on the outside and a pink, juicy interior, you don't have to fire up the grill. Here's how to get perfect burgers on the table with a minimum of fuss using a skillet.

Shaping Burgers

This test kitchen method for shaping burgers quickly packs the meat without mashing and overhandling it.

1. With cupped hands, toss 1 portion of meat back and forth from hand to hand to shape it into loose ball.

2. Using your hands, flatten balls into 1-inch-thick patties.

To Dimple or Not to Dimple?

To prevent hamburgers from puffing up during cooking, many sources recommend making a depression in the center of the patty before placing it on the heat. But we have found the need for a dimple depends on how the burger is cooked. Meat inflates upon cooking when its connective tissue, or collagen, shrinks at temperatures higher than 140 degrees. If burgers are cooked on a grill or under a broiler, a dimple is in order since the meat is exposed to direct heat, not only from below or above but also on its sides. As a result, the edges of the patty shrink, compressing its interior up and out. But when a patty is cooked in a skillet, the edges of the burger never directly touch the heat, so the collagen it contains doesn't shrink much at all, and the burger doesn't puff.

Knowing When Your Burger Is Done

The best way to know when your burger is cooked the way you want it is to take its temperature, just as you would a steak. While we like to hold steaks with tongs and slide a thermometer through the side, this isn't as effective with more delicate burgers that can break apart. Instead, we slide the thermometer into the burger at the top edge and push it toward the center.

Skillet Hamburgers

Serves 4

You can serve these burgers simply with the classic condiments and lettuce and sliced tomatoes, or change things up by adding roasted or caramelized vegetables or a flavorful dressing. Or for a cheesy twist, top with a slice of your favorite cheddar, American, or Swiss or with crumbled blue cheese. Alternatively, mix ¾ cup shredded cheddar, American, or Swiss cheese into the beef mixture in step 1.

- 1½ pounds 80 percent lean ground beef
- 1 teaspoon salt
- ½ teaspoon pepper
- 2 teaspoons vegetable oil
- 4 hamburger rolls

1. Combine beef, salt, and pepper in large bowl. Divide meat into 4 equal portions. With cupped hands, toss 1 portion of meat back and forth to shape it into loose ball, then flatten balls into 1-inch-thick patties.

2. Heat oil in 12-inch skillet over medium-high heat until just smoking. Place burgers in skillet and cook until bottoms are dark brown, about 3 minutes. Flip burgers over and continue to cook until meat registers 120 to 125 degrees (for medium-rare), 3 to 5 minutes. Transfer burgers to buns and top as desired.

Spicy Shrimp-and-Herb-Salad Wraps

Serves 4

✔ **WHY THIS RECIPE WORKS:** Tortilla-wrap sandwiches are certainly a snap to fix, but if you aren't thinking creatively, they quickly become all too formulaic. For a one-of-a-kind, spring-inspired wrap, we developed this shrimp salad recipe that boasts plenty of garden-fresh herbs. We fold half a cup each of mint, parsley, and cilantro into the shrimp salad itself, then we top the shrimp salad with another half cup of each before wrapping it up in flour tortillas to make our sandwiches. Tossing the shrimp in a mix of cayenne, paprika, and garlic before cooking them ensures our wraps also pack plenty of robust flavor.

1	cup fresh mint leaves
1	cup fresh parsley leaves
1	cup fresh cilantro leaves
½	cup mayonnaise
3	tablespoons olive oil
2	garlic cloves, minced
1	teaspoon paprika
½	teaspoon cayenne pepper
	Salt and pepper
1½	pounds large shrimp (26 to 30 per pound), peeled, deveined, and tails removed
4	(10-inch) flour tortillas

1. Combine mint, parsley, and cilantro leaves and chop. Combine half of chopped herbs with mayonnaise in large bowl. Stir together 2 tablespoons oil, garlic, paprika, cayenne, 1 teaspoon salt, and ¼ teaspoon pepper in small bowl. Add shrimp and toss to combine.

2. Heat remaining 1 tablespoon oil in 12-inch nonstick skillet over medium-high heat until just smoking. Add shrimp and cook until opaque throughout, 1 to 2 minutes per side. Transfer to cutting board to cool slightly. Cut shrimp into ½-inch dice and stir into mayonnaise mixture. Season with salt and pepper to taste.

3. Lay tortillas on clean counter. Distribute shrimp mixture evenly among tortillas, leaving 2-inch border at bottom. Sprinkle remaining chopped herbs over shrimp mixture, then roll tortillas, from top to bottom, tightly around filling. Cut each wrap in half on bias and serve.

SIMPLE SIDE CARROT SALAD WITH RAISINS
Grate 4 large carrots on large holes of box grater and transfer to medium bowl. Add ½ cup raisins, ¼ cup chopped parsley, ¼ cup mayonnaise, and 2 tablespoons lemon juice and mix until thoroughly combined. Season with salt and pepper to taste. Serves 4.

Salmon Burgers with Tomato Chutney

Serves 4

✔ **WHY THIS RECIPE WORKS:** Using the food processor ensures the salmon is chopped just right, while panko bread crumbs as a binder (along with a little mayo) help avoid a mushy texture. For fresh flavor, scallions, cilantro, and lemon juice do the trick. Fresh tomatoes cooked with Asian sweet chili sauce, ginger, and lemon juice create a sweet and sour chutney that serves as a bright counterpoint to the salmon's richness.

1   **(1¼-pound) skinless salmon fillet, cut into 1-inch pieces**
½   **cup panko bread crumbs**
½   **cup chopped fresh cilantro**
8   **scallions, minced**
3   **tablespoons lemon juice**
2   **tablespoons mayonnaise**
    Salt and pepper
2   **tablespoons vegetable oil**
1   **tablespoon grated fresh ginger**
2   **tomatoes, cored, seeded, and chopped**
3   **tablespoons Asian sweet chili sauce (see page 310)**
4   **hamburger rolls**

1. Adjust oven rack 6 inches from broiler element and heat broiler. Pulse half of salmon in food processor until even mix of finely minced and coarsely chopped pieces, about 2 pulses. Transfer processed salmon to large bowl and repeat with remaining salmon. Add panko, 6 tablespoons cilantro, 3 tablespoons scallions, 1 tablespoon lemon juice, mayonnaise, ½ teaspoon salt, and ¼ teaspoon pepper to bowl with salmon and stir gently until combined. Form mixture into four 3½-inch patties, arrange on large plate, and refrigerate for 10 minutes.

2. Meanwhile, heat 1 tablespoon oil in 12-inch nonstick skillet over medium-high heat until shimmering. Add ginger and remaining scallions and cook until fragrant, about 1 minute. Add tomatoes, chili sauce, and remaining 2 tablespoons lemon juice and cook until mixture is very thick, about 6 minutes. Stir in remaining 2 tablespoons cilantro and season with salt and pepper to taste. Transfer chutney to bowl and wipe out skillet.

3. Heat remaining 1 tablespoon oil in now-empty skillet over medium heat until shimmering. Add burgers and cook until browned on both sides, about 4 minutes per side. Meanwhile, broil hamburger rolls until lightly toasted, about 2 minutes. Arrange burgers on bottom halves of toasted rolls, top with chutney and other side of rolls, and serve.

SIMPLE SIDE SUGAR SNAP PEA AND RED BELL PEPPER SALAD
Fill large bowl with ice water. Add 1 pound trimmed snap peas and 1 teaspoon salt to 6 cups boiling water in large saucepan and cook until crisp-tender, 1½ to 2 minutes. Drain peas, transfer to ice water, then drain again and dry with paper towels. Whisk together 2 tablespoons toasted sesame oil, 1 tablespoon rice vinegar, and ⅛ teaspoon red pepper flakes in large bowl. Add peas and 1 red bell pepper, stemmed, seeded, and sliced thin, to bowl with dressing and toss to coat. Season with salt and pepper to taste. Serves 4.

Portobello Sandwiches with Pesto Mayonnaise

Serves 4

✓ **WHY THIS RECIPE WORKS:** Giving meaty portobello mushrooms a crispy bread-crumb coating makes for a great vegetarian-friendly sandwich that is also plenty satisfying. While the mushrooms are cooking on the stovetop, we whip together a pesto mayonnaise (made with prepared pesto from the supermarket refrigerated section), which, together with a handful of arugula, gives these sandwiches a good touch of freshness. Dipping the mushrooms in flour, then egg, and finally crispy panko bread crumbs creates a substantial coating that stays put (just make sure the eggs thoroughly coat the undersides of the mushrooms, since that can be tricky). Cooking the breaded mushrooms covered at first steams them and helps them cook through while one side browns. We then finish cooking them uncovered so the moisture can escape and both sides remain properly crisped. Pressing down on the mushrooms with a spatula once they have been flipped over ensures the underside crisps evenly.

½ cup all-purpose flour

2 large eggs

1 cup panko bread crumbs
  Salt and pepper

4 (4-inch-wide) portobello
  mushroom caps, gills removed

½ cup olive oil

½ cup mayonnaise

3 tablespoons basil pesto

4 hamburger rolls

2 ounces (2 cups) baby arugula

1. Spread flour in shallow dish. Beat eggs in second shallow bowl. Combine panko, ½ teaspoon salt, and ¼ teaspoon pepper in third shallow dish. Working with one mushroom at a time, dredge in flour, dip in egg (make sure eggs coat gill side of cap), then coat with bread-crumb mixture, pressing gently to adhere. Transfer to plate.

2. Heat oil in 12-inch nonstick skillet over medium-high heat until shimmering. Add mushrooms, gill side up, and cook, covered, until mushrooms begin to brown, 4 to 5 minutes. Flip mushrooms and cook, uncovered, pressing mushrooms frequently with spatula to ensure even cooking, until second side has browned, 4 to 5 minutes. Transfer mushrooms to paper towel–lined plate and season with salt and pepper to taste.

3. Meanwhile, combine mayonnaise and pesto in small bowl and season with salt and pepper to taste. Spread mayonnaise on both sides of hamburger rolls. Arrange mushrooms on bottom halves of buns, then top with arugula and other side of buns and serve.

SIMPLE SIDE CHERRY TOMATO SALAD
Whisk together 3 tablespoons extra-virgin olive oil and 2 tablespoons red wine vinegar in large bowl. Add 1½ pounds halved cherry tomatoes, ½ cup pitted and chopped kalamata olives, and 1 small red onion, sliced thin, and toss to combine. Season with salt and pepper to taste. Serves 4.

Gouda and Apple Panini with Tangy Cabbage Slaw

Serves 4

✔ **WHY THIS RECIPE WORKS:** For a revamped grilled cheese, we sandwich smoky gouda and crisp Granny Smith apple between slices of pumpernickel, while honey mustard gives it just the right sweetness and spice. A simply dressed cabbage slaw served alongside complements the richness of the sandwich. You can use a 12-inch nonstick skillet here if you don't own a grill pan.

½ cup orange juice

¼ cup lime juice (2 limes)

2 tablespoons honey

6 tablespoons vegetable oil

½ head red cabbage, cored
   and sliced thin (6 cups)

¼ cup chopped fresh cilantro
   Salt and pepper

2 tablespoons Dijon mustard

8 slices pumpernickel bread

8 ounces smoked gouda cheese,
   shredded (2 cups)

1 Granny Smith apple, cored
   and sliced thin

1. Adjust oven rack to middle position and heat oven to 200 degrees. Set wire rack in rimmed baking sheet. Combine orange juice and lime juice in small saucepan, bring to simmer, and cook until reduced by half, about 5 minutes. Stir in 1 tablespoon honey until melted, about 30 seconds. Transfer juice mixture to large bowl and, whisking constantly, drizzle in ¼ cup oil. Add cabbage and cilantro to bowl with dressing, toss to coat, and season with salt and pepper to taste.

2. Whisk mustard and remaining 1 tablespoon honey together in small bowl. Spread mustard mixture evenly over 1 side of 4 slices bread, then top with half of gouda. Shingle apple slices over gouda, then top with remaining cheese and remaining 4 slices bread.

3. Heat 12-inch nonstick grill pan over medium heat for 1 minute. Brush outside of sandwiches lightly with remaining 2 tablespoons oil. Place 2 sandwiches in pan and weight with Dutch oven. Cook sandwiches until bread is crisp and cheese is melted, 4 to 6 minutes per side. Transfer sandwiches to prepared wire rack and keep warm in oven while cooking remaining 2 sandwiches. Serve with cabbage slaw.

EASY PANINI PRESS
For perfectly gooey panini that also hold together, position apples between two layers of shredded gouda cheese. After assembling sandwiches, cook in two batches in grill pan, weighting sandwiches with Dutch oven to mimic texture and signature marks of panini press.

STIR-FRIED PORK WITH SHIITAKES AND SNOW PEAS

Stir-Fries, Curries & Asian Noodles

300 Beef, Green Bean, and Scallion Stir-Fry

302 Stir-Fried Pork with Shiitakes and Snow Peas

303 Chicken, Carrot, and Scallion Stir-Fry with Black Bean Sauce

304 Chicken Teriyaki Stir-Fry

307 Chicken, Snow Pea, and Winter Squash Stir-Fry with Cilantro Rice

308 Chile, Basil, and Chicken Stir-Fry with Coconut Rice

309 Stir-Fried Shrimp and Asparagus with Lemon Sauce

312 Indonesian-Style Pork Fried Rice

313 Vegetarian Lo Mein with Bok Choy and Scallions

315 Udon Noodles with Edamame Pesto

316 Sesame Noodles with Tofu, Scallions, and Cashews

318 Noodle Cake with Spicy Peanut-Chicken Stir-Fry

319 Chicken Yakisoba

321 Stir-Fried Curried Pork Noodles

322 Quick Indian Beef Curry

323 Thai Green Curry with Pork and Zucchini

324 Thai Green Curry with Eggplant

Beef, Green Bean, and Scallion Stir-Fry

Serves 4

✔ **WHY THIS RECIPE WORKS:** By cooking the green beans in the skillet first, then setting them aside so we can follow with the beef (cooked in batches for proper browning) and then the scallions, we make sure each component is cooked through perfectly. Serve with Easy White Rice (page 22).

⅓ **cup low-sodium chicken broth**

¼ **cup oyster sauce**

2 **tablespoons soy sauce**

2 **teaspoons rice vinegar**

1 **teaspoon red pepper flakes**

3 **tablespoons vegetable oil**

1 **pound green beans, trimmed and cut into 2-inch pieces**

1 **(1-pound) flank steak, trimmed and sliced thin across grain**

8 **scallions, cut into 2-inch pieces**

6 **garlic cloves, minced**

1 **tablespoon grated fresh ginger**

1. Whisk broth, oyster sauce, soy sauce, vinegar, and red pepper flakes in bowl; set aside. Heat 1 tablespoon oil in 12-inch nonstick skillet over high heat until just smoking. Add green beans and cook, stirring occasionally, until spotty brown, 4 to 6 minutes. Transfer to large bowl.

2. Heat 2 teaspoons oil in now-empty skillet over high heat until just smoking. Pat steak dry with paper towels. Add half of steak to skillet, break up any clumps, and cook, without stirring, for 1 minute. Stir beef and continue to cook until browned, 1 to 2 minutes. Transfer to bowl with green beans and repeat with 2 teaspoons oil and remaining steak.

3. Add remaining 2 teaspoons oil and scallions to now-empty skillet and cook until spotty brown, about 2 minutes. Clear center of skillet, add garlic and ginger, and cook, mashing mixture into pan, until fragrant, about 30 seconds. Stir mixture into scallions, then return green beans and steak, with any accumulated juices, to skillet and toss to combine. Whisk oyster sauce mixture to recombine, then add to skillet and cook, stirring constantly, until sauce is thickened, about 30 seconds. Serve.

QUICK PREP TIP
SLICING BEEF FOR STIR-FRIES
Using sharp chef's knife, slice steak with grain into 2-inch-wide pieces (freezing steak for 15 minutes first will make it easier to slice). Then cut each piece across grain into very thin slices.

Stir-Fried Pork with Shiitakes and Snow Peas

Serves 4

✔ **WHY THIS RECIPE WORKS:** Tender, mild pork tenderloin pairs well with the earthiness of mushrooms and spinach and the sweetness of snow peas here. A balanced, flavorful sauce made with sweet hoisin sauce, salty soy sauce, and spicy red pepper flakes adds just the right complexity with a minimum of ingredients. To give the dish good textural contrast, we wait until the mushrooms are tender before we add the snow peas to our skillet, cooking them for just a few minutes to make sure they keep their appealing crispness. Freezing the pork tenderloin for 15 minutes will make it easier to slice. Serve with Easy White Rice (page 22).

⅓ cup hoisin sauce

⅓ cup water

2 tablespoons soy sauce

½ teaspoon red pepper flakes

3 tablespoons vegetable oil

1 (1-pound) pork tenderloin, trimmed, halved lengthwise, and sliced thin

1 pound shiitake mushrooms, stemmed and sliced thin

8 ounces snow peas, strings removed

4 garlic cloves, minced

1 tablespoon grated fresh ginger

3 ounces (3 cups) baby spinach

1. Whisk hoisin sauce, water, soy sauce, and red pepper flakes together in bowl. Heat 1 tablespoon oil in 12-inch nonstick skillet over medium-high heat until just smoking. Pat pork dry with paper towels. Add half of pork to skillet, break up any clumps, and cook until no longer pink, about 2 minutes; transfer to plate. Repeat with 1 tablespoon oil and remaining pork.

2. Add mushrooms and remaining 1 tablespoon oil to now-empty skillet and cook until just tender, about 3 minutes. Add snow peas and cook, stirring frequently, until bright green and crisp-tender, about 3 minutes. Clear center of skillet, add garlic and ginger, and cook, mashing mixture into pan, until fragrant, about 30 seconds. Stir mixture into vegetables, then add pork and any accumulated juices and spinach to skillet. Whisk hoisin mixture to recombine, then add to skillet and cook, stirring constantly, until spinach wilts and sauce thickens, about 1 minute. Serve.

SMART SHOPPING SHIITAKE MUSHROOMS
Originally from Asia, shiitake mushrooms have broad caps and slender, fibrous stems (which should be removed before cooking since they are too tough to eat). Available both fresh and dried, shiitakes are prized for their earthy flavor and pleasantly chewy texture. When shopping for fresh shiitakes, look for those that have smooth, brown caps devoid of any bruising.

Chicken Stir-Fry with Black Bean Sauce

Serves 4

✓ **WHY THIS RECIPE WORKS:** The bold flavor of fermented black beans, a traditional Asian condiment, gives this otherwise ordinary combination of chicken, carrots, and scallions a real savory flavor boost. Since carrots can take some time to cook, we speed things up by simmering them in our skillet in a little chicken broth. And because we cook the chicken in the skillet first, once we add the broth we can incorporate the flavorful fond left behind in the pan from browning the meat. When the carrots are about halfway done, we add the scallions, which become tender in the amount of time it takes to cook off what remains of the broth, then the chicken and sauce go into the pan and cook until it reaches the right consistency, only a few minutes more. See page 304 for more about slicing chicken for stir-fries. Serve with Easy White Rice (page 22).

3	tablespoons black bean garlic sauce
3	tablespoons soy sauce
2	tablespoons Chinese rice wine or dry sherry
4	teaspoons packed brown sugar
2	tablespoons vegetable oil
4	(6-ounce) boneless, skinless chicken breasts, trimmed and sliced thin
4	carrots, peeled and sliced thin
2	tablespoons grated fresh ginger
½	cup low-sodium chicken broth
16	scallions, cut on bias into ½-inch pieces

1. Whisk black bean garlic sauce, soy sauce, rice wine, and sugar in bowl. Heat 1 tablespoon oil in 12-inch nonstick skillet over medium-high heat until just smoking. Pat chicken dry with paper towels. Add half of chicken to skillet, break up any clumps, and cook until lightly browned and no longer pink, about 3 minutes. Transfer to plate and repeat with remaining 1 tablespoon oil and remaining chicken.

2. Add carrots and ginger to now-empty skillet and cook until fragrant, about 30 seconds. Add chicken broth and bring to simmer, scraping up any browned bits. Reduce heat to medium-low and cook, covered, until carrots are just tender, about 3 minutes. Add scallions and cook until scallions are bright green and liquid has evaporated, 2 to 3 minutes.

3. Return chicken and any accumulated juices to skillet. Whisk black bean sauce mixture to recombine, then add to skillet and cook, stirring constantly, until sauce is thickened, 1 to 3 minutes. Serve.

SMART SHOPPING BEAN SAUCES
Made from either soybeans or black beans, bean sauces are a staple ingredient in many Asian cuisines. Their consistency can range from thin to thick, and their texture can vary from smooth to chunky. Both soybean-based and black bean-based sauces are made with fermented beans, and while those made from soybeans are usually simply labeled "bean sauce," those made with black beans are labeled specifically as such. Black bean sauce is salty and full-flavored. It typically includes garlic, but it might be sold as simply "black bean sauce." Hot black bean sauce also contains chiles, sesame oil, and sugar.

Chicken Teriyaki Stir-Fry

Serves 4

✔ **WHY THIS RECIPE WORKS:** When made the usual way, the chicken in chicken teriyaki is pan-fried, grilled, or broiled, while the sauce is added during the last stages of cooking. The chicken is most often served off the bone and cut into thin strips. This recipe takes on the essence of authentic teriyaki, pairing chicken with a classic teriyaki sauce, but instead of cooking bone-in chicken pieces and cutting them up just before serving, we precut the meat and use it in a stir-fry. We whisk together our own homemade teriyaki sauce, which requires only five ingredients and beats the store-bought variety hands down. Bell pepper and scallions lend color to this simple dish. We do stray from the traditional teriyaki ingredients by adding a jalapeño, which we like for its fresh flavor and heat. Serve with Easy White Rice (page 22).

⅓ **cup soy sauce**

2 **tablespoons mirin**

¼ **cup sugar**

1 **tablespoon grated fresh ginger**

1 **teaspoon cornstarch**

2 **tablespoons vegetable oil**

4 **(6-ounce) boneless, skinless chicken breasts, trimmed and sliced thin**

1 **red bell pepper, stemmed, seeded, and sliced thin**

1 **jalapeño chile, stemmed, seeded, and sliced thin**

3 **scallions, sliced thin on bias**

1. Whisk soy sauce, mirin, sugar, ginger, and cornstarch together in bowl. Heat 2 teaspoons oil in 12-inch nonstick skillet over medium-high heat until just smoking. Pat chicken dry with paper towels. Add half of chicken to skillet, break up any clumps, and cook until lightly browned and no longer pink, about 3 minutes. Transfer to plate. Repeat with 2 teaspoons oil and remaining chicken.

2. Add remaining 2 teaspoons oil, bell pepper, and jalapeño to now-empty skillet and cook until just softened, about 3 minutes. Return chicken and any accumulated juices to skillet and toss to combine. Whisk soy sauce mixture to recombine, then add to skillet and cook, stirring constantly, until slightly thickened, about 1 minute. Garnish with scallions and serve.

QUICK PREP TIP
SLICING CHICKEN FOR STIR-FRIES
After removing tenderloin from each breast, slice breasts across grain into ¼-inch-wide strips and cut center pieces in half crosswise so they are approximately same length as end pieces. Then cut tenderloin on diagonal to produce pieces about same size as strips of breast meat. Freezing chicken for 15 minutes will make slicing easier.

Chicken and Squash Stir-Fry with Cilantro Rice

Serves 4

✔ **WHY THIS RECIPE WORKS:** This recipe brings together contrasting flavors and textures: spicy and mild, rich and lean, crunchy and tender. Though slightly unexpected, the addition of peanut butter to this sauce gives it a richness that the lean chicken breasts lack. And since we have time, we pair this stir-fry with a flavorful cilantro-infused rice that is surprisingly easy to make. We simply blend fresh cilantro with the water used to cook the rice. See page 304 for more about slicing chicken for stir-fries.

1 cup fresh cilantro leaves
and stems

2 cups water

¼ cup hoisin sauce

¼ cup creamy peanut butter

2 tablespoons rice wine
or dry sherry

1 teaspoon Asian chili-garlic sauce

1 cup long-grain white rice, rinsed
Salt and pepper

3 tablespoons vegetable oil

3 (6-ounce) boneless, skinless
chicken breasts, trimmed and
sliced thin

1 pound butternut squash, peeled,
seeded, and cut into ½-inch
chunks (2⅔ cups)

12 ounces snow peas, strings
removed

½ cup dry-roasted peanuts,
chopped

1. Puree cilantro and 1½ cups water in blender until smooth, 20 to 30 seconds. Whisk remaining ½ cup water, hoisin sauce, peanut butter, rice wine, and chili-garlic sauce together in bowl.

2. Combine cilantro mixture and rice in saucepan, bring to simmer, cover, and cook until tender, about 20 minutes. Season with salt and pepper to taste.

3. Meanwhile, heat 2 tablespoons oil in 12-inch nonstick skillet over medium-high heat until just smoking. Pat chicken dry with paper towels. Add chicken to skillet, break up any clumps, and cook until no longer pink, about 5 minutes. Transfer to bowl. Add remaining 1 tablespoon oil and squash and cook until lightly browned and almost tender, about 7 minutes. Whisk hoisin mixture to recombine. Add snow peas, chicken and any accumulated juices, and hoisin mixture to skillet, cover, and cook until squash is tender and snow peas are bright green and tender, about 2 minutes. Sprinkle with peanuts and serve with cilantro rice.

SMART SHOPPING CREAMY PEANUT BUTTER
We recently tasted several conventional and natural peanut butters, and in the creamy category, tasters sampled 10 brands plain, in cookies, and in a satay sauce. Texture proved paramount. They had to be smooth, creamy, and spreadable; they also had to have a good balance of sweet and salty flavors. The overall champ, a regular hydrogenated oil–based spread, was **Skippy Peanut Butter**. **Jif Natural Peanut Butter Spread**, which tasters praised for its "dark-roasty flavor," was a very close runner-up.

Chile, Basil, and Chicken Stir-Fry with Coconut Rice

Serves 4

✔ **WHY THIS RECIPE WORKS:** Basil gets promoted from accent herb to starring ingredient in this fresh-tasting, unusual stir-fry that boasts big flavor yet requires only a handful of ingredients. And the sauce, made with fish sauce, lime juice, and sugar, has a balance of sour, salty, and sweet that gives this recipe a Thai character. By cooking rice in a combination of coconut milk, water, and fish sauce, we create a creamy coconut rice that serves as the perfect rich counterpoint to the basil-chicken mixture. While the rice cooks, we prepare the chicken, making every minute count. See page 304 for more about slicing chicken for stir-fries.

1	(14-ounce) can coconut milk
1	cup water
3	tablespoons fish sauce
1½	cups jasmine rice
3	tablespoons lime juice (2 limes), plus lime wedges for serving
1	tablespoon sugar
2	tablespoons vegetable oil
4	(6-ounce) boneless, skinless chicken breasts, trimmed and sliced thin
1	jalapeño chile, stemmed, seeded, and sliced thin
1	cup fresh basil leaves

1. Whisk coconut milk, water, and 1 tablespoon fish sauce in medium saucepan until smooth. Bring to boil, add rice, and stir to combine. Reduce heat to low and cook, covered, until rice is tender, about 15 minutes. Remove from heat and let sit for 10 minutes.

2. Meanwhile, whisk together remaining 2 tablespoons fish sauce, lime juice, and sugar in bowl and set aside. Heat 2 teaspoons oil in 12-inch nonstick skillet over medium-high heat until just smoking. Pat chicken dry with paper towels. Add half of chicken to skillet, break up any clumps, and cook until lightly browned and no longer pink, about 3 minutes. Transfer to plate. Repeat with 2 teaspoons oil and remaining chicken.

3. Add jalapeño, ½ cup basil, and remaining 2 teaspoons oil to now-empty skillet and cook until just softened, about 1 minute. Return chicken and any accumulated juices to skillet. Whisk fish sauce mixture to recombine, then add to skillet and cook, stirring constantly, until sauce is slightly thickened, about 1 minute. Sprinkle with remaining ½ cup basil and serve with coconut rice and lime wedges.

SMART SHOPPING JASMINE RICE

With its long, slender grains and assertive popcornlike flavor, this Thai rice is similar to Indian basmati rice but has a stickier texture. Its flavor and fragrance make it a good choice for Thai recipes such as this one. While jasmine rice can be cooked just as you would other varieties of rice, here we cook it in a mixture of coconut milk, water, and fish sauce, which gives it an especially rich flavor.

Stir-Fried Shrimp and Asparagus with Lemon Sauce

Serves 4

✔ **WHY THIS RECIPE WORKS:** For this light and refreshing stir-fry, we marinate the shrimp in soy sauce and rice wine for just 10 minutes to give them an impressive flavor boost. Preparing the sauce and vegetables while the shrimp marinate means we make the most of every minute. Serve with Easy White Rice (page 22).

6	tablespoons low-sodium chicken broth
¼	cup lemon juice (2 lemons)
¼	cup plus 2 teaspoons Chinese rice wine or dry sherry
2	tablespoons plus 2 teaspoons soy sauce
2	teaspoons sugar
2	teaspoons cornstarch
¼	teaspoon pepper
1	pound extra-large shrimp (21 to 25 per pound), peeled and deveined
3	scallions, minced
3	garlic cloves, minced
1	tablespoon grated fresh ginger
5	teaspoons vegetable oil
1	pound asparagus, trimmed and cut on bias into 2-inch lengths
2	carrots, peeled and cut into 2-inch-long matchsticks

1. Whisk together chicken broth, lemon juice, ¼ cup rice wine, 2 tablespoons soy sauce, sugar, cornstarch, and pepper in small bowl. Toss shrimp with remaining 2 teaspoons rice wine and remaining 2 teaspoons soy sauce in medium bowl and let marinate for 10 minutes. Combine scallions, garlic, ginger, and 1 teaspoon oil in another bowl.

2. Heat 2 teaspoons oil in 12-inch nonstick skillet over high heat until just smoking. Add shrimp, break up any clumps, and cook until lightly browned on all sides but not fully cooked, about 1½ minutes. Transfer to clean bowl, cover, and set aside.

3. Heat remaining 2 teaspoons oil in now-empty skillet over high heat until shimmering. Add asparagus and carrots and cook until vegetables are crisp-tender, 3 to 4 minutes. Clear center of skillet, add garlic mixture, and cook, mashing mixture into skillet, until fragrant, 15 to 30 seconds. Stir garlic mixture into vegetables.

4. Return shrimp and any accumulated juices to skillet. Whisk chicken broth mixture to recombine, then add to skillet. Cook, stirring constantly, until shrimp are cooked through and sauce has thickened, 30 seconds to 2 minutes. Serve.

QUICK PREP TIP **GRATING GINGER**

Although we love the floral pungency of fresh ginger, its fibrous texture can be distracting when coarsely grated or minced. What's the best way to avoid ginger's stringy texture? Although fancy kitchen stores sometimes carry porcelain "ginger graters" designed specifically for the job, we prefer to use our rasp-style grater. Its fine blades pulverize the ginger, releasing all of its flavorful juices without any stringy segments. Simply peel a small section of a large piece of ginger, then grate the peeled portion, using the rest of the ginger as a handle. Be sure to work with a large nub of ginger—and watch your knuckles.

ALL ABOUT Asian Ingredients

These days you don't have to go to a specialty store or Asian market to get the ingredients you need to make a flavorful stir-fry or curry. Many supermarkets now carry a wider array of Asian ingredients—look for them in the international foods aisle. Here are some common Asian ingredients that you'll find in many of our recipes.

Hot Chile Sauces

Used both in cooking and as a condiment, these sauces come in a variety of styles. Sriracha (right) contains garlic and is made from chiles that are ground into a smooth paste. Chili-garlic sauce (left) also contains garlic and is similar to sriracha but the chiles are coarsely ground. Sambal oelek (middle) is made purely from ground chiles without the addition of garlic or other spices, thus adding heat but not additional flavor. Once opened, these sauces will keep for several months in the refrigerator.

Sweet Chili Sauce

Unlike the spicy Asian chile sauces (above), which add heat, Thai-style sweet chili sauce lies at the other end of the spicy spectrum. This sweet, thick sauce is made primarily from palm sugar, pickled chiles, vinegar, and garlic. It makes a good dipping sauce for egg rolls and dumplings, it is often served in Thailand with barbecued chicken, and we also use it as a glaze.

Rice Vinegar

Rice vinegar is made from glutinous rice that is broken down into sugars, blended with yeast to ferment into alcohol, and aerated to form vinegar. Because of its sweet-tart flavor, rice vinegar is used to accentuate many Asian dishes. Seasoned rice vinegar is simply rice vinegar with salt, sugar, and sake added. This condiment, whose aliases include sushi vinegar and *awasezu*, makes a flavorful dressing for salads or vegetables.

Mirin

This Japanese rice wine has a subtle salty-sweet flavor prized in Asian marinades and glazes. The most traditional method for making mirin uses glutinous rice, malted rice, and distilled alcohol and requires more than a year to mature. Many supermarket brands, however, combine sake or another type of alcohol with salt, corn syrup (which helps mimic the traditional syrupy consistency), other sweeteners, and sometimes caramel coloring and flavoring. We use mirin to brighten the flavor of stir-fries and various Asian dishes. If you cannot find mirin, substitute 1 tablespoon dry white wine and ½ teaspoon sugar for every 1 tablespoon of mirin.

Soy Sauce

Soy sauce is a fermented liquid made from soybeans and roasted grain, usually wheat, but sometimes barley or rice. It is used throughout Asia to enhance flavor and contribute complexity to food. Though Chinese-style soy sauce is the most familiar, It can vary quite a bit from region to region. It was first brewed in China and later in Japan. Japanese soy sauce, known as *shoyu*, is sweeter and less salty than Chinese soy sauce (left). Meanwhile, Indonesian soy sauce (right), known as *kecap* (pronounced like "ketchup"), a catch-all term for fermented sauces, is sweeter than the Japanese and Chinese styles. There are many varieties of kecap, but *kecap manis*, often labeled "sweet soy sauce," is easily the sweetest. It's very dark and thick, like a syrup, due to the ample palm sugar added during cooking. It's typically seasoned with various ingredients, including garlic and star anise. It can be used in sauces for rice or noodles or as a dipping sauce for dumplings, rolls, or dim sum. In a pinch, sweet soy sauce can be made by combining regular soy sauce with brown sugar or molasses and then boiling until the sugar is dissolved and the sauce is thick and syrupy.

Hoisin Sauce

Hoisin sauce is a thick, reddish-brown mixture of soybeans, sugar, vinegar, garlic, chiles, and spices, the most predominant of which is five-spice powder. It is used in many classic Chinese dishes, including barbecued pork, Peking duck, and kung pao shrimp, and as a table condiment, much like ketchup. The ideal hoisin sauce balances sweet, salty, pungent, and spicy elements so that no one flavor dominates.

Miso

Made from a fermented mixture of soy beans and rice, barley, or rye, miso is incredibly versatile, suitable for use in soups, braises, dressings, and sauces as well as for topping grilled foods. This salty, deep-flavored paste ranges in strength and color from a mild, pale yellow (referred to as white) to stronger-flavored red or brownish black, depending on the fermentation method and ingredients.

Fish Sauce

Fish sauce is a salty amber-colored liquid made from fermented fish. It is used as an ingredient and condiment in certain Asian cuisines, most commonly in the foods of Southeast Asia. In very small amounts, it adds a well-rounded, salty flavor to sauces, soups, and marinades. Note that the lighter the color of the fish sauce, the lighter its flavor.

Chinese Rice Wine

This rich-flavored liquid made from fermented glutinous rice or millet is used for both drinking and cooking. It ranges in color from clear to amber and tastes slightly sweet and aromatic. Chinese rice cooking wine is also called yellow wine, *Shao Hsing,* or *Shao Xing.* If you can't find Chinese rice cooking wine, dry sherry is a decent substitute.

Oyster Sauce

This thick, salty, strong brown sauce is a concentrated mixture of oysters, soy sauce, brine, and seasonings. It is used to enhance the flavor of many dishes and is the base for many Asian dipping sauces.

Five-Spice Powder

Often called Chinese five-spice powder, this aromatic blend of spices most often contains cinnamon, cloves, fennel seed, star anise, and Sichuan peppercorns (white pepper or ginger are common substitutes). Available in the spice aisle of the supermarket, five-spice powder is great in sauces and in spice rubs for grilled foods.

Wasabi Powder

Hot and pungent, wasabi is commonly used as a condiment for sushi and sashimi but is also useful as an ingredient in other Japanese dishes. Fresh wasabi root (also known as Japanese horseradish) is hard to find and expensive (about $8 per ounce). More widely available is wasabi that is sold in paste or powder form (the powder is mixed with water to form a paste). Because fresh wasabi root is so expensive, most pastes and all powders contain no wasabi at all, but instead a mixture of garden-variety horseradish, mustard, cornstarch, and food coloring. Nevertheless, we have found that they do the job just fine in our recipes.

Sesame Oil

Raw sesame oil, which is very mild and light in color, is used mostly for cooking, while toasted sesame oil, which has a deep amber color, is primarily used for seasoning because of its intense and nutty flavor. Toasted sesame oil is frequently used to finish dishes all over Asia. For the biggest hit of sesame flavor, we prefer to use toasted sesame oil. Just a few drops will give stir-fries, noodle dishes, or salad dressings a deep, rich flavor. Sesame oil stored at room temperature will turn rancid if not used within a few months, and it is particularly prone to damage from heat and light. Try to purchase sesame oil in tinted glass and refrigerate it to extend its shelf life.

Indonesian-Style Pork Fried Rice

Serves 4

✔ **WHY THIS RECIPE WORKS:** Sweet, salty, and slightly spicy, Indonesian-style fried rice provides a welcome change from the more familiar Chinese-style versions. Starting with precooked rice makes this recipe no-fuss, while the use of Indonesian sweet soy sauce is key to creating the right flavor profile. Pork tenderloin, mushrooms, scrambled eggs (a traditional Indonesian fried rice inclusion), and cabbage (we opt for prepared coleslaw mix for simplicity) all add heft and texture. Each component gets cooked in the skillet in stages, then it all comes together at the end. Freezing the pork tenderloin for 15 minutes will make it easier to slice.

¼ **cup sweet soy sauce (see page 310)**

3 **tablespoons rice vinegar**

2 **teaspoons hot sauce**

6 **tablespoons vegetable oil**

8 **ounces pork tenderloin, trimmed, halved lengthwise, and sliced thin**

4 **large eggs, lightly beaten**

8 **ounces white mushrooms, trimmed and sliced**

2 **cups (5½ ounces) shredded green coleslaw mix**

8 **scallions, sliced thin, white and green parts separated**

2 **(8.8-ounce) packages Uncle Ben's Original Long Grain Ready Rice**

1 **cup bean sprouts**

1 **cucumber, peeled, halved lengthwise, seeded, and sliced ½ inch thick**

1. Combine soy sauce, vinegar, and hot sauce in bowl. Heat 1 tablespoon oil in 12-inch nonstick skillet over medium-high heat until just smoking. Pat pork dry with paper towels. Add pork to skillet, break up any clumps, and cook until no longer pink, about 2 minutes; transfer to bowl. Add 1 tablespoon oil and eggs to now-empty skillet and cook, stirring constantly, until just cooked through, about 1½ minutes. Transfer scrambled eggs to bowl with pork.

2. Heat remaining ¼ cup oil in Dutch oven until just smoking. Add mushrooms and cook until lightly browned, about 5 minutes. Add coleslaw mix and scallion whites and cook until just softened, about 1 minute. Whisk soy-sauce mixture to recombine, then add rice, soy-sauce mixture, pork and egg mixture, bean sprouts, and scallion greens to pot and cook, stirring constantly, until heated through and sauce is thoroughly incorporated, 1 to 2 minutes. Sprinkle with cucumber and serve.

SMART SHOPPING UNCLE BEN'S READY RICE
Various types of instant rice have been around for years to help time-crunched cooks avoid the process of cooking rice. In addition to boil-in-bag rice and instant rice, there is also fully cooked rice, which is coated with oil to keep the grains distinct and is packaged in microwavable pouches. While we don't love Uncle Ben's Ready Rice plain as a side dish, if time is tight we have found that it works as an acceptable substitute for home-cooked rice when used in combination with other ingredients.

Vegetarian Lo Mein with Bok Choy and Scallions

Serves 4

✔ **WHY THIS RECIPE WORKS:** For a quick Chinese-style lo mein dinner that isn't greasy (like most take-out) and is also vegetarian-friendly, we use a simple combination of hoisin sauce, soy sauce, and chili-garlic sauce to create a robust, spicy flavor profile. Using bok choy in combination with a whole bunch's worth of scallion whites and greens gives the dish freshness, while slices of red bell pepper add sweetness and a half-pound of meaty shiitake mushrooms lend enough heft to keep most carnivores satisfied. Just 2 teaspoons of cornstarch is enough to make the sauce cling to the noodles without making the dish gluey.

1   (9-ounce) package fresh Chinese noodles or 8 ounces dried linguine

1   tablespoon toasted sesame oil

¼   cup water

3   tablespoons hoisin sauce

3   tablespoons soy sauce

1   tablespoon Asian chili-garlic sauce

2   teaspoons cornstarch

1   tablespoon vegetable oil

8   scallions, white and green parts separated and cut into 1-inch pieces

8   ounces shiitake mushrooms, stemmed and sliced thin

1   red bell pepper, stemmed, seeded, and sliced thin

1½   pounds bok choy, sliced crosswise ¼ inch thick

1. Bring 4 quarts water to boil in large pot. Add noodles and cook, stirring occasionally, until noodles are al dente. Drain, rinse with cold water until cool, then toss with sesame oil and set aside. Meanwhile, whisk water, hoisin sauce, soy sauce, chili-garlic sauce, and cornstarch together in small bowl; set aside.

2. Heat vegetable oil in 12-inch nonstick skillet over medium-high heat until shimmering. Add scallion whites, shiitakes, and bell pepper and cook until vegetables are softened, about 5 minutes. Stir in bok choy, scallion greens, and noodles. Whisk hoisin mixture to recombine, then add to skillet and cook, tossing constantly, until sauce is thickened and noodles are heated through, about 1 minute. Serve.

SMART SHOPPING FRESH CHINESE NOODLES
You can find fresh Chinese noodles in the refrigerated section of many supermarkets as well as Asian markets. Some noodles are cut thin (left), and others are cut slightly wider (right). Their texture is a bit more starchy and chewy than that of dried noodles, and their flavor is cleaner (less wheaty) than Italian pasta, making them an excellent match with well-seasoned sauces and soups. Fresh Chinese noodles cook quickly, usually in no more than three to four minutes in boiling water.

Udon Noodles with Edamame Pesto

Serves 4

✔ **WHY THIS RECIPE WORKS:** Here we pair thick, chewy udon noodles (a favorite in Japanese cuisine) with a creative Asian-inspired pesto featuring frozen edamame, parsley, cilantro, and basil (as well as the classic pesto ingredients of olive oil, pine nuts, Parmesan, and garlic). The edamame-based pesto is hearty and naturally protein packed, so all this recipe needs is a vegetable (we opt for asparagus) to turn it into a one-dish meal. The pesto takes minimal time to prepare since all the ingredients are simply added to the food processor and pureed. We cook the asparagus and noodles together in the same pot to save time, so all we have to do once they're drained is combine them with the sauce. The addition of a little reserved pasta cooking water turns the thick pesto into a creamy sauce. We recommend using the thinnest asparagus stalks available to ensure that they'll cook in about the same amount of time as the noodles.

8	ounces frozen edamame, thawed
1	cup fresh parsley leaves
1	cup fresh cilantro leaves
1	cup fresh basil leaves
½	cup pine nuts, toasted
⅓	cup grated Parmesan cheese
¼	cup olive oil
2	tablespoons lemon juice
1	garlic clove, minced
	Salt and pepper
2	(9-ounce) packages fresh udon noodles
1	pound thin asparagus, trimmed and cut on bias into 1½-inch lengths

1. Bring 4 quarts water to boil in large pot. Process edamame, parsley, cilantro, basil, pine nuts, Parmesan, olive oil, lemon juice, and garlic in food processor until smooth, about 20 seconds, scraping down bowl as needed. Transfer to small bowl and season with salt and pepper to taste.

2. Add noodles and asparagus to boiling water and cook, stirring occasionally, until noodles and asparagus are tender, about 4 minutes. Reserve 1 cup cooking water, then drain pasta and asparagus and return them to pot.

3. Stir pesto into pot with noodles. Season with salt and pepper to taste and add reserved cooking water as necessary to adjust consistency. Serve.

SMART SHOPPING UDON NOODLES
These thick Japanese noodles made from wheat are similar to spaghetti and can be round or squared. Available in varying thicknesses, they are typically used in soups and have an appealing chewy texture. You can find them alongside the tofu in the refrigerated section in most grocery stores as well as Asian markets. They may be labeled simply "Japanese-style noodles," but there will likely be a note on the packaging about their use as udon. They can contain quite a bit of salt (as much as 4,000 milligrams of sodium per 12 ounces); because of that, we opt to not add salt to the cooking water in this recipe.

Sesame Noodles with Tofu, Scallions, and Cashews

Serves 4

✔ **WHY THIS RECIPE WORKS:** For a satisfying, flavorful vegetarian Asian-inspired noodle dish, we liven up mild-mannered tofu and noodles with a sesame-based sauce made with tahini, seasoned rice vinegar, and oyster sauce, plus a little heat from ginger and spicy Asian chili-garlic sauce. Draining excess moisture from the tofu helps it crisp up in the skillet and gives it texture, and the draining and sautéing can all happen while the noodles are cooking in a separate pot. We combine our sauce, noodles, and tofu in the skillet, and we add some scallions for brightness. Topping it all off with toasted and chopped cashews lends some richness as well as texture.

14	ounces extra-firm tofu, cut into ¾-inch cubes
¼	cup tahini
3	tablespoons seasoned rice vinegar (see page 310)
2	tablespoons oyster sauce
1	tablespoon Asian chili-garlic sauce
1	tablespoon soy sauce
2	teaspoons grated fresh ginger
2	tablespoons vegetable oil
1	pound fresh Chinese noodles or 12 ounces dried linguine
	Salt and pepper
4	scallions, sliced thin
½	cup raw cashews, toasted and chopped

1. Spread tofu out in single layer on several layers of paper towels and let drain for 10 minutes. Bring 4 quarts water to boil in large pot.

2. Whisk tahini, vinegar, oyster sauce, chili-garlic sauce, soy sauce, and ginger in bowl.

3. Heat oil in 12-inch nonstick skillet over high heat until shimmering. Add tofu and cook, stirring occasionally, until lightly browned and crisp, 8 to 10 minutes.

4. Meanwhile, add noodles and 1 tablespoon salt to boiling water and cook, stirring often, until al dente. Reserve 1½ cups cooking water, then drain noodles and return them to pot. Whisk tahini mixture to recombine. Add tahini mixture, tofu, half of scallions, and ¾ cup cooking water and toss to combine. Season with salt and pepper to taste and add remaining cooking water as needed to adjust consistency. Serve immediately topped with cashews and remaining scallions.

SMART SHOPPING TAHINI

Tahini is a thick paste made from ground sesame seeds that's most often used to flavor Middle Eastern dishes. We tasted five supermarket brands, and **Joyva Sesame Tahini** boasted the most tahini flavor. Tasters called the tahini "very nutty," "buttery," and almost "peanut-butterish."

Noodle Cake with Spicy Peanut-Chicken Stir-Fry

Serves 4

✔ **WHY THIS RECIPE WORKS:** For a change of pace, we swap out the rice you'd typically find served with a stir-fry for a noodle cake. The cake is a snap to make in a skillet and adds great texture and visual appeal. We start by boiling fresh Chinese noodles, then drain them and transfer them to our skillet. Pressing down on the noodles with a spatula, and flipping them over halfway through cooking, is all it takes to form them into a cake. Chicken spiced up with serranos, ginger, and garlic brings bold flavor to this dish. Serve with Steamed Bok Choy (page 161).

1   **(9-ounce) package fresh Chinese noodles**

1   **tablespoon salt**

4   **scallions, sliced thin**

4   **(6-ounce) boneless, skinless chicken breasts, trimmed and sliced thin**

2   **tablespoons soy sauce**

2   **tablespoons Chinese rice wine or dry sherry**

¾   **cup low-sodium chicken broth**

2   **teaspoons cornstarch**

¼   **cup vegetable oil**

½   **cup dry-roasted peanuts, chopped**

2   **serrano chiles, stemmed, seeded, and chopped**

1   **(1½-inch) piece ginger, peeled and cut into 2-inch-long matchsticks**

5   **garlic cloves, sliced thin**

1. Bring 4 quarts water to boil in large pot. Add noodles and salt and cook, stirring often, until tender. Drain and toss with half of scallions. Meanwhile, toss chicken with 1 tablespoon soy sauce and 1 tablespoon rice wine and let marinate for 10 minutes. Whisk remaining 1 tablespoon soy sauce, remaining 1 tablespoon rice wine, broth, and cornstarch together in small bowl.

2. Heat 1 tablespoon oil in 12-inch nonstick skillet over medium-high heat until just smoking, add noodles, and, using spatula, press into even layer. Cook until crisp on first side, 2 to 3 minutes. Place back of baking sheet over skillet and invert noodle cake onto sheet. Add 1 tablespoon oil to skillet and slide noodle cake back into skillet. Cook until browned on second side, about 2 minutes. Slide noodle cake onto serving platter and tent loosely with foil.

3. Heat 2 teaspoons oil in now-empty skillet over high heat until just smoking. Pat chicken dry with paper towels. Add half of chicken to skillet, break up any clumps, and cook until lightly browned and no longer pink, about 3 minutes. Transfer to clean bowl. Repeat with 2 teaspoons oil and remaining chicken.

4. Add remaining 2 teaspoons oil, peanuts, serranos, ginger, and garlic to now-empty skillet and cook, stirring constantly, until fragrant, about 1 minute. Return chicken and any accumulated juices to skillet and toss to combine. Whisk chicken broth mixture to recombine, then add to skillet. Cook, stirring constantly, until sauce is slightly thickened, about 1 minute. Cut noodle cake into wedges and sprinkle with remaining scallions. Serve with chicken.

Chicken Yakisoba

Serves 4

✔ **WHY THIS RECIPE WORKS:** *Yakisoba* is a dish often sold at Japanese festivals and is similar to chow mein. It is made with ramen noodles (not soba, despite the name), which are conveniently quick-cooking, making it a great weeknight choice. We quickly boil the noodles, then stir-fry the chicken and vegetables before adding the noodles. The noodles are typically the main feature of yakisoba, but we turn it into a heartier meal by adding more chicken and vegetables and using fewer noodles. We use a traditional yakisoba sauce made with the clean-tasting combination of soy sauce, Chinese rice wine, and mirin, which we add to the skillet last and cook just until the noodles are coated. See page 304 for more on cutting chicken for stir-fries.

4   **(3-ounce) packages instant ramen noodles, seasoning packets discarded**

     Salt

3   **tablespoons vegetable oil**

2   **(6-ounce) boneless, skinless chicken breasts, trimmed and sliced thin**

1½ **pounds bok choy, cut into 1-inch pieces**

2   **carrots, peeled and sliced thin**

2   **tablespoons grated fresh ginger**

3   **scallions, sliced thin on bias**

¼   **cup soy sauce**

2   **tablespoons Chinese rice wine or dry sherry**

2   **tablespoons mirin**

1. Bring 4 quarts water to boil in Dutch oven. Add noodles and 1 tablespoon salt and boil until noodles are tender, about 2 minutes. Drain and rinse under cold water.

2. Heat 2 tablespoons oil in now-empty pot over medium-high heat until just smoking. Pat chicken dry with paper towels. Add chicken to pot, break up any clumps, and cook until lightly browned and no longer pink, about 3 minutes. Transfer to plate.

3. Add remaining 1 tablespoon oil, bok choy, and carrots to now-empty pot and cook until vegetables are tender, about 3 minutes. Clear center of skillet, add ginger and scallions, and cook, mashing mixture into pan, until fragrant, about 30 seconds. Stir mixture into vegetables. Stir in noodles and cook until heated through, about 1 minute. Stir in chicken and any accumulated juices, soy sauce, rice wine, and mirin and cook, stirring constantly, until sauce is thickened and coats noodles and vegetables, about 1 minute. Serve.

SMART SHOPPING RAMEN NOODLES

Though instant ramen noodles are a favorite among college students because of their extremely affordable price, in the test kitchen as a rule we don't like them if they are prepared either plain or with the salty, stale-tasting seasoning packet they often come with. However, we do sometimes use plain ramen noodles as the pasta component in Asian-inspired recipes; we just get rid of the seasoning packet and add our own mix of fresh herbs and spices (along with other ingredients). Typically fried in oil before they are dried and packaged, ramen noodles take only a few minutes to cook, making them an even more convenient, quicker-cooking choice than other dried-noodle options.

Stir-Fried Curried Pork Noodles

Serves 4

✔ **WHY THIS RECIPE WORKS:** This flavorful, one-of-a-kind meal is often referred to as "Singapore curry noodles" since the flavors are a fusion of Chinese, Indian, and Malaysian cooking. We soak the noodles in hot water rather than boil them to ensure they don't overcook, and we prepare the rest of the recipe while they soak to keep things moving. Snap peas lend both color and texture and cook in a few minutes in the skillet. After cooking the pork, vegetables, and aromatics in a skillet, we add the softened noodles and sauce to the pan and toss to combine. To make the pork easier to slice, we freeze it first for 15 minutes.

8	ounces (¼-inch-wide) rice noodles
¼	cup water
4	tablespoons vegetable oil
3	tablespoons fish sauce
2	tablespoons lime juice
1	tablespoon sugar
1	(1-pound) pork tenderloin, trimmed and sliced crosswise ¼ inch thick
1	onion, sliced thin
8	ounces snap peas, strings removed and halved on bias
4	garlic cloves, minced
1	tablespoon curry powder

1. Cover noodles with boiling water in bowl and soak until softened but not fully tender, about 20 minutes. Drain noodles and set aside.

2. Whisk ¼ cup water, 2 tablespoons oil, fish sauce, lime juice, and sugar in small bowl until sugar dissolves. Set aside.

3. Heat 2 teaspoons oil in 12-inch nonstick skillet over medium-high heat until just smoking. Pat pork dry with paper towels. Add half of pork to skillet, break up any clumps, and cook until lightly browned and no longer pink, 1 to 2 minutes per side. Transfer to plate and repeat with 2 teaspoons oil and remaining pork.

4. Add remaining 2 teaspoons oil, onion, and snap peas to now-empty skillet and cook until vegetables are soft, about 3 minutes. Clear center of skillet, add garlic and curry powder, and cook, mashing garlic into skillet, until fragrant, about 1 minute. Stir garlic mixture into vegetables. Add softened noodles, fish sauce mixture, and pork and any accumulated juices and cook, tossing constantly, until noodles are completely tender, about 2 minutes. Serve.

SMART SHOPPING RICE NOODLES
Rice noodles, used in various Asian cuisines, are made from rice powder and water. They come in several widths (¼ inch wide, which is similar to linguine; ⅜ inch wide; and thin vermicelli). Since they can overcook quickly, we often soften them off the heat in hot water before adding them to whatever dish we're making toward the end of cooking. We've also had some success boiling the noodles as long as we carefully watch the time, and we usually rinse them after draining to ensure they cool quickly.

Quick Indian Beef Curry

Serves 4

✔ **WHY THIS RECIPE WORKS:** Indian curries have a well-deserved reputation for being hearty, satisfying dishes packed with flavor. The downside is that they typically feature lengthy ingredient lists calling for a number of exotic items. Here we simplify the process without sacrificing flavor by using easy-to-find supermarket staples: onion, garlic, curry powder, fresh ginger, and tomato paste. We start by making the sauce, then add the potatoes and the beef and allow them to cook through right in the sauce, which infuses all the components with flavor. Most types of stew meat take hours to turn tender, but well-marbled blade steak needs only a quick braise before it's ready, making this curry weeknight friendly. We cut the potatoes into small chunks and the blade steaks into easily manageable ¼-inch strips so that both will cook through quickly. Serve with Cilantro Chutney and either Easy White Rice (page 22) or naan bread.

2	tablespoons vegetable oil
1	onion, chopped fine
2	tablespoons curry powder
1	tablespoon tomato paste
1	tablespoon grated fresh ginger
3	garlic cloves, minced
1½	pounds blade steaks, trimmed and sliced crosswise into ¼-inch strips
1¼	pounds red potatoes, cut into ½-inch pieces
1	(14.5-ounce) can diced tomatoes
1	cup water
	Salt and pepper

1. Heat oil in 12-inch skillet over medium-high heat until shimmering. Add onion and cook until softened, about 3 minutes. Add curry powder, tomato paste, ginger, and garlic and cook until fragrant, about 1 minute.

2. Add beef, potatoes, tomatoes, and water and bring to boil. Reduce heat to medium-low, cover, and cook until beef is tender, about 20 minutes, stirring halfway through cooking. Season with salt and pepper to taste.

SIMPLE SIDE CILANTRO CHUTNEY
Process 1½ cups fresh cilantro leaves, ½ cup chopped onion, ¼ cup lemon juice (2 lemons), 1 stemmed, seeded, and chopped jalapeño, 2 teaspoons salt, and ¼ teaspoon cayenne pepper in food processor until smooth, 20 to 30 seconds. Serves 4.

QUICK PREP TIP
TRIMMING BLADE STEAK
To remove thin line of gristle running through center of blade steak, halve each steak lengthwise, leaving long, thin piece of gristle attached to 1 half. Cut away gristle from half to which it is still attached and discard.

Thai Green Curry with Pork and Zucchini

Serves 4

✓ **WHY THIS RECIPE WORKS:** Although authentic curry originated in southern India, the word "curry" has evolved into a catchall term used to describe any number of spicy, saucy dishes from all over the globe. For this take on a curry and pork dish, we drew inspiration from the flavors of Thailand by bringing together salty, sweet, sour, and spicy. To deepen and bloom the flavor of our store-bought curry paste, we cook it in the skillet for about 30 seconds before we add the coconut milk, fish sauce, and sugar to the pan. Cooking the pork and the zucchini first, in stages, leaves behind flavorful fond in the pan that we can incorporate into the curry once we add the coconut milk. After we cook down the coconut milk mixture to the proper saucy consistency, all we have to do is return the pork and zucchini to the pan to heat through. A little fresh cilantro and lime juice added at the end give this dish the right balancing brightness.

1	**(1-pound) pork tenderloin, trimmed and cut into ¾-inch pieces**
	Salt and pepper
2	**tablespoons vegetable oil**
2	**zucchini, cut into ¾-inch pieces**
3	**tablespoons Thai green curry paste**
1	**(14-ounce) can coconut milk**
2	**tablespoons fish sauce**
1	**tablespoon packed brown sugar**
½	**cup chopped fresh cilantro**
1	**tablespoon lime juice**

1. Pat pork dry with paper towels and season with salt and pepper. Heat 1 tablespoon oil in 12-inch skillet over medium-high heat until just smoking. Add pork, break up any clumps, and cook until well browned, about 6 minutes. Transfer pork to bowl and set aside.

2. Add remaining 1 tablespoon oil and zucchini to now-empty skillet and cook until browned, 3 to 5 minutes. Transfer zucchini to bowl with pork and set aside.

3. Add curry paste to now-empty skillet and cook until fragrant, about 30 seconds. Stir in coconut milk, fish sauce, and sugar, scraping up any browned bits, and bring to simmer over medium heat. Simmer until sauce thickens, about 6 minutes. Stir in browned pork and zucchini, along with any accumulated juices, and cook until heated through, about 2 minutes. Off heat, stir in cilantro and lime juice. Serve.

SMART SHOPPING COCONUT MILK
Coconut milk is made by steeping equal parts shredded coconut meat and either warm milk or water. The meat is pressed or mashed to release as much liquid as possible, the mixture is strained, and the result is coconut milk. We tasted seven nationally available brands (five regular and two light) in coconut pudding, coconut rice, a Thai-style chicken soup, and green chicken curry. In the soup and curry, tasters preferred **Chaokoh** because of its exceptionally low sugar content. Of the two light brands tasted, we preferred the richer flavor of A Taste of Thai, though neither was nearly as creamy as the full-fat options. Ka-Me brand coconut milk is best suited for sweet recipes.

Thai Green Curry with Eggplant

Serves 4

✔ **WHY THIS RECIPE WORKS:** The combination of sweet, sour, salty, and spicy flavors is a trademark of Thai cooking, and we achieve that complexity here while maintaining a short ingredient list. To begin, we use a store-bought curry paste instead of making our own. We then microwave the eggplant, cut into chunks for faster cooking, to extract moisture, ensuring it will brown quickly when it hits the pan without becoming overcooked and soggy. We rely on quick-cooking frozen peas to add a sweet counterpoint to the other savory flavors in the recipe. And while Thai basil is traditional in green Asian curries, we substitute more widely available Italian basil for convenience. Serve with Easy White Rice (page 22).

2   pounds eggplant, cut into
    ¾-inch chunks

2   tablespoons vegetable oil

8   scallions, white parts minced,
    green parts cut into 1-inch
    pieces

1   (14-ounce) can coconut milk

3   tablespoons Thai green curry
    paste

2   tablespoons fish sauce

2   tablespoons packed brown sugar

1   cup frozen peas

½   cup fresh basil leaves,
    roughly torn

4   teaspoons lime juice

1. Microwave eggplant in large bowl until softened and slightly shriveled, about 10 minutes, tossing halfway through cooking. Heat oil in 12-inch nonstick skillet over medium-high heat until shimmering. Add eggplant and cook, without stirring, until golden brown on 1 side, about 3 minutes. Stir once and continue to cook until golden brown all over, about 2 minutes more. Add scallion whites and cook until fragrant, about 30 seconds. Transfer eggplant mixture to clean bowl and wipe out skillet with paper towels.

2. Whisk together coconut milk, curry paste, fish sauce, and sugar, then add to now-empty skillet. Bring coconut milk mixture to simmer over medium heat, then add peas, scallion greens, and eggplant and any accumulated juices and cook until sauce is slightly thickened, about 5 minutes. Off heat, stir in basil and lime juice, then serve.

SMART SHOPPING GLOBE AND CHINESE EGGPLANT

Of the many eggplant varieties commonly found in supermarkets, the globe eggplant (below left) is the most versatile. Globe eggplants contain fewer seeds than their sister varieties, and their firm flesh retains its shape after cooking, making them an ideal choice for most applications, including frying, roasting, sautéing, grilling, and stuffing. Chinese eggplants (far right) have a comparatively sweet and delicate flavor that is less bitter than larger varieties. They also have thinner, more tender skin. Chinese eggplants are a great choice for stir-fries, but globe will work just fine, too.

Index

A

Antipasto Pizza with Arugula Salad, 280
Apple(s)
    Basil-Parmesan Chicken Salad with, 38, *39*
    Cider-Glazed Pork Chops with Waldorf Salad, *122,*
        130
    cutting into matchsticks, 74
    and Gouda Panini with Tangy Cabbage Slaw, *296,*
        297
    Raita, Curried Chicken Sandwiches with, 285
    Rye-Crusted Pork Schnitzel with Quick
        Applesauce, 146
Apricot(s)
    -Cilantro Couscous, 191
    -Crusted Pork Chops with Radicchio, 134
    dried, about, 134
    Rice Pilaf, Curried Chicken Meatballs with, *84,* 85
Artichoke(s)
    and Chicken Paella, 70
    -Lemon Aïoli, Prosciutto Panini with, 289
    and Mushrooms, Sautéed Shrimp with, 180, *181*
    -Potato Ragout, Strip Steaks with, 95
Arugula
    about, 33
    Basil-Parmesan Chicken Salad with Apples, 38, *39*
    Beets, and Blue Cheese, Farfalle with, 219
    Chorizo, and Pecorino, Penne with, 214
    Lemony Salmon and Roasted Beet Salad, 48
    Pesto and Potato Pizza with Fennel Salad, 282, *283*
    with Roquefort Vinaigrette, 112
    Salad, Antipasto Pizza with, 280
    Salad with Balsamic-Mustard Vinaigrette, 202
    Skillet Tortellini Supper, 224
    Three-Cheese Pesto Lasagna Stacks, 245
Asian Chicken Salad Sandwiches, *286,* 287
Asian ingredients, about, 310–11
Asparagus
    and Chicken, Matzo Ball Soup with, 11
    and Lemony Chicken, Pasta with, 218

Asparagus *(cont.)*
    Salmon, and Leeks, Spring Farfalle with, 236
    and Shrimp, Stir-Fried, with Lemon Sauce, 309
    Steamed, with Olive Oil and Sea Salt, 232
    Udon Noodles with Edamame Pesto, *314,* 315
Avocado(s)
    Chunky Chipotle Guacamole, 129
    and Crab, Gazpacho with, *18,* 19

B

Bacon
    Clam, and Onion Pizza, 281
    Easy Spaghetti Amatriciana with Pancetta Crisps,
        211
    Endive, and Peas, Farfalle with, 210
    Maple-Glazed, Blue Cheese Wedge with, 28
    Skillet Macaroni and Cheese with, 237
Baked Risotto with Shrimp and Zucchini, 240
Balsamic Steak Tips and Tomato Salad, 113
Barley
    about, 87
    Salad, Mustard-Sage Turkey Cutlets and, 87
Basil
    Chili, and Chicken Stir-Fry with Coconut Rice, 308
    chopping, 233
    -Garlic Aïoli, Cod Cakes with, 164
    -Parmesan Chicken Salad with Apples, 38, *39*
    Pine Nut and Parmesan–Crusted Chicken, 67
Bean(s)
    Black, Soup, Quick, 22, *23*
    canned, about, 190
    canned, taste tests on, 190
    edamame, about, 97
    Hearty Chicken and Chorizo Skillet Supper, 79
    Individual Tex-Mex Chicken Pizzas, *274,* 277
    Lima, Ragout, Roast Chicken with, *52,* 57
    Pan-Seared Scallops with Bacon Succotash, 183

Bean(s) *(cont.)*
  Quick All-American Chili with Cheesy Cornbread, 4, *5*
  Quick Southern Fried Chicken Dinner, *76,* 77
  Red, and Rice, Spicy, Skillet Chicken with, 72, *73*
  Refried, Southwestern Steak Tips with, 116
  Smoky Chorizo, Chickpea, and Spinach Soup, 16
  Spanish Tapas Salad, 30, *31*
  Udon Noodles with Edamame Pesto, *314,* 315
  Vegetable Tagine with Chickpeas and Olives, 191
  White, and Tuna Salad, Tuscan-Style, 45
  White, Escarole, and Linguiça Soup, *2,* 15
  White, –Fennel Salad, Mediterranean Tuna and, 170, *171*
  White, Panzanella, 207
  White, Soup, Creamy, with Kale Pesto, 24
  White Chicken Chili, 14
  see also Green Bean(s)
Bean sauces, Asian, about, 303
Bean-Sprout Salad, Spicy, 151
Beef
  Burritos, Spicy, *110,* 111
  Curry, Quick Indian, 322
  Greek Meatballs with Herb and Lemon Orzo, *118,* 119
  Green Bean, and Scallion Stir-Fry, 300, *301*
  Kebabs, Grilled, with Napa Cabbage Slaw, *252,* 253
  Lettuce Cups, Spicy, 120
  Quick All-American Chili with Cheesy Cornbread, 4, *5*
  and Rice Bowl, Korean-Style, 114, *115*
  Skillet Hamburgers, 291
  slicing, for stir-fries, 300
  Spring Rolls with Spicy Mayo, 121
  Stew, Quick Guinness, 6
  USDA grades of, 102
  Wellington, Quick, 117
  see also Steak(s)
Beet(s)
  Arugula, and Blue Cheese, Farfalle with, 219
  preventing stains from, 219
  raw, grating, 35
  Roasted, and Lemony Salmon Salad, 48
  Steak Salad with Creamy Horseradish Dressing, *34,* 35
  -Yogurt Sauce, Couscous Patties with, 195

Blue Cheese
  Arugula with Roquefort Vinaigrette, 112
  Balsamic Steak Tips and Tomato Salad, 113
  Beets, and Arugula, Farfalle with, 219
  Cheesy Gnocchi and Cauliflower Gratin, 241
  Gnocchi with Spinach, Ham, and Gorgonzola, *242,* 243
  Grilled Beef Tenderloin with Watercress Salad, *246,* 250
  Italian Cobb Salad, 37
  Squash, Gorgonzola, and Pancetta Pizza, 278, *279*
  and Walnut Chopped Chicken Salad, 36
  and Walnut–Stuffed Chicken Breasts, 54, *55*
  Wedge with Maple-Glazed Bacon, 28
Bok Choy
  baby, cleaning, 175
  Baby, Teriyaki Pork Chops with, 142
  Chicken Yakisoba, 319
  Chili-Glazed Salmon with, *174,* 175
  and Scallions, Vegetarian Lo Mein with, 313
  Steamed, 161
Bread crumbs, panko, making at home, 176
Breads
  Easy Rouille Croutons, 20
  lavash, about, 276
  naan, about, 285
  Parmesan French Toast with Tomato-Basil Topping, *204,* 205
  Quick Cheesy Breadsticks, 212
  Rosemary-Olive Focaccia, 37
  White Bean Panzanella, 207
Broccoli
  with Balsamic Vinaigrette, 237
  Currants, and Pine Nuts, Orecchiette with, 225
  Lemony Steamed, 60
  Roasted, 146
  Spicy, and Red Pepper, Snapper with, 158, *159*
  trimming, 158
  varieties of, 238
  see also Broccoli Slaw
Broccolini
  about, 238
  Easy Garlicky Risotto with, 238, *239*
  Garlicky, Hoisin-Glazed Boneless Ribs with, 143
  trimming, 143

Broccoli Rabe
about, 238
Chicken Francese with, 78
Parmesan Pork Cutlets with, 147
and Sausage Calzones, 284
Broccoli Slaw
Grilled Salmon Sandwiches with, 271
Spicy Cornmeal Flounder and Lemony Slaw, 156
Steaks with Citrus-Soy Pan Sauce and Slaw, *96, 97*
Broth, vegetable, taste tests on, 25
Buffalo Chicken Lavash Pizza, 276
Burgers
cooking indoors, 291
Grilled Andouille, with Spicy Mayonnaise, 266
Grilled Thai Turkey Sliders, 262
Pork, with Quick Pickled Peaches, 290
Salmon, with Tomato Chutney, 294
Skillet Hamburgers, 291
Burritos, Spicy Beef, *110*, 111
Butter
browning, 228
unsalted, taste tests on, 218
Butternut, Poblano, and Cheese Quesadillas, 198

C

Cabbage
with Kielbasa and Honey-Dijon Dressing, 29
-Mango Slaw and Coconut-Lime Chicken, *26,* 41
napa, about, 33
Napa, Salad, 148
Napa, Slaw, Grilled Beef Kebabs with, *252,* 253
-Potato Hash, Mustard Salmon with, 176
Slaw, Tangy, Gouda and Apple Panini with, *296,* 297
Slaw, Warm, Grilled Glazed Tofu with, 270
see also Coleslaw mix; Sauerkraut
Calzones, Sausage and Broccoli Rabe, 284
Cambodian Chicken Soup, 12, *13*
Capers, taste tests on, 271
Caribbean Chicken Pepper Pot, 61
Carrot(s)
-Parsnip Mash, Flank Steak with, 109
Salad, Orange-Ginger Pork Tenderloin and, 124, *125*

Carrot(s) *(cont.)*
Salad with Raisins, 292, *293*
storing, 109
Cauliflower
and Gnocchi Gratin, Cheesy, 241
Pork Chops with Roasted Red Pepper Sauce, 135
-Potato Mash and Boursin, Steaks with, 99
and Sage Browned Butter, Linguine with, 228
Celery, storing, 38
Celery Root Slaw and Parsley Sauce, Chicken with, 74
Cheese
Antipasto Pizza with Arugula Salad, 280
Boursin, about, 99
Butternut, and Poblano Quesadillas, 198
Cheesy Gnocchi and Cauliflower Gratin, 241
Cheesy Skillet Polenta and Eggplant Bake, 200, *201*
feta, taste tests on, 49
Goat, Chicken, and Cherry Salad, 42, *43*
Goat, Fennel, and Olive Tarts, 206
Gouda and Apple Panini with Tangy Cabbage Slaw, *296,* 297
mozzarella, buying, 280
Pecorino, about, 214
Penne with Arugula, Chorizo, and Pecorino, 214
Prosciutto Panini with Artichoke-Lemon Aïoli, 289
Quick All-American Chili with Cheesy Cornbread, 4, *5*
Ricotta, Basil, and Summer Squash Frittata, 202
Romaine Wedge with Shrimp and Feta Dressing, 49
Sausage and Broccoli Rabe Calzones, 284
semisoft, shredding, 244
Skillet Macaroni and, with Bacon, 237
Skillet Shrimp and Orzo with Feta, 178
Sopa Seca, 244
Spanish Tapas Salad, 30, *31*
Steaks with Boursin and Potato-Cauliflower Mash, 99
storing, 28
Three-, Pesto Lasagna Stacks, 245
see also Blue Cheese; Parmesan
Cheesy Polenta, 59
Cherry(ies)
Chicken, and Goat Cheese Salad, 42, *43*
pitting, 42

Cherry Tomato Salad, 295
Chicken
  and Artichoke Paella, 70
  and Asparagus, Matzo Ball Soup with, 11
  Breasts, Blue Cheese and Walnut–Stuffed, 54, *55*
  Buffalo, Lavash Pizza, 276
  Chile, and Basil Stir-Fry with Coconut Rice, 308
  Chili, White, 14
  and Chorizo Skillet Supper, Hearty, 79
  Coconut-Lime, and Cabbage-Mango Slaw, *26*, 41
  and Corn Chowder, Spicy, 10
  Country Captain, 64
  Curried, Sandwiches with Apple Raita, 285
  cutlets, preparing, 77
  Cutlets with Ginger-Shiitake Sauce, 75
  Date, and Olive Salad, Moroccan-Style, 40
  Fingers, Parmesan, with Marinara Sauce, 80, *81*
  Francese with Broccoli Rabe, 78
  Goat Cheese, and Cherry Salad, 42, *43*
  Grilled, Greek-Style, Pita Sandwiches, 259
  Grilled, with Lemon-Thyme Potato Salad, 258
  Grilled Breaded, with Tomato Salad, *260*, 261
  Grilled Indian-Spiced, with Mango Relish,
    256, *257*
  Italian Cobb Salad, 37
  Lemony, and Asparagus, Pasta with, 218
  Meatballs, Curried, with Apricot Rice Pilaf,
    84, 85
  and Mexican Green Rice Skillet Supper, *68*, 69
  with Mexican-Style Pumpkin Seed Sauce, 71
  with Parsley Sauce and Celery Root Slaw, 74
  -Peanut Stir-Fry, Spicy, Noodle Cake with, 318
  Pepper Pot, Caribbean, 61
  Pie, Sweet and Savory Cuban, 83
  Pine Nut and Parmesan–Crusted, 67
  Pizzas, Individual Tex-Mex, *274*, 277
  and Potatoes, Quick White Wine–Braised,
    62, *63*
  Pozole, Quick, 7
  Prosciutto-Wrapped, with Sage Butter, 66
  Quick Southern Fried, Dinner, *76*, 77
  Roast, Wintry, with Honey-Glazed Parsnips, 56
  Roast, with Lima Bean Ragout, *52*, 57
  rotisserie, buying, 7

Chicken *(cont.)*
  Salad, Basil-Parmesan, with Apples, 38, *39*
  Salad, Blue Cheese and Walnut Chopped, 36
  Salad Sandwiches, Asian, *286*, 287
  shredding, 9
  Skillet, with Spicy Red Beans and Rice, 72, *73*
  Skillet Glazed Drumsticks, 60
  slicing, for stir-fries, 304
  Sopa Seca, 244
  Soup, Cambodian, 12, *13*
  and Squash Stir-Fry with Cilantro Rice, *306*, 307
  Stir-Fry with Black Bean Sauce, 303
  Tarragon, and Egg Noodles, *216*, 217
  tenderloins, buying, 82
  Tenders with Meaty Green Beans, 82
  Teriyaki Stir-Fry, 304, *305*
  Thai Coconut Curry Soup with, *8*, 9
  Thighs with Fennel, Orange, and Olives, *58*, 59
  Yakisoba, 319
Chile(s)
  Butternut, Poblano, and Cheese Quesadillas, 198
  Caribbean Chicken Pepper Pot, 61
  Chicken with Mexican-Style Pumpkin Seed Sauce,
    71
  Chile, Basil, and Chicken Stir-Fry with Coconut
    Rice, 308
  chipotle, powder, about, 116
  poblano, buying, 14
  Pork Chops with Creamy Roasted Poblanos, 132
  sauces, hot, about, 310
  Scotch bonnet, about, 61
  Skillet Summer Vegetable Tamale Pie, 199
  White Chicken Chili, 14
Chili
  Chicken, White, 14
  Quick All-American, with Cheesy Cornbread, 4, *5*
Chili-Glazed Salmon with Bok Choy, *174*, 175
Chili powder, taste tests on, 105
Chinese rice wine, about, 311
Chipotle chile powder, about, 116
Chunky Chipotle Guacamole, 129
Chutney
  Cilantro, 322
  mango, taste tests on, 50

Cider-Glazed Pork Chops with Waldorf Salad, *122*, 130

Cilantro
  -Apricot Couscous, 191
  Chutney, 322
  Rice, 71

Clam(s)
  Bacon, and Onion Pizza, 281
  Quick Bouillabaisse, 20
  Sauce, Spicy White Fresh, Spaghetti with, *234*, 235

Coconut
  cream of, about, 41
  Curry Soup, Thai, with Chicken, *8, 9*
  -Lime Chicken and Cabbage-Mango Slaw, *26*, 41
  milk, taste tests on, 323
  Rice, Chile, Basil, and Chicken Stir-Fry with, 308
  Tropical Shrimp and Rice Salad, 50, *51*

Cod
  Cakes with Garlic-Basil Aïoli, 164
  with Herbed Tomato-Caper Compote, 162, *163*
  Macadamia-Crusted, with Mango-Mint Salsa, 165

Coffee-Rubbed Rib Eye with Creamy Slaw, *92*, 105

Cola-Glazed Pork Chops with Mustard Greens, 140, *141*

Coleslaw mix
  Coffee-Rubbed Rib Eye with Creamy Slaw, *92*, 105
  Indonesian-Style Pork Fried Rice, 312
  Ranch Slaw, 80
  Slaw with Cumin-Honey Dressing, 198

Collard Greens, 91

Corn
  Cakes, Spicy Shrimp with, 179
  and Chicken Chowder, Spicy, 10
  Pan-Seared Scallops with Bacon Succotash, 183
  removing kernels from cob, 131
  Skillet Summer Vegetable Tamale Pie, 199
  Spicy Pork Chops and Summer Vegetable Sauté, 131

Cornbread, Cheesy, Quick All-American Chili with, *4, 5*

Cornbread Croutons, Southwest Beef Salad with, 32

Cornbread mix
  Skillet Summer Vegetable Tamale Pie, 199
  taste tests on, 199

Cornmeal
  Flounder, Spicy, and Lemony Slaw, 156
  see also Cornbread mix

Country Captain Chicken, 64

Couscous
  about, 172
  Apricot-Cilantro, 191
  and Fish Packets, Moroccan, *166,* 167
  Lemon, and Olive Relish, Swordfish with, 172
  Patties with Beet-Yogurt Sauce, 195
  -Stuffed Acorn Squash, 196, *197*

Crab
  and Avocado, Gazpacho with, *18,* 19
  grades of, 19
  -Stuffed Sole with Lemon-Butter Sauce, 160

Creamy White Bean Soup with Kale Pesto, 24

Crème fraîche, about, 62

Crispy Potato Pierogi with Mushroom Ragout, *192,* 193

Crispy Sesame Pork Cutlets, 148, *149*

Crostini, Garlic, Steamed Mussels with Chorizo and, *184,* 185

Cucumber(s)
  Gazpacho with Avocado and Crab, *18,* 19
  Salad, 106
  and Yogurt Salad, 288

Curried dishes
  Country Captain Chicken, 64
  Curried Chicken Meatballs with Apricot Rice Pilaf, *84,* 85
  Curried Chicken Sandwiches with Apple Raita, 285
  Flank Steak with Spicy Peanut Noodles, 106, *107*
  Jasmine Rice Cakes with Vegetable Thai Green Curry, 194
  Quick Indian Beef Curry, 322
  Stir-Fried Curried Pork Noodles, *320,* 321
  Thai Coconut Curry Soup with Chicken, *8,* 9
  Thai Green Curry with Eggplant, 324, *325*
  Thai Green Curry with Pork and Zucchini, 323

Curry paste, Thai green, about, 194

D

Date(s)
  Chicken, and Olive Salad, Moroccan-Style, 40
  chopping, 40
Dutch ovens, ratings of, 17

E

Easy Garlicky Risotto with Broccolini, 238, *239*
Easy Rouille Croutons, 20
Easy Spaghetti Amatriciana with Pancetta Crisps, 211
Easy White Rice, 22
Eggplant
  and Garlic Sauté, 85
  globe vs. Chinese, 324
  and Polenta Bake, Cheesy Skillet, 200, *201*
  Thai Green Curry with, 324, *325*
Egg(s)
  Fried-, and Frisée Salad with Lentils, 44
  hard-boiled, preparing, 48
  Indonesian-Style Pork Fried Rice, 312
  Korean-Style Beef and Rice Bowl, 114, *115*
  Ricotta, Basil, and Summer Squash Frittata, 202
  scrambling, tip for, 173
  Smoked Salmon Scrambled, with Chive Butter, 173
  Spicy Tomato and Pepper Sauce–Poached, 203
Endive
  about, 251
  Bacon, and Peas, Farfalle with, 210
  and Radicchio, Grilled T-Bone Steaks with, 251
Equipment, ratings of
  Dutch ovens, 17
  pepper mills, 65
Escarole
  about, 15
  Linguiça, and White Bean Soup, *2, 15*

F

Fajitas, Skillet Pork, *128,* 129
Farfalle with Bacon, Endive, and Peas, 210

Farfalle with Beets, Arugula, and Blue Cheese, 219
Fennel
  Olive, and Goat Cheese Tarts, 206
  Orange, and Olives, Chicken Thighs with, *58,* 59
  Salad, Arugula Pesto and Potato Pizza with, 282, *283*
  trimming and coring, 170
  –White Bean Salad, Mediterranean Tuna and, 170, *171*
Fish
  canned tuna, taste tests on, 45
  Cod Cakes with Garlic-Basil Aïoli, 164
  Cod with Herbed Tomato-Caper Compote, 162, *163*
  and Couscous Packets, Moroccan, *166,* 167
  Crab-Stuffed Sole with Lemon-Butter Sauce, 160
  and Creamy Coconut Rice Packets, Thai-Style, 161
  Halibut and Potatoes with Lemon-Caper Sauce, 168
  Macadamia-Crusted Cod with Mango-Mint Salsa, 165
  Orange-Tarragon Trout with Smoky Green Beans, 157
  Quick Bouillabaisse, 20
  smoked trout, buying, 47
  Smoked Trout Salad, *46,* 47
  Snapper with Spicy Broccoli and Red Pepper, 158, *159*
  Spicy Cornmeal Flounder and Lemony Slaw, 156
  Swordfish with Lemon Couscous and Olive Relish, 172
  see also Salmon; Shellfish; Tuna
Fish sauce, about, 311
Five-spice powder, about, 311
Flank Steak with Parsnip-Carrot Mash, 109
Flank Steak with Spicy Peanut Noodles, 106, *107*
Flounder, Spicy Cornmeal, and Lemony Slaw, 156
Fragrant Basmati Rice, 272
French Toast, Parmesan, with Tomato-Basil Topping, *204,* 205
Frisée
  about, 33
  and Fried-Egg Salad with Lentils, 44
Frittata, Ricotta, Basil, and Summer Squash, 202

G

Garlic
  Crostini, Steamed Mussels with Chorizo and, *184, 185*
  Easy Garlicky Risotto with Broccolini, 238, *239*
  prepeeled, freezing, 95
Gazpacho with Avocado and Crab, *18,* 19
Ginger
  fresh, shelf life of, 124
  grating, 309
  -Orange Pork Tenderloin and Carrot Salad, 124, *125*
  -Peach Chutney, Quick, Pork Chops with, 138
  -Shiitake Sauce, Chicken Cutlets with, 75
  smashing, 12
Glazed Caribbean Tofu with Rice and Pigeon Peas, 189
Glazed Pork Tenderloin with Creamy Turnip Puree, 126
Gnocchi
  and Cauliflower Gratin, Cheesy, 241
  with Spinach, Ham, and Gorgonzola, *242,* 243
  taste tests on, 243
Gouda and Apple Panini with Tangy Cabbage Slaw, *296, 297*
Grains. *See* Barley; Cornmeal; Polenta; Rice
Greek Meatballs with Herb and Lemon Orzo, *118,* 119
Greek-Style Grilled Chicken Pita Sandwiches, 259
Green Bean(s)
  Beef, and Scallion Stir-Fry, 300, *301*
  and Black Olive Salad, 162
  Meaty, Chicken Tenders with, 82
  Pine Nut and Parmesan–Crusted Chicken, 67
  –Potato Salad, Grilled Dijon Steak with, 248, *249*
  Prosciutto-Wrapped Chicken with Sage Butter, 66
  Skillet, 241
  Smoky, Orange-Tarragon Trout with, 157
Greens
  removing leaves from stems, 24
  for salad, types of, 33
  Winter, Whole-Wheat Pasta with, 229
  see also specific greens
Grilled dishes. *See list of recipes on page 247*
Grills, setting up, 255
Guacamole, Chunky Chipotle, 129

H

Half-and-half, substitutes for, 10
Halibut and Potatoes with Lemon-Caper Sauce, 168
Ham
  Spinach, and Gorgonzola, Gnocchi with, *242,* 243
  see also Prosciutto
Hearty Chicken and Chorizo Skillet Supper, 79
Herb(s)
  -and-Shrimp-Salad Wraps, Spicy, 292, *293*
  Mixed- , Pesto Pasta with Squash, 222, *223*
  Udon Noodles with Edamame Pesto, *314, 315*
  see also specific herbs
Hoisin-Glazed Boneless Ribs with Garlicky Broccolini, 143
Hoisin sauce, about, 311
Hominy
  buying, 21
  Quick Chicken Pozole, 7
  Shrimp Tortilla Soup, 21
Honey, crystallized, reviving, 29
Hot chile sauces, about, 310

I

Individual Tex-Mex Chicken Pizzas, *274,* 277
Indonesian-Style Pork Fried Rice, 312
Ingredients, tastings of
  andouille sausage, 127
  Arborio rice, 240
  California olive oil, 224
  canned beans, 190
  canned diced tomatoes, 79
  canned tuna, 45
  capers, 271
  chili powder, 105
  cider vinegar, 287
  coconut milk, 323
  cornbread mix, 199
  creamy peanut butter, 307
  feta cheese, 49
  gnocchi, 243
  ketchup, 140
  long-grain white rice, 69

Ingredients, tastings of (cont.)
  mango chutney, 50
  maple syrup, 142
  red wine vinegar, 207
  sauerkraut, 150
  spaghetti, 235
  tahini, 316
  tomato paste, 64
  unsalted butter, 218
  vegetable broth, 25
  whole-wheat pasta, 229
Italian Cobb Salad, 37

J

Jambalaya, Quick Pork, 127
**Jasmine Rice Cakes with Vegetable Thai Green
  Curry, 194**
**Jícama-Orange Salad, Mojo Grilled Pork Chops
  with, 264, *265***

K

Kale
  Pesto, Creamy White Bean Soup with, 24
  removing leaves from stems, 24
  Whole-Wheat Pasta with Winter Greens, 229
Ketchup, taste tests on, 140
Korean-Style Beef and Rice Bowl, 114, *115*

L

Lavash
  about, 276
  Pizza, Buffalo Chicken, 276
Leeks
  cleaning, 236
  Creamy, Pepper-Crusted Steaks with, *100,* 101
  Salmon, and Asparagus, Spring Farfalle with,
    236
Legumes. *See* Bean(s); Lentil(s); Pigeon Peas
Lemon grass, mincing, 151

Lemon(s)
  Lemony Salmon and Roasted Beet Salad, 48
  Lemony Steamed Broccoli, 60
  storing, 119
  zest, storing, 78
  zest strips, creating, 168
Lentil(s)
  Frisée and Fried-Egg Salad with, 44
  Salad, Grilled Garlic Sausages with, 267
  varieties of, 267
Lettuce
  Blue Cheese and Walnut Chopped Chicken Salad,
    36
  Blue Cheese Wedge with Maple-Glazed Bacon, 28
  Cups, Spicy Beef, 120
  Italian Cobb Salad, 37
  Romaine Wedge with Shrimp and Feta Dressing, 49
  Southwest Beef Salad with Cornbread Croutons, 32
  Steak Salad with Creamy Horseradish Dressing,
    34, 35
  varieties of, 33
**Linguine with Cauliflower and Sage Browned
    Butter, 228**

M

**Macadamia-Crusted Cod with Mango-Mint Salsa,
    165**
Macaroni Salad, 266
Mango
  -Cabbage Slaw and Coconut-Lime Chicken,
    26, 41
  chutney, taste tests on, 50
  -Mint Salsa, Macadamia-Crusted Cod with, 165
  Relish, Grilled Indian-Spiced Chicken with,
    256, *257*
Maple (syrup)
  -Glazed Bacon, Blue Cheese Wedge with, 28
  Pork Chops with Sweet Potato–Bacon Hash, *136,*
    137
Mashed Potatoes, 101
Mashed Sweet Potatoes, 88
Mashed Sweet Potatoes with Lime Zest, 132
Matzo Ball Soup with Chicken and Asparagus, 11

Matzo meal, buying, 11
Meat
  shredding, 9
  see also Beef; Pork
Meatballs
  Curried Chicken, with Apricot Rice Pilaf, *84, 85*
  Greek, with Herb and Lemon Orzo, *118,* 119
  Turkey, Spanish-Style, 90
Meatloaves, Mini Barbecued Turkey, 91
Mediterranean Tuna and White Bean–Fennel
    Salad, 170, *171*
Microwaving, cookware for, 137
Mini Barbecued Turkey Meatloaves, 91
Mirin, about, 310
Miso, about, 311
Mixed-Herb Pesto Pasta with Squash, 222, *223*
Mojo Grilled Pork Chops with Orange-Jícama
    Salad, 264, *265*
Molasses, about, 60
Moroccan Fish and Couscous Packets, *166,* 167
Moroccan-Style Chicken, Date, and Olive Salad,
    40
Moroccan Sweet Potato Soup, 25
Mushroom(s)
  and Artichokes, Sautéed Shrimp with, 180, *181*
  Chicken Cutlets with Ginger-Shiitake Sauce, 75
  Chicken Marsala Pasta, *208,* 215
  Pasta with Roasted Tomatoes and Porcini Sauce,
    230, *231*
  Portobello Sandwiches with Pesto Mayonnaise, 295
  Quick Beef Wellington, 117
  Ragout, Crispy Potato Pierogi with, *192,* 193
  Rib-Eye Steaks with Tarragon Smashed Potatoes,
    102, *103*
  Roast Chicken with Lima Bean Ragout, *52,* 57
  shiitakes, about, 302
  Stir-Fried Pork with Shiitakes and Snow Peas, *298,*
    302
  white vs. brown, 180
Mussels, Steamed, with Chorizo and Garlic
    Crostini, *184,* 185
Mustard Greens, Cola-Glazed Pork Chops with,
    140, *141*
Mustard-Sage Turkey Cutlets and Barley Salad, 87
Mustard Salmon with Potato-Cabbage Hash, 176

N

Naan, about, 285
Napa Cabbage Salad, 148
Noodle(s)
  Cake with Spicy Peanut-Chicken Stir-Fry, 318
  Cambodian Chicken Soup, 12, *13*
  Chicken Yakisoba, 319
  Egg, Tarragon Chicken and, *216,* 217
  fresh Chinese, about, 313
  ramen, about, 319
  rice, about, 321
  Sesame, with Tofu, Scallions, and Cashews, 316, *317*
  Sesame-Scallion, 120
  Spicy Peanut, Flank Steak with, 106, *107*
  Stir-Fried Curried Pork, *320,* 321
  Thai Pesto, Grilled Flank Steak with, 254
  udon, about, 315
  Udon, with Edamame Pesto, *314,* 315
  Vegetarian Lo Mein with Bok Choy and Scallions,
    313
Nut(s)
  Macadamia-Crusted Cod with Mango-Mint Salsa,
    165
  Noodle Cake with Spicy Peanut-Chicken Stir-Fry,
    318
  see also Pine Nut(s); Walnut(s)

O

Okra
  Caribbean Chicken Pepper Pot, 61
  Quick Southern Fried Chicken Dinner, 76, 77
Olive oil, Californian, taste tests on, 224
Olive(s)
  Black, and Green Bean Salad, 162
  Cherry Tomato Salad, 295
  Chicken, and Date Salad, Moroccan-Style, 40
  and Chickpeas, Vegetable Tagine with, 191
  Fennel, and Orange, Chicken Thighs with, *58,* 59
  Relish and Lemon Couscous, Swordfish with,
    172
  -Rosemary Focaccia, 37
  Sweet and Savory Cuban Chicken Pie, 83
  and Tomato Salad, 164

Onion(s)
chopping in advance, 227
Jam and Wasabi Mayo, Steak Sandwiches with, 288
Pearl, Balsamic-Glazed, London Broil with, 112
sweet, buying and storing, 94
vs. shallots, 217
Orange(s)
Chipotle–Glazed Turkey Tenderloins, Spicy, 88, *89*
Fennel, and Olives, Chicken Thighs with, *58,* 59
-Ginger Pork Tenderloin and Carrot Salad, 124, *125*
-Jícama Salad, Mojo Grilled Pork Chops with, 264, *265*
Skillet Glazed Drumsticks, 60
-Tarragon Trout with Smoky Green Beans, 157
Orecchiette with Broccoli, Currants, and Pine Nuts, 225
Ouzo, about, 178
Oyster sauce, about, 311

P

Paella, Chicken and Artichoke, 70
Pancetta Crisps, Easy Spaghetti Amatriciana with, 211
Panko, making at home, 176
Pan-Seared Scallops with Bacon Succotash, 183
Panzanella, White Bean, 207
Parmesan
-Basil Chicken Salad with Apples, 38, *39*
Cheesy Polenta, 59
Chicken Fingers with Marinara Sauce, 80, *81*
French Toast with Tomato-Basil Topping, *204,* 205
and Pine Nut–Crusted Chicken, 67
Pork Cutlets with Broccoli Rabe, 147
Quick Cheesy Breadsticks, 212
shaving, 282
Three-Cheese Pesto Lasagna Stacks, 245
Tofu, *186,* 188
Parsnip(s)
-Carrot Mash, Flank Steak with, 109
Honey-Glazed, Wintry Roast Chicken with, 56
trimming and cutting, 56

Pasta
Cheesy Gnocchi and Cauliflower Gratin, 241
Chicken Marsala, *208,* 215
Easy Spaghetti Amatriciana with Pancetta Crisps, 211
Farfalle with Bacon, Endive, and Peas, 210
Farfalle with Beets, Arugula, and Blue Cheese, 219
gnocchi, taste tests on, 243
Gnocchi with Spinach, Ham, and Gorgonzola, *242,* 243
Greek Meatballs with Herb and Lemon Orzo, *118,* 119
with Lemony Chicken and Asparagus, 218
Linguine with Cauliflower and Sage Browned Butter, 228
Macaroni Salad, 266
measuring less than a pound of, 221
Mixed-Herb Pesto, with Squash, 222, *223*
Orecchiette with Broccoli, Currants, and Pine Nuts, 225
Penne alla Vodka with Shrimp, 232
Penne with Arugula, Chorizo, and Pecorino, 214
Quick Sausage Ragu with Gemelli, 212, *213*
with Roasted Tomatoes and Porcini Sauce, 230, *231*
Scallops and Angel Hair with Lemon Cream Sauce, 233
shapes, matching with sauces, 220–21
Skillet Macaroni and Cheese with Bacon, 237
Skillet Shrimp and Orzo with Feta, 178
Skillet Tortellini Supper, 224
Sopa Seca, 244
spaghetti, taste tests on, 235
Spaghetti with Spicy White Fresh Clam Sauce, *234,* 235
Spanish-Style Fideos with Swiss Chard, *226,* 227
Spring Farfalle with Salmon, Leeks, and Asparagus, 236
Three-Cheese Pesto Lasagna Stacks, 245
whole-wheat, taste tests on, 229
Whole-Wheat, with Winter Greens, 229
see also Couscous; Noodle(s)
Peach(es)
-Ginger Chutney, Quick, Pork Chops with, 138
Quick Pickled, Pork Burgers with, 290
storing, 290

Peanut butter
    creamy, taste tests on, 307
    Flank Steak with Spicy Peanut Noodles, 106, *107*
Peanut-Chicken Stir-Fry, Spicy, Noodle Cake with, 318
Pea(s)
    Bacon, and Endive, Farfalle with, 210
    pigeon, about, 189
    Pigeon, and Rice, Glazed Caribbean Tofu with, 189
    Snow, and Shiitakes, Stir-Fried Pork with, *298,* 302
    Sugar Snap, and Red Bell Pepper Salad, 294
Penne alla Vodka with Shrimp, 232
Penne with Arugula, Chorizo, and Pecorino, 214
Pepper-Crusted Steaks with Creamy Leeks, 100, 101
Pepper mills, ratings of, 65
Pepper(s)
    Country Captain Chicken, 64
    Easy Rouille Croutons, 20
    Gazpacho with Avocado and Crab, *18, 19*
    Pork-and-Sausage-Stuffed, *152, 153*
    Red, and Spicy Broccoli, Snapper with, 158, *159*
    Red Bell, and Sugar Snap Pea Salad, 294
    Roasted Red, Sauce, Pork Chops with, 135
    roasted red, taste tests on, 135
    Skillet Pork Fajitas, *128, 129*
    Sweet, Ragout, Strip Steaks with, 98
    and Tomato Sauce–Poached Eggs, Spicy, 203
    see also Chile(s)
Pico de Gallo, 22
Pierogi, Crispy Potato, with Mushroom Ragout, *192,* 193
Pies
    Chicken, Sweet and Savory Cuban, 83
    Tamale, Skillet Summer Vegetable, 199
Pigeon Peas
    about, 189
    and Rice, Glazed Caribbean Tofu with, 189
Pine Nut(s)
    Broccoli, and Currants, Orecchiette with, 225
    and Parmesan–Crusted Chicken, 67
    toasting, 225
Pizza dough, buying, 278

Pizza(s)
    Antipasto, with Arugula Salad, 280
    Arugula Pesto and Potato, with Fennel Salad, 282, *283*
    Buffalo Chicken Lavash, 276
    Clam, Bacon, and Onion, 281
    Squash, Gorgonzola, and Pancetta, 278, *279*
    Tex-Mex Chicken, Individual, *274, 277*
Polenta
    Cheesy, 59
    and Eggplant Bake, Cheesy Skillet, 200, *201*
Pork
    -and-Sausage-Stuffed Peppers, *152,* 153
    Burgers with Quick Pickled Peaches, 290
    buying, 133
    Chops, Apricot-Crusted, with Radicchio, 134
    Chops, Cider-Glazed, with Waldorf Salad, *122,* 130
    Chops, Cola-Glazed, with Mustard Greens, 140, *141*
    chops, cooking tip, 142
    Chops, Maple, with Sweet Potato–Bacon Hash, *136,* 137
    Chops, Mojo Grilled, with Orange-Jícama Salad, 264, *265*
    Chops, Spicy, and Summer Vegetable Sauté, 131
    Chops, Teriyaki, with Baby Bok Choy, 142
    Chops with Chorizo and Spanish Rice, 139
    Chops with Creamy Roasted Poblanos, 132
    Chops with Quick Ginger-Peach Chutney, 138
    Chops with Roasted Red Pepper Sauce, 135
    Cutlets, Crispy Sesame, 148, *149*
    cutlets, making your own, 147
    Cutlets, Parmesan, with Broccoli Rabe, 147
    Fajitas, Skillet, *128, 129*
    Florentine Casserole, *144, 145*
    Fried Rice, Indonesian-Style, 312
    Grilled, Vietnamese-Style, Sandwiches, *268, 269*
    Grilled Andouille Burgers with Spicy Mayonnaise, 266
    Hoisin-Glazed Boneless Ribs with Garlicky Broccolini, 143
    Jambalaya, Quick, 127
    Noodles, Stir-Fried Curried, *320,* 321
    Patties, Thai-Style, 151

Pork *(cont.)*
   Schnitzel, Rye-Crusted, with Quick Applesauce, 146
   Stir-Fried, with Shiitakes and Snow Peas, *298, 302*
   Tenderloin, Glazed, with Creamy Turnip Puree, 126
   Tenderloin, Orange-Ginger, and Carrot Salad, 124, *125*
   Tenderloins, Spice-Rubbed Grilled, 263
   and Zucchini, Thai Green Curry with, 323
   see also Bacon; Ham; Sausage(s)
Portobello Sandwiches with Pesto Mayonnaise, 295
Potato(es)
   -Artichoke Ragout, Strip Steaks with, 95
   and Arugula Pesto Pizza with Fennel Salad, 282, *283*
   -Cabbage Hash, Mustard Salmon with, 176
   -Cauliflower Mash and Boursin, Steaks with, 99
   and Chicken, Quick White Wine–Braised, 62, *63*
   fingerling, about, 258
   Flank Steak with Parsnip-Carrot Mash, 109
   –Green Bean Salad, Grilled Dijon Steak with, 248, *249*
   and Halibut with Lemon-Caper Sauce, 168
   with Lemon and Parsley, 98
   Mashed, 101
   Pierogi, Crispy, with Mushroom Ragout, *192,* 193
   Quick Indian Beef Curry, 322
   Ricotta, Basil, and Summer Squash Frittata, 202
   Salad, Lemon-Thyme, Grilled Chicken with, 258
   Smoked Trout Salad, *46, 47*
   Spice-Rubbed Grilled Pork Tenderloins, 263
   Strip Steaks with Tomato–Ancho Chile Sauce, 94
   Tarragon Smashed, Rib-Eye Steaks with, 102, *103*
   see also Sweet Potato(es)
Poultry. *See* Chicken; Turkey
Pozole, Quick Chicken, 7
Prosciutto
   Panini with Artichoke-Lemon Aïoli, 289
   Skillet Tortellini Supper, 224
   Turkey Saltimbocca, 86
   -Wrapped Chicken with Sage Butter, 66
Pumpkin Seed Sauce, Mexican-Style, Chicken with, 71

Q
Quesadillas, Butternut, Poblano, and Cheese, 198
Quick All-American Chili with Cheesy Cornbread, 4, *5*
Quick Beef Wellington, 117
Quick Black Bean Soup, 22, *23*
Quick Bouillabaisse, 20
Quick Cheesy Breadsticks, 212
Quick Chicken Pozole, 7
Quick Guinness Beef Stew, 6
Quick Indian Beef Curry, 322
Quick Pork Jambalaya, 127
Quick Sausage Ragu with Gemelli, 212, *213*
Quick Southern Fried Chicken Dinner, 76, 77
Quick White Wine–Braised Chicken and Potatoes, 62, *63*

R
Radicchio
   about, 251
   Apricot-Crusted Pork Chops with, 134
   and Endive, Grilled T-Bone Steaks with, 251
Ranch Slaw, 80
Rib-Eye Steaks with Tarragon Smashed Potatoes, 102, *103*
Rice
   Arborio, taste tests on, 240
   Baked Risotto with Shrimp and Zucchini, 240
   Basmati, Fragrant, 272
   and Beef Bowl, Korean-Style, 114, *115*
   Chicken and Artichoke Paella, 70
   Cilantro, 71
   Cilantro, Chicken and Squash Stir-Fry with, *306,* 307
   Coconut, Chile, Basil, and Chicken Stir-Fry with, 308
   Creamy Coconut, and Fish Packets, Thai-Style, 161
   Easy Garlicky Risotto with Broccolini, 238, *239*
   fully cooked, buying, 312
   jasmine, about, 308
   Jasmine, Cakes with Vegetable Thai Green Curry, 194

Rice *(cont.)*
  long-grain white, taste tests on, 69
  Mexican Green, and Chicken Skillet Supper, *68,* 69
  and Pigeon Peas, Glazed Caribbean Tofu with, 189
  Pilaf, Apricot, Curried Chicken Meatballs with, *84,* 85
  Pork-and-Sausage-Stuffed Peppers, *152,* 153
  Pork Fried, Indonesian-Style, 312
  Quick Pork Jambalaya, 127
  and Red Beans, Spicy, Skillet Chicken with, 72, *73*
  Saffron, 90
  and Shrimp Salad, Tropical, 50, *51*
  Spanish, and Chorizo, Pork Chops with, 139
  White, Easy, 22
Ricotta, Basil, and Summer Squash Frittata, 202
Risotto
  Baked, with Shrimp and Zucchini, 240
  Easy Garlicky, with Broccolini, 238, *239*
Roast Chicken with Lima Bean Ragout, *52,* 57
Roasted Broccoli, 146
Romaine Wedge with Shrimp and Feta Dressing, 49
Rosemary-Olive Focaccia, 37
Rutabagas, about, 126
Rye-Crusted Pork Schnitzel with Quick Applesauce, 146

S

Saffron, about, 70
Saffron Rice, 90
Salads (main-dish)
  Basil-Parmesan Chicken, with Apples, 38, *39*
  Beef, Southwest, with Cornbread Croutons, 32
  Blue Cheese and Walnut Chopped Chicken, 36
  Blue Cheese Wedge with Maple-Glazed Bacon, 28
  Cabbage with Kielbasa and Honey-Dijon Dressing, 29
  Chicken, Date, and Olive, Moroccan-Style, 40
  Chicken, Goat Cheese, and Cherry, 42, *43*
  Cobb, Italian, 37
  Coconut-Lime Chicken and Cabbage-Mango Slaw, *26,* 41
  Frisée and Fried-Egg, with Lentils, 44

Salads (main-dish) *(cont.)*
  Lemony Salmon and Roasted Beet, 48
  Romaine Wedge with Shrimp and Feta Dressing, 49
  Shrimp and Rice, Tropical, 50, *51*
  Smoked Trout, *46,* 47
  Spanish Tapas, 30, *31*
  Steak, with Creamy Horseradish Dressing, *34,* 35
  Tuna and White Bean, Tuscan-Style, 45
  White Bean Panzanella, 207
Salads (side)
  Arugula, with Balsamic-Mustard Vinaigrette, 202
  Arugula with Roquefort Vinaigrette, 112
  Bean-Sprout, Spicy, 151
  Carrot, with Raisins, 292, *293*
  Cherry Tomato, 295
  Cucumber, 106
  Cucumber and Yogurt, 288
  Green Bean and Black Olive, 162
  Macaroni, 266
  Napa Cabbage, 148
  Ranch Slaw, 80
  Slaw with Cumin-Honey Dressing, 198
  Sugar Snap Pea and Red Bell Pepper, 294
  Sweet Potato, 289
  Tomato and Olive, 164
Salmon
  about, 177
  Burgers with Tomato Chutney, 294
  Chili-Glazed, with Bok Choy, *174,* 175
  Grilled, Sandwiches with Broccoli Slaw, 271
  Leeks, and Asparagus, Spring Farfalle with, 236
  Lemony, and Roasted Beet Salad, 48
  Mustard, with Potato-Cabbage Hash, 176
  Smoked, Scrambled Eggs with Chive Butter, 173
Salsa
  Pico de Gallo, 22
  Tomatillo, 179
Sandwiches
  Chicken Salad, Asian, *286,* 287
  Curried Chicken, with Apple Raita, 285
  Gouda and Apple Panini with Tangy Cabbage Slaw, *296,* 297
  Greek-Style Grilled Chicken Pita, 259
  Grilled Salmon, with Broccoli Slaw, 271

Sandwiches *(cont.)*
 Portobello, with Pesto Mayonnaise, 295
 Prosciutto Panini with Artichoke-Lemon Aïoli, 289
 Sausage and Broccoli Rabe Calzones, 284
 Spicy Shrimp-and-Herb-Salad Wraps, 292, *293*
 Steak, with Onion Jam and Wasabi Mayo, 288
 Vietnamese-Style Grilled Pork, *268,* 269
 see also Burgers
Sauerkraut
 Skillet-Braised Bratwurst and, 150
 taste tests on, 150
Sausage(s)
 andouille, taste tests on, 127
 -and-Pork-Stuffed Peppers, *152,* 153
 Antipasto Pizza with Arugula Salad, 280
 and Broccoli Rabe Calzones, 284
 Cabbage with Kielbasa and Honey-Dijon Dressing, 29
 Chicken and Artichoke Paella, 70
 chorizo, about, 185
 Escarole, Linguiça, and White Bean Soup, *2,* 15
 Grilled Andouille Burgers with Spicy Mayonnaise, 266
 Grilled Garlic, with Lentil Salad, 267
 Hearty Chicken and Chorizo Skillet Supper, 79
 Penne with Arugula, Chorizo, and Pecorino, 214
 Pork Chops with Chorizo and Spanish Rice, 139
 Quick Pork Jambalaya, 127
 Ragu, Quick, with Gemelli, 212, *213*
 Skillet-Braised Bratwurst and Sauerkraut, 150
 Skillet Chicken with Spicy Red Beans and Rice, 72, *73*
 Smoky Chorizo, Chickpea, and Spinach Soup, 16
 Spanish Tapas Salad, 30, *31*
 Steamed Mussels with Chorizo and Garlic Crostini, *184,* 185
Sautéed Shrimp with Artichokes and Mushrooms, 180, *181*
Sautéed Spinach with Garlic Chips, 86
Scallions, storing, 72
Scallops
 and Angel Hair with Lemon Cream Sauce, 233
 buying, 183
 Pan-Seared, with Bacon Succotash, 183
 Seared, with Squash Puree and Sage Butter, *154,* 182

Seared Scallops with Squash Puree and Sage Butter, *154,* 182
Sesame Noodles with Tofu, Scallions, and Cashews, 316, *317*
Sesame oil, about, 311
Sesame-Scallion Noodles, 120
Sesame seeds
 Crispy Sesame Pork Cutlets, 148, *149*
 Tuna with Miso Butter and Sesame Spinach, 169
Shallots vs. onions, 217
Shellfish
 Clam, Bacon, and Onion Pizza, 281
 Quick Bouillabaisse, 20
 Spaghetti with Spicy White Fresh Clam Sauce, *234,* 235
 Steamed Mussels with Chorizo and Garlic Crostini, *184,* 185
 see also Crab; Scallops; Shrimp
Shrimp
 -and-Herb-Salad Wraps, Spicy, 292, *293*
 and Asparagus, Stir-Fried, with Lemon Sauce, 309
 and Feta Dressing, Romaine Wedge with, 49
 Masala, Grilled Spicy, 272, *273*
 Penne alla Vodka with, 232
 and Rice Salad, Tropical, 50, *51*
 Sautéed, with Artichokes and Mushrooms, 180, *181*
 Skillet, and Orzo with Feta, 178
 Spicy, with Corn Cakes, 179
 Tortilla Soup, 21
 and Zucchini, Baked Risotto with, 240
Sides
 Apricot-Cilantro Couscous, 191
 Broccoli with Balsamic Vinaigrette, 237
 Cheesy Polenta, 59
 Chunky Chipotle Guacamole, 129
 Cilantro Chutney, 322
 Cilantro Rice, 71
 Collard Greens, 91
 Easy Rouille Croutons, 20
 Easy White Rice, 22
 Eggplant and Garlic Sauté, 85
 Fragrant Basmati Rice, 272
 Lemony Steamed Broccoli, 60
 Mashed Potatoes, 101
 Mashed Sweet Potatoes, 88

Sides *(cont.)*
  Mashed Sweet Potatoes with Lime Zest, 132
  Pico de Gallo, 22
  Potatoes with Lemon and Parsley, 98
  Quick Cheesy Breadsticks, 212
  Roasted Broccoli, 146
  Rosemary-Olive Focaccia, 37
  Saffron Rice, 90
  Sautéed Spinach with Garlic Chips, 86
  Sesame-Scallion Noodles, 120
  Skillet Green Beans, 241
  Steamed Asparagus with Olive Oil and Sea Salt, 232
  Steamed Bok Choy, 161
  Swiss Chard with Onion and Bacon, 138
  Tomatillo Salsa, 179
  see also Salads (side)
Skillet-Braised Bratwurst and Sauerkraut, 150
Skillet Chicken with Spicy Red Beans and Rice, 72, *73*
Skillet Glazed Drumsticks, 60
Skillet Green Beans, 241
Skillet Hamburgers, 291
Skillet Macaroni and Cheese with Bacon, 237
Skillet Pork Fajitas, *128,* 129
Skillet Shrimp and Orzo with Feta, 178
Skillet Summer Vegetable Tamale Pie, 199
Skillet Tortellini Supper, 224
Slaw with Cumin-Honey Dressing, 198
Smoked Salmon Scrambled Eggs with Chive Butter, 173
Smoked Trout Salad, *46,* 47
Smoky Chorizo, Chickpea, and Spinach Soup, 16
Snapper with Spicy Broccoli and Red Pepper, 158, *159*
Sole, Crab-Stuffed, with Lemon-Butter Sauce, 160
Sopa Seca, 244
Soups
  Black Bean, Quick, 22, *23*
  Chicken, Cambodian, 12, *13*
  Coconut Curry, Thai, with Chicken, *8, 9*
  Escarole, Linguiça, and White Bean, *2,* 15
  Gazpacho with Avocado and Crab, *18,* 19
  Matzo Ball, with Chicken and Asparagus, 11
  preparing, tips for, 17
  pureeing safely, 16

Soups *(cont.)*
  Shrimp Tortilla, 21
  Smoky Chorizo, Chickpea, and Spinach, 16
  Spicy Chicken and Corn Chowder, 10
  Sweet Potato, Moroccan, 25
  White Bean, Creamy, with Kale Pesto, 24
  see also Stews
Southwest Beef Salad with Cornbread Croutons, 32
Southwestern Steak Tips with Refried Beans, 116
Soy sauce, about, 310
Spaghetti, taste tests on, 235
Spaghetti with Spicy White Fresh Clam Sauce, *234,* 235
Spanish-Style Fideos with Swiss Chard, *226,* 227
Spanish-Style Turkey Meatballs, 90
Spanish Tapas Salad, 30, *31*
Spice-Rubbed Grilled Pork Tenderloins, 263
Spices
  about, 65
  see also specific spices
Spicy Bean-Sprout Salad, 151
Spicy Beef Burritos, *110,* 111
Spicy Beef Lettuce Cups, 120
Spicy Chicken and Corn Chowder, 10
Spicy Cornmeal Flounder and Lemony Slaw, 156
Spicy Orange Chipotle–Glazed Turkey Tenderloins, 88, *89*
Spicy Pork Chops and Summer Vegetable Sauté, 131
Spicy Shrimp-and-Herb-Salad Wraps, 292, *293*
Spicy Shrimp with Corn Cakes, 179
Spicy Tomato and Pepper Sauce–Poached Eggs, 203
Spinach
  about, 33
  Ham, and Gorgonzola, Gnocchi with, *242,* 243
  Korean-Style Beef and Rice Bowl, 114, *115*
  Pork Florentine Casserole, *144,* 145
  Sautéed, with Garlic Chips, 86
  Sesame, and Miso Butter, Tuna with, 169
  Smoky Chorizo, and Chickpea Soup, 16
Spring Farfalle with Salmon, Leeks, and Asparagus, 236
Spring Rolls, Beef, with Spicy Mayo, 121

Squash

Acorn, Couscous-Stuffed, 196, *197*

butternut, peeled and halved, buying, 182

Butternut, Poblano, and Cheese Quesadillas, 198

and Chicken Stir-Fry with Cilantro Rice, *306*, 307

cutting into ribbons, 222

Gorgonzola, and Pancetta Pizza, 278, *279*

Mixed-Herb Pesto Pasta with, 222, *223*

Puree and Sage Butter, Seared Scallops with, *154*, 182

Spicy Pork Chops and Summer Vegetable Sauté, 131

Summer, Ricotta, and Basil Frittata, 202

see also Zucchini

Steak(s)

blade, trimming, 322

with Boursin and Potato-Cauliflower Mash, 99

with Citrus-Soy Pan Sauce and Slaw, *96*, 97

Flank, Grilled, with Thai Pesto Noodles, 254

Flank, with Parsnip-Carrot Mash, 109

Flank, with Spicy Peanut Noodles, 106, *107*

Grilled Beef Tenderloin with Watercress Salad, *246*, 250

Grilled Dijon, with Potato–Green Bean Salad, 248, *249*

London broil, about, 112

London Broil with Balsamic-Glazed Pearl Onions, 112

pan-searing, 104

Pepper-Crusted, with Creamy Leeks, *100*, 101

Rib Eye, Coffee-Rubbed, with Creamy Slaw, *92*, 105

Rib-Eye, with Tarragon Smashed Potatoes, 102, *103*

Salad with Creamy Horseradish Dressing, *34*, 35

Sandwiches with Onion Jam and Wasabi Mayo, 288

Southwest Beef Salad with Cornbread Croutons, 32

Strip, with Potato-Artichoke Ragout, 95

Strip, with Sweet Pepper Ragout, 98

Strip, with Tomato–Ancho Chile Sauce, 94

T-Bone, Grilled, with Radicchio and Endive, 251

Tips, Balsamic, and Tomato Salad, 113

tips, buying, 6

Tips, Southwestern, with Refried Beans, 116

and Zucchini Tostadas, 108

Steamed Asparagus with Olive Oil and Sea Salt, 232

Steamed Bok Choy, 161

Steamed Mussels with Chorizo and Garlic Crostini, *184*, 185

Stews

Guinness Beef, Quick, 6

Quick Bouillabaisse, 20

Quick Chicken Pozole, 7

Stir-Fried Curried Pork Noodles, *320*, 321

Stir-Fried Pork with Shiitakes and Snow Peas, *298*, 302

Stir-Fried Shrimp and Asparagus with Lemon Sauce, 309

Strip Steaks with Potato-Artichoke Ragout, 95

Strip Steaks with Sweet Pepper Ragout, 98

Strip Steaks with Tomato–Ancho Chile Sauce, 94

Sugar Snap Pea and Red Bell Pepper Salad, 294

Sweet and Savory Cuban Chicken Pie, 83

Sweet chili sauce, about, 310

Sweet Potato(es)

–Bacon Hash, Maple Pork Chops with, *136*, 137

Caribbean Chicken Pepper Pot, 61

Mashed, 88

Mashed, with Lime Zest, 132

Salad, 289

Soup, Moroccan, 25

Thai Coconut Curry Soup with Chicken, *8*, 9

Swiss Chard

Chicken Cutlets with Ginger-Shiitake Sauce, 75

with Onion and Bacon, 138

Spanish-Style Fideos with, *226*, 227

Swordfish with Lemon Couscous and Olive Relish, 172

T

Tahini, taste tests on, 316

Tarragon Chicken and Egg Noodles, *216*, 217

Tarts, Fennel, Olive, and Goat Cheese, 206

Teriyaki Pork Chops with Baby Bok Choy, 142

Thai Coconut Curry Soup with Chicken, *8*, 9

Thai green curry paste, about, 194

Thai Green Curry with Eggplant, 324, *325*

Thai Green Curry with Pork and Zucchini, 323

Thai-Style Fish and Creamy Coconut Rice Packets, 161

Thai-Style Pork Patties, 151

Three-Cheese Pesto Lasagna Stacks, 245

Tofu
  Glazed Caribbean, with Rice and Pigeon Peas, 189
  Grilled Glazed, with Warm Cabbage Slaw, 270
  Parmesan, *186,* 188
  Scallions, and Cashews, Sesame Noodles with, 316, *317*

Tomatillo(s)
  Chicken with Mexican-Style Pumpkin Seed Sauce, 71
  Salsa, 179

Tomato(es)
  –Ancho Chile Sauce, Strip Steaks with, 94
  -Basil Topping, Parmesan French Toast with, *204,* 205
  -Caper Compote, Herbed, Cod with, 162, *163*
  Cherry, Salad, 295
  Chutney, Salmon Burgers with, 294
  diced, taste tests on, 79
  Easy Spaghetti Amatriciana with Pancetta Crisps, 211
  Gazpacho with Avocado and Crab, *18,* 19
  and Olive Salad, 164
  Parmesan Chicken Fingers with Marinara Sauce, 80, *81*
  and Pepper Sauce–Poached Eggs, Spicy, 203
  Pico de Gallo, 22
  Roasted, and Porcini Sauce, Pasta with, 230, *231*
  Salad, Balsamic Steak Tips and, 113
  Salad, Grilled Breaded Chicken with, *260,* 261
  storing, 113

Tomato paste, taste tests on, 64

Tortilla(s)
  Butternut, Poblano, and Cheese Quesadillas, 198
  Individual Tex-Mex Chicken Pizzas, *274,* 277
  Skillet Pork Fajitas, *128,* 129
  Soup, Shrimp, 21
  Spicy Beef Burritos, *110,* 111
  Spicy Shrimp-and-Herb-Salad Wraps, 292, *293*
  Steak and Zucchini Tostadas, 108

Tostadas, Steak and Zucchini, 108

Tropical Shrimp and Rice Salad, 50, *51*

Trout
  Orange-Tarragon, with Smoky Green Beans, 157
  smoked, buying, 47
  Smoked, Salad, *46,* 47

Tuna
  Mediterranean, and White Bean–Fennel Salad, 170, *171*
  with Miso Butter and Sesame Spinach, 169
  and White Bean Salad, Tuscan-Style, 45

Turkey
  Cutlets, Mustard-Sage, and Barley Salad, 87
  Meatballs, Spanish-Style, 90
  Meatloaves, Mini Barbecued, 91
  Saltimbocca, 86
  Sliders, Grilled Thai, 262
  Tenderloins, Spicy Orange Chipotle–Glazed, 88, *89*

Turnip(s)
  Puree, Creamy, Glazed Pork Tenderloin with, 126
  vs. rutabagas, 126

Tuscan-Style Tuna and White Bean Salad, 45

U

Udon Noodles with Edamame Pesto, *314,* 315

V

Vegetable(s)
  broth, taste tests on, 25
  Tagine with Chickpeas and Olives, 191
  see also specific vegetables

Vegetarian Lo Mein with Bok Choy and Scallions, 313

Vietnamese-Style Grilled Pork Sandwiches, *268,* 269

Vinaigrettes, preparing, 36

Vinegar
  cider, taste tests on, 287
  red wine, taste tests on, 207
  rice, about, 310

Vodka, Penne alla, with Shrimp, 232

W

Walnut(s)
and Blue Cheese Chopped Chicken Salad, 36
and Blue Cheese–Stuffed Chicken Breasts, 54, *55*
Farfalle with Beets, Arugula, and Blue Cheese, 219
Whole-Wheat Pasta with Winter Greens, 229
Wasabi powder, about, 311
Watercress
about, 33
Balsamic Steak Tips and Tomato Salad, 113
Moroccan-Style Chicken, Date, and Olive Salad, 40
Salad, Grilled Beef Tenderloin with, *246, 250*
Smoked Trout Salad, *46,* 47
Tuscan-Style Tuna and White Bean Salad, 45
White Bean Panzanella, 207
White Chicken Chili, 14
Whole-wheat pasta, taste tests on, 229
Whole-Wheat Pasta with Winter Greens, 229
Wine
Chicken Marsala Pasta, *208,* 215
Marsala, about, 215
white, for cooking, choosing, 57
Wintry Roast Chicken with Honey-Glazed Parsnips, 56

Y

Yogurt
-Beet Sauce, Couscous Patties with, 195
and Cucumber Salad, 288
Curried Chicken Sandwiches with Apple Raita, 285

Z

Zucchini
Jasmine Rice Cakes with Vegetable Thai Green Curry, 194
and Pork, Thai Green Curry with, 323
and Shrimp, Baked Risotto with, 240
Skillet Summer Vegetable Tamale Pie, 199
and Steak Tostadas, 108